Jazz
The First Century

Edited by
John Edward Hasse

Forewords by
Quincy Jones and Tony Bennett

with contributions by

Larry Appelbaum	*Gerald Early*	*Rainer E. Lotz*
David Baise	*Sascha Feinstein*	*Steven Loza*
David Baker	*Rusty Frank*	*Jeff Magee*
Philippe Baudoin	*Krin Gabbard*	*Jack Stewart*
Bob Blumenthal	*Deborah Gillaspie*	*Neil Tesser*
Michael Brooks	*William H. Kenney*	*Michael White*
Donna M. Cassidy	*Ann K. Kuebler*	*Kevin Whitehead*
James Dapogny	*Tad Lathrop*	*Calvin Wilson*
	John Litweiler	

William Morrow
An Imprint of HarperCollinsPublishers

Also by John Edward Hasse:
  Beyond Category: The Life and Genius of Duke Ellington
  Discourse in Ethnomusicology (Co-Editor)
  Ragtime: Its History, Composers, and Music (Editor)

Produced by The Grayson Lathrop Group, San Francisco
  Producer and Editorial Director: Tad Lathrop
  Art Director: Nancy Carroll
  Copy Editor: Jacqueline Dever Celenza
  Production and Editorial Assistants: Curtis Carroll,
    Francis H. Gilbert, Fredrick Schermer

Book and Cover Design by Nancy Carroll

Image, p. 136 (left), from *Infants of the Spring* by Wallace Thurman. Cover design: Leah Lacoco. Cover painting: *Black Belt,* 1934, by Archibald Motley, Jr., oil on canvas, 31 7/8" x 39 1/4", Hampton University Museum, Hampton, Virginia. Modern Library © 1999, Random House, Inc.

Cover of *Invisible Man* by Ralph Ellison. Copyright © 1995 by Random House, Inc. Reprinted by permission of Vintage Books, a division of Random House, Inc.

HarperCollins books may be purchased for educational, business, or sales promotional use. For information please write: Special Markets Department, HarperCollins Publishers, Inc., 10 East 53rd Street, New York, NY 10022.

First Edition

Library of Congress Cataloging-in-Publication Data
Jazz : the first century / edited by John Edward Hasse.
    p. cm.
  Includes discographies
  Includes bibliographical references (p. 235) and index.
  ISBN 0-688-17074-9
    1. Jazz—History and criticism. I. Hasse, John Edward, 1948–
  ML3506 .J47 2000
  781.65'09 21—dc21
                                                          99-046071

00 01 02 03 04   10 9 8 7 6 5 4 3 2 1

Acknowledgments

Tad Lathrop, a San Francisco-based book producer, and I independently conceived of this book and decided to join forces. That our idea became a reality is due to two musically hip men of publishing: the energetic Andrew Stuart of the Literary Group and Paul Bresnick, executive editor at William Morrow. Both recognized the importance of the music and the need for a book such as this one and warmly backed the project.

Tad proved to be a wonderful collaborator, directing the editorial process, acquiring images, and facilitating the production gracefully while under the pressure of deadlines. He is one of the best "line" editors, and photo caption writers, in the business, and his expertise and judgment show on every page. Among his masterstrokes was signing up Nancy Carroll, who devoted months to the book's design and production. Her dedication, artistic judgment, and visual acumen have made this book as handsome as it is.

My good friends David Baker and Bruce Talbot made a number of invaluable suggestions throughout the project. In Paris, Philippe Baudoin read several portions of the manuscript and generously and repeatedly supplied helpful pieces of information. In New Orleans, Bruce Boyd Raeburn of Tulane University and Jack Stewart reviewed sections of the manuscript and kindly helped track down images.

The undertaking was greatly aided by copy editor (and jazz-song aficionado) Jacqueline Celenza; production assistant Curtis Carroll; editorial assistants Fredrick Schermer and Francis Gilbert; and Ben Schafer, who guided the book through its final production phase. Special thanks are due to Bill Hollowell and Craig Matthews for their generous support throughout.

Tom Alexios, *Down Beat* magazine's director of special projects, made an invaluable contribution by helping to acquire photos and, in particular, arranging the loan of images from the magazine's archive; *Down Beat* editorial director Frank Alkyer cheerfully facilitated that loan in countless ways.

For their gracious help with photographs, thanks also to Bill Claxton, Frank Driggs, Ken Franckling, William Gottlieb, Herman Leonard, Jan Persson, Duncan P. Schiedt, and Lee Tanner. Phil Elwood generously loaned record albums, as did Fred Hill, Vince Littleton, and John and Ann Carroll.

Thanks, of course, to the book's two dozen knowledgeable contributors, as well as to Larry Appelbaum, Lida Belt Baker, Bob Blumenthal, Jerry Brock, Myles Faulkner of Allegro Distributing, Krin Gabbard, Deborah Gillaspie, Vince Giordano, Beverly Hennessey, Arnold Hirsch, Andy Jaffe, Ann K. Kuebler, Kevin Lathrop, Stacey Lewis, Don Lucoff, Wynn Matthias, José Rizo, Lina Stephens, Sasha Taskaev, Steve Teeter, Michael Ullman, and Jim Wilke.

Special thanks to my dear daughter Leanne, who brightens my life every day. And to Holly for her patience, support, and sweet self-sacrifice that allowed me space to work on this book.

Finally, appreciation above all to the men and women who created the first century of jazz, for their art has enriched the lives of hundreds of millions of people around the world.

JOHN EDWARD HASSE
December 1999

Foreword

One of the things I'm most grateful for in my life—after my children, of course—is that I grew up at a time when I was able to witness, and play a role in, the maturation of the only true indigenous American art form: jazz.

When I first began performing, in 1945, in Seattle, it was as if I'd been bitten by a vampire and the music was the blood that would sustain me. I was hooked, and there was no going back—even if I'd wanted to. At fourteen years old, it was music twenty-four hours a day, 365 days a year. That's how powerful it was.

Seattle was a hotbed of it, and everybody came through there: Billie Holiday, Lionel Hampton, Oscar Pettiford, Clark Terry—just everyone. At the time, I was playing in Bumps Blackwell's band, and soaking up as much as I possibly could. And it was then that I met Mr. Ray Charles. Ray was sixteen at the time, and we formed an instant bond, which has lasted to this day. Ray helped me get inside the music by teaching me how to write arrangements, opening up yet another wonderful world.

It was truly a beautiful time—playing the music that moved us, all night long. It was the beginning of a journey that would carry me all over the world and put me onstage and in the recording studio with my idols. There were Dizzy and Miles, Charlie Parker, Sarah Vaughan, Dinah Washington, Count Basie, Duke Ellington, Billy Eckstine, Benny Carter, and a host of others. Those were the cats who were my Beatles and Rolling Stones.

From Chicago to Seattle, New York, and the "chitlin" circuit, from Sweden to Paris to Tokyo, jazz opened up a whole new world for me. Jazz is like a beautiful mistress who makes you do whatever you have to, to be with her. My affair with her has lasted fifty-three years. And in that time, I have seen her power firsthand. The power to make men forget their differences and come together. To make one's heart swell until it feels like it's going to jump out of your chest. The power to make you laugh, cry, jump, dance, think, and love. It's a power that doesn't recognize color, class, religion, or geographic boundaries—it's universal.

Jazz has left an indelible handprint on America's history, a central thread woven through the fabric of our country. Morphing itself, and giving birth to a host of other musical genres. It is part of the bedrock of pop, R&B, and rock music, and it's an intricate road map to our culture.

As we celebrate the first hundred years of jazz, many of the men and women who were responsible for it are no longer with us. But wherever they are, I know there is one killer jam session going on. I believe that a hundred years from now, when people look back at the twentieth century, they will view Bird, Miles, and Dizzy as our Mozarts, Bachs, Chopins, and Tchaikovskys. I can only hope that one day America will recognize what the rest of the world already has: that our indigenous music, jazz, is the heart and soul of all popular music, and that we can not afford to let its legacy slip into obscurity.

Jazz. Yes, she is my mistress. And in the immortal words of Duke Ellington, I love her madly.

QUINCY JONES
December 1999

Foreword

[Sincere jazz musicians] aim at excellence and apparently nothing else. They are hard to buy and if bought they either backslide into honesty or lose the respect of their peers. And this is the loss that terrifies them. In any other field of American life, great reward can be used to cover the loss of honesty, but not with jazz players—a slip is known and recognized instantly. And further, while there may be some jealousies, they do not compare with those in other professions. Let a filthy kid, unknown, unheard of and unbacked sit in—and if he can do it—he is recognized and accepted instantly. Do you know of another field where this is true?

—JOHN STEINBECK

I love jazz more than any other form of music. The music and the musicians who have dedicated their lives to jazz have had a profound effect on me both professionally and personally.

As a teenager growing up in New York City I would frequent all the jazz clubs, and the great performances I saw were an inspiration.

There were many jazz musicians who helped me at the start of my career. One of my first shows, held at the Piccadilly Club in Paramus, New Jersey, featured bandleader Earle Warren, who had played alto saxophone for Count Basie. With Earle's guidance I was able to get through the show. Very early on, I was given a break by the trombonist Tyree Glenn, who had played with Louis Armstrong, when Glenn asked me to perform with him one night at a nightclub in Astoria, New York, called the Shangri-La. It turned into a regular gig until he left to tour with Duke Ellington. Soon after, I met Al Cohn and Zoot Sims, who worked with me on several albums.

I was fortunate to realize that if I surrounded myself with jazz musicians, whether on live shows or on recordings, the music would always be alive. Jazz performers understand that in music, movement is the most important element—they improvise, and by so doing they reinvent the music every night.

The best singing advice I was ever given was from my vocal coach, Mimi Spear. She had a studio on 52nd Street, across from all the jazz clubs that featured such greats as Art Tatum, Erroll Garner, Billie Holiday, Lester Young, and so many more. She would tell me, "Don't imitate another singer; you'll end up sounding like they do. Instead, find a musician and study his phrasing, and you'll develop your own style." Instinctively or not, this is what all the greatest jazz musicians have done.

Every civilization is known by its culture, and jazz is America's greatest contribution to the world—it is our "classical" music. Jazz is spontaneous, honest, and natural, and it is a celebration of life itself.

TONY BENNETT
October 1999

Shadow image: William Claxton/DPM
Billie Holiday, Charlie Parker: © William P. Gottlieb

Contents

Introduction

Anew form of musical expression emerged at the outset of the twentieth century. One hundred years later it was still vital. And somehow, in the intervening years, it had become the most expansive and influential approach to music-making introduced during that time.

That music was jazz. And the idea behind it was powerful: Employ improvisation, hot rhythm, and other enlivening devices in the performance of music from an array of sources—in effect, making something new and exciting from something old and familiar. The concept proved fruitful, its creative possibilities inexhaustible. The music grew accordingly, and it accrued the history and the qualities that make for enduring art.

Among those qualities is universality. Today, jazz offers something for everyone. A listener may not understand bebop, yet that same person may thrill to jazz-infused hip-hop. Others might find "free jazz" unsettling but can't resist the verve and pulse of swing. Someone might not "get" Betty Carter yet can't get enough of Benny Carter. Another might reject Charlie Byrd but relish Charlie "Bird" Parker.

When called upon, jazz delivers on many levels. It can serve as soothing background music or as challenging art that requires—and rewards—undivided attention. It can convey deep emotion—the pain of John Coltrane's *Alabama*, the reverence of Duke Ellington's *Come Sunday*, the exaltation of Louis Armstrong's *Stardust*. And it can provide food for thought—as do the Modern Jazz Quartet's *Vendome*, Lennie Tristano's *A Ghost of a Chance*, and Anthony Braxton's *Composition No. 91*.

Jazz is both visual and visceral. It encompasses unforgettably vivid sonic paintings—witness Ellington's eerie *The Mooche* or Miles Davis and Gil Evans' piercing *Saeta*. And it can induce a nearly irresistible urge to move—Benny Goodman's *Stomping at the Savoy*, Herbie Hancock's *Watermelon Man*, and Tito Puente's *Oye como va*.

From the realm of jazz came some of the century's greatest creative artists and most colorful personalities: Armstrong, as an instrumentalist and singer, the most influential of American musicians; Ellington, the greatest all-around American composer and performer; Davis, who, like Pablo Picasso, frequently and boldly reconceived himself and his art.

And jazz has inspired creation in other fields, by dancers, choreographers, novelists, poets, painters, classical composers, and filmmakers.

Jazz didn't progress slowly. In the course of just one century, it recapitulated the centuries-long evolution of European classical music from a localized dance accompaniment to an international art with an avant-garde edge. Separated by only twenty actual years, Louis Armstrong's *West End Blues* of 1928 and Charlie Parker's *Parker's Mood* of 1948 nonetheless seem light years apart. This contrast bespeaks the extraordinary rate of change in jazz, matching the velocity of transformation in other sectors of twentieth-century life.

As jazz evolved, the shapes it took made it a musical analog to historic events and trends. Nightclub jazz and dance-hall swing of the 1920s and thirties, for example, rose on a wave of postwar optimism and a surging youth culture. The music's multiethnic flavors—heard, for instance, in the Afro-Cuban beat of Dizzy Gillespie's *Manteca*, the calypso of Sonny Rollins' *St. Thomas*, and the bossa nova of Stan Getz's *The Girl from Ipanema*—emerged with both the growth of U.S. immigration and the increasing interconnectedness of world cultures due to advances in communications and transportation. Progressive bebop of the 1940s articulated the new assertiveness of African Americans, and the even more progressive free jazz of the sixties echoed the anti-repressive call of the civil-rights and counterculture movements. Post-sixties jazz synthesizers and electronics signaled alliance with the digital information revolution, while the kaleidoscopic sonic arrays of some late-century jazz reflected the increasingly fractured and data-bombarded state of late-century consciousness.

Jazz not only mirrored social and cultural change but also brought it on. Long before American society was racially integrated, jazz musicians were recording in multihued bands and becoming celebrities across the color line. Jazz moved many African American musical practices right into the musical mainstream, thereby transforming American music and spurring the creation of new styles, including rock and roll, R&B, and soul.

Jazz did all those things because, at its core, it's about honest, instantaneous, high-level communication. The jazz musician improvises, and the immediacy of that approach to invention ensures that the message comes from the heart. At the same time, the depth and scope of the jazz language—on a par with the most complex "classical" music—make that communication as deep and articulate as musical expression can be. The reflection of life in all its complexity has no truer image than that found in jazz.

It wouldn't be that way if not for the freedom jazz affords and encourages. "If jazz means anything," wrote Duke Ellington, "it is freedom of expression." For early New Orleans players, jazz could also mean freedom from anonymity, poverty, and powerlessness. For 1920s "Jazz Age" adherents, it could mean freedom from old, tired social mores. For people living under totalitarian regimes, it could symbolize individualism and freedom from regimentation.

Jazz is as much about the personal as it is about the collective. The jazz musician, through inflections and stylings, puts his or her own distinctive stamp on the material, making something personal out of something shared. Like democracy at its best, a jazz band maintains an optimum balance between the individual and the group and upholds the value of both.

In a century rife with the predictable, the dehumanizing, and the dispiriting, jazz affirmed the fresh, the human, the hopeful. It came to represent humanity at its best: striving for beauty, personal achievement, and perfection, and communicating a message that brings pleasure to the world.

Jazz flourished in thousands of places and in millions of performances, enriching the aesthetic life of its first century and promising, through the indelibility of recordings, to do so in the next. How it all came to pass is one of the great stories of the twentieth century.

JOHN EDWARD HASSE
November 1999

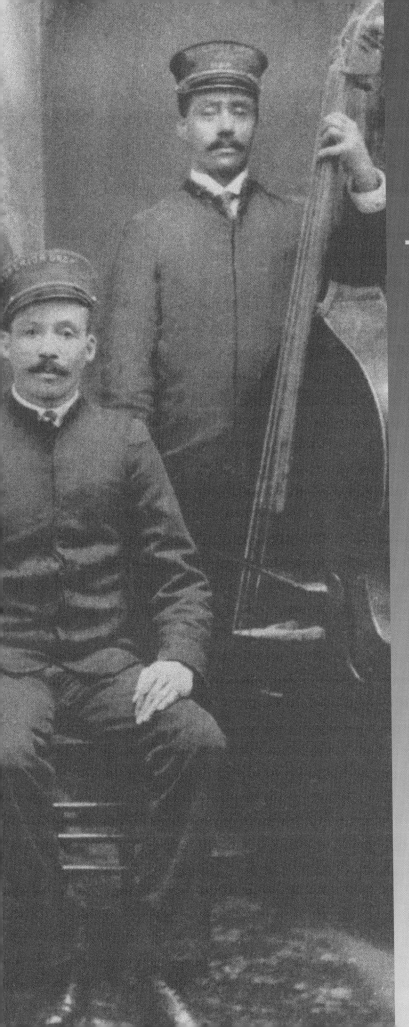

CHAPTER 1

The Emergence
of Jazz

John Edward Hasse

The Original Superior Brass Band, New Orleans, ca. 1900, with acclaimed cornetist Bunk Johnson (standing, second from left).

New Orleans cornet king Freddie Keppard left the city in 1914, taking his sound west to Los Angeles and north to Chicago.

Jazz, according to popular lore, was born and raised in Storyville, the New Orleans red-light district. When, to protect sailors, the U.S. Navy forced the area's closure in 1917, jazz musicians left the city and took the new music up the Mississippi River to Chicago. From there it spread across the nation.

Is that the way jazz actually came into being? Well, not really. This widely embraced notion is freighted with five misconceptions—about where the music started, where it was played in New Orleans, when the exodus of jazz musicians began, why the migration began, and where musicians went.

Jazz did not originate in Storyville, and it was played not only in that district but all over New Orleans. Some musicians left New Orleans long before 1917, while others didn't leave for a number of years or never left. Those who did leave were motivated by the promise of greater economic opportunity elsewhere. None of the adventurers took the Mississippi River to Chicago (it doesn't go anywhere near Chicago). Some of the musicians who left went north, some went west to California, and others toured widely.

But historians are still far from unanimity about the origins and early development of jazz. In fact, the early years of jazz are shrouded in a kind of fog, which the passing decades have thickened rather than cleared.

In the years leading up to the making of the first jazz records in 1917, the evidence—the prehistory of the music—is mostly silent. Lacking recordings of jazz musicians before 1917, the historian must rely on far less direct sources of information: contemporaneous recordings of other kinds of music, the reminiscences of musicians (which frequently are at odds with each other), newspaper notices, and photographs.

The very origin of the word *jazz* is in doubt—there are at least a half-dozen theories about its derivation. One holds that the word is an Afro-Caribbean term for "speed up." There are multiple indications that in early twentieth-century San Francisco, the word was in the air, meaning something like pep, enthusiasm, or "play with energy," while in New Orleans, the word was used to mean sexual intercourse. The first verified written use of it was in a San Francisco newspaper in 1913. In fact, the word was spelled variously "jas," "jass," "jaz," and "jazz" until at least 1918. In New Orleans, until the 1920s at the earliest, most musicians used the term *ragtime* for the music they played.

The early history of jazz may never be known precisely. Yet it's possible to identify a number of phenomena, conditions, and events that in combination seem to have given rise to the music and brought it into the public consciousness.

Old-World Roots

The story of jazz begins with two of the most consequential population shifts in modern history: European emigrants seeking a better life in the New World, and black Africans being brutally uprooted and transported to the Americas to be sold into slavery. In the Western Hemisphere, European- and African-derived cultural traditions—including musical traditions—intermingled gradually over a period of several hundred years, creating an array of syntheses that included jazz.

African Influences

Understanding jazz requires a look at a few facts about African music, and in particular the music of West Africa, where most of the slaves came from. A number of the characteristics of jazz are found in African music. They include group participation, a link with dancing, an emphasis on rhythm, a structure based on *call and response*, the use of improvisation, the application of vocal sounds to instruments, and the prevalence of short,

repeated melodic phrases—called *riffs* in jazz. African music also tends to be passed on aurally, rather than in written form.

In Africa, music is such an integral and omnipresent part of the daily fabric that life without it is inconceivable. Music involves group participation, and it is frequently performed to accompany dancing.

Drumming is a crucial mode of musical expression in West Africa. But it is just one aspect of the all-important twin hallmarks of African music: rhythm and percussiveness. West African music is marked by "hot rhythm"—rhythm that swings or has a strong forward-propelling motion. Musical ensembles often play polyrhythms and polymeters—several different rhythms and meters going on simultaneously.

A related dominant trait of West African music is a percussive approach to articulation. Musical instruments, whether struck or not, are given a crisp, precise attack, creating a kind of kick at the beginning of the note, a practice that would come to mark a great deal of jazz.

An early-nineteenth-century West African community performs ceremonial music and dance as British explorers look on.

The formal structure of much African music is responsorial. It entails call and response—a kind of dialogue (often of an interlocking, overlapping nature) between a leader and a chorus. Call and response also characterizes interplay between drummers in a drum ensemble and between a singer and accompaniment. In addition, it's reflected in African dance: sometimes a skilled dancer will step into a circle of dancers and take a solo that mirrors a call-and-response pattern in the music.

Call and response typically involves improvisation: the soloist will spontaneously invent musical statements and melodic variations and embellishments. The chorus responds to each improvised statement with a more stable melodic "answer" to the soloist. Both improvisation and responsorial patterns came to suffuse African American music, including jazz. Examples can be heard in the music of 1930s big bands, in which a lead instrument improvises a melody over a background chorus of repeating riffs played by a horn section.

African music also makes use of the natural melodic quality of spoken language, applying it to both vocal and instrumental music. Most African languages are built on a melodic relationship between syllables (up-down, down-up, same-same), and thus speech patterns are easily transformed into song. African vocal music has such other speechlike characteristics as glissandi, dips and bends, a rising attack, and a falling release. Similar sounds can be produced with some instruments—the famous African "talking drums," for example, as well as such melody-producing instruments as flutes, trumpets, and xylophones. Jazz trumpeters and trombonists would carry on this tradition by developing ways of using mutes and half-valving techniques to make their brass instruments "talk."

Long forms comparable to the European rondo or sonata are rare in traditional West African music, which prefers short, iterative forms—the kind that would show up in jazz as riffs and the repeating bass lines of boogie-woogie. While some African patterns are repeated verbatim, often there is subtle variation.

Thus, traditional West African music can generally be characterized as participatory, polyrhythmic and polymetric, percussive, responsorial, interlocking, varying or improvisatory, iterative, and aurally learned. These traits would, in varying degrees, come to mark jazz as it progressed through the twentieth century.

European Influences

Other characteristics of jazz came from European music. First, even though there is a basic kind of harmony in some African music, and while the African scale is similar to the European, jazz took its harmonic system more from Europe. Second, jazz, when written down, is expressed using the European system of musical notation, slightly modified. Third, jazz derived most of its instruments—cornet, trumpet, trombone, the saxophone family, clarinet, piano, bass, and guitar—from European music. (Exceptions included the drum set, which was an American amalgamation of percussion instruments of various origin, and the banjo, an American commercial adaptation of an instrument, the *banza,* made by West African slaves in the New World.) Fourth, European music served as the source of several compositional forms common in jazz, notably the thirty-two-bar popular-song form and the multi-strain form used in marches, rags, and such early jazz pieces as *Tiger Rag* (1917) and Jelly Roll Morton's *Kansas City Stomp* (1923).

The banjo, its origins traceable to West Africa, has a brittle and trebly tone that can match the volume of horns and drums, making the instrument a staple of early jazz. The banjo had long been used in minstrel shows—traveling revues that were among the conduits through which nineteenth-century U.S. listeners heard the music of the day and such proto-jazz sounds as syncopation.

Lavish performances like this European production were staged at New Orleans' French Opera House, which, from 1859 to 1919, was the city's most celebrated, and celebratory, house of entertainment and revelry. In addition to French-language opera, it hosted masquerade balls and other festive events.

Black audiences attended French Opera House performances, though they were sequestered in the venue's fourth tier of seating.

One example of Europe's impact on jazz: European and especially Italian opera exerted a powerful influence on trumpeter Louis Armstrong. It can be heard in Armstrong's improvised quotations from various operas and, moreover, in his dramatic bursts of melody; florid embellishments; operatic, bravura musical gestures; and way of theatrically placing himself, as soloist, in the sonic foreground. Armstrong, through his clarion example, would make these characteristics common in jazz.

New Orleans

Many syntheses of African and European traditions took place in the Americas, and one of them was jazz. In the creation of that music, one American locale looms largest: New Orleans.

New Orleans was established in 1718 as an outpost in the French colony of Louisiana, and during its first century it had more in common geographically, economically, and culturally with the French and Spanish colonies in the Caribbean than it did with New York or Boston. One example: while the U.S. populace was largely Protestant (with some puritanical influence) and English-speaking, that of New Orleans was Roman Catholic and French-speaking. The French in the New World, through their cultural and religious worldview, were noted for exercising tolerance of local cultures, which would help lay the groundwork for jazz in New Orleans.

At first, French culture predominated in New Orleans, reinforced by an influx of French and Creoles—New

World natives of European, African, and mixed descent—from Saint-Domingue (now Haiti) around 1810. At that time the city was awash in French-language opera (established in 1791, the first in North America), theater, and newspapers. Before the Civil War, New Orleans was often called "the Paris of America."

In 1800, more than half the population had African origins; the scent of African cooking, the sounds of African music, and the sight of Afro-Creole dancing flavored the cultural environment. The African influence was reinforced by the importation of slaves directly from Africa; although the federal government outlawed the practice in 1808, some slaves were brought in illegally up to the eve of the Civil War. The city boasts the oldest urban black community in the United States.

Following the Caribbean pattern, New Orleans developed something of a three-tiered racial structure: whites, blacks, and people of mixed descent.

Events in the city's history added to its ethnic plural-ism. In 1783, France ceded Louisiana to Spain, which returned it to France in 1803. That year, the Louisiana Purchase transferred ownership to the United States. A flood of Anglo-American immigrants then challenged the Franco-African host culture of the city. Before the Civil War, the city took in many German and Irish immi-grants and, after the war, an influx of Italians. Although Anglo-Americans were ascendant, New Orleans boasted an ethnic composition—including French, African, Carib-bean, Italian, German, Mexican, and American Indian—of a diversity unprecedented in the South.

New Orleans' Six Jazz-Creating Conditions

New Orleans, with its multiethnic populace and pivotal location, claimed a unique set of six conditions that gave rise to jazz.

Fluid Cultural Boundaries. New Orleans possessed the loose boundaries needed for the exchange of culture.

Until the Civil War, it was the second-largest port of immigration in the Western Hemisphere—both the Mississippi River and the Gulf of Mexico served as capa-cious musical highways.

The city's residential patterns and musical activities promoted cultural intermingling. In most other U.S. cities, many ethnic groups typically lived in their own neigh-borhoods. New Orleans, however, had no such ghettos. People of one race lived cheek by jowl with another: the black trumpeter Buddy Bolden lived two doors down from the white clarinetist Larry Shields and his musical family, and the black bassist Pops Foster lived next door to the Sicilian American clarinetist Leon Roppolo. Part of the city's fluid multiculturalism, this proximity pro-vided many opportunities for musical interchange and helped jazz spread quickly beyond color lines.

Active Afro-Caribbean Culture. The city hosted a large contingent of free blacks—proud Afro-French Creoles, who established their own culture and small-market economy. By the late eighteenth century, on Sun-days and religious holidays, slaves and free people of color gathered in an open field that became known as the Place de Nègres, later called Place Congo or Congo Square. It and a couple of other grassy commons in the city became probably the only places in North America where Afri-can dancing, drumming, and music-making could occur openly. (Drumming also figured in ceremonies of an

A thriving port, accessible by both the Gulf of Mexico and the Mississippi River, New Orleans (depicted here in 1873) absorbed immigrants and musical influences from many different locales and cultures.

The Eighth Cavalry Mexican Band opened at the Cotton Centennial Exposition in New Orleans in 1884. Audiences embraced its sound, and the band's popularity helped bring what Jelly Roll Morton called the "Spanish tinge" to jazz.

African-derived religion called *voudon* or voodoo, which some Africans and African descendants kept alive.)

New Orleans also absorbed elements of Caribbean cultures. Among them were the Cuban *habanera* and other rhythms and dances.

Dancers carried on African and Caribbean traditions in Congo Square until the mid-1850s, when increasing Americanization, with its more restrictive laws on matters of public amusement, drove those traditions out. But they lived on in cultural memory. Clarinetist Sidney Bechet wrote of the "remembering song"—"the long song that started back there in the South…. There's so much to remember."

Vital Musical Life. In nineteenth-century New Orleans, music played an important role in community and civic life. "Of all the cities in North America," wrote cultural historian Berndt Ostendorf, "New Orleans had the oldest and most active musical public sphere." New Orleanians loved a good melody, and the city was awash with operatic airs such as the quartet from Verdi's *Rigoletto* (1851); French music-hall songs; such Creole tunes as *Eh la bas*; *Old Dan Tucker* (1843) and other minstrel songs; spirituals such as *Down by the Riverside*; African American folk songs such as *Careless Love*; Italian, German, Mexican, and Cuban tunes; polkas and marches; and the latest popular songs from New York City. When an enormous Mexican military band played the city's Cotton Centennial Exposition in 1884–85, it created a sensation and sparked interest in Latin-influenced music. After the band broke up, some of its members remained in New Orleans, helping to extend the Latin musical influence in the city.

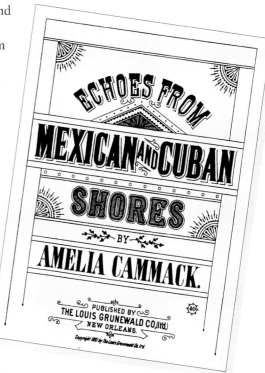

Music publishers responded to the demand for Latin-influenced music by issuing printed versions of songs and instrumentals.

Though jazz didn't originate in New Orleans' red-light district, it was played there. The pianist pictured above, at Hilma Burt's "house" in Storyville, is thought to be Jelly Roll Morton.

An 1867 carnival parade reflected New Orleans' infatuation with festivities and pageantry.

Strong Dance Tradition. Like its active musical sphere, the city's long-standing, insatiable demand for dancing transcended all boundaries of class and race. Dancing was the cheapest and most feasible form of entertainment in the frontier days; it jumped language barriers better than song. (Louisiana's first U.S.-appointed governor, William Claiborne, reportedly complained that the locals were ungovernable because they were preoccupied with dancing.) Early on, New Orleans hosted discrete dance traditions, but by the end of the nineteenth century it had developed a citywide dance culture. Out of this culture grew jazz, thanks to the bands that provided dance accompaniment.

Pervasive "Good Times" Atmosphere. The Big Easy loves to party, savors a holiday, relishes any festive occasion, and exercises a laid-back attitude toward sex and revelry. New Orleans is the only large U.S. city with a tradition of pre-Lent Carnival or Mardi Gras, and *Laissez les bons temps roulez* (Let the good times roll) is the city's unofficial motto.

Early on, New Orleans earned notoriety for its bohemian streak and for its elegance, extravagance, colorfulness, and, yes, wickedness. (During the twenty-year period ending when Storyville was closed down in 1917, as many as 800 registered prostitutes worked 175 "houses," making Storyville the largest red-light district in the nation.)

Whatever the setting for good times—whether dances, parties, parades, cabarets, sporting events, riverboat excursions, or even brothels—jazz was on hand to provide the accompaniment.

Prevalence of Brass Bands. By the late nineteenth century, brass bands were popular across the U.S., but in New Orleans especially so: the city adored marching bands and parades, as observers going back at least as far as 1830 noted. During the Civil War and Reconstruction, brass bands proliferated in the city at large and among black musicians. By 1888, *Metronome* magazine was reporting that New Orleans had "twenty to twenty-five bands averaging twelve men apiece. The colored race monopolize the procession music." Such bands as the Excelsior and Onward, both established in the 1880s, were often hired by black fraternal organizations for parades and funeral marches—events that reflected African notions of responsorial group participation. These bands, which sometimes doubled as dance bands, provided musical training for many jazz musicians, contributed pieces to the jazz repertory, and influenced dance bands to change over from stringed instruments to the brass instruments that became central to jazz.

Particularly noteworthy—and colorful—were the funerals with brass bands, a tradition that continues to this day. Typically sponsored by local fraternal societies, the processions are subdued and reverent in the march toward the interment ceremony, but on the way out, the musicians, as Jelly Roll Morton put it, "just tear loose," spiritedly celebrating the life of the departed.

Parading with a Brass Band

Boom!...Boom!...Boom! Those first thunderous blasts from the big bass drum signal the start of a musically led passage deep into the soul of New Orleans. Whatever the context of the drum call and improvised brass-band music that follow, be it a funeral march, a social club's annual parade, or a church anniversary, everyone is welcome to participate in the spirited—and often spiritual—occasion.

One, two, even three ten-piece brass bands—each member wearing a uniform and band cap—may line up for the procession. Each group might have three trumpets to improvise melodies, two trombones to slide and growl, a clarinet to sing and dance above the ensemble, and two saxophones to lay down powerful riffs. The foundation is a swinging rhythm section with a lightly rapping snare drum, a roaring bass drum to pour out endless syncopated rhythms, and a whopping tuba to anchor

everything with bass lines. Whether jazzing up a standard religious hymn, a traditional march, a popular song, a rag, or a blues, the band struts along and marks the time in easy, neither-too-fast-nor-too-slow dance tempos.

Each band is led by an elegantly dressed grand marshal, who waves his handkerchief and carries a decorated umbrella as he gracefully dances along, establishing processional order amid the surrounding chaos. Then there are dozens of club members, who spend thousands for the special day. Club divisions attempt to outdo each other in dance and dress. One group may wear boiled-shrimp-colored outfits from head to toe; another may wear cranberry red or avocado green.

As the parade proceeds, it collects an endless number of "second liners"—hundreds of anonymous onlookers who follow and dance alongside the parade. The music

and dance interact in countless ways. Standard music rules are broken, twisted, and stretched in favor of fresh creative expression that matches the wild passion of the dances and provides a taste of the freedom sought by its creators in everyday life. It's easy to become disoriented in this spirit world. As the dancing and the music reach ever-higher levels of intensity, the participants may feel they're losing themselves in a swirling sea of people, motion, heat, scents, and sounds. For many, undoubtedly, the four-to-six-hour duration of the experience seems like mere minutes.

The parade ends with a rousing finale, and normalcy slowly sets in. Musicians and others begin to feel the ache of fatigue and the sting of blistered feet. But chances are that everyone has the same thought: it'll be a long wait until the next weekend, when they can do it all again.
—Michael White

Parade and funeral regulars Henry Allen, Sr., and his brass band in Algiers, Louisiana, ca. 1905. Standing, left to right: Jack Carey, unidentified musician, Jimmy Palao, August Rousseau, unidentified musician, Joe Howard, Oscar "Papa" Celestin, Henry Allen, Sr.

Blues Bedrock

Ask a music industry executive what the blues is and you'd be pointed to a body of music exemplified by Robert Johnson, Muddy Waters, and B.B. King. Ask an English professor, and you'd be pointed to a three-line, AAB, poetic form. But ask a jazz musician, and you'd be pointed to a twelve-bar musical structure which, at its most basic, contains just three chords that always pull you back to the home, or *tonic*, chord. The following prototypical blues chorus, from W.C. Handy's *St. Louis Blues* (1914), contains space (shown in yellow) for a soloist to answer the singer:

Bar 1	Bar 2	Bar 3	Bar 4
I hate to see	the evenin' sun go	down.	.
C	F	C	C7
Bar 5	**Bar 6**	**Bar 7**	**Bar 8**
Hate to see	the evenin' sun go	down.	
F	F	C	C
Bar 9	**Bar 10**	**Bar 11**	**Bar 12**
'Cause my baby	he done lef' this	town.	
G	G7	C	C

The simple and expressive but extraordinarily elastic blues "progression" (typically twelve bars, but sometimes eight or sixteen) runs throughout jazz—indeed, is its most basic musical structure. Within this simple form, however, jazz musicians have created dozens of variations and thousands upon thousands of blues tunes.

Sometimes blues are easy to spot: obvious ones include the traditional *Careless Love* and *Frankie and Johnny,* the Original Dixieland Jazz Band's *Livery Stable Blues* (1917), King Oliver's *Chimes Blues* (1923), Count Basie's *One O'Clock Jump* (1937), Billie Holiday's *Fine and Mellow* (1939), Charlie Parker's *Now's the Time* (1945), and Miles Davis's *All Blues* (1959). In other cases, the composer camouflages the blues "changes": examples are Duke Ellington's *Creole Love Call* (1928) and *Ko-Ko* (1940), Thelonious Monk's *Misterioso* (1948) and *Straight, No Chaser* (1951), John Coltrane's *Chasin' the Trane* (1961), and Chick Corea's *Matrix* (1968).

Ironically, such songs as *Birth of the Blues* (1926), *Basin Street Blues* (1928), and *Blues in the Night* (1941) are not considered blues by jazz musicians: none follow the blues chord progression. To recognize a real blues, you have to use your ears. —*John Edward Hasse*

Musical Antecedents: The Blues

While jazz drew on numerous cultural traditions, it also grew from, and built on, several preceding U.S.-originated musical forms. One of them was the blues, whose evolved three-chord structure ultimately served as a popular framework for jazz compositions, and whose characteristic bent and slurred notes became common in jazz melodies.

The blues, like jazz, has roots in Africa. In his provocative book *Origins of the Popular Style*, scholar Peter van der Merwe argues that "the raw materials of the blues already existed in Africa, but mixed with an enormous wealth of other material. Gradually and unconsciously this other material was winnowed away, and what was left was the blues." At the same time, European influence—especially through settlers of Scots-Irish ancestry who found their way to Mississippi and other Deep South states—not only simplified complex African rhythms but added a few new rhythmic twists and exerted some sway over the structure and melodic contour of the blues.

The blues may have begun when a nineteenth-century African American thought up the idea of accompanying a field holler (an extemporaneous, solo cry used in cotton-picking and other work settings)—probably at first with a one-chord accompaniment. In this scenario, elaborations developed over time, and eventually the blues' familiar three-chord pattern coalesced. Tunes employed a "framework of melodically sensitive notes interspersed with less sensitive notes," as van der Merwe put it, emphasizing "blue notes" (slightly flattened third, fifth, sixth, and seventh notes of the scale) in syncopated rhythm.

Blues lyrics typically comprise three lines, the second often repeating the first. While many people think the blues have to be woeful or complaining, in fact many blues songs are celebratory. But either way, they're packed with emotion and spirituality. When a jazz musician really plays the blues, he or she is dipping into a deep river of tradition that speaks of struggle, community, affirmation, and transcendence over adversity. The blues brings release to the performer as it uplifts the audience.

The blues no doubt arose in rural areas of the Deep South—W.C. Handy recalled hearing it in the 1890s—and then found its way into southern cities and eventually into the North. The music existed strictly in aural tradition until sheet music published in New Orleans and St. Louis began to reveal it in the first decade of the twentieth century. In the 1910s, following the lead of Handy, songwriters began publishing bluesy pieces. Beginning in 1920, blues tunes were recorded on discs by Ma Rainey, Bessie Smith, and others. By then, the blues chord progression, blue notes, and even a blues sensibility had become firmly entrenched in jazz, and the blues would continue to evolve as a related but separate music.

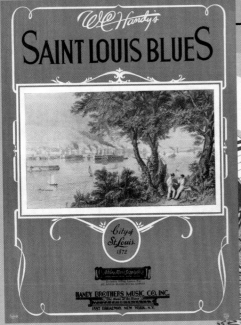

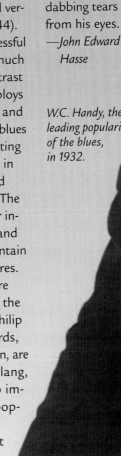

In 1909, Memphis bandleader W.C. Handy, inspired by the folk blues he had heard while traveling the South, composed a song called *Memphis Blues*. When published in 1912, it sparked a fad for blues songs and eventually became a jazz standard. Two years later, he published *St. Louis Blues*, which far surpassed *Memphis Blues* to became one of the most familiar, widely performed jazz standards and American songs of all time.

St. Louis Blues caught on slowly; it wasn't until the 1920s that it became a jazz staple. In that decade, more than sixty jazz recordings were made of it, and the number increased in the 1930s. Ultimately, *St. Louis Blues* became the second-most recorded American song (Hoagy Carmichael's *Stardust* is first), with versions by such artists as the Original Dixieland Jazz Band, Louis Armstrong, Duke Ellington, Sidney Bechet, Dave Brubeck, Herbie Hancock, and Sun Ra.

The piece has been arranged for dozens of instrumental combinations and undergone numerous variations. Pianist Earl "Fatha" Hines recorded it as *Boogie-Woogie on Handy's St. Louis Blues* (1940), and Glenn Miller and

His Orchestra issued a recorded version as *St. Louis Blues March* (1944).

Why was this the most successful blues of all time? The piece is much richer in musical form and contrast than typical blues tunes. It employs an AABC structure. Both the A and C sections comprise twelve-bar blues progressions, while the contrasting B section is a sixteen-bar strain in *habanera* rhythm (Handy's band had traveled to Cuba in 1900). The A and C strains provide further interest by building in "breaks," and those in the final, C section contain some boogie-woogie bass figures. The three different melodies are singable and memorable. And the lyrics are striking; as scholar Philip Furia has pointed out, the words, particularly in the middle section, are "laced with more truncated slang, telegraphic syntax, and sharp imagery than would appear in popular lyrics until the 1920s."

The song was used in about forty motion pictures, most notably the 1929 sixteen-

minute short subject *St. Louis Blues*, in which Bessie Smith, in her only screen appearance, sings the song with great power and majestic sorrow. The song also served as the title of a patronizing 1958 Hollywood biopic starring Nat "King" Cole as W.C. Handy. In the 1956 documentary *Satchmo the Great*, made two years before Handy's death, the cameras captured a touching moment in which Louis Armstrong performs *St. Louis Blues* while the aged, now-blind Handy, in the front row, listens transfixed to his masterpiece, dabbing tears from his eyes.

—John Edward Hasse

W.C. Handy, the leading popularizer of the blues, in 1932.

The publication of sheet music helped popularize ragtime.

The perceived wildness of ragtime proved an attractive subject for parody—and met with the disapproval of musical conservatives.

Musical Antecedents: Ragging and Ragtime

Another musical precursor of jazz—ragtime—emerged in the late nineteenth century.

It started out, probably far back in U.S. history, as a practice of "ragging"—creatively altering and syncopating—an existing piece of music. In 1876, the Georgia-born poet Sidney Lanier wrote, "Syncopations… are characteristic of Negro music. I have heard Negroes change a well-known melody by adroitly syncopating it…so as to give it a bizarre effect scarcely imaginable."

Over time, the technique was applied to new compositions. Songs and pieces for banjo and piano would be composed in a "ragged" or "raggy" style, with the syncopations an inherent, not an added-on, part of the music. Ragtime's characteristics, apart from syncopation, included polyrhythm, a strong rhythmic polarity between treble and bass, and multisectional forms.

In the 1880s, ragtime could be heard in the Midwest, even as its reverberations radiated to surrounding parts of the country. By 1892, composer Charles Ives had come across ragtime in minstrel shows in his hometown of Danbury, Connecticut, and at the 1893 Chicago World's Fair, many people evidently heard the style for the first time. By 1896, the first pieces labeled "rag time" were being published. In 1897, twenty-some piano rags were published, and by 1899, the number had reached more than 120, including some issued in New Orleans. Ragtime became the "new thing" in music, appealing to young people across the nation (though their parents often hated it).

Ragtime was played largely on the piano, and two traditions of doing so developed: most amateurs played pieces from sheet music largely as written, while many professional pianists "faked"—that is, embellished and even improvised on the melodies, playing, in everything but name, an early form of jazz. So many pianists were showing off and taking liberties that by 1905, Scott Joplin, the "King of Ragtime Writers," felt compelled to mark his rags "Notice! Don't play this piece fast." And in 1913, ragtime composer Artie Matthews admonished: "Don't fake."

While the composition and publication of ragtime died out in the late 1910s, the music's characteristics were absorbed into the new jazz style.

Jazz: An Improvisational Music

The jazz style involved not only reading written music but also improvising—composing or making up melodies spontaneously, on the spot. The practice comes largely from the African side of the music's Afro-European heritage (although European music of the Baroque and Classical periods employed kinds of improvisation). "Jazz," observed Berndt Ostendorf, "is the result of a confluence of rural ear music and urban eye music, of Western musical literacy and African musical memory"—in other words, jazz represents a merging of aural traditions (such as the blues) with notated forms of music.

Once jazz got under way in New Orleans, most of the city's jazz bands could both read notation and fake, or play by ear, which increasingly included improvising. The latter would eventually come to be regarded as a fundamental part of jazz. Players' ability to improvise satisfyingly would become at least as important as their technique, style, sound, choice of repertory and bandmates, and ability to communicate musically and connect with the audience.

Maple Leaf Rag

But when Maple Leaf was started
my timidity departed.
I lost my trepidation
you could taste de admiration.
Oh go 'way man.
I can hypnotize dis nation.
I can shake de earth's foundation
wid de Maple Leaf Rag.

—from *The Maple Leaf Rag Song* (1904),
words by Sydney Brown

Throughout the twentieth century, one ragtime piece has stood above all others: Scott Joplin's *Maple Leaf Rag*.

Born near Texarkana, Texas, to ex-slaves, probably in 1868, Scott Joplin settled in 1894 in the modest, maple tree–lined railroad town of Sedalia, Missouri, where he wrote his most celebrated rag. *Maple Leaf Rag*, published in 1899, sold only 400 copies its first year. But it gradually picked up steam, selling 500,000 copies within ten years and earning Joplin the rightful title of King of Ragtime Writers.

For a well-trained pianist, the notes on the pages don't look daunting. But perfecting the right-hand rhythms, establishing a groove with the bass part, and coordinating the two hands at a medium tempo or faster—that's a challenge. Embellishing the melody makes the task even tougher. And that's precisely what professional piano "perfessers" and "ticklers" were doing with *Maple Leaf Rag*—taking liberties, embellishing, and improvising. Although they also did it with other rags, *Maple Leaf* was a universally known "test piece" among them. In 1938, recording for Alan Lomax at the Library of Congress, Jelly Roll Morton made a famous demonstration of the "Missouri" or ragtime style of playing the *Maple Leaf*, followed by his own jazz version, showing how adaptable the piece is.

By the 1950s, there were about seventy versions on 78-rpm records, with dozens more to come on LPs and CDs. The tune has always been a favorite among pianists, but the range of artists who recorded it spans the century and an array of musical styles. They include the U.S. Marine Band; New Orleans musicians Sidney Bechet and Kid Ory; swing bandleaders Tommy Dorsey and Benny Goodman; the revivalist Lu Watters' Yerba Buena Jazz Band; the country-blues guitarist Reverend Gary Davis; the Brazilian guitarist Carlos Barbosa-Lima; the cutting-edge jazzmen Anthony Braxton, Ran Blake, and Archie Shepp; the Australian folk-rock group the Seekers; and the rock band Emerson, Lake, and Palmer.

Why the appeal? First, there's the allure of ragtime's toe-tapping rhythms and the magical polarity between the rhythms of the right and left hands. Then there's the *Maple Leaf's* originality. Though it's not as highly developed as some of Joplin's late rags, none can match its exuberance, rhythmic drive, and triumphant note of optimism, especially as the last strain goes out with a burst of energy.

—*John Edward Hasse*

Scott Joplin, the "King of Ragtime Writers," 1904.

Jazz: A Dance Music

Jazz started as a music primarily intended for dancing, and it would remain so for decades. European dance steps—the mazurka, polka, lancer, schottische, and variety—were prevalent in nineteenth-century New Orleans, accompanied by such bands as those under the leadership of John Robichaux and William Braun, whose members normally read music rather than improvised.

In the 1890s, New Orleans dancers began displacing the European steps with the American two-step and such erotic dances as the Grizzly Bear, Turkey Trot, Texas Tommy, and Todolo—some of which may have originated locally. As New Orleans experienced an influx of blacks migrating from other parts of Louisiana as well as Mississippi and Alabama, these new residents danced to other vernacular steps, including the Black Bottom and the Funky Butt. As the racier dances became popular, the bands focused more on improvisational music, especially after midnight when the "nice people" went home and the remaining dancers got down and dirty. The dancers idolized such musicians as the African American cornetists Buddy Bolden and Bunk Johnson, who played a looser, hotter, bluesier style of dance music than did the Creoles.

There may have been a hundred or more bands in New Orleans at the time: besides Robichaux's long-lived orchestra, leading bands around 1910 were the Magnolia and Superior orchestras, Manuel Perez's Imperial Orchestra, Freddie Keppard's Olympia Orchestra, Frankie Dusen's Eagle Band, Frank Christian's Ragtime Band, and those led by Papa Celestin, Armand J. Piron, Kid Ory, Happy Schilling, Johnny Fischer, and Jack Laine. These bands kept the dozens of dance halls that were scattered throughout the city and in outlying communities—including Economy Hall, Masonic Hall, Globe Hall, Artesian Hall, Tuxedo Hall, Funky Butt Hall, Perseverance Hall, the Tin Roof Café, and the 101 Ranch—packed with dancers.

As the Grizzly Bear and other racy dances gained popularity, so did dance bands that improvised and played hotter, bluesier music than that of their more "polite" counterparts.

John Robichaux (seated, right) led one of New Orleans' most active dance bands from the 1890s into the new century.

New Orleans Jazz Shrines

The Preservation Hall Jazz Band: (left to right) Jim Robinson, Cie Frazier, James Prevost, Percy Humphrey, Willie Humphrey, Sing Miller, and Narvin Kimball.

No city, except perhaps for New York, regularly receives more visiting jazz aficionados than New Orleans. For the lover of New Orleans jazz, what is there to see in the Crescent City?

First of all, stroll through the French Quarter and soak up the atmosphere: the old Spanish buildings with their iron balconies, the humidity that hangs in the air like a weight during the hot months, the calliopes sounding from the Mississippi riverboats a few blocks away. You might hear some jazz or blues coming out of a nightspot, perhaps even the sound of a trumpet floating out of an upstairs window. On occasion, you might even witness a brass band marching through the Quarter or on nearby city streets.

Many devotees head to the heart of the Quarter, to Preservation Hall (726 St. Peter Street), a bare-bones pair of wooden rooms that since 1961 has served as a shrine of sorts to the traditional New Orleans sound, as heard in nightly performances by the resident Preservation Hall Jazz Band.

Most of the legendary buildings associated with the heyday of New Orleans jazz—Economy Hall, Funky Butt Hall, Lulu White's Mahogany Hall—are long gone. But, at century's end, some remained standing, if not open to the public. They included the Odd Fellows Hall (1116 Perdido), where Buddy Bolden, King Oliver, Bunk Johnson, and Louis Armstrong once held forth; Bolden's haunt, the adjoining Eagle Saloon (410 South Rampart); the notorious Red Onion (762 South Rampart), where Jelly Roll Morton, Armstrong, Sidney Bechet, and Johnny Dodds played; Perseverance Hall (more recently a church, 1644 Villere), where Bolden and Freddie Keppard entertained dancers; and the Halfway House (102 City Park Avenue), where Leon Roppolo, Abbie Brunies, and others performed.

In 1994, the U.S. Congress authorized the establishment of the New Orleans Jazz National Historical Park, with exhibits, tours, educational programs, and visitors' facilities providing information on the early history of jazz. The planned site for the visitors' facilities is the city-run Louis Armstrong Park, whose grounds feature statues of Armstrong and Bechet and include the old Congo Square (North Rampart and Orleans), where slaves and free blacks once kept African traditions of music and dance alive. Listen closely, and you might hear faint echoes of footfalls and drumbeats.

—John Edward Hasse

Perhaps the very first jazz band, led by cornetist Buddy Bolden (standing, second from left). This photograph, the only known image of Bolden, was probably taken between 1895 and 1900.

New Orleans Notables

Early on, nearly all New Orleans ragtime, jazz, and dance musicians had to have "day gigs"—jobs as barbers, carpenters, laborers, longshoremen, brick masons, cigar rollers—to support themselves. By the early 1910s, some were able to pursue music full-time, which must have looked enticing. At a time of growing racial discrimination, the profession of musician was one of only three (the others were teacher and minister) open in any numbers to African Americans, and music held out the hope of escape from poverty, anonymity, and powerlessness. For all, it provided a means of self-expression and opportunities to impress others; for many, it offered a chance to travel, to escape routine, and to earn good tips. But to pursue that profession, musicians found that they had to leave the city, which was in a gradual economic decline; in the 1910s most of the best—or at least the most ambitious—players migrated to pastures with more "green."

No one can say who was the first jazz musician in New Orleans. Cornetist and bandleader Charles "Buddy" Bolden was among the earliest. By 1895 Bolden was leading his own group, and by 1901, it comprised cornet, trombone, clarinet, guitar, bass, and drums, which became a prototypical lineup of instruments. He became famous playing in New Orleans dance halls, in outlying communities, and in the city's Johnson Park, where his band would "cut," or outplay and outdraw, the polite dance band of John Robichaux, who performed across the street in the more respectable Lincoln Park. Bolden is said to have been inspired by the music of a "holy roller" church, and he delivered sounds in many forms, from rough and loud to slow and low-down. A legend has it that he made a cylinder recording, but if so, it has never been found. He did leave indelible memories of the rhythmic and emotional power and the clarion example of his playing on such numbers as *Make Me a Pallet on the Floor; If You Don't Shake, You Don't Get No Cake*; and his signature tune, *Funky Butt* (recorded as *Buddy Bolden's Blues* by Jelly Roll Morton). In 1907, Bolden, suffering from apparent dementia, was institutionalized, and he remained so for the rest of his life. He assumed the status of a legendary father figure in jazz.

Drummer and bandleader George "Jack" (or "Papa") Laine was one of the oldest of the pioneers, born in 1873, four years earlier than Bolden. In the 1890s, he established his Reliance Brass Band and a series of offshoots that included both "readers" and "fakers." Through his bands passed many of the white players who would make their names in jazz of the 1910s and 1920s in such groups as Tom Brown's Band from Dixieland, the Original Dixieland Jazz Band, Jimmy Durante's Original New Orleans Jazz Band, and the New Orleans Rhythm Kings. Though the Reliance bands never recorded, Laine achieved lasting importance as a nurturer of jazz talent.

Cornetist Freddie Keppard began his professional career in 1906. At that time, Keppard led the Olympia Orchestra and worked in other bands. In 1914, he headed west to Los Angeles, where he joined the Original Creole Band. Though they never recorded, this important band of New Orleans musicians played the vaudeville circuit for mostly white audiences for four years, spreading the city's novel jazz sound across the nation. Other musicians found Keppard's youthful skills praiseworthy: "There was no end to his ideas," recalled Jelly Roll Morton. "He could play a chorus eight or ten different ways." Legend has it that Keppard, like many vaudeville performers leery of having others "steal their stuff," turned down an offer from the prestigious Victor Talking Machine Company to become the first New Orleans band to record; the honor of making the first jazz record then went to a white group, the Original Dixieland Jazz Band. By the time Keppard would record in the 1920s, he was past his influential period and would sound dated and archaic compared to the cutting-edge Louis Armstrong.

It was in approximately 1907 that Joe Oliver began playing in dance bands, brass bands, and small units across New Orleans. Another cornet "king," he developed an expressive vocabulary of blueslike pitches and rhythmic nuances. He also became an early master of mutes, creating "wah-wah" and other effects

Brass-band pioneer "Papa" Jack Laine (seated) with an edition of his Reliance Brass Band, New Orleans, 1910. Laine's bands nurtured musicians who would later make more widely heard music with such acts as the Original Dixieland Jazz Band and the New Orleans Rhythm Kings.

Having built a reputation in New Orleans, cornetist Joe "King" Oliver (third from left) moved to Chicago and made history with his Creole Jazz Band. In 1921, the band—shown here in San Francisco—included clarinetist Johnny Dodds (third from right) and pianist Lil Hardin (fourth from left). Cornet prodigy Louis Armstrong would join later—and would marry Hardin.

that would be copied by many a musician, the Ellington trumpeter Bubber Miley, for one. After moving to Chicago in 1919—part of a general migration, during and after World War I, of blacks seeking more opportunity and a better life in the North—Oliver formed his own band in 1920 and became a respected bandleader. He played in California before returning to Chicago in 1921 and establishing King Oliver's Creole Jazz Band, which, when joined by the younger Louis Armstrong on second cornet, would make history.

From 1912 to 1919, trombonist Edward "Kid" Ory led one of New Orleans' most respected bands. Settling in California, he formed a unit known as Kid Ory's Original Creole Band, which, in 1922, became the first African American New Orleans group to make a record. He was the best-known trombonist in the loud, smeary, "tailgate" style, and he composed the standard *Muskrat Ramble* (1926).

Pianist, entertainer, and composer Jelly Roll Morton (born Ferdinand Joseph LaMothe) was descended from free Creoles of color who had roots in Saint-Domingue. Raised with the colored Creoles' social and ethnic sensibilities, Morton preferred to work with other downtown mulattoes more than with the uptown African Americans.

In 1907, after playing the Storyville district, he began touring in vaudeville and working sometimes as a solo pianist, with a drummer, or as a bandleader. His travels took him through the Gulf Coast and on to Memphis, St. Louis, New York, Texas, and the Midwest. He settled in Chicago from 1914 to 1917 and then on the West Coast from 1917 to 1922. Like Oliver, Keppard, Bechet, and Louis Armstrong, Morton remained unrecorded until 1923. But in the 1910s he had already composed a number of works (by then probably including *New Orleans Blues, King Porter Stomp, Georgia Swing,* and *Winin' Boy Blues*);

published an important early blues (*Jelly Roll Blues*, 1915); and registered a composition with the copyright office (*Frog-I-More Rag*, 1918).

A colorful personality who made money as a pool shark and wore a diamond in his tooth, Morton bragged that he "invented" jazz in the first decade of the century—an assertion that was met with derision by many. Yet by the 1910s he was already a piano wizard of the first rank who could evidently transform all sorts of music into jazz, embellishing, paraphrasing, and improvising, smoothing out the rhythms of ragtime, and making everything flow and swing.

Two years older than Morton was trombonist Tom Brown, who played in Jack Laine's Reliance bands before starting his own in about 1910. After opening for a short but influential run at Chicago's Lamb's Café in May of 1915, his Brown's Band from Dixieland became one of the first New Orleans jazz acts to make a splash—for itself and the new music—in the North.

Among the second generation of pioneer jazzmen, clarinetist and soprano saxophonist Sidney Bechet stands the tallest. By 1910, when he was in his teens, he had found work as a clarinetist in New Orleans jazz bands; in 1916, he left to play in touring shows, and in 1917 he settled briefly in Chicago, where he picked up the soprano saxophone, which became his primary instrument. In 1919, he became one of the first Americans to spread jazz to Europe, prompting the Swiss conductor Ernest Ansermet to famously call him "an extraordinary clarinet virtuoso…an artist of genius" who played blues "equally admirable for their richness of invention, force of accent, and daring in novelty and the unexpected." Bechet played with great intensity, soaring passion, and, like Armstrong, operatic bravura that, heard on recordings, can still raise goosebumps. At the end of his life, he wrote an autobiography, *Treat It Gentle* (1960)—as warm, lyrical, and eloquent as the best of his music.

Pianist and composer Jelly Roll Morton in Chicago, ca. 1923.

Sidney Bechet (far right) played Paris with Benny Peyton's Jazz Kings in 1921. He had already been hailed as a genius in Europe.

The Original Dixieland Jazz Band (ODJB) in 1917: (left to right) Tony Sbarbaro, Eddie Edwards, Nick LaRocca, Larry Shields, and Henry Ragas.

The ODJB's 1917 recording of Livery Stable Blues sold a phenomenal 1.5 million copies. Ironically, given the denigrating caricature on the sheet-music cover, the music owed a great debt to African American musicians.

The Sicilian American cornetist Nick LaRocca was a mainstay of the Original Dixieland Jazz Band (ODJB), a dance outfit, organized in Chicago in 1916, that comprised five New Orleans musicians. Clarinetist Larry Shields became known as its best player. In January of 1917, the ODJB opened at Reisenweber's Restaurant in New York City, where they played for eighteen months. They created a sensation and became the first jazz band to make recordings, in February of that same year. Although their recordings reveal a band short on improvisational ability, they were also full of drive and energy and were considered strikingly novel by the American public; their 1917 recording of Livery Stable Blues sold an extraordinary 1.5 million copies. They performed in England in 1919–20 and played a leading role in spreading jazz to a mass audience abroad as well as in the United States. Five of the band's numbers—two from 1917, Tiger Rag and Dixieland Jass Band One-Step (later called Original Dixieland One-Step), and three 1918 pieces, LaRocca's and Shields' At the Jazz Band Ball and Fidgety Feet, along with Clarinet Marmalade (by Shields and the ODJB's H.W. Ragas)—became jazz standards.

New Orleans Style and "Jass" Variants

The style developed by New Orleans musicians weaved separate melody lines into a captivating counterpoint—a "hot" sound of group embellishment and improvisation. The melody was typically passed from instrument to instrument, but by the 1920s, the cornet usually punched out the melody, the trombone smeared a countermelody or doubled the bass line, and the clarinet filled in with filigree. "In the early days…[n]one of the guys took their horns down for a chorus to let another guy play a solo," recalled Pops Foster. "About 1920 or '21 guys started taking down their horns, after they'd blown a chorus." In the 1920s, especially through the influence and genius of trumpeter Louis

Tiger Rag

First recorded by the Original Dixieland Jazz Band on August 17, 1917, in New York City, *Tiger Rag* is the quintessential New Orleans jazz composition and one of the best known and most often recorded jazz pieces of all time.

A long-running controversy shrouds its origins. Although the song was published by the Leo Feist company in New York, with the ODJB's cornetist Nick La-Rocca listed as the composer, pianist-composer Jelly Roll Morton later claimed he developed the piece from an old French quadrille popular in New Orleans. Legendary New Orleans bandleader Jack Laine and his men said it was alternately known as *Meatball, Praline, Number One, Number Two,* and the *Reliance Rag* and that it was a "put-together" piece. LaRocca explained that the piece resulted from combining many elements. These include an extension of a popular two-bar phrase known as "Get Over Dirty," a simplified stop-time version of the children's song *London Bridge Is Falling Down,* a chorus melody built on the chord progressions of the standard march *National Emblem* (1906), and a downward "rip" after the lyric "Hold that tiger" that imitates the alto horn part in German bands. *Tiger Rag* as recorded by the ODJB also incorporates an eight-bar excerpt from Schubert's *Sixteen German Dances, Opus 33.*

Tiger Rag's source material turned up in other songs as well. The *National Emblem* chord progressions appear in many popular pieces from the time—including *Zacatecas March* (1891), *Bill Bailey, Won't You Please Come Home* (1902), and *Washington and Lee Swing* (1910).

By 1942, jazz musicians had recorded *Tiger Rag* more than 130 times. It became a favorite of Louis Armstrong and every traditional-style New Orleans jazz band, as well as guitarist Django Reinhardt, pianist Art Tatum, and bandleader Duke Ellington. Lyrics by Harry de Costa were added in 1932, and pop artists ranging from the Mills Brothers to Liberace to Bobby Short recorded the piece. *Tiger Rag* also became one of the fight songs of the Louisiana State University Tigers football team.

Tiger Rag achieved enduring popularity because it contains many simple yet effective devices that hold interest and build intensity. Through two 32-bar verses and a 128-bar chorus, it uses appealing chord progressions, two key changes, three different extended riffs, numerous breaks, and the signature tiger "rip" to build to a rousing finish in a "ride-out chorus." It has often been noted that everyone played the *Maple Leaf Rag,* and it can also be said that everybody played, and still plays, *Tiger Rag.* —*Jack Stewart*

Armstrong and saxophonist Sidney Bechet—and the indelibility of recordings—jazz would become a soloist's art.

The growing diaspora of Crescent City players spread the sound, and it caught the fancy of many young people at a time when, across the nation, public dancing was becoming a craze and nightlife was increasing as a sphere of urban culture. However much the youngsters liked the new jazz sound, though, many oldsters resisted it on musical or moralistic grounds, joining a heated controversy that had raged over ragtime and now erupted into a war over jazz. "Does Jazz Put the Sin in Synco-pation?" asked a 1921 article in *Ladies Home Journal,* answering its own question with an emphatic affirmative.

But opposition couldn't contain jazz. New Orleans wasn't the only source of the music in the 1910s. During the middle and late teens, early jazz was emerging in Los Angeles, San Francisco, Chicago, Kansas City, New York, and Washington, D.C. There and elsewhere, musicians were experimenting. They were trying out looser rhythms, exploring syncopation, bending notes, embellishing melodies, varying familiar songs, devising their own "breaks," and creating their own tunes.

Some of the musicians leading the way worked in New York City, the hub of show business and the home of storied Tin Pan Alley. By 1913, pianist James P. Johnson was playing dance halls in the "Jungles" section of the rough Manhattan neighborhood Hell's Kitchen, working out a driving keyboard style that, beginning in 1917, was captured on player-piano rolls. He and fellow pianists Abba Labba, Luckeyth Roberts, and Eubie Blake were creating an eastern style of ragtime—flashy, tricky, with syncopation in the left hand as well as the right—that would develop into the Harlem "stride" style of jazz piano.

By the close of the 1910s, jazz had emerged outside the confines of New Orleans, lighting up nightspots on the South Side of Chicago, in Hell's Kitchen and Harlem, and on the West Coast. While expanding geographically, jazz had also moved from the tenderloins into dance halls and vaudeville houses. Through sheet music, piano rolls, and especially phonograph recordings, jazz had entered the parlors and living rooms of average Americans, undergoing a transformation from a localized style of music-making to a budding and controversial national phenomenon. It had sailed the ocean and penetrated Europe. In the next decade, jazz would, along with its associated dance steps, bring an unprecedented number of Americans into dance halls and ballrooms, capture the imagination of painters and writers and composers, and produce the first momentous evidence of its foremost practitioners' depth and genius when Sidney Bechet, Jelly Roll Morton, Louis Armstrong, and Duke Ellington made records. ◠

Sheet music, piano rolls, and phonograph recordings were early means of distribution, exposing the public to the music that would give rise to jazz.

Key Recordings

Atlantic Jazz: New Orleans. Atlantic. The persistence of the New Orleans jazz tradition and repertory is attested to by recordings of Paul Barbarin, George Lewis, the Eureka Brass Band, and others made in the 1950s and sixties. Included are infectious versions of *Bourbon Street Parade, Sing On,* and *Tiger Rag.*

The Blues: A Smithsonian Collection of Classic Blues Singers. This four-disc anthology, spanning sixty-two years of recordings, provides an excellent overview of blues song, beginning with such important figures of the 1920s as Blind Lemon Jefferson, Ma Rainey, and Bessie Smith, and continuing through Robert Johnson, Joe Turner, T-Bone Walker, Jimmy Rushing, Jimmy Witherspoon, Muddy Waters, Ray Charles, Bobby "Blue" Bland, and others. A follow-up Smithsonian set, *Mean Old World: The Blues from 1940 to 1994,* is also superb.

Blues Roots. Rhino. This disc (Volume 10 in Rhino's Blues Masters series), recorded in the field, examines various origins of the blues, beginning with West African music and continuing through prison work songs, minstrel songs, and religious tunes. Rich Amerson's unaccompanied, haunting "field blues" *Black Woman* will give you goosebumps. Compiled and annotated by the blues expert Samuel Charters.

Hyman, Dick. *Scott Joplin: Piano Works, 1899–1904.* RCA. Best known as a versatile jazz pianist, Hyman interprets sixteen of Joplin's early rags—including *Maple Leaf Rag*—with precision, verve, and zest, making this collection a standout in the field of Joplin recordings.

Jazz: New Orleans, 1918–1944. Fremeaux. This two-disc French release provides a useful sampling of bands from New Orleans, including the Original Dixieland Jazz Band, Sam Morgan's Jazz Band, Piron's New Orleans Orchestra, and Celestin's Original Tuxedo Jazz Orchestra.

Johnson, James P. *Carolina Shout.* Biograph. Back before African American jazz musicians were making records, piano wizard Johnson was making player-piano rolls of his athletic and rhythmic Harlem stride style. His *Carolina Shout* became a favorite of Ellington; also included is his emblem of the 1920s, *Charleston.*

Morton, Jelly Roll. *The Library of Congress Recordings.* Rounder. These recordings—among the great sound documents in American culture—capture the early development of jazz, as Morton embodied it, in piano solos, songs, and stories. His contrasting versions of *Maple Leaf Rag* alone are worth the price of admission. Rounder also issued these as four separate CDs, titled *Kansas City Stomp, Anamule Dance, The Pearls,* and *Winin' Boy Blues,* originally comprising dozens of 78-rpm sides. The label excluded most of Morton's fascinating anecdotes, boasts, and recollections, but a promised release will rectify those omissions.

New Orleans in New Orleans. EPM. Not all the good jazz musicians left New Orleans in the rush to the North and West. This French disc features fourteen bands that remained behind and were captured in recordings made, with one exception, in New Orleans itself between 1923 and 1929. The artists include Sam Morgan, Celestin's Original Tuxedo Jazz Orchestra, Fate Marable's Society Syncopators, and Tony Parenti.

Ragtime to Jazz, 1 and 2. Timeless. These two Dutch releases, the first covering recordings from 1912 to 1919 and the second from 1916 to 1922, trace ragtime as it merged and morphed into jazz, at the hands of James Reese Europe, the Original Dixieland Jazz Band, Wilbur Sweatman, the Louisiana Five, and others.

The Spirit of Ragtime. ASV Living Era. Recordings from 1910 to 1947 on this UK release spotlight piano rolls, ragtime songs, and piano rags transformed into jazz by such artists as James P. Johnson, Jelly Roll Morton, Fats Waller, and Art Tatum. —*John Edward Hasse*

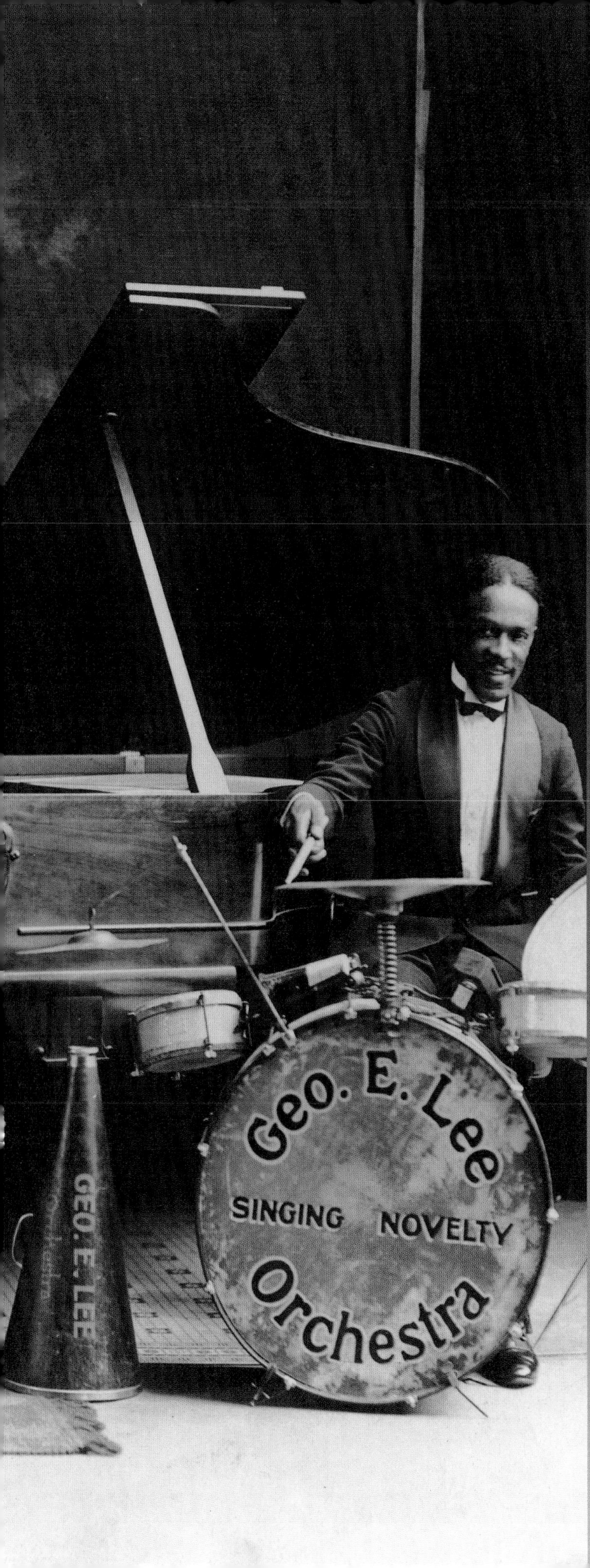

CHAPTER 2

The Flourishing of Jazz

Michael Brooks

SIDEBARS

The George Lee Orchestra, one of the top Kansas City bands of the 1920s, with Lee (fourth from left) on saxophone and his sister Julia on piano (shown here in 1926).

Trumpeter and singer Louis Armstrong, one of the most beloved entertainers of the twentieth century and the model for all jazz soloists to come.

Jazz began as a music associated with dancing, and it remained that way as it moved into the 1920s, with one overriding difference: In earlier years, live jazz, still in embryonic form, was hard to find outside of New Orleans and a few other cities. But in the 1920s it took shape as a distinct musical style known and embraced by young audiences the world over.

Its first creative geniuses—Louis Armstrong, Duke Ellington, Sidney Bechet, and Jelly Roll Morton—produced key work during the twenties, transforming what had once been a rough iteration of ragtime, the blues, and marching music into an art of sophistication and depth. Through vision and force of personality, they established new artistic benchmarks and conventions that would last through the remainder of the century: Where jazz had once been an ensemble sound, artists in the wake of Armstrong shifted the focus to soloists. Where jazz composition had formerly been narrowly conceived, new artists envisioned it as broader, more open-ended. Where band sounds had been limited, innovators expanded the sonic palette, introducing new timbres and combinations of instruments. And making their accomplishment all the more remarkable was the fact that they did it in the restrictive sphere of popular entertainment, where the first order of business was to keep the crowds coming.

Nightlife and the surrounding social whirl, whatever the creative limitations it placed on performers, had everything to do with jazz coming into public favor. New trends in the use of leisure time—trends that favored the public consumption of music—had emerged in the years surrounding and during World War I. Burgeoning and diversifying populations in urban industrial centers, combined with changing social attitudes, had spiked demand for new kinds and places of entertainment. A dance craze swept U.S. cities from 1912 to 1916, fueled by a new permissiveness that made public dancing socially acceptable for both women and men. The opening of New York City's Roseland Ballroom in 1919 heralded a boom in dance halls in the 1920s, and dance bands played for young people who wanted to forget the war and instead look forward to a brighter future.

With the passage of the Volsted Act in 1919, Prohibition had come into force, outlawing the manufacture and sale of alcohol. But instead of eliminating consumption, Prohibition drove it underground, where nightclubs, cabarets, and speakeasies lured late-night crowds with the promise of illegal booze and unregulated revelry.

The "Roaring Twenties," with its taste for the new, the exciting, and the exotic, found in jazz the perfect sonic accompaniment. So great a part of the cultural fabric was the new music that novelist F. Scott Fitzgerald dubbed the 1920s the "Jazz Age."

Jazz also rode in on the coattails of a growing white fascination with African American culture. In August 1920, singer Mamie Smith made the first blues record, *Crazy Blues*, which opened the floodgates for "race records"—discs made expressly for blacks, but that whites also purchased. In New York, the home of the largest concentration of African Americans in the United States, all-black revues and musicals were the rage on Broadway, fueling a market for other types of black entertainment and art. But even more key was the explosion of interest in African American–derived dancing. One 1923 revue, *Runnin' Wild,* popularized the Charleston. The step became a national fad for several years and created a vogue for other dances—and for the jazz that accompanied them.

Further laying the groundwork for the spread and development of jazz in the 1920s were advances in communications and recording technology. Radio became a mass medium in the middle part of the decade, exposing listeners all over the U.S. to the sound of the new music. At the same time, phonograph recording shifted from acoustic to electrical reproduction techniques, vastly improving the quality of recorded sound and inspiring such jazz composers as Duke Ellington to create more detailed and intricate musical arrangements.

In the 1920s, New York remained the center of the entertainment industry, but, thanks to a still-vital vaudeville circuit, musical acts spread across the country on lengthy tours, bringing up-to-date entertainment into any town large enough to have a theater. Jazz, too, especially as black musicians moved north and east from the economically waning South, found its way into other cities. Chief among them were Chicago and Kansas City.

The Charleston and other popular dances of the 1920s came out of musical revues such as those produced and choreographed in Harlem by Clarence Robinson (center, ca. 1925).

Chicago

Because of its central location and access to waterways, Chicago has long been one of the great commercial hubs of North America, and at the dawn of the 1920s it was especially active. The city's population was booming, Prohibition had given rise to a thriving black market in vice, money was pouring in from illicit liquor stills, and booze was being smuggled in from Canada. Speakeasies, brothels, nightclubs, movie houses, and dance halls were proliferating—all of them craving musical entertainment. The musicians followed, coming into LaSalle Station from the South with cases containing not submachine guns but trumpets and saxophones.

It took a few years for white musicians from New Orleans—who made most of the first Chicago jazz records—to shake off their Crescent City roots, but by the mid-1920s a distinctive new style of jazz had emerged. It was quite different from the sound produced in New Orleans; here, the music had an edgy 4/4 rhythm with angry staccato solo work that was not out of keeping with the trigger-happy philosophy of the surroundings.

There were few black jazz records until 1923, when Joe "King" Oliver returned from a stint in California to take up residence in Chicago's Lincoln Gardens—along with a new addition to the band, the young cornetist Louis Armstrong—and the Gennett Record Company invited his Creole Jazz Band to cut some sides in their Richmond, Indiana, studios. Gennett's outside-the-hub location and lack of a nationwide distribution system ordinarily meant they couldn't attract big-name artists. But a year earlier, they'd recorded the New Orleans Rhythm Kings (NORK), a group of young white musicians in residence at Chicago's Friar's Inn, and the records were selling well. Inspired by both the Original Dixieland Jazz Band and cornetist King Oliver, the NORK, with solid ensemble playing and memorable solos by clarinetist Leon Roppolo, created a sound—on such recordings as *Weary Blues* and *Tin Roof Blues* (both 1923)—that would influence a coterie of white Chicago players.

In April 1923 King Oliver made his first recordings for Gennett. His records followed the classic New Orleans pattern of ensemble playing, but with an important difference: the interplay between Oliver and Armstrong drove the listeners wild, making them more aware of individual instrumentalists. The same phenomenon was happening with the New Orleans clarinetist Roppolo, whose biting tone cut through the other instruments and whose expressive solos with the NORK (*Panama*, 1922; *Wolverine Blues*, 1923) caused the crowds to demand that he be featured.

But the most significant break from the New Orleans small-group sound came with the legendary Louis Armstrong Hot Five and Seven sides, made for OKeh Records in Chicago from 1925 to 1928. The group never existed outside of the recording studios, but the music they made under the direction of A&R man Richard M. Jones is as important as any jazz in the twentieth century. On their first recording (1925), *My Heart* essentially follows the old formula, with a few short solo breaks and Armstrong playing a strong lead. But on the flip side, *Gut Bucket Blues*, Armstrong introduces each sideman,

Joe "King" Oliver

When cornetist and bandleader Joe Oliver hired Louis Armstrong in 1922, the two turned Chicago on its ear. Their paths then diverged. Armstrong moved on to New York and international stardom. Oliver's career went into decline and his health began to fail; he eventually moved to Georgia, where his final job was that of a pool-room attendant.

Leading Labels: Columbia, Victor, and OKeh

Of all the record companies involved in early jazz, the three most prominent were Columbia, Victor, and OKeh.

The oldest record label still in existence, Columbia can lay claim to recording the first jazz record when the Original Dixieland Jazz Band entered the studios in New York's Woolworth Building and cut *The Darktown Strutters' Ball* and *Indiana* in 1917. Appalled at the noise, management rejected the sides until they noticed that tracks recorded by the same group for the Victor label later in the year—especially *Livery Stable Blues* and *Dixie Jass Band One-Step*—were racking up huge sales. The Columbia pairing was hurriedly released and it did well, but by then the group had signed with Victor.

This burst of competitive activity between the two labels was not soon repeated. Initially, Victor showed little or no interest in cashing in on the jazz craze, and Columbia was content to record pre-jazz bandleaders Wilbur Sweatman and W.C. Handy, whose output was not substantially different from that of the popular white orchestras.

It was left to the struggling American branch of a German company to lead the way in jazz recording. In February 1920 a young black vaudevillian named Mamie Smith persuaded the management of OKeh Records to cut two of her songs. Hedging their bets, they used a group of white musicians to accompany her. The record sold well enough for her to be invited back to make two more sides, this time with a black group. The result, *Crazy Blues* backed with *It's Right Here for You,* smashed all sales records and proved that there was an audience of African Americans hungry for their own music and willing to pay for it.

OKeh Records act Mamie Smith's Jazz Hounds, 1920, with Willie "The Lion" Smith on piano.

In 1921 OKeh launched a series of "race records" directed by artists-and-repertoire (A&R) men Ralph Peer, Clarence Williams, and, later, Tommy Rockwell. Columbia followed with its own series in 1923; one of its first artists was singer Bessie Smith, signed by Frank Walker. The Victor company held off until 1926, when it signed Jelly Roll Morton and Bennie Moten; in 1928 it launched its own line of black-music recordings with some sides by McKinney's Cotton Pickers and Duke Ellington. Ralph Peer left OKeh for Victor, where he handled most of the race records, while Nat Shilkret and Leroy Shield oversaw the bulk of the white material. Columbia diversified: in 1925 it introduced the budget Harmony label, for which some Columbia jazz artists recorded under various pseudonyms; then, in 1926, Columbia purchased OKeh.

In the wake of the Depression, OKeh artists were gradually absorbed into Columbia, and the OKeh label disappeared in 1934 (although it was revived in World War II as a budget line). Victor was bought by the RCA Corporation; that company's low-price Bluebird label, introduced in 1932, would offer reissues of early classic jazz, country artists, hotel dance bands, and, in the late 1930s, sides by Glenn Miller, Artie Shaw, Muggsy Spanier, Earl Hines, and Fats Waller. —*Michael Brooks*

the first time this had occurred on record, and gives each one generous space. The floodgates for soloists had opened, and a new era was born.

On *Big Butter and Egg Man* (1926), Armstrong delivers one of his most celebrated, perfectly constructed solos, while *Potato Head Blues, Struttin' with Some Barbecue,* and *Hotter Than That* (all 1927) reveal his growing gifts as cornetist and improviser: technical mastery of his instrument; a big, beautiful tone; rhythmic daring; a fertile imagination as a soloist; and the ability to personalize his material. With these talents, Armstrong would assert more influence on the course of jazz than any other musician in the twentieth century.

By 1923 OKeh Records had hired black pianist Clarence Williams as its director of "race records"; the Columbia and Brunswick labels also recognized the commercial possibilities of signing black artists. Only the Victor Company stood aloof, but it finally capitulated in 1926, signing Jelly Roll Morton to an exclusive contract.

Morton is now recognized as the first great jazz composer and arranger—a pioneer in working variety and improvisation into the structure of his compositions—and as one of the most meticulous of early bandleaders, who would spend hours rehearsing for each record date. His piano solos reflect the ragtime style of his youth, and there are echoes of gavottes and mazurkas, too (*Seattle Hunch* and *Pep,* both 1929). His early Red Hot Peppers sides are equally impressive. *Grandpa's Spells,* recorded with a seven-piece band in 1926, is a wondrously complex piece of arranging, replete with breaks and a variety of contrasting textures and dynamic levels. His masterpiece *Black Bottom Stomp,* from the same year, is rich in structure, contrast, and musicality, using stop-time (an intermittent statement of the beat), breaks, varying rhythms, exchanges of four-bar phrases, and outstanding improvised solos. *Doctor Jazz,* also from 1926, burns up the wax with trumpeter George Mitchell's tight, economical lead and clarinetist Omer Simeon's long, sustained notes and liquid phrasing.

The Lincoln Gardens—the site of King Oliver's 1923 post-California stint—was situated on Chicago's South Side. Until the Crash of 1929, the zone had three times as many theaters and nightclubs as New York. Along the "Stroll," a nine-block stretch of South State Street, jazz lovers had a choice of the Panama, Dreamland, and Elite cafés, or they could take in two silent movies and a musical program at the Monogram or Vendome theaters. At the latter, Erskine Tate led a big band with Louis Armstrong and Earl "Fatha" Hines among its sidemen. The one record they made, *Static Strut* backed with *Stomp Off, Let's Go* (1926), is a heavy-footed yet immensely exciting pairing, with Armstrong spraying out notes with the ferocity of a double-crossed gangster. The black music scene later shifted to 35th and Calumet (honored by a 1934 Mezz Mezzrow recording), where you could hear Armstrong at the Sunset Café, drummer Sonny Clay or King Oliver at the Plantation, or clarinetist Jimmie Noone and Earl Hines at the Apex Club.

Although this was the black neighborhood, there was no segregation in force, and it quickly became the haunt of some white students who attended the Austin High School. The nucleus of jazz-seeking teenagers included cornetist Jimmy McPartland, tenorman Bud Freeman, drummer Dave Tough, and reedman Frank Teschemacher. They were joined in their obsession by such future stars as guitarist Eddie Condon, cornetists Muggsy Spanier and Leon "Bix" Beiderbecke, and pianist Joe Sullivan. The youngsters bought

Jazz on the Stroll

Bronzeville. The old black Chicago neighborhood is steeped in memories of music that was once the heart and soul of the city's South Side. At century's end, visitors saw vacant lots. But in earlier years, it was different.

Chicago was a hot town in the 1910s and 1920s. The North Side had its famous clubs: the Green Mill, College Inn, Blackhawk, Kelly's Stables, and Friar's Inn. But the hottest music could be found by following a musician after a gig. No matter where a player worked, he'd end up on the South Side "Stroll"— where so much music was in the air, people said an instrument held outside at midnight would play itself.

Starting with the Pekin Inn at 27th Street, the Stroll's clubs, speakeasies, theaters, and ballrooms sat practically door-to-door along State Street and across 31st and 35th. Like the old Times Square, the Stroll ran twenty-four hours a day, and offered similar attractions. But what drew musicians was a concentration of musical talent that would be unrivaled until New York's 52nd Street became ascendant in the 1930s.

Some of the most famous spots were the Lincoln (formerly Royal) Gardens and the Dreamland, where Louis Armstrong debuted with King Oliver, and the Plantation and Sunset cafés, where they played in rival bands and Oliver threatened nightly to blow Armstrong off 35th Street. There was also the DeLuxe Café, where Jelly Roll Morton and Freddie Keppard played; the Grand Terrace and Regal Theater, where Earl Hines appeared; and Jimmie Noone's Apex Club. Erskine Tate could be found at the Monogram, Vendome, and Grand theaters, and blueswomen Ethel Waters, Alberta Hunter, and Bessie Smith performed in all the big houses.

The kids who hung on every note would be the next generation, the originators of "Chicago style" jazz: Bix Beiderbecke, Eddie Condon, Bud Freeman, Benny Goodman, Jim Lanigan, Gene Krupa, Dave Tough, Muggsy Spanier, Milt Hinton, Frank Teschemacher, Jimmy McPartland. They listened, they sat in, they created something new, and the next generation learned from them.

By the end of the twenties, the jazz exodus to New York had begun. Now, much of the Stroll is gone, found only in photos, oral histories, and such jazz tunes as *Royal Garden Blues* and *State Street Blues*. But as long as the music is played, the memories live on. —*Deborah Gillaspie*

Chicago's Sunset Café in 1923, with violinist Carroll Dickerson's band backing singer Mary Stafford (center, arms out) and dancer Frankie "Half Pint" Jaxon (front).

Cornetist Bix Beiderbecke, 1923.

Eddie Condon: banjo player, guitarist, and Bix Beiderbecke associate, 1921.

records by King Oliver and the New Orleans Rhythm Kings, played them till the grooves wore flat, and dreamed of making their own mark on recorded jazz. This dream became reality in 1926 when they met up with a St. Louis disc jockey named William "Red" McKenzie, whose lack of musical ability was counterbalanced by his genius for promotion. In quick succession he persuaded the Chicago A&R man of the prestigious OKeh Record Company to record four sides in December 1927, including *Nobody's Sweetheart* and *Liza*. Two months later he wangled a date with Paramount Records; the date included *Sister Kate* and *Bullfrog Blues*. On the strength of the OKeh session, most of the musicians left for New York, where the local talent frowned on their use of 4/4 rhythm and the standard of competition was much tougher.

One of the most romantic of the early jazz figures was Bix Beiderbecke, out of Davenport, Iowa. When he hit Chicago with the Wolverines, a midwestern group of dubious talent, his drive and tone on such records as *Jazz Me Blues* and *Copenhagen* (both 1924) set the other musicians on their collective ear. Eddie Condon and the Austin High gang claimed him as one of their own, but he never recorded with them, and judging by his later work among the more sophisticated New York musicians, it is difficult to imagine him in their company.

Beiderbecke became known for his lyrical, well-constructed solos and distinctive tone. (His notes, said his friend Hoagy Carmichael, "weren't blown—they were hit, like a mallet strikes a chime.") And he made a series of influential recordings—perhaps none more revered by musicians than *Riverboat Shuffle; I'm Coming, Virginia;* and especially *Singin' the Blues* (all with Frank Trumbauer's band, 1927). But his recording career was brief. Though Beiderbecke was both talented and sweet-natured, he had little capacity for dealing with day-to-day living. Saxophonist Trumbauer, who met Beiderbecke while they were with the Jean Goldkette band, tried to be a father figure to him, but it was a losing battle. Time ran out for Beiderbecke and he died, alone, of acute alcoholism, in 1931 at the age of twenty-eight.

Inexplicably, another major figure on the Chicago jazz scene, Earl Hines, went little noticed by later generations of jazz musicians. Inexplicably because in the 1920s he revolutionized jazz piano, releasing it from the exciting but musically limiting constraints of ragtime and stride and paving the way for such higher-profile figures as Bud Powell and Thelonious Monk. Before he made a remarkable series of piano solos in 1928—including *Caution Blues, 57 Varieties,* and *Off Time Blues*—most jazz pianists relied heavily on the unfaltering rhythm of the left hand to propel the music along. Hines departed from the regular left-hand patterns of alternating chords and single

Chicagoan Ben Pollack (fourth from left) employed musicians who went on to far greater fame than he; in 1928 they included Jack Teagarden (second from left) and Benny Goodman (fourth from right).

Earl "Fatha" Hines, one of the leading pianists in all of jazz, ruled the Chicago scene with Louis Armstrong in the 1920s. His career stretched into the 1980s.

notes, instead introducing countermelodies or his own inventive harmonies while still retaining a strong beat. For the right hand he created the celebrated "trumpet style," interjecting single notes or octave doublings to cut through the sound of the orchestra. He also developed a devastating tremolo on the keyboard to imitate the vibrato of a wind instrument.

From 1926 to 1928 Hines and Louis Armstrong were musically joined at the hip, recording a series of small-group master-pieces under the banner of the resuscitated Hot Five. Their output included one of the greatest jazz records of all time, *West End Blues,* with Armstrong's breath-taking opening cadenza, and culminated in their brilliant and assured duet *Weather Bird* (both 1928).

As the Great Depression unfolded, Chicago underwent a transformation. Money dried up, gangster Al Capone's stranglehold on Chicago was broken by federal tax laws, Prohibition was repealed, and a new type of club rose from the ashes, while the surviving ballrooms were taken over by legitimate businessmen who favored the "sweet" bands of such leaders as Hal Kemp, Don Bestor, or Guy Lombardo. Jazz continued to thrive, but a new set of players arrived on the scene, and most of the older ones either retired or moved on to other cities.

Bennie Moten (in black) had the most successful band in Kansas City in the 1920s. In 1931, it included Bill (later "Count") Basie (second from left), "Hot Lips" Page (third from left), Eddie Durham (front, sixth from left), and Jimmy Rushing (top right).

Pianist Bill Basie followed his tenure in the Moten band by forming his own outfit and taking the nickname "Count."

Kansas City

Like a seedling planted in fertile soil, jazz burst into opulence in the fecund atmosphere of Kansas City, Missouri. Because of the city's economic importance, bands from all over the South and Southwest, the Great Plains, and the Midwest passed through, some to play local dates, others to use the city as a stopover where they indulged in fierce cutting contests with local musicians. Kansas City became known for a style of big-band jazz steeped in the blues of the South and old Southwest and rich with riffs and rhythmic drive.

Kansas City jazz thrived in a setting not unlike that of Prohibition-era Chicago. The city's nightlife—its unbridled vitality assured by the fact that it lined the pockets of political boss Tom Pendergast—spilled forth in such storied clubs as the Reno, Hey-Hay, Cherry Blossom, Harlem Club, Lucille's Band Box, and the Sunset Crystal Palace. "Most of the [K.C.] nightspots were run by politicians and hoodlums, and the town was wide open for drinking, gambling, and pretty much every form of vice," recalled pianist Mary Lou Williams. "Naturally, work was plentiful for musicians."

The biggest name in Kansas City in the 1920s was that of pianist Bennie Moten. Born in 1894, he studied with former pupils of composer Scott Joplin and began playing in the city as early as 1916. By the mid-1920s he had the most successful band in town, with whom he made many recordings for the Victor Company. His records from the 1926–28 period, such as *Kansas City Shuffle* (1926) and *South* (1928), employ a heavy, rolling rhythm, prominent banjo and tuba, and novelty effects. Although the Moten band was immensely popular in Kansas City and attracted big crowds on the road, its music was old-fashioned even for its time. In 1928, Moten staged a battle of the bands with Walter Page's Blue Devils and was so impressed by the latter group that he hired away trumpeter Oran "Hot Lips" Page and vocalist Jimmy Rushing. Later, a young pianist from Red Bank, New Jersey, by the name of William (later "Count") Basie took over the piano chair, leaving Moten to concentrate on leading. These and other personnel changes, including the additions of trombonist Eddie Durham, bassist Walter Page, and tenorman Ben Webster, transformed Moten's band into a powerhouse. Their final session came in 1932 when, broke and hungry, they crashed Victor's studios in Camden, New Jersey, where a local entrepreneur persuaded Victor's Eli Oberstein to let them cut ten tunes, including *Toby, Lafayette,* and *Prince of Wails.* These recordings—which capture the band's swinging rhythm section (featuring Basie), "horizontal" flow of rhythm, exciting breakneck tempos, and impressive virtuosity—exploded off the wax in much the same way as the first Parker-Gillespie sides would in the next decade. Although these last Moten discs sold abysmally on their first release, their ultimate influence brought the 1930s into the Swing Era. Basie would prove a dominant figure in that era with his own band, composed in part of former Moten sidemen.

Trumpeter Oran "Hot Lips" Page.

Another prominent group in Kansas City was that of George E. Lee, a singer who had learned to play saxophone after military service. His band, with his sister Julia on piano and vocals, can be heard on *Paseo Street* and *Won't You Come Over to My House?* (both 1929). Julia possessed an earthy, full-throated delivery and a mean left hand, but she wasn't to achieve full recognition until the 1940s, when she made the West Coast her home.

Kansas City also served as the base for the band of Andy Kirk. In 1929 he hired the beautiful, willowy Mary Lou Williams, whose fragile appearance belied hands that could leave other pianists in the dust. She also possessed a keen musical intelligence; such Williams arrangements as *Mess-a-Stomp* (1929), *Walkin' and Swingin'* (1936), and *A Mellow Bit of Rhythm* (1937)—with their combination of drive and subtlety—would make the Kirk outfit one of the top bands of the mid-1930s. Her vital contribution to the Kirk ensemble would be aptly celebrated in their 1936 recording *The Lady Who Swings the Band.*

Trombonist–guitar player Eddie Durham.

Walter Page's Blue Devils generated excitement in the Southwest in the late 1920s. Members Hot Lips Page, Jimmy Rushing, and, later, Walter Page himself went to work for Bennie Moten and eventually became the core of the Count Basie band.

The Lafayette, at 131st Street in Harlem, hosted vaudeville shows. 1927's Jazzmania revue featured Duke Ellington's band.

New York

If Chicago and Kansas City were the nation's cultural mixing bowls, New York City was the full store of ingredients. Immigrants from almost every country on earth streamed through Ellis Island until its closure in 1954, bringing their music with them as a reminder of the Old Country and incorporating it into the strains of other nationalities.

At the same time, New York hosted a growing black population, fueled, during World War I, by a massive migration from the southern states. By the 1920s, African American cultural life had found its center in the Harlem section of uptown Manhattan, and in that decade—during what is now called the Harlem Renaissance—music, entertainment, literature, and art were thriving.

But early New York jazz owed as much to Italians and Jews as it did to blacks. Manhattan's Jewish ghetto

Pianist, arranger, and bandleader Fletcher Henderson.

on the Lower East Side was one of the most densely populated areas on earth, while on the southernmost tip of the island Irish and Italians lived cheek by jowl in far-from-harmonious conditions. Yet harmony emerged. One of the earliest New York jazz bands, the Original Memphis Five, was composed of three Italians, a Jew, and a white Protestant. All New

Yorkers, they took the name from W.C. Handy's 1912 standard Memphis Blues. This frequently recorded group, under the leadership of trumpeter Phil Napoleon, favored pop tunes of the day that would appeal to the general public, with carefully tailored solo passages. Their later recordings, including Fireworks (1928) and Kansas City Kitty (1929), both of which featured Napoleon's strong trumpet and Tommy Dorsey's trombone, are particularly appealing.

The first important big band was led by Fletcher Henderson, a classically trained pianist from Georgia. Henderson eventually became known as one of the fathers of the swing big-band sound, but his earliest recordings, such as Dicty Blues (1923) and Teapot Dome Blues (1924), are remembered primarily for the contributions of such outstanding musicians as alto saxophonist Don Redman and tenorman Coleman Hawkins.

Hawkins was a pioneer of his instrument; prior to his arrival on the scene, the saxophone (usually the alto or C-melody) was employed as a novelty instrument in dance orchestras. Hawkins kept some of the flashiness but combined it with ferocious, stop-time "bombs"; a lyrical, romantic approach on slow tempos; and, above all, a sense of swing hitherto unheard on the instrument. His solos with Henderson (*The Stampede*, 1926; *Wherever There's a Will, Baby*, 1929; and *It's the Talk of the Town*, 1933) influenced an entire generation of tenor reedmen, and his fat tone remained the ideal until Lester Young, in the late 1930s, pioneered a light, airy sound.

Late in 1924, Henderson, who had just begun what would become a long-running association with New York's Roseland Ballroom, hired Louis Armstrong away from King Oliver. Armstrong was the alchemist who turned a collection of first-rate but disparate ingredients into gold. His clarion sound, swinging rhythm, and natural genius, evident in his solos on *Shanghai Shuffle* (1924) and *When You Do What You Do* and *Sugar Foot Stomp* (both 1925), cloaked the Henderson band in a sheen of brilliance that lasted even after he returned to Chicago in 1925. Right into the early 1930s, on such recordings as *D Natural Blues* (1928), *Comin' and Going* (1931), and *Queer Notions*

Other Early Jazz Labels

After Columbia, Victor, and OKeh, Brunswick-Vocalion was the most important early label for jazz recordings. Mayo Williams was in charge of the company's Chicago sessions, and Jack Kapp, later co-founder of American Decca, headed the New York operation. By far the biggest names on the labels were Red Nichols, King Oliver, and Johnny Dodds, and Duke Ellington made dozens of sides under the pseudonym of the Jungle Band. The label's "race record" series included recordings by the erratic but exciting trumpeter Jabbo Smith. But Brunswick's distribution was poor in comparison to the major companies, and these records are rare today.

The Pathé-Perfect group, whose products were badly recorded and pressed on cheap brown shellac, cut numerous jazz and blues titles in the 1920s, as did the Plaza Music group (home of the Oriole, Cameo, Romeo, Domino, Jewel, and Banner imprints), but these were budget labels, bought by the young and fickle, played to death, then tossed aside. Most of the artists represented were obscure or not considered good enough for the major labels, but there were gems to be found, including sides by Cab Calloway, Duke Ellington, Luis Russell, and Red Nichols, all under colorful pseudonyms.

Headquartered in Port Washington, Wisconsin, Paramount made recordings mostly in New York City and Chicago. Unlike the larger labels, its products and advertising were aimed mainly at African American audiences. Its jazz output was relatively sparse, with sides by such artists as Charles Pierce, Lovie Austin, Freddie Keppard, and Jimmy O'Bryant. But the company excelled in recording blues artists, including Ma Rainey. The Depression hit the company's audience particularly hard, and Paramount issued its last disc early in 1932.

The main recording studio of Gennett Records, a division of the Starr Piano Company, sat so close to railroad tracks in Richmond, Indiana, that recording had to be suspended when a train came by. The company first started making records in 1917 but by the early 1920s found that lack of capital and distribution made it impossible to compete in classical music with the likes of Victor and Columbia, so it concentrated on popular music and jazz. Artists who made their debuts on the navy-blue and gold label include Johnny Dodds, King Oliver, Louis Armstrong, Hoagy Carmichael, Bix Beiderbecke, and the New Orleans Rhythm Kings, and Jelly Roll Morton recorded his first solo piano efforts for the label. These gems came to be sought after as great rarities by the 78-rpm collector, but the Gennett recording process was primitive and the discs wore out quickly, so it is almost impossible to locate clean copies of them. Hurt by the Depression, Gennett released its last record at the end of 1930, but its subsidiary, the lower-priced Champion, limped along until 1934. —*Michael Brooks*

Trumpeter Red Nichols, one of Brunswick-Vocalion's leading recording artists.

(1933), Henderson's was the premier black band, often challenged but never vanquished, despite numerous personnel changes. Its ultimate demise was due to its lack of a top-notch manager and its leader's decreasing ambitiousness, probably caused by the after-effects of a serious car accident in 1928.

Louis Armstrong's and Coleman Hawkins' chief rival in the mid-1920s was the brash soprano saxophonist Sidney Bechet. He was away from the U.S. music scene for long periods and during the Depression retired temporarily, opening a tailor's shop in Harlem with Henderson alumnus Tommy Ladnier. That hiatus, and Bechet's adherence to the notoriously difficult soprano saxophone, have led him to be overlooked by some jazz historians. Few jazz musicians even attempted to make the soprano sax their instrument of choice in the 1920s. Johnny Hodges (with Ellington) and Charlie Holmes (with Luis Russell)

Saxophonist Johnny Hodges, a mainstay of the Ellington band.

occasionally employed it in solo work, but both preferred the more stable alto. Bechet, perhaps mindful of its tendency to go out of tune, used it like a blowtorch. So strong was his attack that on most small-group recordings he dominated even the brass instruments.

Armstrong was one of the few who could take him on head to head. Some of Bechet's best work (and some of the greatest jazz ever recorded) are his records with Armstrong under the leadership of pianist-composer Clarence Williams, including *Texas Moaner Blues* (1924) and *Santa Claus Blues* (1925). Armstrong and Bechet did not like one another; their work together resembles a shootout rather than a cutting contest. Probably their finest effort is Williams' OKeh version of *Cake Walking Babies from Home* (1925), in which, still keeping the traditional New Orleans format, they weave and intertwine; it's like a death battle between a cobra and a mongoose, set to music. Some find Bechet more acceptable in a big-band setting, where his aggression fuels the excitement rather than upsets the balance, as some feel it did in a small group. He is arguably at his best with the Noble Sissle Orchestra on such tracks as *The Basement Blues* and *Roll On, Mississippi, Roll On* (both 1931).

In the first five years of the 1920s, the two most prominent white bands were Paul Whiteman's orchestra and Ed Kirkeby's California Ramblers. Whiteman was a Denver-born violinist who laid aside his instrument for a baton. He made for an imposing presence on the bandstand—he was tall and heavily built—which he matched with a mastery of self-promotion. He soon became known as the "King of Jazz": he didn't believe the hype, but the public did.

Whiteman did recognize talent in others. He helped advance the career of composer George Gershwin, staging the first public performance of his *Rhapsody in Blue* at a famous 1924 concert at New York's Aeolian Hall and recording many of his early compositions. But his band was stilted and fussy and its arrangements pretentious. It wasn't until 1927, when he hired a number of musicians from the defunct Jean Goldkette Orchestra and added arrangers Tom Satterfield, Bill Challis, and William Grant Still, that jazz could be applied to the name of Whiteman. His biggest coup was acquiring from the Goldkette band those disparate but inseparable musical twins, Bix Beiderbecke and Frank Trumbauer. The former was pure blazing heat with an unearthly tone; the latter cool and languid, with a vibratoless tone and phrasing that oddly predated the bebop players of the 1940s.

Whiteman's augmented personnel produced his greatest recordings of this, or any other era, including *Changes* (1927) and *From Monday On* and *Louisiana* (both 1928).

The California Ramblers, led by former recording executive Wallace T. "Ed" Kirkeby and anchored by the massive bass saxophone of Adrian Rollini, packed its repertoire with ephemeral pop tunes and novelty items—including *She Knows Her Onions* (1926) and *Crazy Words, Crazy Tune* (1927)—and became immensely popular with the fast college crowd. Despite the superficiality of the Ramblers' output, Kirkeby filled the band with top white jazz players of the period. In 1930 trumpeter Jack Purvis joined the band. A blazing talent who spent much of his life in prison, he electrified such otherwise mundane dance records as *Charming* and *The Stein Song* (both 1930). Heard today, the sides hint at what the Jay Gatsby crowd might have danced to in West Egg.

In the middle and late 1920s, the finest white musicians held lucrative jobs playing dance music in hotel bands or radio house orchestras.

Trombonist Tommy Dorsey and his reedman brother, Jimmy, worked with Fred Rich's Astor Hotel band; Joe Venuti, Eddie Lang, Miff Mole, and Fud Livingston were with Roger Wolfe Kahn; and Red Nichols was with CBS's Don Voorhees.

Violinist Guiseppe "Joe" Venuti had a short fuse and a penchant for practical jokes that made him a liability in the eyes of some orchestra leaders. But he collaborated with guitarist Eddie Lang on a series of remarkable duet and small-group recordings—including *Stringin' the Blues* (1926) and *My Honey's Loving Arms* (1928)—that amply displayed his rich tone and facile technique and made him the first to gain the violin acceptance as a jazz instrument. Lang was known for his single-string solos and his consummate accompanying, favored by such top vocalists as Bing Crosby. He also recorded guitar duets with bluesman Lonnie Johnson, including *Two Tone Stomp* (1928) and *Bullfrog Moan* (1929).

Many of these musicians supplemented their regular incomes with freelance jazz record dates under various names, some real, some fictitious. Most of the lucrative recording work was in the hands of trumpeter Loring "Red" Nichols.

Shaped by musical training at a military academy, Nichols' playing tended to be stiff and formal, the solos logically thought out but rarely exciting. Nonetheless, he was an astute judge of talent. At the age of twenty-one, in 1926, he made the first of his sides under the name of the Five Pennies with trombonist Miff Mole. The latter's deft, understated work, playing seemingly random notes until, suddenly, a musical portrait was complete, made him the pointillist of jazz (as on *Original Dixieland One-Step* and *Slippin' Around*, both 1927). They were joined by Jimmy Dorsey, who would become a bandleader during the Swing Era, but whose pioneering alto sax work—heard to good advantage on *That's No Bargain* (1926) and *Oh! Peter* (1931)—would make him the idol of the young Lester Young and Charlie Parker. Nichols later employed Chicagoans Eddie Condon, Bud Freeman, and Joe Sullivan. Together they produced some memorable records (*Shim-Me-Sha-Wabble*, 1928; *Rose of Washington Square*, 1929; *China Boy*, 1930), though personal animosities made the collaboration a brief one.

In 1928 a new star hit town. Jack Teagarden came roaring in from Texas like an uncapped oil well and set the town on its ear. If Miff Mole was the Seurat of jazz, Teagarden was Gauguin, all exotic colorings and broad sensual tones, as on *Knockin' a Jug* with Louis Armstrong (1929) and *Makin' Friends* under the name of the Whoopee Makers (1930). He became a fixture at the Park Central Hotel with Ben Pollack's Orchestra, alongside clarinetist Benny Goodman, trumpeter Jimmy McPartland, and trombonist Glenn Miller. Drummer Pollack was another impeccable judge of talent, and his 1933 orchestra formed the nucleus of the outstanding Bob Crosby big band.

New York during the period 1926–30 hosted what may have been the richest cultural life in North American history. Theater, literature, art, and music flourished as never before or since. Broadway theater alone served as the stomping ground for playwrights Phillip Barry, Eugene O'Neill, and Sydney Howard; actors Alfred Lunt and Lynne Fontanne, the Barrymores, Katharine Cornell, and Jeanne Eagels; and songwriters Jerome Kern, George and Ira Gershwin, Richard Rodgers and Lorenz Hart, Vincent Youmans, Cole Porter, Harold Arlen, and Dorothy Fields and Jimmy McHugh.

Bandleader Paul Whiteman was not the "King of Jazz" he was promoted as, but he did hire talented musicians, and he commissioned George Gershwin to write the jazz-infused masterwork Rhapsody in Blue.

Jazz and Classical Music

In 1895, when Antonín Dvořák heard the future of American music in "Negro melodies or Indian chants," the "Negro melodies" he had in mind were spirituals, not ragtime or jazz. Yet Dvořák proved remarkably prescient. Much of the vitality and distinctively "American" qualities of twentieth-century classical music have links to African American song and rhythm, and the reason is jazz.

The seeds were sown in the ragtime era. Among the composers taking Dvořák's charge to heart, Henry Gilbert stands out as the most committed, with a series of works spanning two decades, including *The Dance in Place Congo* (1908). Charles Ives alludes to it in a few works, most notably *Central Park in the Dark* (1906), featuring a "ragtime war" leading to a cacophonous climax. Meanwhile,

Scott Joplin, the "King of Ragtime Writers," strove to compose in larger European forms and realized his dream in the operas *A Guest of Honor* (1903) and *Treemonisha* (1911).

When jazz and blues began to reach larger audiences in the late 1910s and early 1920s, composers for the concert hall were quick to respond. In fact, jazz was soon enlisted in the effort to define a modern American classical music. Jazz was nothing less than "the voice of the American soul," as George Gershwin put it. The Chicago composer John Alden Carpenter made an early impact with his "jazz pantomime," *Krazy Kat* (1921), based on a popular comic strip, and with his ballet *Skyscrapers* (1924).

But the key figure was Gershwin. Despite success and wealth as a

composer of popular songs and Broadway shows, this Brooklyn-born son of Russian-Jewish immigrants wanted to be taken seriously. With *Rhapsody in Blue* (1924), commissioned by Paul Whiteman, Gershwin put the classical music world on notice that he had arrived. From the opening, siren-like clarinet to the blues-drenched melodies and infectious rhythms—all embedded in a conception heavily indebted to nineteenth-century European Romantics such as Franz Liszt—Gershwin threw down the gauntlet for American composers seeking a distinctively modernist American idiom.

As if taking up Gershwin's challenge, Aaron Copland (another native Brooklynite of Russian-Jewish parentage) answered with his own *Piano Concerto* (1926), whose two movements illustrated what Copland believed to be the two moods of jazz: the "blues and the snappy number." Copland had already engaged jazz in such works as *Music for the Theater* (1925), but the *Piano Concerto* raised the stakes, as it was premiered by the prestigious Boston Symphony Orchestra under the direction of the great conductor Serge Koussevitzky.

Meanwhile, several European composers found in jazz a bracing medium through which to escape the burdensome weight of Teutonic Romanticism. The impulse was especially strong in France. Erik Satie ignited interest with his unique ballet *Parade* (1917). Darius Milhaud soon followed with his own ballet score, *La creation du monde* (1923), featuring a jazzy blues theme as a fugue subject. And Maurice Ravel embraced jazz in the "Blues" movement of his *Sonata for Violin and Piano* (1927) and a piano concerto. Igor Stravinsky, a transplanted Russian in Paris, also captured the new spirit in such works

George Gershwin composed such jazz-inflected concert works as Rhapsody in Blue *(1924) and the opera* Porgy and Bess *(1935).*

as *Ragtime* (1919) and the *Ebony Concerto* (1945), composed for Woody Herman's big band after the composer had immigrated to the U.S. For the same group Leonard Bernstein composed his memorable *Prelude, Fugue, and Riffs* (1948), though ultimately it was Benny Goodman, not Herman, who played its premiere.

In the first half of the century, most composers who adopted jazz—whether in the U.S., France, or elsewhere—did so as outsiders seeking modernist energy in a musical idiom beyond their own cultural heritage. And none of their works invited improvisation. In the second half of the century, however, the most notable developments in concert-hall hybrids came from jazz musicians writing in extended musical forms that provided space for improvisation. Duke Ellington paved the way with his landmark *Black, Brown, and Beige* (1943), a multimovement "tone parallel to the history of the Negro in America," premiered at Carnegie Hall. Ellington composed several other large-scale works mixing notated and improvised music, including *Harlem* (1950), commissioned by Arturo Toscanini and the NBC Symphony (though never played by them), and his and Billy Strayhorn's witty, swinging versions of Grieg's *Peer Gynt Suite* and Tchaikovsky's *Nutcracker Suite* (1960).

Inspired, in part, by Ellington's model, other jazz composers followed suit. Charles Mingus's masterpiece *The Black Saint and the Sinner Lady* (1963) combines written composition, extensive improvisation, and considerable editing and overdubbing overseen by the composer. At a time when Ellington was conceiving and performing a series of sacred concerts, Mary Lou Williams composed several jazz masses, most notably

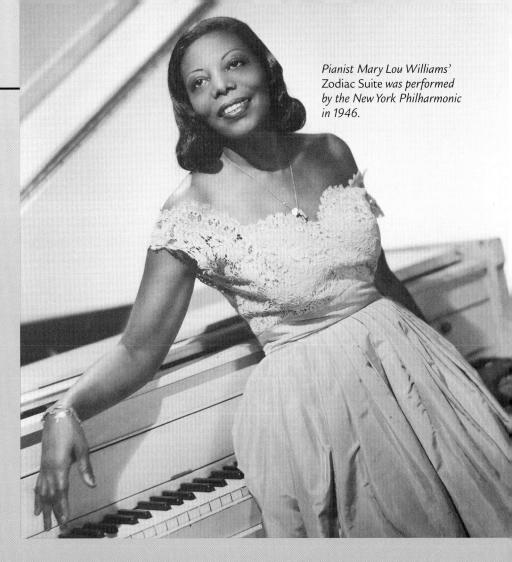

Pianist Mary Lou Williams' *Zodiac Suite was performed by the New York Philharmonic in 1946.*

Mary Lou's Mass (1971). The renowned jazz musician, composer, and educator David Baker contributed such works as *Le chat qui peche,* for soprano, orchestra, and jazz quartet (1974); *Three Ethnic Dances,* a clarinet concerto (1992); and *Roots II* for piano trio (1992).

Gunther Schuller, the omnivorous composer, conductor, crossover French-horn player, and a later president of the New England Conservatory, acted as a figurehead among jazz musicians pursuing serious composition. In 1957, Schuller coined the term *third stream* to acknowledge and encourage compositions that blended genuine jazz elements and classical forms and techniques. Schuller's own works, such as *Transformations* (1957) and *Seven Studies on Themes by Paul Klee* and *Abstractions* (both 1959), put his ideas into

practice. Other key third-stream composers included Jimmy Giuffre, John Lewis, and George Russell.

In the 1980s and 1990s, jazz itself enjoyed a newly elevated status as a kind of classic music, and as a result, efforts to blend jazz and classical elements seemed less urgent. Yet such efforts continue in surprising, artistic, and ambitious ways. Perhaps the most prominent transformation of the impulse at century's end could be found in the work of Wynton Marsalis, who wrote a series of works for Jazz at Lincoln Center. His *In This House, on This Morning* (1992) and his jazz oratorio *Blood on the Fields* (1997), which won a Pulitzer Prize, demonstrated the ongoing possibilities of extended, jazz-based concert music. And they answer Dvořák's call beyond his wildest imaginings. —*Jeffrey Magee*

The Duke Ellington Orchestra at New York's Fulton Street Theater, 1930; (left to right) Freddie Jenkins, Cootie Williams, Sonny Greer, Duke Ellington, Arthur Whetsol, Juan Tizol, Wellman Braud, Johnny Hodges, Harry Carney, Joe "Tricky Sam" Nanton, Freddy Guy, and Barney Bigard.

Much of the city's cultural glow emanated from Harlem, and Broadway's leading lights had a way of sneaking uptown incognito, uninvited but not unwelcome. The Harlem clubs may not have been as sumptuous as those downtown, but the music more than compensated for the lack of silk brocade. The Savoy Ballroom opened in 1926, and blacks and whites happily mingled there, much to the chagrin of the authorities. The equally famous Cotton Club had a white-patrons-only policy, and the socialites flocked there.

Before his Cotton Club tenure, Duke Ellington led a smaller group at the Kentucky Club in midtown Manhattan. His first recordings, still using outmoded acoustic technology (*Trombone Blues*, 1925; *L'il Farina*, 1926), show little indication of what was to come. But once he signed with Columbia and Victor he quickly embraced the new electrical recording techniques that permitted clearer, more detailed sound. The results included such beautifully realized tracks as *East St. Louis Toodle-Oo* (1926) and *Black and Tan Fantasy* (1927).

Ellington's move to the Cotton Club in December 1927 was the break of a lifetime for the young Washingtonian. Taking advantage of the sophisticated clientele, the first-class floor shows, and the media coverage, he shrewdly combined Fields-McHugh tunes written for the club revues (*Freeze and Melt*, 1928; *Hot Feet* and *Arabian Lover*, both 1929) with his own three-minute masterpieces (*Black Beauty, Creole Love Call*, both 1927, and *The Mooche*, 1928) and further broadened his fan base by recording for every major record label, under a barrage of pseudonyms. Ellington has been rightly acclaimed as one of this century's greatest composers—for his distinctive harmonic language and tonal palette, among many other attributes—but not enough tribute has been paid to his genius for shaping an orchestra as a showcase for his work, penning arrangements to highlight his soloists' strengths, and hiring musicians from other bands only to totally retool their styles to suit his needs.

A case in point is his transformation of conventional soloists Bubber

Miley and Cootie Williams (trumpets) and Joe "Tricky Sam" Nanton (trombone) into masters of the mute. Other beneficiaries of the Ellington touch include Lawrence Brown, an unheralded musician with the Los Angeles–based Paul Howard Orchestra whom Ellington helped transform into the most lyrical of trombone soloists (*The Sheik of Araby*, 1932), and Albany "Barney" Bigard, whose work with the 1926–27 King Oliver band barely merits a second listen yet whose liquid, New Orleans clarinet Ellington used to perfection in such classics as *Mood Indigo* (1930) and *Slippery Horn* (1932). Few of Ellington's soloists who moved on ever duplicated the successes of their time with him.

Ellington, under the management of Irving Mills, stayed at the Cotton Club for three years, until February 1931, when he and his band began nonstop touring. During an absence in 1930 when he and his orchestra went to Hollywood to be featured in RKO's Amos and Andy film *Check and Double Check*, they were replaced by the singer-showman Cab Calloway.

The Cotton Club

Harlem's nightlife became a magnet in the 1920s, and one of its greatest attractions was the Cotton Club.

Of New York City's illegal drinking establishments, numbering an estimated 32,000 to 100,000, the Cotton Club was a standout. Its owners were gangsters. The employees were black. The customers were white. And the entertainment included a heady mix of dancing, vaudeville, and such musicians-on-the-rise as Duke Ellington and Cab Calloway.

Located on 142nd Street near Lenox Avenue, the Cotton Club opened in the fall of 1923. It had a log-cabin exterior and interior and featured jungle decor, a proscenium stage, and a dance floor.

Cab Calloway, who first performed there in 1930, vividly recalled the venue as "a huge room. The bandstand was a replica of a southern mansion with large white columns and a backdrop painted with weeping willows and slave quarters.... The waiters were dressed in red tuxedos, like butlers in a southern mansion,

and...there were huge cut-crystal chandeliers."

During Ellington's tenure, which began in 1927, the club typically opened at 10 p.m. and closed at 3 a.m. Showtimes were specifically designed to attract a high-spending after-theater crowd.

"There were brutes at the door," observed Carl Van Vechten, "to enforce the Cotton Club's policy which was opposed to [racially] mixed parties." Occasionally, however, a star performer such as Ethel Waters or Bill "Bojangles" Robinson could get a table for friends.

Beginning in 1926, the shows were staged and produced by singer, dancer, and comic Dan Healy. Jimmy McHugh wrote the songs, usually with Dorothy Fields, through 1929.

The performers' costumes were sensational, as Calloway observed: "The soloists, dancers, and singers were always dressed to the hilt—the women in long flowing gowns, if that was appropriate, or in the briefest of brief dance costumes.... Low cut and very, very risqué."

The cast could be large: The spring 1929 revue had thirty in the company, plus Ellington's orchestra.

The Cotton Club provided a hell of a good show. But it also exposed whites to African American culture—a rarity at a time when such opportunities were circumscribed in many ways. What's more, the club provided Ellington with an opportunity to work out many important musical ideas and, via its radio wire, to reach a national audience.

The original club closed in 1936. Late that year, the owners opened a new Cotton Club at 48th Street, which closed in 1940.

—*John Edward Hasse*

The Ellington orchestra accompanies Ethel Waters at the Cotton Club, 1933.

Jazz and Tap

The Three Eddies in the Ellington-penned Chocolate Kiddies, *1925.*

Tap dancer Bill "Bojangles" Robinson.

Who was responsible for the evolution of jazz, the musicians or the tap dancers? Ask a tap dancer, and he'll tell you. Ask a jazz musician, and she just might admit it. The truth is, during the first half of the twentieth century, tap dance and jazz music were intricately intertwined and affected one another more than most realized.

In early twentieth-century American entertainment, musicians and tap dancers lived and worked in the same world—that of vaudeville, Broadway, and nightclubs. In these environments, the tap dancers were the stars and the musicians played the dancers' charts. The musicians watched and listened in wonder to the confoundingly complex syncopated rhythms tapped out by the dancers.

"Tap dancers had a big influence on drummers, no doubt about it," bandleader Jay McShann recalled. "They taught drummers when to play and when to stay out of the way. Reading music had little to do with it; it was a matter of developing your instincts."

Musicians listened day after day, night after night, year after year as tap dancers stretched the boundaries of early jazz to swing, from swing to bop, and from bop to modern jazz. According to the tap dancers, the musicians replicated their rhythmic ideas, and musical changes constantly followed.

By the mid-1930s, vaudeville was on its way out and a new form of entertainment called *presentation* was taking its place. While vaudeville consisted of a lineup of variety artists, presentation focused on the music. The musicians were taken out of the orchestra pit and placed right up on the stage. And the bands were top-drawer swing orchestras. It was bandied about that every band had a tap-dance act and every tap dancer had a band. To name a few: Jimmy Slyde worked with Count Basie and Duke Ellington; Coles and Atkins with Cab Calloway and Basie; the Condos Brothers with both Jimmy and Tommy Dorsey, Benny Goodman, Ellington, Basie, and Sammy Kaye; Bunny Briggs with Ellington, Charlie Barnet, Earl Hines, and Basie; Bill Bailey with Ellington; Jeni LeGon with Fats Waller and Basie. Peg Leg Bates, perhaps the most ubiquitous of all, danced with Jimmy Dorsey, Barnet, Ellington, Erskine Hawkins, Calloway, Basie, Jimmie Lunceford, Claude Hopkins, Louis Armstrong, and Billy Eckstine.

So who changed jazz, musicians or tap dancers? Answers may differ depending on whom you ask. But without a doubt, jazz wouldn't have happened the way it did without music and dance interacting. —*Rusty Frank*

Another Irving Mills aggregate was the Blue Rhythm Band, which was assigned the role of benchwarmer, standing in for Ellington, Calloway, Henderson, and other Harlem big bands when they were playing on the road. While the Blue Rhythm Band lacked great soloists (except for the pianist, Edgar Hayes), they had a gritty brass section that snarled its way through such tunes as *Blue Rhythm* and *Levee Low Down* (both 1931).

More torrid fare was available at the Saratoga Club, where the resident band was led by Panama-born Luis Russell and a bunch of mainly New Orleans musicians front-lined by trumpeter Henry "Red" Allen, the son of noted New Orleans brass-band leader Henry Allen, Sr. Russell was content to write simple frameworks for his ten-piece band then let the musicians' solo artistry take over. In addition to Allen (*Feelin' Drowsy* and *Swing Out*, both 1929), there was trombonist J.C. Higginbotham, whose shouting style resembled a revivalist preacher at full throttle (*Feeling the Spirit*, 1929; *Song of the Swanee*, 1930); the lyrical Charlie Holmes on alto (*Poor L'il Me* and *Give Me Your Telephone Number*, both 1930), unfairly overshadowed by Ellington's Johnny Hodges up the street; Albert Nicholas on clarinet; Teddy Hill or Greely Walton on tenor; and a relentless rhythm section. Some jazz aficionados rate the group as the best Harlem had to offer.

Along with New York's larger clubs, there were dozens of speakeasies whose owners could only afford a pianist and maybe a singer. Here, and at Harlem rent parties, the great Harlem stride pianists thrived. The aptly dubbed "Father of the Stride Piano" was James P. Johnson, whose serpentine fingers seemed to draw energy through the keyboard on such compositions of his own as *Carolina Shout* (1921) and *You've Got to Be Modernistic* (1929). There was also Willie "The Lion" Smith—so called because of his bravery in World War I—who could whip off the impossible *Fingerbuster* (1934) and then slip into the lacy *Morning Air* or *Passionette* (both 1938). But the greatest entertainer of all was the rotund Thomas "Fats" Waller. Some years away from his small-group recording triumphs of the mid-1930s, and still better known as a composer and pianist, Waller could produce dazzling uptempo pyrotechnics on *Gladyse* and *Valentine Stomp* (both 1929); switch to a vocal rendition of his own composition *Ain't Misbehavin'* (1929); then steal out to the local church and perform the most beautiful pipe-organ renditions of *Lenox Avenue Blues* (1926) and *Tanglefoot* (1929).

After their regular gigs, these and other members of the stride fraternity would rouse the remaining customers with some ferocious cutting contests, all conducted with the greatest good humor, with the vanquished returning the next night and, more often than not, besting the victor of the night before.

James P. Johnson, the "Father of the Stride Piano," 1921.

Entertainer and Ain't Misbehavin' *composer Fats Waller, 1936.*

Vocalists

Though often thought of as a city blues singer, Bessie Smith, who began her recording career in 1923, must be considered one of the great jazz singers, for her accompanists (especially Louis Armstrong, as heard on *St. Louis Blues*, 1925, and James P. Johnson, as heard on *Back Water Blues*, 1927); for her repertory, which included many jazz standards; and for her emotional depth, communicative power, and musicality.

But within bands, jazz vocalists were a rarity during the 1920s. When vocals were called for, they were usually delivered by members of the band. The most influential was Louis Armstrong, who—with his rhythmic elasticity (*The Last Time*, 1927); melodic reinvention (*I Can't Give You Anything but Love*, 1929); and scat singing (*Heebie Jeebies*, 1926)—revolutionized jazz singing for men and women alike.

Blues vocalists such as Bessie Smith and Ma Rainey had little success in New York, where glossier, showier fare was the rule. Indeed, in the mid-1930s Bessie Smith attempted a comeback in Manhattan with a repertoire of current pop songs, including *Smoke Gets in Your Eyes*.

Blues singer Ma Rainey and her Georgia Jazz Band at Chicago's Grand Theatre, 1925.

The rest of the black singers, male and female, had their roots in vaudeville and, in many respects, were no more jazz-oriented than such white stars as Sophie Tucker, Blossom Seeley, Ruth Etting, Eddie Cantor, and Al Jolson. One notable anomaly was Broadway star Cliff Edwards, better known as Ukelele Ike. While never feigning to be anything other than an entertainer, he possessed an advanced sense of rhythm and timing, allowing him to take liberties with the tempo and beat that were not common until the early 1930s.

Singer and showman Cab Calloway followed Duke Ellington into the Cotton Club in 1930 and became a mainstay there. Calloway matched his flashy suits, physical gyrations, flying lock of hair, and infectious humor with a top-flight band whose members, at various times, included Chu Berry, Milt Hinton, Mario Bauzá, and Dizzy Gillespie.

Cab Calloway took his liberties with both singing and stage presentation, which were often way over the top, much to the delight of customers who caught him at the Cotton Club and elsewhere in the 1930s. Calloway's singing wasn't limited to the flash, scat-singing, and pyrotechnics demonstrated on his greatest hit, *Minnie the Moocher* (1931). On such recordings as *Gotta Darn Good Reason Now* (1930) and *Evenin'* (1933) Calloway displays a restrained vocal technique, an impressive range, and a firm grasp of the subtleties of jazz singing.

Paul Whiteman was probably the first leader to use a resident vocalist when, in 1927, he hired the Rhythm Boys—Bing Crosby, Harry Barris, and Al Rinker (*Changes*, 1927; *Rhythm King*, 1928). Two years later Rinker's sister, Mildred Bailey, became a member of Whiteman's orchestra, going on to a successful solo career in the 1930s. She possessed the toughness necessary to withstand long and debilitating bus trips between gigs, and to work in an all-male environment. Although working conditions didn't improve until the mid-1930s, the horrors of the Depression and the need for work at any cost meant that women learned to fend for themselves; by the end of the decade female band singers were the norm.

Early big-band singer Mildred Bailey.

Jazz Arrangers of the 1920s

In the early 1920s, jazz had few formal arrangements, though arranger Ferde Grofé did help to standardize the instrumentation of jazz orchestras into choirs of brass, reeds, and a rhythm section. Mostly, orchestra leaders were content to get their stock arrangements from music publishers, while small jazz groups mainly improvised or relied on informal, unwritten "head" arrangements. The introduction of electrical recording in 1925, which employed microphones and thus abolished the need for musicians to cluster around a large acoustic horn used to capture sound, opened up new possibilities. On records, reed sections evolved from mud to clearly delineated instruments; strings became crystal-clear, so the grunting tuba and cutting banjo were replaced by the more flexible string bass and guitar.

By the second half of the decade, jazz arranging was beginning to emerge, in the scoring for Fletcher Henderson's band by Don Redman (*Copenhagen*, 1924); by Henderson himself (*King Porter Stomp*, 1928); by Benny Carter (*Keep a Song in Your Soul*, 1930); and in John Nesbitt's work for McKinney's Cotton Pickers (*Put It There*, 1928). Redman is widely credited for pioneering the clarinet trio scoring in jazz. When questioned years later, Redman laughed and said, "Oh, I stole that from the polka bands."

Other arrangers included Bill Challis (who scored for Whiteman, as on *Changes*, 1927) and reedman Walter "Fud" Livingston, noted for angularity (Frank Trumbauer's *Humpty Dumpty*, 1927) and a preference for stop chords, in which staccato phrasing and sudden changes of key were employed to build excitement (*Oh! Baby*, 1928). His technique was also favored by Don Redman and adopted in the early work of Livingston's prodigy, Glenn Miller. The flowering of the big bands in the 1930s saw jazz arranging come into its own as a vital addition to the big-band sound.

Regional Bands

Every major city in the country had one or more jazz bands, but aural documentation is sparse. The major record companies had offices and recording studios in New York, Chicago, and Los Angeles, but there was a lot of country in between. All that survives of regional or "territory" bands under the names of Speed Webb, Thamon Hayes, Peck Kelly, Doc Ross, Ligon Smith, Leslie Sheffield, and countless others are fading memories, since they never recorded. The few that did were usually confined to one session on a label's field trip. Examples include Hal Kemp's *Peg-Leg Stomp* (Atlanta, 1926); Jesse Stone's *Boot to Boot* (St. Louis, 1927); and Celestin's Original Tuxedo Jazz Orchestra's *Black Rag* (New Orleans, 1927).

Two regional bands that did record prolifically, and thus achieved a national following, were the Detroit-based Jean Goldkette Orchestra and McKinney's Cotton Pickers. Both groups used Detroit's gigantic Graystone Ballroom as their base and both were under the management of the French-born Goldkette. McKinney's was led by alto saxophonist and arranger Don Redman, who had left Henderson. Although much of the Cotton Pickers' output was dance music and novelty material with commercial vocals (*There's a Rainbow 'Round My Shoulder*, 1928; *Never Swat a Fly*, 1930), the group could play with rhythmic complexity (*Peggy*, 1929); with ensemble precision (*Stop Kidding*, 1928); or with abandon (*Milenberg Joys*, 1928), justifying the claims that on "coloreds-only night" three thousand people packed the place.

Early Jazz Standards

Jazz standards are pieces that jazz musicians keep alive in performance because the tunes are fun, especially beautiful, interesting, comfortable, nostalgic, or challenging to play. They then become part of a shared repertoire that musicians expect one another to know.

The recordings of the Original Dixieland Jazz Band tell us much about both the sources and the nature of early jazz standards. The group's three sources were the traditional pieces they had shared with their fellow New Orleans musicians, including *Tiger Rag;* their own compositions, such as *Original Dixieland One-Step* and *Sensation;* and popular tunes of the day, including *Darktown Strutters' Ball* and *(Back Home Again In) Indiana* (both published in 1917).

The structural template for much of the shared New Orleans jazz repertoire is the multi-strain piece, often with changes of key. This is the same form used in the social-dance pieces, marches, and, in particular, rags that nourished jazz during its development. Most of King Oliver's and Jelly Roll Morton's early pieces, and even many of Duke Ellington's early works, are also of this multi-strain type.

Other early jazz tunes that became standards are William H. Tyers' *Panama* (1911), Artie Matthews' *The Weary Blues* (1915), the Original Dixieland Jazz Band's *At the Jazz Band Ball* and *Clarinet Marmalade* (1918), the New Orleans Rhythm Kings' *Farewell Blues* (1922) and *Bugle Call Rag* (1923), and Jelly Roll Morton's *Wolverine Blues* and *King Porter Stomp* (both 1923). King Oliver and Louis

Armstrong's *Dipper Mouth Blues* (1923) and Charlie Davis's *Copenhagen* (1924) also became standards.

Some early jazz pieces were the result of a process that survives to this day: that of using preexisting pieces, or parts of them, as bases for new ones, called *contrafacts*.

Early on, perhaps the most popular contrafact was *Milenberg Joys* (1925). This multi-strain piece by

STAR DUST
by Hoagy Carmichael

MILLS MUSIC
Music Publishers

Jelly Roll Morton and the New Orleans Rhythm Kings was fashioned by varying the last strain of *Tiger Rag* to create all three different strains of the new composition. Contrafacts of *Tiger Rag* were numerous, beginning in the 1920s.

Jazz musicians applied their new style to pop tunes that were already well known, perhaps partly as a way to engage a wider public with something familiar. Older pop tunes adopted as jazz numbers include *My Gal Sal* (1905), *Some of These Days* (1910),

Alexander's Ragtime Band (1911), *Ballin' the Jack* (1913), *St. Louis Blues* and *That's A-Plenty* (both 1914), and *I Ain't Got Nobody* (1916).

African American composers wrote pieces that became standards of popular music—and often of jazz as well. Among them are *After You've Gone* (1918), *Royal Garden Blues* (1919), *(I Wish I Could Shimmy Like My) Sister Kate* and *'Way Down Yonder in New Orleans* (1922), *Charleston* (James P. Johnson, 1923), *Everybody Loves My Baby* and *Shine* (1924), *Sweet Georgia Brown* (1925), *Sugar* (1928), and *Ain't Misbehavin', Black and Blue,* and *Honeysuckle Rose* (the last three by Fats Waller, 1929).

By 1930's end, many other popular songs had been—or were about to be—adopted into the jazz standard repertoire. They included *The Sheik of Araby* (1921), *Somebody Loves Me* (1924), *Tea for Two* (1925), and *Someone to Watch Over Me* (1926). There were also *Stardust, 'S Wonderful,* and *My Blue Heaven* (1927); *How Long Has This Been Going On?* and *Makin' Whoopee* (1928); *Just You, Just Me* (1929); and *Body and Soul, Love for Sale, I Got Rhythm, On the Sunny Side of the Street, You're Driving Me Crazy, Exactly Like You,* and *What Is This Thing Called Love?* (1930). Songwriters included George Gershwin, Cole Porter, Irving Berlin, Hoagy Carmichael, and Walter Donaldson.

Many of these songs became bases for new jazz tunes in the 1930s and 1940s. Among these, a particular favorite is Gershwin's *I Got Rhythm.* (See "Old Chords, New Melodies," page 93, for other examples.)
—James Dapogny

The Jean Goldkette Orchestra, with saxophonist Frank Trumbauer (top row, third
from left) and cornetist Bix Beiderbecke
(fourth from right). Based in Detroit, the
band was one of the few regional outfits
to earn national recognition.

The Goldkette band boasted an array of star jazz soloists—including
Beiderbecke, Trumbauer, Venuti, Lang, Tommy and Jimmy Dorsey, and arranger
Bill Challis—and on one famous occasion in 1926 even bested the Fletcher
Henderson band on its home turf at the Roseland Ballroom in Manhattan. But
Victor's A&R man confined the Goldkette band's studio dates to commercial
fare, leaving only a few recordings—*My Pretty Girl* and *Clementine* (both
1927)—for the annals of jazz.

Goldkette's band broke up in 1927, but eighteen months later he took on
a band out of Toronto called the Orange Blossom Orchestra. The name was
changed to the Casa Loma Orchestra, and in the fall of 1929 they went down
to play at the Roseland. A recording date was set at OKeh's Union Square
studios, and early in the morning of October 29, 1929, a weary band cut their
first record date, including *Happy Days Are Here Again*. Meanwhile down on
Wall Street the world was ending: it was Black Thursday. The tune became
the anthem of the Great Depression and the band one of the harbingers of
the Swing Era.

During the "Jazz Age" of the 1920s, Louis Armstrong had transformed
jazz from a group art into a soloist's art; Morton and Ellington had set the
standard for jazz composition; Redman and Henderson had worked out the
fundamental format for big-band arrangements; and a varied group of voices—
from Bessie Smith to James P. Johnson to Bix Beiderbecke—had established
clarion, individual styles that would resonate for decades to come. Jazz, now
a widely known style of music, was poised to enter its period of greatest
commercial success. 🎧

Key Recordings

Armstrong, Louis. *Portrait of the Artist as a Young Man.* Four discs, Legacy/Smithsonian. A magnificent, Grammy-winning retrospective of Armstrong's career from 1923 to 1934. It covers his earliest recorded work with King Oliver's Creole Jazz Band, Fletcher Henderson, the legendary Hot Fives and Sevens, and his first big-band recordings and culminates in the remarkable sides he made in Paris in 1934.

Beiderbecke, Bix. *Bix Beiderbecke: Vol. 1, Singin' the Blues; Vol. 2, At the Jazz Band Ball.* Sony Legacy. These recordings were made for the OKeh label after Beiderbecke had left the Jean Goldkette band and come to New York to join Paul Whiteman's orchestra. Most of the sidemen are also Whiteman alumni, alongside some of New York's best studio musicians. The music ranges from free-swinging small-group jazz to some early experimental "cool" arrangements penned by Bill Challis and Fud Livingston.

Ellington, Duke. *The OKeh Ellington.* Two discs, Sony Legacy. A chronological set of Ellington's entire 1927–31 recorded output for OKeh, Columbia, and Harmony, including such classics as *Mood Indigo* and *Black and Tan Fantasy.* The earliest tracks highlight Ellington's "jungle" period, with growl trumpet and plunger-mute trombone heavily featured. Later music is more sophisticated and daring, evidence of how Ellington's experience at the Cotton Club reshaped his musical thinking.

Hines, Earl. *The Earl Hines Collection: Piano Solos, 1928–1940.* Collector's Classics (Denmark). Hines' complete recorded solo output of the period, demonstrating how he revolutionized piano jazz and paved the way for the modernists. Included are rare sides cut for a piano-roll manufacturer and afforded limited distribution, plus alternate takes of *Down Among the Sheltering Palms* and *Love Me Tonight.*

Jazz from the Windy City. Timeless (Holland). The driving Chicago style as purveyed by Eddie Condon, Charles Pierce (his legendary Paramount sides), and others. The disc also contains most of the recorded work of clarinetist Frank Teschemacher, who might have been the greatest Chicagoan of all if he hadn't lost his life in an accident at the age of twenty-six.

Mole, Miff. *Miff Mole's Molers.* Two discs, Frog (UK). Mole's complete output with Red Nichols, Jimmy Dorsey, Eddie Lang, and others. Most of the titles on the first disc are by Red Nichols and His Five Pennies, although, for contractual reasons, they weren't issued under that name. Titles on the second disc break away from the early Five Pennies format, feature trumpeters such as Leo McConville and Phil Napoleon, and substitute Jimmy Dorsey, on clarinet and alto saxophone, for Fud Livingston and/or Pee Wee Russell. Whether the music is early chamber-jazz or hot dance music aimed at the 1920s "fast" set, Miff Mole's trombone is dominant throughout, setting the tone and demonstrating that early jazz could be both hot and melodic.

Morton, Jelly Roll. *Jelly Roll Morton.* BMG (Canada). Morton's recording career was spasmodic in the extreme, encompassing a few primitive band sides, some piano solos in 1924, then the marvelous Red Hot Pepper tracks of 1926-28 for Victor. After Morton's contract with the label expired in 1930, he made no more records until 1938, aside from a couple of tunes as a sideman in 1934. In 1939 Victor re-signed him, and his career went out in a blaze of glory. This set features the best of his Victor output.

New York, 1926–1929, Vol. 1. Frog (UK). Harlem during the melting-pot years, with bands coming in from the hinterlands and trying to establish themselves in the big time. The big bands of Duke Ellington and Charlie Johnson are here, as are the Savoy Bearcats and others. Some of the music is rough, but all of it is adventurous and exciting, with such future stars as Benny Carter, Dicky Wells, and Jabbo Smith battling it out with veterans from the early 1920s.

The Real Kansas City, 1924–1940. Sony Legacy. A survey of the Kaycee music scene, emphasizing its importance as a music hub for bands passing through from all points of the compass. Such important bands as Bennie Moten's, George E. Lee's, Count Basie's, and Jay McShann's are featured heavily, but we also hear lesser-known territory bands, including Jesse Stone's and the Carolina Cotton Pickers; some boogie-woogie piano with blues shouter Joe Turner; and a fascinating track played by Basie sidemen and led by a young Texas trumpet player named Harry James. Produced by this author.

Russell, Luis. *The Luis Russell Collection, 1926–34.* Collector's Classics (Denmark). Harlem jazz at its best: fierce, uninhibited, and swinging, with some of the greatest New Orleans soloists on record. The Russell band was the supreme example of the dictum "Less is more." Simple arrangements lay down a framework for superb soloists, creating a fierce and terrible beauty that even now can send shivers down your spine. —*Michael Brooks*

CHAPTER 3

The Swing Era

John Edward Hasse

Duke Ellington entertaining at the Hurricane Club, New York, 1943.

Harry James paid dues in territory bands before becoming one of the most popular Swing Era bandleaders.

f novelist F. Scott Fitzgerald had it right when he called the 1920s the Jazz Age, then the 1930s through the mid-1940s could even more aptly be termed the Swing Era. That's because during that time, the swing pulse and impulse transformed jazz— and through it, much of American vernacular music.

Swing music and dancing became a huge phenomenon, almost a national obsession, taking jazz to heights of popularity never achieved before or since. More jazz musicians gained favor with the general public, more audiences turned to jazz as a backdrop for dancing and entertainment, than at any other time in history. Never before had jazz so dominated the field of popular music. At no other time was jazz such a catalyst for thousands of fans queuing up for a performance, for turn-away crowds so large and enthusiastic that the police had to be called in to keep order, for so many live radio broadcasts carrying the music to waiting listeners coast-to-coast, and for heated band battles that became the stuff of legends.

Many people helped create swing, but two musicians, Fletcher Henderson and Louis Armstrong, were especially influential.

In the 1920s, Fletcher Henderson's orchestra had popularized a fundamental format for, and style of, big-band arranging. Henderson and his principal arranger, Don Redman, fully developed a basic framework that featured sections of reeds and brass pitted against each other, sometimes in call-and-response patterns, and sometimes with one section playing supporting motifs or riffs (short, repeated phrases).

What separated swing from jazz that preceded? Most of all, its rhythm. Louis Armstrong's rhythmic innovations loosened up the beat of jazz, provided a greater variety of rhythms, and made its momentum more flowing. Between 1930 and 1935, Armstrong influenced other musicians to play slightly ahead of the beat and, in so doing, transformed the rhythmic feel of jazz.

In its most original and most fundamental sense, *swing* is a verb meaning to play with that perceptible forward momentum, the propulsive rhythmic quality that is found in much African-rooted music. It's a looseness, almost an elasticity of the pulse. "Swing is not a kind of music," Duke Ellington told an interviewer in 1939. "It is that part of rhythm that causes a bouncing, buoyant, terpsichorean urge."

The change in the rhythms of jazz became more pronounced as bands, over time, began replacing traditional instruments and introducing new instrumental techniques. The plodding tuba, originally used to keep a two-to-the-bar beat, gave way to the fleeter string bass, which promoted an even, flowing feel of four to the bar. The banjo

Frank Sinatra's popularity echoed the success of big bands in the thirties. The singer first rose to fame with the Harry James and Tommy Dorsey orchestras.

was abandoned in favor of the more versatile guitar. Drummers shifted the fundamental pulse from the drum itself to the high-hat cymbal. These changes made the music feel less staccato and jerky, more long-lined, forward-moving, and, well, swinging.

Singers also became an important part of the Swing Era. Paul Whiteman was among the first bandleaders to feature a vocalist (Bing Crosby), and in 1931 Duke Ellington hired Ivie Anderson. Other bandleaders began to follow their lead: in the 1930s, Benny Goodman offered singer Helen Ward, Count Basie had Jimmy Rushing, Chick Webb featured Ella Fitzgerald, Earl Hines engaged Billy Eckstine, Harry James employed Frank Sinatra, and Artie Shaw presented Helen Forrest and Billie Holiday.

At its essence, however, swing was an instrumental music. "In the middle and late thirties," wrote Barry Ulanov, "swing lost its standing as a verb and was elevated to the stature of a noun and a category. Jazz was dead, long live swing."

To most people, swing meant big-band jazz.

Jazz, the Mass Attraction

The 1920s and 1930s were, as Russell Nye has observed, the time when "public dancing in America reached its highest point of popularity and profit, and the dance hall became one of the nation's most influential social institutions."

Café Society, in Greenwich Village, offered a varied musical menu that included swing. The club's opening in 1939 featured Billie Holiday with Frankie Newton's band, the Boogie Woogie Boys, Albert Ammons, Meade "Lux" Lewis, Joe Turner, and Pete Johnson.

The kind of dance hall that drew the largest attendance was the dance palace: "Huge, brilliantly lighted, elaborately decorated with columns, gilt, drapes, mirrors, and ornate chandeliers, often with two bands, these became synonymous with glamour and romance," wrote Nye. The most celebrated dance palaces were the Roseland and Savoy in New York City, the Trianon and Aragon in Chicago, the Graystone in Detroit, the Indiana Roof Garden in Indianapolis, and the Avalon Casino on Santa Catalina Island, California. A step down in space and luxury were the Marigold in Minneapolis, the Pla Mor in Kansas City, and the Madrid in Louisville, Kentucky. Several nightclubs with big ballrooms became famous, including Glen Island Casino in New Rochelle, New York; Castle Farm in Cincinnati; and Shadowland in San Antonio, Texas.

Public dancing became, by the 1930s, one of the key American courtship rituals. For many young people, swing music and dancing served as important emotional outlets; for others, they offered much-needed escape from the economic difficulties of the lingering Depression. With partner in hand, caught up in shared euphoria and momentary forgetfulness, dancers could stomp and swing themselves into states of transcendence. While the music's time surged forward, real-world time, paradoxically, seemed to stop. Ears flooded with irresistible melodies and intoxicating rhythms, skin flushed with excitement (and perhaps desire), and pulses quickened as dancers Lindy-Hopped, Susy-Q'ed, Shim-Shammed, and Shagged the nights, and their cares, away. If ballrooms had won public acceptance in the 1920s and offered a diversion from the Depression of the early 1930s, in the late thirties they reached their all-time height of popularity. Most of the dancers were young people, and swing took center stage in American youth culture, just as rock and roll would two decades later.

Swing may have been a national phenomenon, but Manhattan was the music's capital and Harlem its absolute epicenter. There, "uptown," one could catch swing at such ballrooms as the Savoy and Renaissance; such theaters as the Apollo and the Harlem Opera House; such nightclubs as Monroe's Uptown House, Small's Paradise, and the Rhythm Club; and all sorts of lesser spots. Outside of Harlem, swing venues dotted the map of New York City, but they were concentrated in three areas of Manhattan: One ran along a stretch of West 52nd Street (also known as Swing Street or simply the Street), where the basements of brownstones crammed in dozens of nightspots, among them the Onyx Club, the Famous Door, the Three Deuces, and the Hickory House. The prominent midtown hotels—among them the Waldorf, the Edison, the New Yorker, and the Pennsylvania—provided another locus for swing dancing and listening, albeit for affluent white people. And finally, Greenwich Village offered such swinging clubs as the Village Vanguard, Black Cat, and Café Society.

Throughout the nation, swelling masses of listeners and dancers created an explosion in the popularity of jukeboxes, on which swing recordings were increasingly heard. The number of jukeboxes in the United States jumped dramatically from 25,000 in 1933 to 300,000 in 1939, by then consuming 13 million discs a year. Spurred on by the swing-music craze, the recovering economy, the popularity of the phonograph, the jukebox boom, and the new low-priced (35-cent) discs issued by music-industry upstart Decca Records and others, the record industry climbed back to recovery. From a low of 10 million units sold in 1933, sales surged to 33 million in 1938 and 127 million in 1941.

The Swing Dances

From the beginning, ragtime, jazz, and often blues had been music to dance to, spawning a progression of famous steps—the Slow Drag, the Grizzly Bear, Ballin' the Jack, the Mooche, the Shimmy, the Black Bottom, the Charleston, and others. Most of the steps originated among southern African Americans in down-home juke joints and, in expurgated versions, eventually reached the stages of northern nightclubs, vaudeville theaters, and Broadway.

During the Swing Era, jazz dancing reached its apex of public participation, attention, and virtuosity. "The beat," asserted dancer Norma Miller, "is what swing dancing is all about.... Swing music. There's never been any music so perfectly attuned to what the body can do."

As always, hip dancers were open to new steps, and the 1930s saw a parade of them, including the Shim-Sham (also known as the Shim-Sham-Shimmy) and the Big Apple, which featured a "caller" shouting out the steps. Some dances originated in Harlem ballrooms or as Cotton Club production numbers—Truckin' (1933), the Suzy-Q (1936), Peckin' (1937), and the Scronch (1937)—and then, as fads, spread widely to dance halls and ballrooms.

The most spectacular and exciting dance step of the Swing Era, the fast, furious Lindy Hop, had burst forth in 1928—probably from the Savoy Ballroom. It was developed there in the 1930s and taken to exceptional heights, literally and figuratively. The dance, encompassing a tension between partnering and individual expression, featured improvised "breakaways" and athletic aerial movements or "air" steps—pioneered by the Harlem dancer

Frankie Manning—in which women were tossed into the air like rag dolls. As the Lindy Hop caught on, energetic young dancers expanded its routine of floor and aerial steps at ballrooms and competitions. Known in white communities as the Jitterbug, the step drew young enthusiasts across America. Twirling dancers, swirling skirts, exuberant smiles, youthful energy, virtuosic displays, the night charged with excitement—this was the Lindy Hop.

A dancing audience gave musicians a charge, too. "Outstanding musicians inspire great dancers and vice versa," observed saxophonist Lester Young. "The rhythm of the dancers," he added, "comes back to you when you're playing." Duke Ellington, when performing in stage shows became routine for his musicians, liked to take his band out for a string of dance gigs, because "when they see people moving around the floor, they've got to put snap and ginger into their work."

And so the musicians and the dancers would form a swinging union, the band's music interplaying with the dancers' limbs and feet, creating what novelist Ralph Ellison called "that feeling of communion which was the true meaning of the public jazz dance. The blues, the singer, the band, and the dancers formed the vital whole of jazz as an institutional form, and even today neither part is quite complete without the rest." —*John Edward Hasse*

Dancing and jukeboxes were both on the rise in the 1930s.

57

Big Band, Big Sound

Much of the appeal of big bands had to do with the sheer depth, breadth, textural variety, and volume of their sound. Where combos of two to five or six musicians tended to thrive in small, intimate surroundings, big bands were geared to fill vast spaces and envelop large audiences.

To create that sound, they employed instrumentation that filled the entire sonic spectrum, from the string bass anchoring the low end to clarinets, trumpets, and piano defining the highest limits of the music's range.

In between, musical events varied depending on the band but generally unfolded along the following lines:

The rhythm section (drums, string bass, piano, and guitar) served as the foundation of the sound. The drums would keep time, generally on the high-hat cymbal and bass drum, and provide rhythmic kicks, accents, and fills on snare drum, tom-toms, and other cymbals. The string bass would serve a double function, reinforcing a steady beat by "walking" in sync with the drums and simultaneously outlining the harmony by playing the lowest notes of the changing chords or providing "counterpoint"—complementary melodies—to the main melody. The guitar would also keep time and establish harmony with chords generally played four to the bar, with occasional rhythmic accents. The piano served a somewhat freer role, keeping time and providing chordal accompaniment while sometimes playing melody and inserting melodic "fills" in musical spaces. In some bands, vibraphone was used in much the same way as a piano, adding an airy yet percussive timbre to the overall sound.

Melody and solos would be played by any of a number of instruments, including clarinet, saxophone, trumpet, or trombone.

The distinctive big-band quality came from the use of brass (trumpets and trombones) and woodwind, or "reed," instruments (primarily clarinet, alto saxophone, tenor sax, baritone sax) to fill out the sound. They were used in "sections" to create chordal blocks of sound that could be used to punch out rhythmic accents or provide smooth harmonic textures under and around the melody. They could also play repeating melodic figures (riffs) or serve as a kind of chorus answering the main melody.

The different tonal qualities of the instruments—crisp, bright, and metallic brass (sometimes greatly altered with the use of mutes) and warm, reedy woodwinds—allowed for contrast, with the brass and the winds often interacting as separate sections. In Duke Ellington's band, however, instruments were frequently combined in unusual ways to create entirely new tonal colors and moods. —*Tad Lathrop*

The 1950 Gene Krupa band's front line of saxes, second tier of brasses, and four-piece rhythm section typified the instrumentation of big swing bands.

Bands had always competed for popularity, but in the Swing Era competition between dance bands came to the fore, taking on the characteristics of rivalry between great athletic teams. Bands attracted ardent followers, orchestras engaged in sometimes epic band battles, and jazz magazines and black newspapers ran readers' polls to select the top groups. Fans kept track of changes in bands' personnel and argued the merits of one band over another.

One cause of swing's ability to draw so many passionate adherents was the depth of its meaning: it affirmed the joys of dance, music, and youthful courtship; of risk-taking improvisation; of a dynamic African American force challenging and changing mainstream America. Like rock and roll would a generation later, swing drew young people powerfully, giving rise to a musical subculture. And swing affirmed the human spirit at a time when the country was still struggling to come out of the Great Depression.

In 1937, swing bands and Hollywood films had comparable clout in the marketplace. Theater operators doubled their drawing power by pairing the two types of entertainment.

Swing also provided a context for forward strides in race relations, contributing to the development of a more inclusive concept of American identity. Before the Swing Era, jazz reflected the nationwide racial divide between blacks and whites. When, in 1935, Benny Goodman established a racially mixed band, he made it safe for other bands to do so. Some swing bands became interracial institutions a decade before baseball and the armed forces were integrated.

Prior to the Swing Era, most white Americans had been only vaguely aware of black jazz musicians, whom the record companies relegated to their "race" catalogs marketed mainly to black buyers. In the 1930s, however, swing led jazz of all colors into the American mainstream.

Jazz began as a local music, deeply rooted in African-American vernacular musical traditions. Prior to the 1930s, most jazz and dance bands, whether headquartered in Atlanta, Kansas City, or Chicago, played in a limited region or territory (and thus were called "territory bands") and found limited access to radio and recording—the means of reaching greater numbers of listeners. But by the height of the Swing Era, jazz was dominated by national bands managed by white businessmen and marketed to a mass, predominantly white, nationwide audience.

Twelve national swing bands—some black and some white—stand out for their excellence, influence, and historical importance. None of these bands played jazz exclusively; surviving in the entertainment marketplace meant their band "books" had to include pop vocals and commercially oriented fare. But at their best, these groups produced jazz of enduring quality.

Fletcher Henderson's last push as a bandleader came in the mid-thirties when his outfit boasted Chu Berry (left) and Roy Eldridge (foreground, leaning on piano).

Singer Ella Fitzgerald.

The Great Black Bands

In the 1920s, Fletcher Henderson and his orchestra had served as a model for Duke Ellington and other bandleaders. Henderson was esteemed for his talented musicians—such as Louis Armstrong, cornetist Rex Stewart, and tenor saxophonist Ben Webster—and his pioneering arrangements, but he possessed neither business acumen nor a shrewd manager. In 1934, not long after recording two of his best compositions, *Down South Camp Meeting* and *Wrappin' It Up,* Henderson's band broke up. He went to work as an arranger for Benny Goodman, and when Goodman and swing became hugely popular, it was, ironically, Henderson's arranging that provided the framework.

The short, hunchbacked Chick Webb may have lacked physical stature, but he made up for it in the respect he earned as a bandleader and drummer. His excellent control of dynamics, imaginative drum breaks and fills (abundantly displayed in *Stompin' at the Savoy* and *Blue Lou,* both from 1934, and *Liza* from 1938), and plucky personality won him many avid fans. Webb's band played at the Savoy Ballroom from 1927 on, and from 1931 to 1939 it served more or less as the house band; he routinely defeated other groups in band battles. In 1934, Webb hired Ella Fitzgerald as vocalist. Upon Webb's untimely death from tuberculosis in 1939 at the age of thirty, Fitzgerald became the nominal leader of his group until it disbanded in 1942 and she went out as a solo singer.

Soon after attracting acclaim with his 1928 recordings with Louis Armstrong, pianist Earl "Fatha" Hines established a band at Chicago's posh Grand Terrace, where he would hold many residencies until 1940. Unlike Ellington or Basie, Hines never built a consistent sonic personality for his band, who nonetheless made a number of solid, impressive recordings, such as *Cavernism* (1933) and *Grand Terrace Shuffle* (1939). A great talent scout, in the 1940s Hines employed Dizzy Gillespie and Charlie Parker, who were on their way to developing an advanced style that would be dubbed bebop.

Stompin' at the Savoy

The unassuming marquee of the Savoy Ballroom belied the venue's reputation as a shrine of dancing and popular style.

"Three nights a week, we were at the Savoy Ballroom," recalled the painter Romare Bearden. "The best dancing in the world was there, and the best music." Opened on March 12, 1926, in Harlem, the Savoy became famous for its hot jazz music, torrid dancing, and special events. Adroit showmanship and promotion helped make the Savoy the most talked-about ballroom in America, "the home of happy feet," as new dances originated there, songs were written about it (*Stompin' at the Savoy, Savoy, House of Joy*), and radio "remotes" broadcast the music coast-to-coast. Normally two bands held forth at a time, alternating sets between two bandstands, so the dance music never stopped.

Situated at 596 Lenox Avenue, it ran the length of the block between 140th and 141st streets. The Savoy boasted a spacious lobby, a marble staircase leading to the ballroom on the second floor, and a 50-by-200-foot polished-maple dance floor. Management billed it as "the world's most beautiful ballroom." The Savoy employed 120 people, including fifteen bouncers to keep order, and its dress code required male customers to wear coats at all times.

Most of the important bands of the Swing Era played there, including those of Duke Ellington, Cab Calloway, Andy Kirk, Count Basie, Roy Eldridge, and Benny Carter. A shrine of public dancing and a center of popular style, the Savoy was not only a highly influential venue but also a demanding one for the bands. "If you didn't swing, you weren't there long," recalled trombonist Dicky Wells.

The Savoy hosted legendary band contests, positioning the contesting groups on adjoining bandstands. On May 15, 1927, the Savoy hired four bands and promoted a battle of New York versus Chicago, which brought out the riot squad. Another contest featured six bands in a battle of the North versus the South. Legendary battle royales pitted Chick Webb's band (the house favorite) against Count Basie's and Webb's against Duke Ellington's. Most sensationally, on May 11, 1937, in "The Music Battle of the Century," Webb's black band battled the white band of Benny Goodman, who had gotten several of his biggest hits from Webb's arranger Edgar Sampson. As the two bands competed heatedly, reported the *New York Age*, thousands "battled mounted cops and patrolmen for places near enough to the Savoy to hear the music of the two great orchestras." The verdict: Webb beat Goodman.

The Savoy welcomed black and white patrons alike. "At one stage, about half the people at the Savoy were white and half were colored," Savoy manager Charles Buchanan recalled. "The cops used to hate it."

By the time the Savoy closed its doors in 1958 and was demolished to make way for a housing project, 250 bands had performed there for an estimated 30 million stomping feet. —*John Edward Hasse*

Band battles, like a 1938 face-off between the Chick Webb and Count Basie outfits, were hot attractions at the Savoy.

A HISTORY MAKING........BATTLE OF SWING

SUNDAY JAN. 16'

The King OF THE DRUMS

The Royalist OF THE KEYBOARD

Chick **WEBB** & AMERICAS OUTSTANDING...SWING BAND *vs* **Count BASIE** & HIS ORCHESTRA *The Aristocrat of Rhythm*

Ella FITZGERALD FEATURED WITH CHICK

Chick Webb & HIS FAMOUS ORCHESTRA WILL PLAY NIGHTLY AT THE SAVOY

Special Matinee 3 P.M. No Increase in Admission

Billie HOLLIDAY FEATURED WITH THE COUNT....

LENOX AVE at 140' STREET.

SAVOY

Earl "Fatha" Hines, pianist and bandleader.

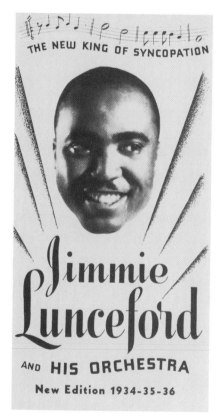

Jimmie Lunceford's orchestra was unmatched for its showmanship, which kept the band at the top of the swing scene for a decade starting in 1934.

Though Hines' orchestra lacked a consistent arranging style, the leader's forceful gifts as a pianist firmly marked the band's sound and, in fact, propelled Hines into the jazz pantheon. Indeed, some jazz critics consider him the greatest of all jazz keyboard artists, for he freed jazz piano from the formalized strictures of blues and the ragtime-derived Harlem "stride" style—in his right hand, replacing ragtime's chords with single notes and octaves; in his left, replacing ragtime's steady oom-pah with suspensions of the beat, and creating dialogues between the hands. With his linear lines, unpredictable phrasing, use of silence, razor-sharp inventiveness, and technical skills (for example, extending a tremolo for two minutes), he deeply influenced other pianists, notably Teddy Wilson. Hines' piano recordings spanned a half century; his Swing Era masterworks included the showpieces *Pianology* (1937), *Rosetta* (1939), and, taken at the dizzying tempo of 276 beats per minute, *Piano Man* (1939).

Like Paul Whiteman and Cab Calloway, Jimmie Lunceford stood in front of his band to conduct it. His band emphasized ensemble playing over solos, offered a joyous swing, and projected infectious enthusiasm in such numbers as *Organ Grinder's Swing* (1936), *For Dancers Only* (1937), and *Margie* (1938); many were arranged by Sy Oliver, whose apparently simple arrangements often masked deep sophistication and offered imaginative contrasts in dynamics and tonal colors.

Lunceford's band established a strong reputation for its "three p's": precision, polish, and presentation. While other bands matched its musicianship, none matched its showmanship. His players always wore sharp outfits; the trombonists would point their slides skyward; the trumpeters would, in unison, toss their instruments into the air and catch them; and the audience could watch everyone in the band enjoying a contagiously good time.

While swing bands typically followed the lead of Fletcher Henderson and voiced their instruments in discrete sections (sax section, trumpet section, trombone section), Duke Ellington often mixed instruments together in unusual ways, creating distinctive and unique tonal colors—for example, pairing a tightly muted trumpet with a low-playing clarinet and a high-playing trombone in *Mood Indigo* of 1930. In contrast to bandleaders Goodman, Basie, Lunceford, Webb, and Tommy and Jimmy Dorsey, Ellington was not merely a gifted instrumentalist and leader; he personally created most of the music played by his orchestra. Unlike many other bandleaders, Ellington wasn't interested primarily in establishing a good beat for dancing; he wanted to explore his musical imagination. Memories, sound colors, moods, emotions—these were his focal points, as you can hear in the astonishing train ride conveyed in *Daybreak Express* (1933), the quiet daydream of *Azure* (1937), the intense drama of *Ko-Ko* (1940), and the sexuality and sensuality of *Warm Valley* (1940).

With musical insight and sensitivity, Ellington composed pieces with his players in mind—for example, *Concerto for Cootie, Cotton Tail,* and *Jack the Bear* (all 1940) were each written for a specific musician in his band (respectively, trumpeter Cootie Williams, tenor saxophonist Ben Webster, and bassist Jimmie Blanton)—and in so doing, lifted individuality within his band to an artistic zenith.

The scope of his musical interests—and his success in pursuing them—set Ellington apart from other leaders of big bands: historically, he ranks as the supreme composer and orchestrator for the medium of the jazz orchestra or big band.

But Ellington's work transcended jazz. Many consider him beyond category—a musician whose body of recordings ranks, as Gary Giddins has written, as "surely the finest representation of a composer's work since Edison invented the phonograph." More than just a snapshot of a particular musical style at a particular time, Ellington's music reflects, in the most sensuous terms, much of life in twentieth-century America—making him not only a quintessential jazz musician but one of the greatest composers, from any stylistic background, that America has produced.

In some obvious ways Ellington was part of swing: he shared with the swing bands a similar instrumentation, employed a singer, played pop songs and original instrumentals, and performed rhythmic music typically for dancing. But overall, Ellington operated in an artistic sphere different from swing's. His music expressed a greater range of emotions than did the swing bands, employed more sensitive dynamics and more of a sense of theater than most, featured the most distinctive players and most varied sounds, experimented and innovated more than any others, was less prone to fads, and presented more original (and challenging) pieces, particularly on records.

Caravan was one of the classics originating with the Duke Ellington Orchestra.

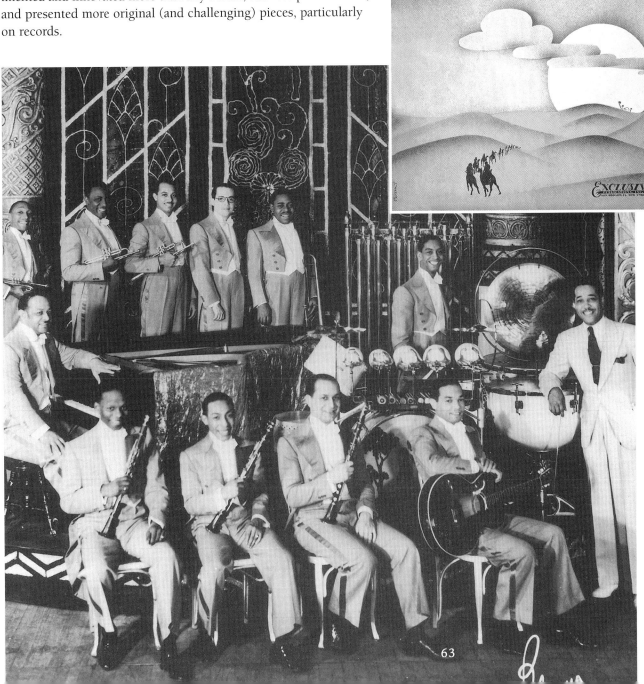

In a swing band, the drummer kept the time and drove the band—examples include the great Jo Jones in the Count Basie band, Chick Webb in his own orchestra, and Gene Krupa with Benny Goodman. Ellington's drummer Sonny Greer took a different course: he was less a driver of the band than a master colorist, with his subtle brush playing, tasteful stick work, and novel use of percussive effects (for example, on the evocative *Caravan*, 1937). Producer-entrepreneur John Hammond called Greer "the most intricate of all percussionists."

Even the best of the other big bands suffer a certain sameness if their recordings are listened to one after the other, but Ellington's recordings, taken together, offer variety, contrast, and even surprise. The Duke Ellington Orchestra predated the swing craze by a decade, helped in fact to foster it, popularized its catchphrase—"It don't mean a thing if it ain't got that swing"—and provided its highest benchmarks of originality.

Count Basie's band, with singer Jimmy Rushing (shown here in 1943), rode its blues-drenched Kansas City swing to international fame.

Other than the Ellington aggregation, the greatest Swing Era ensemble was led by pianist and bandleader William "Count" Basie. His band, which he organized in Kansas City, was steeped in the blues and its traditions, from blues chord progressions and blue notes (certain "bent" notes) to bluesy riffs—short, repeated phrases often rendered behind soloists.

Soon after the band arrived in New York in 1936, it became champion of the hotly competitive Harlem ballrooms, edging out the orchestras of Ellington, Webb, and Lunceford. Basie's band became famous for its outstanding soloists and its peerless "rhythm section"—Basie on piano, Freddie Green on guitar, Walter Page on string bass, and Jo Jones on drums—whose light but relentlessly forward-moving propulsion, or swing, was the envy of many other bands. The Basie rhythm section influenced others to play more flexibly and more responsively to the horn players. In such recordings as *Taxi War Dance* (1939), Basie's rocking Kansas City rhythm proved irresistible to dancers. His use of freewheeling "head" (unwritten) arrangements, in which a player might blow for several choruses, made his performances even more exciting.

By 1939, the band comprised fifteen instrumentalists and two singers, Helen Humes (who replaced Billie Holiday in 1938) and Jimmy Rushing. Basie's band was dominated by great soloists: tenor saxophonists Lester Young (*Lester Leaps In*, 1939) and Herschel Evans (*Doggin' Around*, 1938); trumpeters Buck Clayton (*One O'Clock Jump*, 1937) and Harry "Sweets" Edison (*Shorty George*, 1938); trombonist Dicky Wells (*Texas Shuffle*, 1938); and Basie himself (*Doggin' Around*). His own early playing followed the two-handed ragtime approach, but in the middle 1930s he switched to a relaxed, spare style—imbued with subtlety and wit—that led beautifully into his instrumentalists' solos. From the piano keyboard, Basie cued, directed, and "swung" the band.

From the 1950s on he chose a style rather different from his classic 1930s sound, but Basie's band remained an enduring musical institution, swinging on toward the new millennium.

Big-Band Theme Songs

During the Swing Era, every name band had at least one signature tune or "theme song" that was considered a kind of musical trademark. The bands—the most prominent of which are listed below—typically played the tunes at the beginnings or endings of dances and radio broadcasts. —*John Edward Hasse*

Louis Armstrong	*When It's Sleepy Time Down South*
Charlie Barnet	*Cherokee*
Count Basie	*One O'Clock Jump*
Bunny Berigan	*I Can't Get Started*
Tiny Bradshaw	*Fascination*
Les Brown	*Sentimental Journey*
Cab Calloway	*Minnie the Moocher*
Benny Carter	*Melancholy Lullaby*
Casa Loma Orchestra	*Was I to Blame for Falling in Love with You?, Smoke Rings*
Bob Chester	*Sunburst*
Larry Clinton	*The Dipsy Doodle*
Bob Crosby	*Summertime*
Jimmy Dorsey	*Contrasts*
Tommy Dorsey	*I'm Gettin' Sentimental over You*
Duke Ellington	*East St. Louis Toodle-Oo* (to 1940), *Sepia Panorama* (1940–41) *Take the "A" Train* (1941 on)
Benny Goodman	*Let's Dance* (opening theme), *Good-bye* (closing theme)
Lionel Hampton	*Flying Home*
Erskine Hawkins	*Tuxedo Junction*
Edgar Hayes	*Stardust*
Fletcher Henderson	*Christopher Columbus*
Woody Herman	*Blue Evening, Blue Prelude, Blue Flame* (1942 on)
Earl Hines	*Deep Forest*
Claude Hopkins	*I Would Do Anything for You*
Harry James	*Ciribiribin*
Stan Kenton	*Artistry in Rhythm*
Andy Kirk	*Cloudy* (until 1936), *Until the Real Thing Comes Along* (1936 on)
Gene Krupa	*Apurksody, Star Burst, That Drummer's Band*
Jimmie Lunceford	*Jazznocracy, Uptown Blues, Rhythm Is Our Business*
Hal McIntyre	*Moon Mist*
Glenn Miller	*Moonlight Serenade*
Don Redman	*Chant of the Weed*
Artie Shaw	*Nightmare*
Claude Thornhill	*Snowfall*
Chick Webb	*Let's Get Together*
Paul Whiteman	*Rhapsody in Blue*

Bandleader Cab Calloway.

The Swing Era   65

The Casa Loma Orchestra, led by Glen Gray (in black), in 1936. Noted for technical precision, the Casa Lomans earned the admiration of their musical peers.

The Great White Bands

Established in Detroit in 1927 as the Orange Blossoms, the Casa Loma Orchestra became the first noted white swing band and a model for later bands. With such arrangements as *Casa Loma Stomp* and *San Sue Strut* (both 1930), arranger Gene Gifford transformed the Casa Loma Orchestra from a semi-hot dance band into a jazz outfit known for its precise ensemble playing, fast tempos, and rhythmic energy that could bring dancers to the floor and raise the temperature of any ballroom.

Their flashy uptempo numbers (up to 250 beats per minute) such as *White Jazz* (1931) required great teamwork. When asked later how the Casa Lomans managed to play such demanding charts, clarinetist Clarence Hutchenrider—the band's leading soloist—quipped, "We practiced hard between drinks." But the Casa Loma Orchestra balanced its repertory, mixing fast numbers with such slow-dance ballads as *Smoke Rings* (1932).

The band enjoyed its greatest popularity from 1930 to 1935. Its youthfulness and exuberance attracted followers on the college circuit, while it also performed for older dancers at plush hotels, including New York's Essex House, where it held a residency for nearly two years, in 1933–34.

When compared with music by the best black bands of the 1930s, the Casa Loma Orchestra's recordings reveal more technical virtuosity (some would say mechanical exactness) than soulfulness or soloistic creativity, and they lack the looseness evident in the best of swing. Nonetheless, the ensemble exerted a strong influence, even on black bands. (Eddie Barefield, who played and arranged for the Bennie Moten band in the early 1930s, recalled that "we all admired the Casa Loma band, and tried to ape them.") Its precise ensemble playing, well-crafted arrangements, and appeal to college students provided a model for Benny Goodman and other bandleaders.

Clarinetist and bandleader Benny Goodman played a key role in moving jazz from the margins of American culture to the mainstream. He boasted superb technique on his instrument, excellent control, and a clear, light tone. He led the most influential, for a time the most popular, and perhaps the most polished of the big bands of the period. They sent a ripple of excitement through the nation after wowing an audience at the Palomar Ballroom in Los Angeles on August 21, 1935, and, for many who hadn't been paying close attention, seemed to launch the Swing Era. In 1937 his band attracted screaming bobby-soxers at the Paramount Theatre in New York City, and their performances often ignited audience passions to the point that fans rushed the stage to jitterbug to Goodman's music.

A perfectionist and strict taskmaster, Goodman demanded a high level of musicianship from his players and became famous for his glare, dubbed "the ray." His band suffered legendary turnover; singer Helen Forrest said she left the band "to avoid having a nervous breakdown."

Like Louis Armstrong, but unlike Duke Ellington, Goodman took most of the band's solos himself. But it wasn't for lack of talent among his employees. Goodman's band boasted possibly the most esteemed trumpet section—Ziggy Elman and Harry James were key players—of any big band of the Swing Era. Trumpeter Bunny Berigan sparkled on Goodman's recordings of *King Porter Stomp* and *Sometimes I'm Happy* (both 1935). Drummer Gene Krupa swung *Sing Sing Sing* (1937). Goodman himself shone on *Riding High* (1937), *Blue Room* (1938), and *Mission to Moscow* (1942).

Goodman pioneered interracial bands: in 1935 he formed the Benny Goodman Trio, with Gene Krupa on drums and Teddy Wilson on piano; the following year he added vibraphonist Lionel Hampton. His combos—later including the guitar virtuoso Charlie Christian—produced some of the most classic of small-group swing, exemplified by such performances as *After You've Gone* (the Benny Goodman Trio, 1935), *Avalon* (the Quartet, 1937), and *Breakfast Feud* (the Sextet, 1941).

Clarinetist Benny Goodman (front) came to prominence as a leader of a big band. Later, he established a trio, a quartet, and a sextet. His orchestra is shown here at Chicago's Congress Hotel shortly after a 1935 breakthrough engagement at the Palomar in Los Angeles. With him at the time were vocalist Helen Ward and drummer Gene Krupa.

Jazz Controversies

Controversy swirled around jazz almost from its birth. When media commentators weren't decrying it as a "musical vice" (*New Orleans Times-Picayune*, 1918), others were blaming it for a range of social ills.

"Ellington Refutes Cry That Swing Started Sex Crimes!" blared one *Down Beat* headline in 1937. At issue was a prominent educator's charge that a wave of sexual assaults stemmed from the "hot" jazz that was in vogue at the time.

The debate over jazz was actually a continuation of a long-running war of words about ragtime. The opponents of ragtime—conservative members of the older generation, people with vested interests in classical music, and defenders of public morality—attacked that music on multiple grounds: its words, its racial (that is, African American) origins, and its supposed perils. "In Christian homes," wrote the *Musical Observer* in 1914, "where purity and morals are stressed, ragtime should find no resting place.... Let us purge America and the Divine Art of Music from this polluting nuisance."

When jazz became the focus of controversy, traditionalists linked it with sinful sexuality and with public dancing, which in the early 1920s was still controversial. "Moralists," wrote John Edward Hasse, "drew a close link between dancing, loose language, immodest dress, sex, and jazz."

Opposition to the music occurred not just among whites. In many middle-class black homes, parents opposed jazz and blues as disreputable and even as "the devil's music." Clarinetist Garvin Bushell

recalled of the 1920s, "You usually weren't allowed to play blues and boogie-woogie in the average Negro middle-class home. That music supposedly suggested a low element."

But if some saw jazz as "appealing only to the lover of sensuous and debasing emotions" (Lucien White, in *New York Age,* ca. 1921), others saw the music as posing life-threatening danger: in 1936 a series of suicides were attributed to the Billie Holiday song *Gloomy Sunday,* resulting in its being banned from the radio airwaves.

Many, apparently, shared a view of jazz as "an atrocity in polite society...[with great] possibilities of harm" (*New Orleans Times-Picayune,* 1918) or as "a return to the humming, hand-clapping, or tomtom beating of savages" (the *New York Times,* 1924).

When a U.S. Senate committee conducted an investigation of the American Federation of Musicians'

1942–44 ban on recording, they concluded that "if the ban on recording wipes out jitterbug music, jive, and boogie-woogie, it might be a good thing all around."

But some of the most heated controversy occurred within the jazz community itself.

An ongoing point of dissension was any new form of jazz. Musicians often voiced the loudest opposition to the latest styles—or any styles that differed from their own. "Of all the cruelties in the world, bebop is the most phenomenal," Fletcher Henderson said, while Louis Armstrong charged that "bop is ruining music...and the kids that play bop are ruining themselves."

Writers did their parts to raise the critical decibel level. In 1961, critic John Tynan decried a free-jazz performance by John Coltrane and Eric Dolphy as "a horrifying demonstration of what appears to be a growing anti-jazz trend...Coltrane and Dolphy seem intent on deliberately destroying [swing]. They seem bent on pursuing an anarchistic course in music."

None of the controversy should have been surprising. Jazz was born with a rebellious streak; Alain Locke wrote that jazz represented "a reaction from Puritan repressions...an escape from the tensions and monotonies of a machine-ridden...form of civilization." If Hoagy Carmichael was right in calling jazz a rejection of "the accepted, the proper, the old," jazz was bound to stir up antipathy among those with a stake in the accepted, the proper, and the old.
—*Tad Lathrop*

Tommy Dorsey (standing, with trombone) led a band that in 1941 included vocalist Jo Stafford (back row, second from left), Frank Sinatra (back row, right), and the Pied Pipers.

Offering a cool contrast to the hot playing style of Goodman was fellow clarinetist Artie Shaw. From the first bars of his dark theme song, *Nightmare* (1938), one could tell that Shaw was a bandleader of a different order. After failing to win public acceptance for a group based around a string quartet, he formed a conventional big band in 1937; in 1938 he enjoyed an enormous hit with the challenging 108-bar Cole Porter tune, *Begin the Beguine*. Propelled by this success, Shaw became a rival to Goodman, and even a matinee idol. But the introspective Shaw, conflicted about his huge celebrity and unhappy about playing the same hits over and over again, broke up his band in 1939. Thereafter his disbandings became almost as frequent as his marriages (eight, including those to Lana Turner and Ava Gardner).

Between its hiatuses, however, the Shaw band produced some of the finest jazz of the era, such as *Traffic Jam* (1939) and *Lucky Number* (1945). With celebrated choruses by trumpeter Billy Butterfield, trombonist Jack Jenney, and Shaw himself, the band's *Stardust* (1940) ranks as a masterpiece of jazz, the quintessential big-band recording of Hoagy Carmichael's perennial. Shaw assembled a small group called the Gramercy Five in 1940, 1945, and 1954 to make such memorable recordings as *Summit Ridge Drive* and *Special Delivery Stomp* (both 1940) and *Yesterdays* (1954).

Trombonist Tommy Dorsey and his younger brother clarinetist Jimmy Dorsey formed the Dorsey Brothers Orchestra in 1934, but in 1935 Tommy Dorsey walked off the stage in a pique, his famous hot temper showing, and formed his own band. He turned heads with his silky-smooth, lyrical playing, especially on such ballads as *I'm Getting Sentimental over You* (1935). Many of the band's recordings were of novelty tunes and pop songs in uninspired arrangements, though his soloists (trumpeters Bunny Berigan and Yank Lawson, drummer Buddy Rich) could sometimes transform this kind of mediocre material into an artistic creation: for example, Berigan's solo on Dorsey's *Marie* (1937) became one of his most polished, enduring statements.

Moonlight Serenade (1939) and many other hits helped earn the Glenn Miller Orchestra a vast following of swing fans.

Still, prior to 1939, Dorsey's dance band had little to do with jazz. Then when Dorsey hired Sy Oliver (who had been with the Jimmie Lunceford band) as his chief arranger in 1939, the bandleader finally achieved something he had lacked: a swinging jazz sound and style, as Oliver's masterful *Well, Git It!* (1942) and *Opus One* (1944) so amply demonstrate. After Oliver's arrival, the band's repertory proceeded on two lines: the jazz-swing material and the romantic pop vocals sung by Jo Stafford, Frank Sinatra, and the Pied Pipers; the band reached its peak of popularity from 1940 to 1942.

Like Dorsey, his friend Glenn Miller was a bespectacled trombone player who emerged as a bandleader during the late 1930s, becoming a driving taskmaster and a successful musician-businessman. During the late 1930s and early 1940s, Miller led the most popular swing band of its day. Never a remarkable trombone soloist, he left his mark as a band arranger, organizer, and especially leader. Miller's band was known not so much for its rhythmic drive or great improvisatory ability—it boasted only one important jazz soloist, Bobby Hackett—as for its precision and musicianship. The band's most characteristic sound featured a clarinet playing the melody an octave above four saxophones.

Miller organized his first band in 1937. He leapt to national fame in 1939 through live radio broadcasts from the Glen Island Casino and the Meadowbrook Ballroom, and through his own *Moonlight Serenade* radio series.

In its brief four-year life, the Miller orchestra enjoyed many hit recordings, including pop ballads and novelties, but it's best remembered for riff-based instrumental pieces such as *In the Mood* (1939), *Tuxedo Junction* (1940), and *A String of Pearls* (1941). He disbanded his group in 1942 to join the U.S. Army Air Force and in the service organized a first-rate band, which entertained extensively in Britain. In December 1944, Miller's airplane disappeared over the English Channel; widely mourned, he was hailed as a war hero.

Woody Herman's band formed in 1936 when Isham Jones retired and six of his players decided to form a new group, electing clarinetist Herman as front man. The new group became known as "the band that plays the blues," and with the million-selling head arrangement *Woodchopper's Ball* (1939), it attracted national attention.

By 1944, his band, now dubbed Woody Herman's Herd, featured such outsized personalities as tenorman Flip Phillips, trombonist Bill Harris, drummer Dave Tough, and bassist Chubby Jackson, as well as arrangers Neal Hefti and Ralph Burns. The Herd built a reputation for its modern, progressive swing, as on such 1945 recordings as *Caldonia, Bijou,* and *Northwest Passage,* and the driving, stand-up-and-cheer exuberance of *Apple Honey* (based on *I Got Rhythm* chord changes). The band won numerous polls, a sign of the respect Herman commanded for the originality, force, and influence of his music. Two works from 1946 pushed the limits of the jazz-band repertoire: Ralph Burns' twelve-minute *Summer Sequence* and *Ebony Concerto,* which Igor Stravinsky wrote for Herman's band (augmented by harp and French horn) and which the band premiered at Carnegie Hall.

Herman disbanded the Herd in 1946. A year later he formed his Second Herd, rooted in bebop, with a front line of saxophonists—Stan Getz, Serge Chaloff, Zoot Sims, and Herbie Steward—that became famous as the Four Brothers after being featured on a recording by that name. The Second Herd disbanded in 1949, but Herman continued to lead bands for the rest of his career. His greatest talent was for organizing and sustaining ensembles boasting exceptional arrangements and bright young musicians and for balancing changing musical tastes with his fundamental musical integrity.

Woody Herman's bands—which were numerous over his long career—became known as incubators of talented young players. Saxie Mansfield (front, second from left) was a key man in this 1938 edition of the group.

Big-Band Care and Maintenance

As swing became the rage, hundreds of bands were formed to satisfy young Americans' craving for the music. By 1939, there would be an estimated two hundred "name" bands, employing some three thousand musicians, playing swing across the United States.

The leaders of the big bands—from Charlie Barnet and Count Basie to Claude Thornhill and Chick Webb—received the most publicity and, generally, the greatest adulation. But they also endured the headaches of keeping a bunch of mostly single young men in line on the road, meeting a payroll, dealing with booking agents and dance-hall operators, and confronting other challenges. Maintaining order and discipline was demanding, in part because most of the swing bandleaders of the 1930s were themselves relatively young men; most were in their thirties, and Goodman and Shaw were only in their twenties. Some leaders—Goodman and Lunceford, for example—were strict disciplinarians, while others, notably Ellington, took a laissez-faire attitude toward band-member behavior.

If leading a swing band presented many challenges, playing in the bands wasn't an easy job, either. Apart from the demands of the leaders and audiences, the constant travel, and the late hours (no wonder the swing bands were composed mostly of young people), the musicians had to perform under great pressure, most of all in the recording studio. Whereas in later styles of jazz, musicians often soloed for a chorus or more, during the Swing Era the tight arrangements typically allowed soloists only six or eight bars in which to make a musical statement. You had to be concise, coherent, and consistently good; if you frequently flubbed your solo spot, you were out.

Charlie Barnet (on sax) and his band going for a "keeper" with the tape rolling, 1949. The dark-shirted trumpet player (center), Doc Severinsen, would go on to lead the Tonight Show *band during Johnny Carson's tenure as host of that long-running television program.*

The constant travel was hard on both the leaders and the players; while many of the white bands had the luxury of playing in theaters, hotels, or ballrooms for extended stays, many of the black bands had to tour constantly. For example, in 1942 Lunceford estimated that "we do a couple of hundred one-nighters a year, fifteen to twenty weeks of theaters, maybe one four-week location, and two weeks of vacation. All in all, we cover about forty thousand miles a year!" For the black bands, travel invariably meant bad hotel rooms (or splitting up to sleep in homes in black neighborhoods), spotty access to food, racial insults, and sometimes threats.

Conservatory-trained Tommy Douglas (standing), one of Charlie Parker's musical influences, fit a large band into a small tour bus in 1938.

Shapers of the Sound

To sonically fill the cavernous dance halls and theaters, and to create additional musical interest, the bands had been expanding their personnel. As larger bands became the norm in the late 1920s and the 1930s, they required more-skilled orchestrations. After all, even an aggregation of the best musicians will be severely limited without good material to play. Most of the famous bandleaders—Goodman, Dorsey, Webb—possessed neither the skills, inclination, nor time to do their own arranging. Rather, they relied on the talents of behind-the-scenes orchestrator-arrangers, who actually determined the characteristic style of a band more than did the soloists, singers, or bandleaders. In the hotly competitive environment of the Swing Era, with each band seeking its own sound, the arrangers—however invisible to the public—were crucial.

For his band's arrangements, Fletcher Henderson supplied his own while also turning to his brother Horace Henderson as well as to Don Redman and Benny Carter. Chick Webb had Edgar Sampson and Charlie Dixon. Jimmie Lunceford depended on Sy Oliver and Eddie Wilcox. Tommy Dorsey employed Sy Oliver, Axel Stordahl, Deane Kincaide, and Bill Finnegan.

Benny Carter: saxophonist, multi-instrumentalist, bandleader, sideman, and arranger.

What Does an Arranger Do?

Bandleaders hired arrangers to prepare charts of given pieces of music, specifying the parts to be played by each instrument in the band—in essence, turning a skeletal melody-and-chords composition into a fully orchestrated score customized to the band's sound and style.

In jazz, an arranger usually begins with certain specifications. Knowing which ensemble has commissioned the work, he or she will know the instrumentation and perhaps the players and the context (a dance piece? concert piece? record date? telecast?) and will have a general idea of the desired length.

During the big-band era, some parameters were givens—especially duration and instrumentation. Until the advent of long-playing recordings in the 1950s, most arrangements were tailored to fit on a ten-inch 78-rpm record, which could hold three or four minutes of material. And big bands had a fairly standard instrumental lineup. In 1940, for example, Duke Ellington, Benny Goodman, and Artie Shaw each fielded a band of fifteen instrumentalists including themselves (all told, three trumpets, three trombones, five reeds, and a rhythm section of four).

But within these bounds, the arranger would have considerable leeway, deciding on the key; the general tempo (a ballad? a medium bounce? a "killer"?); the degree of reference to, or departure from, the original song or an earlier arrangement; the spirit and feel (sweet or sharp? droll or solemn? nostalgic or contemporary?); the overall architecture (include an altered verse or chorus? a new introduction and ending? a transitional passage?); the number of instruments that play at any given moment (should the trumpets drop out here?); which instruments state the melody, and which take solos and at what points; changes in the original piece's harmony, melody, and rhythm; and specific instrumental voicings and tonal colors.

Anatomy of an Arrangement

Much as different painters would render different still-life interpretations of the same assemblage of household objects, each arranger who tackled, say, *Mood Indigo* perceived its artistic possibilities in an individual way. When Ellington first arranged the composition (which he and his clarinetist Barney Bigard composed) for his band, the maestro voiced the main theme for tightly muted trumpet, trombone, and low-register clarinet, producing a brand-new tonal color. By the early 1950s, he had rearranged the theme for two trombones and bass clarinet, and in 1966, for trumpet, flute, and bass clarinet.

Indeed, the Ellington musical archives at the Smithsonian Institution include no fewer than ten different arrangements of *Mood Indigo,* which he reworked every few years to feature different players or to try a new sonic approach. Russell Procope commented that "a new arrangement would freshen [*Mood Indigo*] up, like you pour water on a flower, to keep it blooming. They'd all bloom—fresh, fresh arrangements."

Most of these were instrumental versions; four featured vocalists: Ivie Anderson (1940), Kay Davis in a wordless vocal (1945), Yvonne Lanauze (1950), and Rosemary Clooney (1956). The 1945 version, recorded for RCA Victor (reissued on the album *Black, Brown, and Beige*), features an outrageous series of key changes and dissonant chords. Billy Strayhorn's 1950 arrangement for

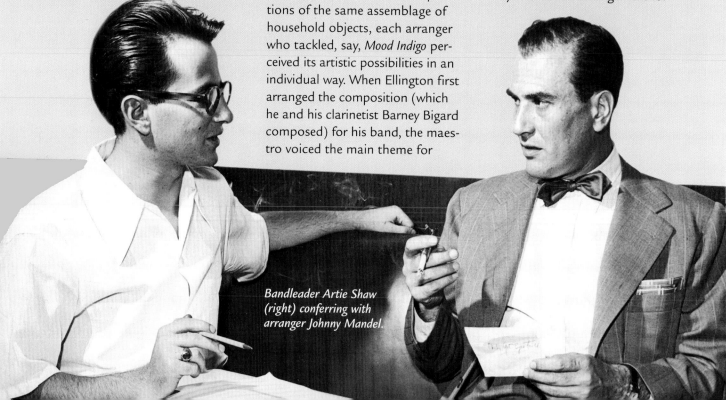

Bandleader Artie Shaw (right) conferring with arranger Johnny Mandel.

the album *Masterpieces by Ellington* extends the piece to seventeen choruses and fifteen minutes, through three keys and many contrasting sonorities, densities, and timbres.

Although Ellington "owned" the piece, a few other big bands recorded their own versions, among them Jimmie Lunceford (arrangement below by Willie Smith, 1934), and Hal McIntyre (arranged by Syd Schwartz, 1944).

The charts below show that Ellington made varying decisions regarding instruments stating the melody, inclusion of the piece's second theme, the length of the arrangement, and other elements. While Ellington's arrangements maintained the dreamy mood of the original, Lunceford's version, with its punchy countermelodies, created an entirely different feeling.
—*John Edward Hasse*

Duke Ellington and His Orchestra (12 players total), recorded on December 10, 1930, for RCA Victor

16 bars	4 bars	16 bars	16 bars	16 bars
Theme A	Passage	Solo	Solo/Theme B	Theme A
trumpet, trombone, clarinet	piano	muted trumpet	clarinet with band	trumpet, trombone, clarinet

Duke Ellington and His Orchestra (15 players total), filmed on March 14, 1952, for Snader Telescriptions (for TV stations)

4 bars	16 bars	16 bars	16 bars	16 bars	16 bars	2 bars
Intro	Theme A	Solo	Solo	Solo	Theme A	Coda
piano	2 trombones + bass clarinet	clarinet	trumpet	piano	2 trombones + bass clarinet	band

Duke Ellington and His Orchestra (15 players total), recorded on May 11, 1966, for RCA Victor *(The Popular Duke Ellington)*

16 bars	16 bars	16 bars	16 bars	16 bars	4 bars	4 bars
Introduction (a rubato variation on Theme A)	Theme A	Solo (variation on Theme B)	Theme A	Solo (variation on Theme B)	Passage	Coda (Theme A)
piano	8 bars trumpet, flute, bass clarinet; 8 bars add tenor sax obbligato	piano	12 bars band + 4 bars band w/clarinet obbligato	clarinet	piano	band

Jimmie Lunceford and His Orchestra (13 players total), recorded on September 11, 1934, for Decca

4 bars	16 bars	4 bars	16 bars	16 bars	16 bars	2 bars
Intro	Theme A	Passage	Solo	Theme A (embellished)	8 bars Theme A, 4 bars new material, 4 bars Theme A	Coda
band	muted brass (reeds play a punchy countermelody)	2 bars trumpet, 2 bars trombone	trumpet (band plays smooth background riffs, mostly based on Theme A)	muted trumpet (band plays staccato chords; piano, guitar, drums lay out)	8 bars trumpet, 4 bars sax tutti, 4 bars trumpet	band

These charts provide outlines of the musical events that occur in four Mood Indigo arrangements. To fully appreciate the differences, one must listen to the recordings.

Benny Goodman used arranger Fletcher Henderson, Edgar Sampson, Mel Powell, and Eddie Sauter. Glenn Miller was a good arranger, but he also employed Bill Finnegan, Jerry Gray, and Billy May to write his arrangements. Bob Crosby used Deane Kincaide, Matty Matlock, and Bob Haggart. Artie Shaw wrote some arrangements himself and also relied upon Jerry Gray and Lennie Hayton.

Some of the Count Basie band's pieces were "head" arrangements—made up collectively during rehearsals or recording dates, not credited to any one individual, and often not written down. Basie also secured written-out arrangements from Jimmy Mundy, Herschel Evans, Buster Smith, Andy Gibson, and Eddie Durham.

Small Groups and Solo Artists

If the Swing Era remains for many people the time of the big bands, it should also be remembered for its classic small groups, engaging singers, and remarkable soloists.

Between 1935 and 1941, Ellington made 140 recordings with small groups, comprising six to ten musicians drawn from his big band. These sessions yielded such enduring recordings as the mournful *Mobile Bay* (1940), released under the nominal leadership of cornetist Rex Stewart, and the exquisite *Passion Flower* (1941), under the name of Ellington's alto saxophone star Johnny Hodges. There were small groups within other big bands, too: the Count Basie Ensemble, the Benny Goodman Trio, Tommy Dorsey's Clambake Seven, Bob Crosby's Bob Cats, Chick Webb and His Little Chicks, Artie Shaw and His Gramercy Five, and Woody Herman's Woodchoppers.

In the 1920s, Louis Armstrong had emerged as the dominant soloist in jazz and as the individual who would, more than anyone else, take the role of soloist to new heights in American music. Now, in the 1930s, following in Armstrong's footsteps, soloists and singers emerged who boasted individual styles that clearly differentiated them from others and would project their voices well into the future.

Solo Instrumentalists

Among the most radiant soloists was tenor saxophonist Coleman Hawkins, who, during his tenure with Fletcher Henderson (1923–34), helped transform the saxophone from a novelty instrument into an expressive, recognized vehicle for jazz. After returning to the U.S. in 1939 from a five-year residency in Europe, he recorded the stunning *Body and Soul*. This recording—one of the most celebrated saxophone solos in history—instantly established Hawkins as a star soloist. With his emphatic attack, rhythmic flexibility, full-bodied vibrato, rich tone, and emotional conviction, he founded a whole school of tenor saxophone playing that would include Don Byas, Chu Berry, Herschel Evans, and Ben Webster.

If Hawkins' style was hot, with a pronounced vibrato and rhythmic emphasis, then tenorman Lester Young's style was cool, with a lighter swing and virtually no vibrato. As a member of the Count Basie band in 1936–40 and 1943–44, the soft-spoken Young gradually established his tenor style—more delicate and detached—as a counter to Hawkins'. One of Young's earliest recordings, *Oh! Lady Be Good* (1936, with a quintet from the Basie band), displays such hallmarks of his style as a relaxed sense of swing; a

Coleman Hawkins' 1939 recording of Body and Soul *established him as a giant of the tenor saxophone.*

A musical sensualist, Ben Webster excelled at conjuring a wide range of spell-binding sounds.

compression of the wide, arpeggio-inspired lines characteristic of Hawkins into more compact melodic shapes; and a freeing of improvisation from the underlying harmonic sequence. This latter innovation would have far-reaching consequences for jazz in the bebop era and beyond. Young's star vehicle, *Lester Leaps In* (1939, with a septet from the Basie band), showcases his superior choice of notes and interlinking melodic ideas. Young's new aesthetic, along with his long, flowing lines, made him the most influential musician in jazz between the rise of Louis Armstrong in the 1920s and that of Charlie Parker, beginning in the mid-1940s.

A focused pitch wasn't a priority for tenor saxophonist Ben Webster, who reveled in sheer sound and tone. With his breathy timbre and sensuality, Webster was a romantic of the highest order, spinning out eloquent solos on such ballads as *Stardust* and *All Too Soon* (both 1940 with the Ellington band). The fast and flashy *Cotton Tail* (also 1940) became a Webster trademark during his 1940–43 years with Ellington, but in fact Webster had a wide tonal and emotional range that encompassed the powerful, driving, and raspy as well as the warm, eloquent, and lyrical. These opposites led to the apt title for the biographical film *The Brute and the Beautiful* (1991).

The soft-spoken Lester "Prez" Young spoke volumes on the tenor sax, and the message registered with a generation of later musicians.

Swing-Era Standards

The Swing Era's *standards*—songs that earned lasting popularity—included both old and new compositions. *King Porter Stomp,* composed by Jelly Roll Morton in 1924, made a comeback as a big-band perennial during the Swing Era. A number of riff-based jazz originals became standards: *Stompin' at the Savoy* (1934), Count Basie's jam session–like *One O'Clock Jump* (1937), Erskine Hawkins' *Tuxedo Junction* (1940), *Jersey Bounce* (1941), Juan Tizol's *Perdido* (1942), and Sy Oliver's *Opus One* (1944). *Cherokee* (1938), by the English bandleader Ray Noble, was a ballad until Count Basie sped up the tempo. Pianist-composer Fats Waller contributed two bouncy, enormously popular tunes to the standard repertory: *Ain't Misbehavin'* and *Honeysuckle Rose* (both 1929).

From Broadway musicals came the jazz standards *Blue Skies* (1927) by Irving Berlin, *Exactly Like You* (1930) by Dorothy Fields and Jimmy McHugh, and *Tea for Two* (1925)

and *Hallelujah!* (1927) by Vincent Youmans. George Gershwin's *Oh! Lady Be Good* (1924) found continued favor with swing musicians, as did his *Liza* (1929) and his *I Got Rhythm* (1930), which beginning in the 1940s would become the harmonic basis for scores of other jazz tunes. Victor Young's *Sweet Sue* (1928) was one of the free-standing songs, independent of musical theater, that became Swing Era jazz standards, as were Hoagy Carmichael's jazz-inflected songs *Georgia on My Mind* and *Rockin' Chair* (both 1930).

This era saw ballads become popular in jazz for the first time. The most recorded was Carmichael's romantic *Stardust* (1927), whose haunting melody seemed to have the improvisations already built in; he also wrote *The Nearness of You* (1937) and *Skylark* (1942). Pianist Earl Hines penned the lovely *Rosetta* (1933), and Duke Ellington co-authored several ballads: the dreamy *Mood Indigo* (composed with his clarinetist Barney Bigard, 1930),

Sophisticated Lady (1933), *Solitude* (1934), and *In a Sentimental Mood* (1935). After Coleman Hawkins' extraordinary 1939 recording of John Green's challenging *Body and Soul* (1930), that song became a must-play among jazz instrumentalists.

Such standards gave musicians and listeners the comfort of recognizing familiar structures, the freshness of experiencing new renditions, and benchmarks for assessing other reinterpretations. —*John Edward Hasse*

Roy Eldridge dominated the jazz-trumpet field post–Louis Armstrong and pre–Dizzy Gillespie.

Trumpet star Bunny Berigan.

After Armstrong, Roy Eldridge became the most original trumpeter in jazz until Dizzy Gillespie came to the fore in the 1940s. Taking his deep tone and arpeggio-laden style from Coleman Hawkins, Eldridge became a powerful, virtuosic player, boasting dexterity over a three-octave range, as on the dazzling *After You've Gone* (1937). With its ease, authority, shape, and skill, his *Rockin' Chair* (1941, with Gene Krupa's orchestra) ranks among the greatest recorded jazz solos. The exuberant, good-humored, and keenly competitive Eldridge loved jam sessions and cutting contests. He helped to dismantle the color barrier in jazz during his stints with the bands of Gene Krupa (1941–43) and Artie Shaw (1944–45).

Trumpeter Bunny Berigan combined influences of Louis Armstrong and Bix Beiderbecke into a personal voice noted for its tone, lyricism, technical assurance, power and projection, exploitation of the trumpet's low register, and clarity of structure. These trademarks can all be heard on his masterpiece (and hit recording), *I Can't Get Started* (1937). Like Beiderbecke, Berigan suffered from alcoholism; he died at the age of thirty-three.

Following in the footsteps of his fellow New Orleans trumpeter Louis Armstrong, Henry "Red" Allen brandished a style brimming with energy and authority. Known for his daring, rhythmic freedom, and large arsenal of timbral devices (slurs, growls, rips, trills, and half-valve effects), Allen was an outstanding interpreter of the blues. Three of his best solos were made in 1933 with Fletcher Henderson's orchestra: *King Porter Stomp, Queer Notions,* and *Nagasaki.*

The pianist Art Tatum, who was 85 percent blind, typically performed in small clubs and was at his best as a solo pianist, for he played a full, orchestral style that needed latitude so he could shape dramatic contrasts. His arpeggios and runs in the right (and even the left) hands astonished fellow musicians and the public; beneath his speed and dazzling, classically trained technique lay Tatum's daring and inventive reharmonizations—one could even say recompositions—of pop songs and show tunes. He favored formulas (many recordings followed a format of free/strict/free tempo) and worked out most solos in advance.

Art Tatum set new technical standards for jazz piano playing.

Though he came to prominence during the Swing Era, his playing was never really of that era, nor of bebop or modern jazz—rather it stood apart, like Ellington's, in a class of its own. Tatum's style continued to mature, as demonstrated by such later masterpiece recordings as *Willow Weep for Me* (1949) and *Sweet Lorraine* (1955), recorded the year before he died.

In contrast to Tatum, Teddy Wilson was very much of the Swing Era; was, in fact, its most important pianist. His style combined elements of Earl Hines' and Tatum's piano styles into one tailored for playing in ensembles.

In comparison to Tatum's splash and unrelenting energy, Wilson—with his clean lines and light textures—sounded more legato, subtle, reserved. As his left hand rendered a series of tenths and his right executed brief melodic figures in octaves, Wilson would sit board-upright at the keyboard, the very model of poise and control. He was the perfect pianist to play the Benny Goodman Trio's kind of chamber jazz—notably on *After You've Gone* and *Body and Soul* (both 1935)—and to accompany Billie Holiday (*Nice Work if You Can Get It*, with Wilson's septet, 1937).

What Coleman Hawkins did for the tenor saxophone, Red Norvo did for the xylophone: took it out of vaudeville and put it firmly in the realm of jazz. Difficult to categorize, Norvo played with pre-swing, swing, and bebop musicians, first on xylophone and later on vibraphone as well. With his light sound, Norvo created a gentle sonic world of subtle surprises, swing, and imaginative solos, as on *In a Mist* and *Dance of the Octopus* (both 1933) and *Remember* (1937).

The guitarist Charlie Christian was one of the first to amplify his instrument so that it could be heard among the winds and brass. His recording career lasted only from 1939 to 1941, his life cut short at age twenty-five by tuberculosis, but in those two years he set musicians and the public on their ears with his fluid and inventive single-line soloing, which for the first time gave the guitar the same kind of expressive power as the trumpet or saxophone. As a member of Benny Goodman's Sextet (*Breakfast Feud*, 1940 and 1941; *I Found a New Baby*, 1941) and big band (*Solo Flight*, 1941), Christian lifted his instrument to prominence in jazz and exerted an enormous influence on later guitarists from a wide range of musical styles.

Exposed as a youth in Texas to African American spirituals at tent revival meetings, Jack Teagarden developed a deceptive ease of technique and forged a singing, lyrical, bluesy sound on the trombone (*Dinah*, with Red Nichols, 1929, and *Jack Hits the Road*, with Bud Freeman, 1940) and an equally personal, blues-drenched vocal style. Indeed, Gunther Schuller has called him "the finest white blues singer." Nowhere is his brilliance better demonstrated than on *St. James Infirmary* (with Louis Armstrong, 1947), which Teagarden transforms into a haunting masterpiece.

Trumpeter Louis Armstrong mugs with trombonist Jack Teagarden on other musicians' instruments.

Louis Armstrong's reputation as a singer and entertainer grew in the 1930s and began eclipsing his renown as a trumpeter.

Singers

One of the greatest jazz singers of them all, Louis Armstrong, flowered in the 1930s, becoming a cultural hero of epic proportions, above all to musicians. He developed a vocal style—marked by his unique gravelly tone, passionate delivery, and superb vowel coloration—as distinctive as his seminal style on trumpet. On such recordings as *Stardust* and *Lazy River* (both 1931), he projected a sense of exultation somewhere between singing and shouting, as Henry Pleasants has noted, and this required singing at both a high volume and pitch. Just as Armstrong lived his life, so he sang with feeling, energy, infectious *joie de vivre*, and good humor—listen to *I'll Be Glad When You're Dead, You Rascal You* (1931) or *Laughin' Louie* (1933) and you can't help smiling. He boasted an extraordinary ability to overcome commonplace material, often—with the force of his musical personality—transforming lackluster pop songs into enduring art (*Sweethearts on Parade,* 1930). And he set the standard for scat singing (*Basin Street Blues,* 1933), his example clarion and timeless. The title of Leslie Gourse's book on jazz singers—*Louis' Children*—is an apt reflection of Armstrong's profound influence on generations of jazz vocalists.

The novelist Ralph Ellison, who grew up in Oklahoma City listening to another local son, the big-voiced tenor Jimmy Rushing, wrote of that singer's "imposition of a romantic lyricism upon the blues…a romanticism which is not of the Deep South but the Southwest." The featured singer with Count Basie's band from 1935 to 1948, Rushing combined the sensitivity and precision of a ballad singer with the authority, earthiness, and robustness of a blues shouter, as on *Sent for You Yesterday* (1938), *Goin' to Chicago* (1941), *I'm Gonna Move to the Outskirts of Town* (1942), and especially the mournful *I Left My Baby* (1939), all with Basie.

The Boswell Sisters, from New Orleans, achieved their peak of popularity and influence from 1931–35, becoming, in the estimation of Will Friedwald, "the greatest of all jazz vocal groups." The trio sang in beautifully blended three-part harmony, with a remarkable sense of rhythm. Connee Boswell did most of the group's imaginative arrangements, replete with reharmonizations, scat singing, the instrument-like use of their voices, frequent tempo changes, and other creative elements that typically recomposed the original material (*Roll On, Mississippi, Roll On,* 1931; *Charlie Two-Step* and *Everybody Loves My Baby,* both 1932). Ella Fitzgerald cited Connee Boswell as among her main musical influences.

The Boswells and the plaintive-voiced Mildred Bailey were the first white singers to absorb and master the African American jazz idiom of the 1920s. Bailey boasted fine diction; a pure, warm, and beautiful natural tone; and an ability to project a song's lyrics and convey sweetness, sincerity, and conviction. She performed Hoagy Carmichael's *Rockin' Chair* (notably a classic version

Singer Connee Boswell.

John Hammond: Talent Scout, Jazz Catalyst

As a discoverer of talent, John Hammond had few if any peers. That's because many of the performers he helped lift from obscurity to the international spotlight went on to validate his sponsorship to a spectacular degree. Singer Billie Holiday, bandleader Count Basie, pianist Teddy Wilson, and guitarists Charlie Christian and George Benson—not to mention soul singer Aretha Franklin and the rock world's Bob Dylan and Bruce Springsteen—are just a few whom Hammond championed before they rose to the highest ranks of the twentieth century's popular artists.

Born in 1910 to a wealthy family (his grandfather was the railroad magnate Cornelius Vanderbilt), Hammond became enamored of jazz as a teenager. He began his career as a disc jockey and producer of jazz stage shows, worked as a music critic for *Down Beat* and *Melody Maker*, went on to serve as a talent scout and tour manager for Benny Goodman (his future brother-in-law), and spent a number of years as a record producer and executive, most notably at Columbia.

Using his inherited wealth, he financed jazz recording sessions at a time when record sales were in the Depression-era basement. During one week in November 1933, he supervised the last recordings of Bessie Smith and the first sessions of Billie Holiday. "She was 17," he later said of Holiday. "I never heard anyone sing like this—as if she was the most inspired improviser in the world." The music business types gave him a hard time, he recalled: "Scratchy, unmusical voice. Where was the tune?"

When Hammond heard the little-known Basie band over a car radio in 1936, the excited producer traveled to Kansas City to hear them in person. As he'd done with Holiday, Hammond brought the Basie band to the attention of his contacts in the music business and helped set the wheels in motion for the group's entry onto the national stage.

Others who benefited from Hammond's support included arranger Fletcher Henderson, trumpeter Bunny Berigan, xylophonist Red Norvo, and saxophonists Benny Carter, Chu Berry, and Lester Young.

But Hammond's impact went well beyond the careers of individual musicians. In 1938 and 1939 he organized two landmark Carnegie Hall concerts of African American music, "From Spirituals to Swing," that helped legitimize jazz. Through his association with Goodman he helped spearhead the Swing Era. He sparked public interest in boogie-woogie by promoting the careers of pianists Meade "Lux" Lewis, Albert Ammons, and Pete Johnson. And Hammond, who called himself "a social activist," served as an important catalyst for racial integration in jazz. —*Tad Lathrop*

John Hammond at Columbia Records, 1939.

Billie Holiday—Lady Day—the most hauntingly distinctive of jazz vocalists.

recorded in 1937) so definitively that she became known as "the Rockin' Chair Lady." Her art also sings on in such memorable sides as *A Porter's Love Song to a Chambermaid* (with husband Red Norvo's band, 1936) and *Darn That Dream* (with Benny Goodman's orchestra, 1939).

Billie Holiday ranks close to Louis Armstrong among the greatest jazz singers. Acknowledging great inspiration from him, she practiced an instrumental approach to singing as she ranged freely over the beat, flattened out the melodic contours of tunes, and, in effect, recomposed songs to suit her range, style, and artistic sensibilities. Her voice was physically limited, but she achieved shadings, nuances, color, and variety by sliding along the thin line separating speech and song. Her collaborations with Lester Young (*I Must Have That Man* and *This Year's Kisses*, both recorded with Teddy Wilson's group, 1937) are justifiably celebrated, as is her courageous recording of the harrowing anti-lynching song *Strange Fruit* (1939) and her haunting studio recording, with strings, of *Lover Man* (1944).

Swing music, whether played by big bands or small groups, was not all that was happening in jazz during the Swing Era.

At universities such as Yale and Princeton, young men were collecting "hot" records of the 1920s, encouraged by articles in the men's magazine *Esquire*. In 1935, from within his big band, Tommy Dorsey organized the Clambake Seven, an octet to play Dixieland jazz, an offshoot of New Orleans jazz, and was followed within two years by Bob Crosby and his Bob Cats.

In the 1930s, partly as a reaction against what some saw as the overly arranged and overly commercialized character of swing, some musicians began consciously reviving the older, uncluttered, small-group jazz styles from New Orleans and Chicago. Attention to these styles took a big step forward in 1938: the year saw the first "Spirituals to Swing" concert at Carnegie Hall, which stimulated interest in the history of jazz; the establishment of two independent record labels—Commodore and H.R.S.—that issued pre-swing jazz; and renewed recording activity

for the New Orleans pioneers Sidney Bechet, Johnny Dodds, and Jelly Roll Morton (whose recordings that year, made by Alan Lomax for the Library of Congress, rank among the great sound documents in American music).

Nineteen thirty-nine was a milestone year, with cornetist Muggsy Spanier forming his so-called Ragtime Band and making a series of influential recordings that included *At the Jazz Band Ball* and *Riverboat Shuffle*. That same year, the landmark book *Jazzmen* was issued, drawing attention to New Orleans jazz and notably to Morton and the forgotten trumpeter Bunk Johnson. Within months of the book's publication, Morton was rediscovered by RCA Victor, which began recording him again (it had dropped him in 1930). Morton's rejuvenation was short-lived, however; he died in 1941 following an illness, his dream of a major comeback unfulfilled. Another independent, Blue Note Records, emerged in 1939 and immediately recorded Sidney Bechet.

Also in 1939, trumpeter Lu Watters organized the Yerba Buena

Jazz Band in the San Francisco Bay Area to revive small-group New Orleans music in the style of King Oliver. In 1941, his band began recording old rags (*Maple Leaf Rag, Black and White Rag*) and early jazz pieces (*Tiger Rag, Fidgety Feet, Muskrat Ramble*) with the polyphony of interweaving clarinet, trumpet, and trombone lines harking back to the music's early years. The band helped spark an international revival of New Orleans and Chicago jazz.

In the early 1940s, a number of African American jazz musicians, some of them, like Kid Ory and Bunk Johnson, in retirement from jazz, were recorded by younger white enthusiasts, by small but influential jazz-specialist magazines—notably *The Record Changer* and *The Jazz Record*—published articles on early figures. In 1944 Orson Welles' CBS radio program put Kid Ory's band—with clarinetist Jimmie Noone and trumpeter Mutt Carey—on the national map. The traditional jazz revival built up steam after World War II, and in 1947, Louis Armstrong dropped his big band in favor of a small-group format, the All Stars, with a traditional New Orleans lineup.

The old styles and the new bebop appealed largely to different groups of listeners, and a war of words broke out between the modernists and the traditionalists, whom the former derisively labeled "moldy figs." Each camp carried a vision of one true jazz; the combatants failed to recognize that by the 1930s, jazz had become a music of multiple styles that could exist side by side. Increasingly jazz would become a music synonymous with variety and, like the American population, pluralism.

—*John Edward Hasse*

After recording the memorable *All or Nothing at All* in 1939 with Harry James' band, Frank Sinatra joined the Tommy Dorsey orchestra and, with his new kind of natural phrasing, rich baritone, jazzy inflections, and depth of feeling, helped lead the band to its greatest acclaim with such recordings as *Everything Happens to Me* (1941). Not one to improvise, his singing nonetheless was influenced by—and in turn much admired by—jazz musicians. By the 1950s, he had become the quintessential American pop singer through his gift for conveying lyrics and ability to take a three-minute song and transform it into a virtual three-act play (*One for My Baby,* 1958).

The Decline and Revival of Swing

A major rupture in the Swing Era came on August 1, 1942, when the American Federation of Musicians, ruled by union boss James Petrillo, enjoined its musicians to cease recording for record companies. At issue was the companies' refusal to contribute a payment per recording to the union's pension fund. In response, musicians were forced to stop making records for sale to the public indefinitely, with the exception of a few transcription recordings intended exclusively for radio stations. It took Victor and Columbia, the two largest companies, until November 1944 to finally cave in to the musicians' union.

During the recording ban of 1942–44, a group of young players had been experimenting in Harlem, and in 1945 they made their first important recordings. Employing heightened melodic and rhythmic complexity, they introduced a music that was intended far less for dancing than for listening in small clubs. Initially known onomatopoeically as "rebop" or "bebop," it finally took the shortened label "bop."

The bebop musicians worked outside previously standard career paths that required being entertainers or dance musicians; they relied for their livelihoods on an intense circle of jazz fans to an extent that a musician of the Swing Era generation would have found uncomfortable. Now, led by African American musicians searching for their own music not co-opted by the white-controlled music industry, many younger jazz players found swing too highly arranged, too formulaic, and too commercial and took up the new, startlingly different bop.

The musical developments occurred partly as a result of societal events. World War II brought more than a million blacks into uniform, and fighting abroad for freedom raised the expectations of returning servicemen. Hundreds of thousands of blacks moved north and west to work in war plants, and they helped support a style of black popular music that would in 1949 be dubbed "rhythm and blues." What became known as R&B was really a diverse group of styles. Sung by the likes of singer-saxophonist Louis Jordan and his Tympany Five, Wynonie Harris, Big Joe Turner, and Ruth Brown and accompanied by guitar, piano, bass, drums, and saxophone, R&B offered accessible songs, a strong dance beat, and a fresh sound.

The pop music world was changing markedly. Exempt from the 1942–44 recording ban, many singers, despite the wartime shortage of shellac used on records, were continuing to make them and were gaining in popularity. This development, combined with an increase in the number of singers leaving

Louis Jordan's jump blues helped usher in the post-swing era.

Boogie-Woogie

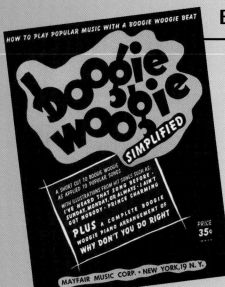

Swinging, eight-to-the-bar figures rumbling way down in the piano bass, meshing with bluesy, complex patterns higher up; a pianist, close to the audience, working the keyboard so powerfully that the piano and the floor could literally rock: this was boogie-woogie.

Jelly Roll Morton and W.C. Handy recalled hearing boogie-woogie in the South during the first decade of the twentieth century, and ragtime sheet music of that time began to hint at it. Taking its name from a dance step developed in the South by African Americans, boogie-woogie piano playing went north with the great black migration after World War I; St. Louis and Chicago became hotbeds. Pianists played boogie-woogie in barrelhouses, saloons, juke joints, honky-tonks, and rent parties, where its loud, rolling sound cut through the din, dominating the atmosphere and providing an all-but-irresistible call to the dance floor.

By the mid-1920s, boogie began to appear on "race records"—for example, Clay Custer's *The Rocks* (1923), Jimmy Blythe's *Chicago Stomp* (1924), and Pine Top Smith's *Pine Top's Boogie Woogie* (1928, with Smith shouting out dance instructions).

The general public "discovered" the style in 1938, after John Hammond presented three masters—Albert Ammons, Pete Johnson, and Meade "Lux" Lewis—in the landmark "Spirituals to Swing" concert at Carnegie Hall. A vogue for boogie then ensued during the late 1930s and the World War II years: the authentic boogie pianists such as Jimmy Yancey were widely recorded, and publishers put out method books for the masses of amateur pianists. There were big-band versions (Count Basie's *Boogie Woogie [I May Be Wrong]*, 1936, and Benny Goodman's *Roll 'Em*, 1937) and pop songs hopping on the boogie bandwagon (*Boogie Woogie Bugle Boy [of Company B]*, 1941); but the music was quintessentially a piano style.

As with ragtime, the tension between the right and left hands' opposing roles made boogie-woogie at once discordant and appealing. Its expressive range was limited and its format highly stylized (almost entirely eight- and twelve-bar blues progressions with a repetitive bass, typically fast and percussive). But within these limitations, the music's complex figures and powerful cross-rhythms could be insistent, hypnotic, and exciting. The style was virtuosic in its way and took great endurance.

Lewis ranks as the most stylistically advanced of the boogie artists. His masterpiece was *Honky-Tonk Train Blues,* a colorful evocation of a train in motion, which he recorded eleven times between 1927 and 1961. Observers recall that he could improvise on this tune for thirty minutes, his fingers cascading over the keys, relentlessly rolling out the rhythms, dazzling everyone within earshot. —*John Edward Hasse*

their big-band employers and striking out on their own (Frank Sinatra and Perry Como in 1942, Dick Haymes in 1943, and Jo Stafford and Peggy Lee in 1944) helped create an era of the "big singer."

The increasing popularity of singers and such emerging styles as R&B and bebop combined with other factors to push the big bands into a sharp decline, effectively ending the big-band era. In November and December 1946, eight of the bands disbanded either permanently or temporarily, including those of Benny Goodman, Harry James, Woody Herman, Tommy Dorsey, Benny Carter, and Les Brown. Additional reasons were numerous: higher costs, a short-lived postwar boom in movie-going, and preoccupation among returning servicemen with settling down and starting families. A new, suburban lifestyle, along with the imminent advent of network television, would create serious adjustments in social habits. Most younger listeners, some of whom in previous years would have become big-band fans, were attracted to more accessible vocal sounds or fresher and newer styles of music. "After the war," bandleader Les Brown recalled, "families settled down and the ballrooms went to hell. Before the war every town with 20,000 people had a ballroom, and my band could spend a month just doing one-nighters in Texas."

But if the era when big bands predominated came to an end in the mid-1940s, the bands themselves never completely disappeared. Indeed, Duke Ellington kept his band together—and made many important recordings—up until his death in 1974. And in the decades after Ellington's death, big bands enjoyed something of a renaissance: jazz programs at American high schools and colleges and growing numbers of archival bands (for example, the Smithsonian Jazz Masterworks Orchestra) kept the canonical repertory alive, while others (the Muhal Richard Abrams Orchestra, for example), focused on newly written works for large jazz ensembles.

Swing rhythm became such an accepted and expected element of jazz that it came to be taken for granted. Swing rhythm also spread into R&B, into the western swing music of Bob Wills, into the propulsive beat of bluegrass, and into other kinds of pop music in the United States and elsewhere. Indeed, as the new millennium approached, North America saw a revival of swing dancing among young people, and new retro pop bands—the Squirrel Nut Zippers, the Brian Setzer Orchestra, and the Royal Crown Revue—attracted younger fans by playing a revved-up, edgy kind of swing. Reinventing itself, in the grand tradition of American music, and adapting itself to changing musical times, swing continues to capture the ears of new generations. ⌒

Key Recordings

An Anthology of Big Band Swing, 1930–1955. Two discs, GRP. Drawn from the Decca catalog, the forty selections include Fletcher Henderson's *Down South Camp Meeting,* the Casa Loma Orchestra's *Casa Loma Stomp,* Bob Crosby's *South Rampart Street Parade,* and Duke Ellington's *Rockin' in Rhythm.*

Armstrong, Louis. *The Vocalist.* Two discs, Fremeaux (France). Spanning the years 1924–40, this collection draws from multiple labels to include *Laughin' Louie, Lazy River, I'll Be Glad When You're Dead, You Rascal You,* and thirty-three others from one of jazz's greatest, most influential singers.

Big Band Jazz: From the Beginnings to the 1950s. Four discs, Smithsonian Recordings. Selected and annotated by Gunther Schuller and Martin Williams. A counterpart to the canonical *Smithsonian Collection of Classic Jazz,* this invaluable anthology draws from seven record companies to survey the idiom. Contains celebrated recordings of all the bands discussed in this chapter. The follow-up set, *Big Band Renaissance: The Evolution of the Jazz Orchestra* (five discs, Smithsonian), continues the survey from the 1940s into the 1990s.

Boogie Woogie Stomp. ASV Living Era (UK). Includes pioneers Clay Custer and Pine Top Smith, as well as masters Albert Ammons, Pete Johnson, Meade "Lux" Lewis, and Jimmy Yancey.

Ellington, Duke. *The Blanton-Webster Band.* Three discs, BMG/RCA Victor. The middle years of Duke Ellington's fifty-year recording career are best represented in this indispensable set covering the 1940–42 period when the band recorded *Take the "A" Train, Cottontail, Concerto for Cootie, Ko-Ko, Jack the Bear, Warm Valley,* and many other masterpieces.

Goodman, Benny. *The Complete RCA Victor Small Group Recordings.* Three discs, BMG/RCA Victor. Made between 1935 and 1939, these recordings feature ample space for the clarinet of Goodman as well as his sparkling Trio and Quartet in *After You've Gone, Avalon, Body and Soul,* and sixty-four others.

Hot Jazz on Blue Note. Four discs, Blue Note/Smithsonian. While no one album satisfyingly covers all the major figures in the revival of New Orleans jazz, this collection is a good place to start, with generous samplings of Sidney Bechet and Sidney DeParis, as well as Edmond Hall, George Lewis, Baby Dodds, and the earthy pianist Art Hodes. Includes a first-rate, eighty-page essay by Dan Morgenstern.

Jazz of the 1930s: Greatest Hits. BMG/RCA Victor. From Victor's vaults, this compilation offers Louis Armstrong's *Basin Street Blues,* Tommy Dorsey's *Song of India,* Artie Shaw's *Begin the Beguine,* and more.

Swing That Music: The Big Bands, the Soloists, and the Singers, 1929–1956. Four discs, Smithsonian. An offshoot of the Smithsonian's *Big Band Jazz* box, this important anthology focuses on the big-band era's soloists and singers, including Red Allen, Charlie Christian, Roy Eldridge, Coleman Hawkins, Jack Teagarden, Mildred Bailey, Billie Holiday, Frank Sinatra, and Jimmy Rushing.

Swing Time: The Fabulous Big Band Era, 1925–1955. Three discs, Columbia. Useful anthology from the vaults of the Columbia family of labels. Includes Harry James' *All or Nothing at All,* Tommy Dorsey's *Marie,* Artie Shaw's *Nightmare,* Basie's *One O'Clock Jump,* and Chick Webb's *Stompin' at the Savoy.*
—*John Edward Hasse*

©Herman Leonard

The Birth of Modern Jazz

Bob Blumenthal

Charlie Parker, Miles Davis, Allen Eager, and Kai Winding, New York, 1948.

Trumpeter and bebop innovator Dizzy Gillespie, 1944.

©William P. Gottlieb

The decline of the big bands and of jazz's status as popular music was precipitous during the World War II years. In 1940, the creative and commercial success attained by the bands of Duke Ellington, Count Basie, Benny Goodman, Artie Shaw, and others appeared beyond challenge. A mere five years later the big-band era was waning and swing was passé. In its place, complex new sounds were entering the jazz lexicon.

Several musical movements emerged to supplant the big bands as the leading forms of popular music. Singers, already critical components in the success of the bands, became even greater commercial forces. The phenomenal popularity of Frank Sinatra, who rose to fame with Tommy Dorsey's band but soon went off on his own, helped shift public taste from a swing beat to romantic ballads. Sinatra had been touched by jazz, and African American singing stars such as Nat Cole, Billy Eckstine, and Ella Fitzgerald reflected an even stronger jazz foundation in their work; yet public taste had turned to lushly arranged pop fare. Soon, even singers with unimpeachable jazz credentials, including Sarah Vaughan and Dinah Washington, were pulled into these more placid pop waters.

There was also the strong tidal pull of a more blues-based, dance-oriented development that can be traced back to the big bands through alto saxophonist Louis Jordan (a Chick Webb alumnus) and various editions of Lionel Hampton's orchestra. Originally referred to as jump blues or rhythm and blues and ultimately evolving into rock and roll, this extroverted style sustained the dynamic power of the big bands in a context that accommodated a more pronounced backbeat and the new sound of the electric guitar.

While pop balladeers and jump bands became music's new commercial champions, young, mostly African American improvisers were adding new elements to jazz and moving it far from the realm of pop entertainment. These players tended to be virtuoso instrumentalists who were schooled in the discipline of the big bands but were unwilling to settle for the limited solo opportunities available to orchestral sidemen. Further, any dissatisfaction they felt with the swing-band modus operandi drew additional fuel from what Scott DeVeaux, in *The Birth of Bebop,* called "entrenched patterns of segregation…[giving] white musicians a nearly insuperable advantage in the mainstream market." Such forces helped push the younger generation of jazz players toward a more assertive mode of expression. The blues and popular song structures still served as the bases of their creations, but these artists favored more complex and irregularly accented melodies, more sophisticated harmonic modulations, faster tempos than those favored by the big bands. In effect, the young jazz players were establishing a new inner circle, an exclusive counter-cultural "club" that required virtuosity of musicians and an open-eared attentiveness on the part of listeners as qualification for membership.

Several heroes from the previous generation had paved the way for this new style. Tenor saxophonist Coleman Hawkins had exemplified the stream-of-consciousness creativity of the improvising soloist with his classic 1939 recording of *Body and Soul* and was among the first to demonstrate the feasibility of an instrumental soloist's playing for listeners rather than dancers—*sans* singers or large orchestral accompaniment. As DeVeaux has pointed out, Hawkins was *the* proto-bebopper: too proud to sing or otherwise ingratiate himself to a mass audience and not inclined to make a go at leading a big band. Pianist Art Tatum, with his stupendous technique and harmonic knowledge, had

revealed in such solo recordings as *Moonglow* (1934) and *Tea for Two* (1933) the complex potential of simple-seeming pop songs. The Count Basie band practiced a flowing, liberating sense of tempo, while Basie's star soloist, Lester Young, introduced an oblique, floating approach that pointed soloists toward musical abstraction. Charlie Christian, the electric guitar innovator, was reflecting a similar attitude in his solos with Goodman, and Ellington's new star, Jimmie Blanton, was revealing the untapped potential of the string bass.

Parker, Gillespie, and the Birth of Bebop

Even before the United States entered World War II, new ideas were germinating among young players inspired by their innovative predecessors. The disciples fueled the evolutionary process by refining and sharing discoveries after hours in Harlem spots such as Minton's Playhouse and Monroe's Uptown House. Several players were central

After Hours at Minton's

Jazz's modern era was nurtured in the clubs of Harlem, where musicians would go to try out new ideas—or simply to seek playing opportunities that the big bands did not provide—after completing club, theater, and ballroom gigs. The jam sessions that resulted, with musicians testing their limits and challenging others to keep up with the latest discoveries, have become legendary; the center of the legend was at 210 West 118th Street, where the former dining room of the Hotel Cecil was converted by M. Henry Minton into the Playhouse, a club we now know simply as Minton's.

The Playhouse opened in 1938 but attracted little attention until two years later, when saxophonist and bandleader Teddy Hill signed on to manage the room. Hill decided to institute more musician-friendly policies, including a Monday-night jam session that set the tone for the innovations that followed. The key to Minton's success was its house band, a quartet co-led by Hill's former drummer Kenny Clarke and trumpeter Joe Guy and including an iconoclastic young unknown, Thelonious Monk, on piano. As word spread about Monk's adventurous harmonies and the daring rhythmic notions Clarke was adding from his drum kit, other musicians began frequenting Minton's to test their own new ideas. Dizzy Gillespie, another Teddy Hill alumnus, was a regular, and electric-guitar fountainhead Charlie Christian left an amplifier in the room so he could drop in as soon as his boss, Benny Goodman, was through

From left to right: Thelonious Monk, Howard McGhee, Roy Eldridge, and Teddy Hill at Minton's Playhouse, New York, 1948.

for the night. Established stars, including Don Byas, Ben Webster, and Lester Young, often visited. Billie Holiday and Charlie Parker preferred Clark Monroe's Uptown House at 198 West 134th Street, which, as Barron Wilkins' Exclusive Club, had been the site of Duke Ellington's first steady New York job, in 1923; but they passed through Minton's as well. Some of the earliest evidence of the modern movement was captured at Minton's on a portable disc recorder by Columbia University student Jerry Newman, who documented Christian, Clarke, Gillespie, and Monk in full after-hours flight. —*Bob Blumenthal*

to this effort, none more so than alto saxophonist Charlie Parker, ultimately known via his legend to even the non-jazz world as "Yardbird" or "Bird."

Parker was born in 1920 and grew up in the fertile musical environment of Kansas City. By 1941 and his initial recorded solos with Jay McShann's band, on such tracks as *Swingmatism* and *The Jumpin' Blues*, he was displaying a heady approach that merged the virtuosity of Tatum and the melodic daring of Young—topped off with a blues-rooted intensity uniquely his own. When Parker finally recorded as a solo artist, in 1945, he could draw upon additional big-band experience with Earl "Fatha" Hines and Billy Eckstine and the ideas he had shared with such contemporaries as trumpeter John Birks "Dizzy" Gillespie, who had apprenticed in the big bands of Teddy Hill and Cab Calloway; drummer Kenny Clarke, another Teddy Hill alumnus who had been among the first to introduce complex polyrhythms behind soloists; and pianist-composer Thelonious Monk, whose work was filled with startling dissonance and rhythmic displacements.

This core group of innovators—particularly the charismatic Parker—first demonstrated their discoveries in jam sessions, then landed nightclub engagements on New York's 52nd Street, before the new music was disseminated widely through recordings. As a result, a slightly younger group of talented musicians had already rallied around Parker and Gillespie before the larger audience learned of their existence. Pianists Earl "Bud" Powell and Al Haig, trumpeter Miles Davis, trombonist J.J. Johnson, saxophonist Edward "Sonny" Stitt, and drummer Max Roach were among the most prominent of these disciples, and together they represented a loose yet identifiable modernist school.

Charlie Parker and trumpeter Red Rodney absorb the sound of Dizzy Gillespie at New York's Club Downbeat, 1948. Rodney, a professional musician from the age of fifteen, worked with Parker in 1949–50. Fame for his role in bop eluded Rodney until thirty years later, when he released a series of widely noticed albums with trumpeter and saxophonist Ira Sullivan.

©William P. Gottlieb

The lack of recorded evidence of the experimenters' early efforts resulted from the 1942–44 ban on recording ordered by the American Federation of Musicians. When the ban ended in late 1944, the new music was poised to emerge from its period of incubation, and it spread quickly in the following year on a series of historic 78-rpm records issued under Gillespie's and Parker's names. Gillespie began 1945 by recording composer Tadd Dameron's *Good Bait* and the trumpeter's own composition *Bebop*, which quickly lent its name to the new style. Then Gillespie held two recording sessions—with Parker as a sideman—that introduced the trumpeter's pieces *Salt Peanuts* and *Groovin' High* as well as Dameron's *Hot House*. Each of these recordings became modern classics. Parker's first session as a leader, which featured Miles Davis, Max Roach, and (on piano as well as trumpet) Gillespie, yielded its own classics: the blues themes *Now's the Time* and *Billie's Bounce* and the virtuosic variation on *Cherokee* called *Ko Ko*.

Few recordings in jazz history proved as influential—and controversial—as these titles. Unsympathetic listeners disparaged the allegedly "thin" tones of the horn players, who had dispensed with the expressive vibratos of traditional soloists; lamented the irregular accents and such dissonant harmonic trademarks as the interval of the flatted fifth; and predicted that any music presenting such challenges to dancers had no future. Gillespie's former boss Cab Calloway had once called the trumpeter's more confounding experiments "Chinese music," and veterans as respected as Louis Armstrong were heard to attack the new sounds in similar terms.

Such reactions were further indicators of the uphill battle faced by the emerging modernists. Swing, as DeVeaux put it, had been "an integral part of the burgeoning entertainment industry.... All of the bebop musicians began their careers within this system. Their decision to break, or at least radically revise, their relationship to it was no casual act. Nor, given the realities of power in American society, could it hope to be entirely successful."

Not all of the older players rejected the music known as bebop or, more simply, bop. Ellington sax star Ben Webster loved to join the jam sessions at Minton's, pianist Mary Lou Williams became a mentor to the likes of Gillespie and Monk, and the harmonically audacious Coleman Hawkins hired Monk and other young innovators. A new generation of musicians and non-dancing listeners—smaller than the audience that sustained the swing bands yet equally passionate—rallied to the modern sounds. The new fans responded to the music's restless energy and sophisticated virtuosity, and they identified with the countercultural trappings that already set the style's leading players apart. Jazz had been born outside the mainstream, and after the mass acceptance of the swing bands, bebop was returning the music to its niche of unconventionality. The new wave of players seemed intent on breaking rules both musical and nonmusical.

The most committed of the modern fans lived for each new Parker and Gillespie 78, just as earlier listeners had devoured the Armstrong Hot Fives and Sevens and the Count Basie sides with Lester Young; and where the older disciples had copied the slang and mannerisms of Armstrong and Young, the new acolytes became similarly absorbed with their bop role models. Sporting Gillespie-inspired goatees, berets, and glasses was benign, but when Parker's heroin addiction became widely known and his followers mistakenly assumed that emulating this aspect of his lifestyle would allow them to produce music of similar brilliance, the hero worship had a far more destructive effect.

Fashions popularized by such boppers as Dizzy Gillespie and Thelonious Monk proved more than a rapidly passing fad; they spawned the berets-and-shades look associated with the "beatnik" counterculture of the 1950s.

In his brief and often sensationalized lifetime, and to an even greater extent after his death in 1955 at the age of thirty-four, Parker became the emblematic modernist, the individual whose music and accompanying experiences evoked more passion—pro and con—than that of any of his contemporaries. Parker stood more clearly apart from previous jazz generations than did Gillespie, who still preferred to work in orchestral settings and still practiced such crowd-pleasing gambits as dancing and scat singing. Parker was also more extroverted and less alienating than the inscrutable Monk. Parker's music had a searing emotional quality that was taken by some as a fitting soundtrack to the drug and alcohol abuse, erratic behavior, and occasional hospitalizations that fueled his legend. Yet while Parker complained that many who came to hear him were only seeking a glimpse of "the world's greatest junkie, the supreme hipster," even his most casual fans were responding to a visceral intensity that gave jazz—and most particularly the blues sensibility so central to jazz—a contemporary immediacy. Together with the more commercial rhythm-and-blues players (who turned his *Now's the Time* into the pop hit *The Hucklebuck* in 1948) and such raw urban-music innovators as Muddy Waters, Parker was taking the blues into the postwar era.

For most of the decade (1945–55) during which he reigned as the acknowledged leader of the modernists, Parker's working life involved leading a combo—usually a quintet in which his alto saxophone was joined by trumpet, piano, bass, and drums—on recording sessions or in club and concert performances. Parker had played for dancers during his years of big-band apprenticeship, yet his new ideas were better suited for listeners. This shift to jazz as listening music not only helped the nightclubs that were now the centers of instrumental music performance but also sustained a growing number of independent jazz labels that could not marshall the production budgets required for recording larger ensembles. (Coleman Hawkins and Lester Young had anticipated the shift to combos, club work, and independent jazz labels before and during the war years.)

The configuration of Parker's most famous group—with Miles Davis on trumpet, Duke Jordan on piano, Tommy Potter on bass, and Max Roach on drums—was ideal for expressing the premium the new music placed on speed of thought and execution. Parker recorded with these musicians for both the Dial and Savoy companies in 1947 and '48, and the resulting performances, including *Scrapple from the Apple, Bird Gets the Worm,* and *Dexterity,* redefined the sonorities and textures of small-group playing. The shift in Parker's customary performing venues during these years—from the after-hours Harlem spots to the nightclubs on and around 52nd Street (which ultimately included a room named Birdland in Parker's honor) and finally to the bohemian haunts of Greenwich Village— also reflected the broader route this new style of jazz was traveling, out of the black community via commercial thoroughfares to the precincts of the so-called intelligentsia.

Charlie "Bird" Parker playing at Birdland in 1949. The club's name was a nod to the alto saxophonist—and to his impact on the jazz world.

Old Chords, New Melodies

Many of the compositions created by bop-era musicians were contrafacts: new melodies written to the harmonic structures—what musicians call the chord changes (or simply "the changes")—of pre-existing songs.

The practice is as old as jazz itself. It could be argued that every twelve-bar blues is this type of "contrafact"; but the technique was applied to popular song forms as well, by some of the greatest jazz composers. Duke Ellington made use of the final harmonic sequence in the classic composition *Tiger Rag* (the "hold that tiger" strain) often in the early days of his orchestra, in such pieces as *The Creeper* (1928) and *High Life* (1929), and built *In a Mellotone* (1940) on the chords of *Rose Room,* while his collaborator Billy Strayhorn's immortal *Take the "A" Train* (1941) borrows harmonies from *Exactly Like You.* Such appropriations were hardly confined to Ellington's circle; witness the Kansas City staple *Moten Swing,* written in 1932 on the changes of the pop song *You're Driving Me Crazy.*

With the arrival of the modern-jazz era, the creation of such contrafacts grew exponentially. In a sense, using a familiar harmonic sequence simply verified the continuity between the new jazz and earlier styles, while also underscoring the melodic, rhythmic, and (through the addition or substitution of more complex passing chords) harmonic distinctions that the modernists had introduced. It was also an economic strategy to reap financial benefits from these new creations. While an improvised solo could not serve as the basis for generating earnings, at least the crafting of a new melody over chords that (like solos) enjoyed no copyright protection

provided a source of royalties. Some record companies, determined to solidify their own profits and avoid payments to established composers, even insisted that musicians record original material with the label acting as publisher—a practice that generated even more contrafacts.

It did not take long for *I Got Rhythm* (1930) to become the jazz world's favorite harmonic sequence after the blues, and for Charlie Parker to become the king of the *Rhythm* remakers. The harmonic motion of the Gershwin classic was ideal for jazz improvisation, and Parker mined it constantly with such new-melody reworkings as *Red Cross* (1944), *Anthropology* (1946), *Cheers*

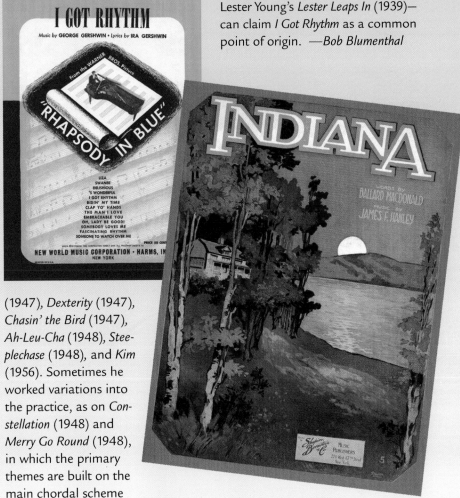

(1947), *Dexterity* (1947), *Chasin' the Bird* (1947), *Ah-Leu-Cha* (1948), *Steeplechase* (1948), and *Kim* (1956). Sometimes he worked variations into the practice, as on *Constellation* (1948) and *Merry Go Round* (1948), in which the primary themes are built on the main chordal scheme

of *Honeysuckle Rose* and the second theme (or bridge) is based on the bridge of *I Got Rhythm.* Parker liked to play compositions based on other songs as well: Tadd Dameron's *Hot House* (1945), Miles Davis's *Donna Lee* (1947), and Benny Harris's *Ornithology* (1946), based on *What Is This Thing Called Love?, Indiana,* and *How High the Moon,* respectively.

When it came to such contrafacts, virtually everybody was doing it in the forties and fifties. That is why such classic compositions of the period as Thelonious Monk's *Rhythm-a-ning* (1941), Bud Powell's *Wail* (1946), and Sonny Rollins' *Oleo* (1954)—not to mention Duke Ellington's *Cotton Tail* (1940) and Lester Young's *Lester Leaps In* (1939)—can claim *I Got Rhythm* as a common point of origin. —*Bob Blumenthal*

The Street

It was called "Swing Street" and "the street that never slept." In its nightclub heyday—which lasted roughly from 1933 to the late forties—the stretch of Manhattan's 52nd Street that ran between Fifth and Seventh Avenues served as a vibrant center of jazz activity.

Clubs such as the Onyx, the Famous Door, and the Three Deuces lit the street in neon. Over time, they also cast light on the changing face of jazz. In the late thirties, a walk past a club marquee and downstairs into a basement would plunge a visitor into a crowded, smoke-filled setting alive with the sound of swing. Ten years later, that same descent would immerse the clubgoer in the hyperkinetic energy of bebop.

The Street offered a grab bag of options for fan and player alike. On any given night, a jazz seeker could snake from one brownstone to another and catch sets by Art Tatum, Coleman Hawkins, and Billie Holiday. The musicians themselves would hop from club to club, finishing up their regular shows and then rushing across the street or a couple of doors away to sit in with other bands. With new ideas and players circulating freely, tested for durability in late-night "cutting sessions," 52nd Street became a hothouse of innovation and evolving styles.

It was on the Street that many musicians heard sax innovator Charlie Parker for the first time, when he would drop in unannounced to jam. "Everybody just flipped," clarinetist Tony Scott recalled. Parker's influence would course through the Street's echoing basements and on into future jazz.

The clubs were numerous, and each had its own minihistory.

There was the Onyx, one of the Street's earliest jazz venues, where

52nd Street, New York City, 1948.

in 1933 one could hear Tatum and the swing quintet Spirits of Rhythm; two years later, audiences could catch the sextet of violinist-singer Stuff Smith, who had a novelty hit in 1936 with *I'se A-Muggin'*. By the mid-forties Dizzy Gillespie was there, playing virtuosic bop trumpet with a group that included bassist Oscar Pettiford and drummer Max Roach.

Across the street was the Famous Door, which played host, over the years, to the likes of Count Basie's

big band, Gillespie, Lester Young, Ben Webster, and Jack Teagarden.

Another club, the Hickory House, opened its doors in 1934. By 1936 it was showcasing one of 52nd Street's first racially mixed groups, led by clarinetist Joe Marsala and featuring Red Allen on trumpet. Marsala seemingly couldn't leave: he played at the Hickory House off and on through 1945.

At the Club Downbeat, featured acts included Holiday, guitarist Tiny

Grimes and his group, and Hawkins, who worked there with Thelonious Monk in 1944, at around the same time Gillespie was bringing bop to the Onyx.

Gillespie also played the Three Deuces. And in 1947 young trumpeter Miles Davis could be heard there, earning his stripes in a quintet led by saxophone sensation Parker and propelled by Max Roach.

Kelly's Stable was the site, in 1939, of Hawkins' debut engagement after an extended stay in Europe. Hawkins' classic Bluebird recording of *Body and Soul* was a product of his Stable stint. Nat Cole, Holiday, and Hot Lips Page were others heard there.

Two doors down from the Onyx was Jimmy Ryan's, a site that specialized in traditional jazz: Page, Allen, Earl Hines, Sidney Bechet, and Bob Wilber played there. The club outlasted the Street itself, closing in 1962.

After the war, the Street's jazz began to slip away, drawn to clubs in other parts of town—clubs such as Bop City, the Royal Roost, Birdland, and Greenwich Village's Café Society and the Village Vanguard. Strip joints and pockets of vice replaced it. Several decades later, following its transformation into a gray stretch of nondescript office buildings, the "street that never slept" finally turned out the lights for good. —*Tad Lathrop*

Parker was not confined exclusively to combos and clubs, however; a significant portion of his recorded legacy reveals that the new music was already functioning elsewhere. In addition to such studio triumphs as *Ornithology, Yardbird Suite,* and the Gillespie composition *A Night in Tunisia,* all from 1946, some of the key products of Parker's often traumatic stay in California between 1945 and 1947 include recorded performances with Jazz at the Philharmonic, a forum in which he and Gillespie demonstrated, to listeners who had open ears and minds, that their approach was perfectly compatible with that of predecessors Roy Eldridge, Coleman Hawkins, and Lester Young. When Norman Granz, the producer of Jazz at the Philharmonic, expanded upon the success of recordings from the concerts to create his own independent jazz label in 1949, Parker was among his first featured artists. Several of the saxophonist's studio projects under Granz's supervision announced even more far-reaching aspects of the new music.

Granz began by recording Parker with Machito's Afro-Cubans, the orchestra fronted by vocalist Frank Raúl "Machito" Grillo. Under the musical direction of Machito's brother-in-law, multi-instrumentalist Mario Bauzá, the Afro-Cubans had successfully merged Latin American rhythms and forms with big-band concepts. Dizzy Gillespie, who had been introduced to Latin rhythms by Bauzá while both were members of the Cab Calloway trumpet section, had established himself as the prime champion of this Latin-jazz fusion by featuring Cuban conga drummer Chano Pozo with the Gillespie orchestra on *Manteca* and *Cubana Be, Cubana Bop* in 1947. This stylistic conjunction continued to develop in the years before Parker's death. Stan Kenton paid tribute in a piece entitled *Machito* (1947), such Latin bandleaders as Tito Puente and Tito Rodriguez followed Machito's lead and made frequent room for guest jazz soloists, and popular jazz combos of the early fifties—led by pianist George Shearing and vibraphonist Cal Tjader—returned the compliment by incorporating Latin percussionists.

Granz also recorded Parker with a string section, fulfilling one of the saxophonist's lifelong ambitions and inspiring a small but steady stream of similar performances from soloists with the artistic or commercial clout to merit such lavish treatment. Despite the often saccharine settings, Parker was extremely proud of his work with strings, especially his stunning interpretation of the standard *Just Friends* (1949), and the *Charlie Parker with Strings* recordings (1949) were easily his most popular.

Parker's die-hard fans were able to preserve many of his more typical quintet performances, since his music was broadcast frequently from nightclubs on radio "remotes" and could be saved through the use of new home-recording technology. Fans made their own copies of such "airchecks" as well as in-person dubs of concerts, club sets, and even informal rehearsals and jam sessions. This activity generated an astounding number of unauthorized Parker recordings, which began surfacing before his death and continued to emerge in the ensuing decades. These multiple versions of the same staple bebop compositions, together with many alternate studio takes saved by the labels for which Parker recorded, testify to his inexhaustible creativity. Several location recordings are masterpieces, such as the 1953 Massey Hall concert in Toronto in which Parker, Gillespie, Powell, Roach, and bassist Charles Mingus held something of a bebop summit. Even the rough and unpolished snippets of Parker alto preserved elsewhere, with ensembles and solos by other band members omitted to save precious tape or discs, include brilliant improvisations and reinforce Parker's status as a cult figure.

Norman Granz and Jazz at the Philharmonic

Norman Granz: producer, record executive, and energetic jazz promoter.

Along with the annual Carnegie Hall concerts that Duke Ellington embarked on in 1943, producer Norman Granz's Jazz at the Philharmonic concert series was among the gathering indications that jazz could find a new home in formal settings that typically hosted symphony orchestras and classical soloists. Not that JATP, as it quickly became known, confined itself to the esoteric aspects of the music. The concerts were organized jam sessions, loose and extroverted and frequently derided for the solo displays of such regulars as tenor saxophonists Illinois Jacquet and Flip Phillips that approached the exhibitionism of rhythm and blues. In honoring Granz's preference for the spontaneous, JATP drove home the point that all "serious" music was not necessarily committed to manuscript paper; and at its best, as in the 1946 concert that produced Charlie Parker's solo on *Lady Be Good,* JATP presented informal cross-generational summit meetings in which young innovators like Parker and Dizzy Gillespie could stand shoulder-to-shoulder with such influential elders as Lester Young and Roy Eldridge.

JATP's 1944 debut concert at Hollywood's Philharmonic Auditorium had been organized by Granz to raise funds for Mexican American defendants in a murder case, and the producer's commitment to civil rights was further demonstrated by his insistence that integration take place both onstage and in the audience at all JATP concerts. The 1944 debut was also recorded, later appearing on twelve-inch, 78-rpm records. These became the first commercially issued live jazz recordings, and their popularity made JATP an international concert phenomenon and Granz the first acknowledged jazz impresario. He continued to present JATP through 1957, generally with vocalist Ella Fitzgerald and the trio of pianist Oscar Peterson as the centerpieces of the star-heavy packages.

Granz also excelled as a recording executive and personal manager. He owned the labels successively known as Clef, Norgran, and Verve, which dominated independent jazz production throughout the 1950s by presenting Fitzgerald, Stan Getz, Gillespie, Billie Holiday, Parker, Peterson, Art Tatum, Young, and other stars. After selling Verve in 1961, Granz returned to recording with his Pablo label in 1973, where Basie, Fitzgerald, Peterson, and guitarist Joe Pass all found a home. Granz also personally oversaw the careers of Fitzgerald and Peterson and enjoyed a productive if less exclusive business relationship with Duke Ellington. —*Bob Blumenthal*

JATP concert recordings proved Norman Granz's entré into the jazz record business.

Big Bands in the Modern Era

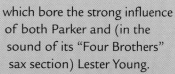

A combination of changing economics and changing tastes may have brought a close to the big-band era, but it hardly extinguished all big bands. In addition to the ongoing enterprises of jazz's orchestral Olympians, Duke Ellington and Count Basie, a number of newer large ensembles emerged as jazz entered the modern era.

Unfortunately, the two big bands that became known as the incubators of the modern era were victims of the 1942–44 recording ban. These were the Earl Hines Orchestra of 1943, which included Dizzy Gillespie, Charlie Parker, and Sarah Vaughan, and the first edition of the band formed by Hines vocalist Billy Eckstine, which featured Gillespie, Parker, and Vaughan as well as such other leading modernists as trumpeter Fats Navarro, tenor saxophonists Gene Ammons and Dexter Gordon, and drummer Art Blakey. By the time Eckstine's band recorded, Gillespie and Parker had moved on.

The big band was a natural setting for Gillespie's virtuosic trumpet and extroverted showmanship, however; and in the latter half of the 1940s he led an orchestra of his own. The compositions *Things to Come* (1946), *Cool Breeze* (1947), and others demonstrated that the innovations heard most frequently in combos could also be applied to larger ensembles, while *Algo Bueno* (1947) and the two-part *Cubana Be, Cubana Bop* (1947) revealed the potential in merging jazz with Afro-Cuban music.

Modern ideas also drove what came to be known as the First and Second Herds of veteran bandleader Woody Herman— especially the 1947–49 Second Herd, which bore the strong influence of both Parker and (in the sound of its "Four Brothers" sax section) Lester Young.

Another variety of modernism was purveyed by the bands of Stan Kenton, who used Jimmie Lunceford as the initial model for his band, yet by the end of the forties was the exemplar of all things "progressive." There was much pretense in Kenton's music (particularly in his constant recasting of 1943's *Artistry in Rhythm*), but much innovation as well, beginning with his use of bassist Eddie Safranski and the Kai Winding–led trombone section on such performances as *Collaboration* and *Minor Riff* (both 1947). Early-fifties editions featured the challenging scores of Bob Graettinger (*City of Glass*, 1951) and Bill Russo (*23° North–82° West*, 1952). By that time, trumpeter Shorty Rogers, saxophonist Gerry Mulligan (who wrote the influential *Young Blood* [1952] but did not play in the band), and others had introduced ideas into Kenton's orbit that would also prove to be forerunners of "cool" jazz.

Ultimately, however, the economics of bandleading proved prohibitive. By 1950, Gillespie had disbanded, Herman and Kenton only toured for parts of each year, and even Count Basie was temporarily reduced to leading a combo. Only Duke Ellington, in a class of his own as always, remained on the road, the exception that proved the rule that big bands had become an unaffordable luxury.
—Bob Blumenthal

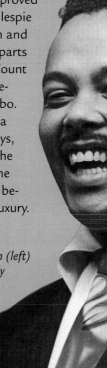

Both vocalist Sarah Vaughan (left) and vocalist/bandleader Billy Eckstine (right) survived the demise of the big bands that launched their respective careers.

Parker's image as a self-destructive outsider established an unfortunate stereotype for his musical generation that inhibited a more serious appreciation of jazz for years after the saxophonist's death. This romantic notion of the doomed jazz genius done in by his or her addictions actually predates Parker and can be traced back at least as far as twenties cornetist Bix Beiderbecke. Still, the identification of jazz with drug abuse grew stronger in the 1940s, boosted by Gene Krupa's and Lester Young's marijuana-related run-ins with authorities, Parker's erratic behavior leading to his commitment in California's Camarillo State Hospital, and Billie Holiday's imprisonment for heroin possession. Frank Sinatra's portrait of fictional drummer Frankie Machine in *The Man with the Golden Arm* (1955) plus later biopics of Holiday and Parker contributed to an environment in which extramusical notoriety often overshadowed artistic achievement. Notwithstanding the distortions and racial double-standards that fed such sensational depictions of many great musicians, there is no denying that substance abuse was a particularly devastating scourge in the jazz world during this period and interrupted the careers of many prominent musicians; for such innovators as baritone saxophonist Serge Chaloff, tenor saxophonist Wardell Gray, and trumpeter Theodore "Fats" Navarro, as well as Parker and Holiday, these addictions would prove fatal before the 1950s ended.

©Herman Leonard

*Piano modernist
Bud Powell.*

Piano Modernists

Even in the face of such problems, players in the forties and early fifties generated a vast quantity of great music, beginning with the work of those who formed Parker's immediate circle as his style took hold. Much of the most interesting music came from the era's pianists. Bud Powell—the musician who best transferred the speed and complexity of Parker's alto playing to the piano—worked with Parker only infrequently, yet he defined the standard for modern piano in several early trio, solo, and quintet recordings and became, arguably, the most influential modernist after Parker. Powell was at best an erratic presence. Psychiatric problems that had apparently been caused or exacerbated by a police beating in 1945 led to lengthy incarcerations, during which Powell underwent shock treatments that left the pianist even more disoriented and withdrawn. The toll taken on Powell's technique became increasingly audible in his playing; yet the pianist's initial recordings for the Roost, Verve, and Blue Note labels between 1947 and 1951, including *Dance of the Infidels*, *Tempus Fugit*, *Parisian Thoroughfare*, and *Un Poco Loco*, capture some of the era's most brilliant and completely realized music.

Tadd Dameron also played piano but is primarily remembered as one of the era's most gifted bandleaders and composers

©William P. Gottlieb

*Pianist, composer, and
bandleader Tadd Dameron.*

(*Good Bait,* 1944; *Hot House,* 1945; *Our Delight,* 1946; *If You Could See Me Now,* 1946). During his period of greatest activity, 1947–49, Dameron led a significant band at the Royal Roost on 52nd Street. The featured trumpeter was Fats Navarro, whose melodic gifts and balanced technique were easier for other trumpeters to emulate than those of the more virtuosic Gillespie. Prior to his death in 1950, Navarro made several important studio recordings with Dameron (*The Squirrel,* 1947, and *Lady Bird,* 1948) and Powell (*Bouncing with Bud* and *52nd Street Theme,* 1949), as well as aircheck recordings with Dameron and Parker, that would enhance his legend decades after his death.

Thelonious Monk at Minton's, 1949.

© Herman Leonard

The late forties marked the first recordings by a third important pianist-composer, one who had mentored Powell at Minton's and collaborated actively with Parker and Gillespie in defining the modern-jazz vocabulary. It took far longer, though, for the public and even many musicians to see beyond Thelonious Monk's personal idiosyncrasies and hear beyond the passing dissonances of his bold, unpredictable creations.

Wearing dark glasses and a variety of distinctive hats and given to occasional cryptic pronouncements, Monk was an ideal candidate for the role of jazz's leading eccentric, an image only reinforced by the distinctive spaces and astringencies of his music and his billing as "the high priest of bebop." From his first Blue Note recordings in 1947 until he began his influential series of albums for the Riverside label eight years later, Monk was a man ahead of his time, valued, if at all, for his quirky

The melodic trumpet style of Fats Navarro (left, shown with Illinois Jacquet) was easier to emulate than that of the more virtuosic Dizzy Gillespie.

yet undeniably fascinating compositions (*Misterioso, Evidence, 'Round [About] Midnight, Little Rootie Tootie*) and frequently challenged regarding his percussive, jarring keyboard attack. It did not help that Monk had taken a drug rap for one of his musician friends, losing, in the process, the "cabaret card" license that was required for performers seeking work in New York establishments where alcohol was served. For years, Monk did much of his playing in his West Side apartment, where young musicians, including tenor saxophonist Sonny Rollins and pianist Randy Weston, would come for intensive tutorials. Monk's day would arrive in the late 1950s. But during the period he helped inaugurate, Monk's brilliant recordings were widely ignored, and he remained a prophet without honor.

'Round Midnight

'Round Midnight (also known as *'Round About Midnight*), with music by Thelonious Monk and Cootie Williams and lyrics by Bernie Hanighen, is one of the most enduring compositions to come out of the modern-jazz era. In the many years—well over half a century—since its birth, there have been more than two hundred recordings of this remarkable piece by such diverse artists as Miles Davis, Wes Montgomery, Ella Fitzgerald, Bobby McFerrin and Chick Corea, Cecil Taylor, the Art Ensemble of Chicago, Sun Ra, June Christy, Laurindo Almeida, Linda Ronstadt, Eydie Gorme, Eileen Farrell, the Kronos Quartet, and virtually every major modern-jazz instrumentalist and singer.

'Round Midnight dates from 1944, when it was first recorded by trumpeter Williams. Like so many other works by Monk, it stands successfully as a composition with or without improvisational embellishment; unlike the great majority of jazz pieces, it is almost always presented with the written introduction and coda intact.

The piece was the focal point of collegial reciprocity between Monk and Dizzy Gillespie, whom Monk introduced to the harmonic and compositional potential of the half-diminished chord (also known as the minor 6th chord) with the 6th in the bass. In turn, the introduction of *'Round Midnight* drew from Gillespie's use of the chord in the ending of his own *I Can't Get Started* (recorded in 1945). The coda of *'Round Midnight* is, again, Gillespie's invention, based loosely on the chord changes to the bridge of Gillespie's *Con Alma* (1954).

The half-diminished chord, which Gillespie also used in *Woody 'n' You* (1944) and other tunes, and which composer Tadd Dameron used so prominently in *Hot House* (1945), seems to hold a special fascination for both jazz and art-music composers and performers. Few classically trained musicians escape a discussion of this so-called

Tristan chord, so named because of its prominence in the Tristan theme of Richard Wagner's opera *Tristan und Isolde*.

The body of *'Round Midnight* is beautifully structured, with a perfect balance between chordal and scalar lines, rising and falling phrases, constantly unfolding sequences, and the illusion of inevitability of resolution without a hint of predictability. Its two main themes are among the most alluring, haunting, and memorable in jazz literature—romantic without being sentimental or maudlin, tender but with muscularity and sinew, and capable of capturing both heart and mind.

The piece is one of a very few works by jazz composers (Ellington excepted) that have become popular successes as well as jazz standards. It's one of two works of Monk that have become titles of successful movies: *Straight, No Chaser* (a biographical documentary) and *'Round Midnight* (a fictional story of a jazz musician who is a loose composite of Lester Young and Bud Powell). In the minds of many, *'Round Midnight* is Monk's magnum opus. —*David Baker*

Bebop-Era Standards

Charlie Parker and Dizzy Gillespie at Birdland, 1951.

Pieces that became standards during the bebop era tended to combine memorability with challenges to the improviser in the form of complex harmonies and rhythms and angular, chromatic melodies. They were either original compositions, popular songs (including ballads, blues, and Tin Pan Alley and show tunes), or contrafacts (tunes based on pre-existing chord progressions or changes).

The following are some of the bop era's contrafacts that became standards among jazz musicians:

Moose the Mooche (1946) by Charlie Parker and *Anthropology* (1946) by Parker and Dizzy Gillespie are both based on the changes to George Gershwin's *I Got Rhythm* (1930), a song that served as the basis for literally hundreds of bebop tunes.

Hot House (1945), penned by Tadd Dameron, is noted for its chromatic, serpentine melody. One of the most distinctive recordings of the tune is from the May 15, 1953, recording of the Massey Hall concert with Charlie Parker, Gillespie, Bud Powell, Charles Mingus, and Max Roach.

Donna Lee (1947) by Miles Davis is one of bebop's most virtuosic and exciting melodies, most often played at impossibly fast tempos. Among the many interpretations available on record is a dazzling version by bassist Jaco Pastorius.

Scrapple from the Apple (1947) by Parker combines the changes to Fats Waller's standard *Honeysuckle Rose* (A section) and *I Got Rhythm* (B section). At jam sessions the piece was—and still is—ubiquitous.

Ornithology (1946), by Parker and Benny Harris, is often referred to as the bebop national anthem because of the frequency with which it was played and the popularity of its harmonic progression. It is based on the 1940 pop song *How High the Moon*. Parker's Dial recording of *Ornithology* from March 1946 is particularly noteworthy.

Among the most played non-contrafact jazz originals are *Confirmation,* written in 1946 by Charlie Parker and recorded by most of bebop's major figures, and Dizzy Gillespie's *A Night in Tunisia* (1944), which evidenced the trumpeter's interest in Latin rhythms. One of the most inspired performances of *Tunisia* can be found on the 1946 Dial recording by Parker, in which he plays an incredible four-measure break to begin his solo.

Dizzy Gillespie penned three other key bop compositions, *Bebop* (1945), *Things to Come* (1946), and *Things Are Here* (1965), all of which use the same harmonic progression and exemplify many of the characteristics that define bebop. They are instrumentally conceived, virtuosic in concept, and—because of the supersonic tempos at which they're often played—not for the faint of heart. A performance of these three works demands the highest degree of technical skill, a quick and inventive mind, much imagination, and a historically informed sense of their importance to the legacy of bebop. In many circles they still serve as a rite of passage for the incipient and aspiring bebopper.

Thelonious Monk contributed more than just *'Round Midnight* to the era's standard repertoire; *Ruby, My Dear* (1945), *Straight, No Chaser* (1951), and *Blue Monk* (1954) were among his memorable pieces.

Other songs of the era that became standards were composed by musicians working outside bebop. Notable among them were Billy Strayhorn's haunting ballad *Lush Life* (1949), Duke Ellington and Strayhorn's enormously popular *Satin Doll* (1953), and the rocking *Night Train* (1952), which was liberally borrowed by Jimmy Forrest from Ellington's *Happy-Go-Lucky Local* (1945).

George Shearing created a perennial with *Lullaby of Birdland* (1952), John Lewis composed the celebrated homage *Django* (1954), and Bronislaw Kaper penned the swinging *On Green Dolphin Street* (1947) and the harmonically and formally challenging *Invitation* (1953). Finally, Johnny Mercer contributed lyrics to two jazz instrumental ballads, the finespun *Early Autumn,* composed by Ralph Burns and Stan Kenton (1949), and the smoldering *Midnight Sun,* by Sonny Burke and Lionel Hampton (1947), which furthered the songs' popularity among jazz singers such as Jo Stafford, Ella Fitzgerald, and Mel Tormé.

—David Baker

Another pianist and bandleader often considered as "far out" as Monk had a more immediate impact. While still in his native Chicago, Lennie Tristano developed a personal philosophy of improvisation and began attracting what would become a significant number of students. His musical approach relied on learning classic recorded performances of Armstrong, Eldridge, Young, and others by ear, and he placed a premium on unfettered melodic invention by eliminating such expressive devices as strong tonal inflection and rhythmically active accompaniment. The style was best captured in a series of 1949 recordings in which Tristano was joined by his two leading disciples, alto saxophonist Lee Konitz and tenor saxophonist Warne Marsh. Two of these performances—*Digression* and *Intuition*—were totally improvised and are now viewed as harbingers of the free-jazz movement that emerged a decade later. While Tristano's influence was significant, particularly in Europe via the recordings and appearances of Konitz, it might have been more keenly felt had the pianist not made teaching his priority from 1951 until his death in 1978.

Tristano's systematic methods and the perception of his music as somewhat dispassionate, perhaps reinforced by the fact that he and his circle were Caucasians rather than African Americans, made it seem to some that his was a more cerebral or "progressive" alternative to bebop. In fact, Tristano was one of Parker's most individualistic disciples, the creator of a music that could not have existed without bebop and the harmonic discoveries of Art Tatum as primary sources. Then again, with rare exceptions (such as Erroll Garner, a pianist who rose to popularity with a merger of swing and modern elements, or young classicists such as cornetist Ruby Braff and clarinetist Bob Wilber, who played in more traditional styles with older players), it is hard to identify any young musicians from the period who were not working from a bebop foundation.

Metronome All-Stars Eddie Safranski (bass), Charlie Parker, and Lennie Tristano, 1949.

Cool Jazz and the West-Coast Scene

Also based on bop, though often viewed as independent of it, was the music that came to be known as "cool" or "West Coast" jazz. As it gained popularity and turned briefly into a marketable commodity, cool jazz became identified with lighter, vibrato-free lines (similar in this respect to Tristano's music); the use of flute, French horn, tuba, and other instruments that were uncommon in earlier jazz styles; and a greater emphasis on counterpoint and other supposedly classical techniques. The style was identified with California, even if such leading cool lights as Stan Getz, Gerry Mulligan, and Shorty Rogers had grown up on the East Coast. Cool was also taken by many to be the exclusive domain of white musicians, even though the leader of the recordings that mark the style's emergence was Miles Davis and the ensemble most deeply immersed in European influences was the Modern Jazz Quartet. Once again, nomenclature disguised evolutionary continuity, for cool jazz was as rooted in the Kansas City continuum of Count Basie, Lester Young, and Charlie Parker as it was in any alternative geographical or cultural soil.

A primary source for the light, floating sounds of cool jazz was the dance orchestra led in the 1940s by pianist Claude Thornhill, which employed

The rich, understated sound of pianist Claude Thornhill's orchestra (here with Lee Konitz, back row, third from left, on alto sax), shaped in part by arranger Gil Evans, offered a moody alternative to the high energy of bop and helped pave the way for the cool-jazz movement.

symphonic brass and woodwinds in addition to the more standard big-band instruments. Gil Evans, Thornhill's primary arranger beginning in 1941, was fascinated by the colors these additional instruments placed at his disposal and began employing them to obtain a range of impressionistic tonal effects. At the same time, Evans embraced the new sounds of the modern-jazz combo. In 1947, he orchestrated the Parker recordings *Yardbird Suite* and *Donna Lee* and the Parker-Gillespie collaboration *Anthropology* for Thornhill as features for the band's distinctive new alto sax soloist, Tristano student Lee Konitz. Evans also began sharing ideas around this time with younger musicians from the Parker quintet such as Miles Davis and future Modern Jazz Quartet leader John Lewis, as well as composers Gerry Mulligan, John Carisi, and George Russell. Their interaction produced the short-lived but seminal Miles Davis Nonet, a compact version of the Thornhill band featuring the solos of Davis, Konitz, and Mulligan and the writing of Evans (*Boplicity*), Mulligan (*Jeru*), Lewis (*Move*), and Carisi (*Israel*).

The Davis Nonet obtained only one booking, in the fall of 1948, but it managed to record on three later occasions, and the dozen titles it produced—which were later collectively dubbed *Birth of the Cool*—had a powerful impact. Their influence extended most directly to the work of Milton "Shorty" Rogers, a young trumpet player and arranger who made similar use of a midsize ensemble in recordings by his Giants group (*Popo, Didi*) that began to appear in 1951. Rogers also drew heavily on the riff-based example of the Count Basie band and the surface restraint of Lester Young, whose influence on young soloists predated Parker's and was still widely felt. The "cool" that Rogers came to exemplify thus echoed jazz's most emphatically swinging sources, as did the playing of a favorite Rogers collaborator, alto saxophonist Art Pepper.

Like many other former big-band sidemen adjusting to shifts in the music industry, Rogers found a new outlet for his playing and writing in the Hollywood studios, where music for films and television began to take on a jazz flavor. (As time went on, studio work for the film, television, and advertising industries—as well as for popular-music recordings—would become a key source of income for some jazz musicians.)

The movie industry's growing infatuation with jazz scores was only the latest of Hollywood's interactions with jazz, which had long included the use of jazz as subject matter for dramatic, musical, and comedic films. But racial discrimination had prevailed in Hollywood, helping to explain the predominance of white jazz musicians in California (although African American veterans such as Benny Carter and Harry "Sweets" Edison were quietly cracking barriers in the segregated system).

Stan Getz's sound, ideally suited for ballads, became a mainstay of West Coast jazz.

Miles Davis's 1949–50 Birth of the Cool *sessions employed Claude Thornhill alumni Gil Evans and Lee Konitz, reflecting Davis's growing interest in impressionistic, texturally varied sounds.*

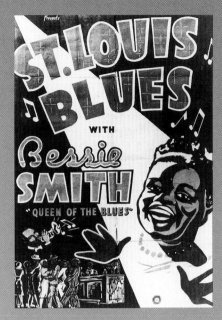

They grew up together. At the same time in the late nineteenth century that audiences were first paying to see images projected on a screen, musicians in New Orleans were stirring up a musical gumbo we now call jazz. Both movies and jazz started out as scandalous, "low" entertainment but quickly won huge popular followings; today they are regularly hailed as art. From the outset, however, jazz and the movies have both been typically American, typically romantic means of expression in which artists and audiences alike have explored their dreams and aspirations.

The two art forms interacted from the beginning. Musicians improvised in theaters while customers watched such "silent films" as *The Jazz Bandits* (1920) and *Children of Jazz* (1923). By 1927, key jazzmen like Duke Ellington and Bix

Beiderbecke were creating ground-breaking work. In that same year the movies first began to talk, appropriately in a film called *The Jazz Singer.* Two years later, Ellington was playing a serious composer and bandleader in Dudley Murphy's eighteen-minute short, *Black and Tan.*

The dignity afforded Ellington in *Black and Tan* was not typical of the film industry's treatment of jazz musicians, however. Also in 1929, director Murphy cast Bessie Smith in *St. Louis Blues* as an abused, gin-swilling woman who sings not because she is an artist like Ellington but simply because her man has left her. Jazz musicians fared much better if they happened to be white, like Paul Whiteman, who regally presided over the bizarre revue *The King of Jazz* (1930).

In the 1930s jazz artists of color were more likely to appear in short subjects or even cartoons than in full-length features. Eubie Blake played the piano, Nina Mae McKinney sang, and the Nicholas Brothers danced

their hearts out in the nine-minute *Pie, Pie, Blackbird* (1932). Louis Armstrong played a cannibal in a 1932 Betty Boop cartoon, and Cab Calloway was cast as an animated dancing walrus in another short feature with Ms. Boop. In the full-length films *Check and Double Check* (1932), *The Big Broadcast* (1932), and *King of Burlesque* (1935), artists such as Ellington, Calloway, and Fats Waller were carefully segregated in brief segments that could easily be edited out for people who were unnerved by the sight of black men.

Jazz in the movies probably came of age in the 1940s. Films with all-black casts—among them *Cabin in the Sky* (1943) and *Stormy Weather* (1943)—offered great performances by Ellington, Armstrong, Calloway, Waller, and Lena Horne. Interracial casts appeared in *Birth of the Blues* (1941), inspired by the Original Dixieland Jazz Band, and *Syncopation* (1942), which cast the great trumpeter and jazz writer Rex Stewart as a character based on cornetist King Oliver. Audiences were given behind-the-scenes dramas about the immensely popular swing

bands in *Orchestra Wives* (1942) and *The Fabulous Dorseys* (1947). *Jivin' in Be-Bop* (1947) served as a vehicle for Dizzy Gillespie and his orchestra, and *Rhythm in a Riff* (1946) featured the early bebop band of Billy Eckstine. In 1948's *A Song Is Born*, jazz was portrayed as an art form with a history (albeit a history so willfully misconceived that it emphasized Spanish explorers and ignored the slave trade).

Some filmmakers found jazz to be useful as a sign of corruption and criminality. In Frank Capra's *It's a Wonderful Life* (1946) the jazz that plays in bars and nightclubs signifies the decadence of "Pottersville," the nightmare alternative to the small-town paradise of Bedford Falls. In *The Wild One* (1953) a gang of motorcyclists in black leather listen not to rock and roll but to big-band music that suggests Stan Kenton. And in *The Rat Race* (1960) a group of talented jazz musicians steal Tony Curtis's saxophones and flutes at a fake audition.

After jazz ceased to be a popular music in the 1950s, it was most

likely to be heard in nostalgic biopics about bandleaders from the Swing Era (among them, *The Benny Goodman Story*, *The Glenn Miller Story*, and *The Five Pennies*); in grainy, "independent films" like *Shadows* (1960) and *The Connection* (1961); or in such documentaries as *Jazz on a Summer's Day* (1960) and *The Last of the Blue Devils* (1974). Jazz also became a musical flavor of choice in movie soundtracks, most memorably in *A Streetcar Named Desire* (1951), *Man with the Golden Arm* (1955), and *The Pawnbroker* (1964), not to mention *Anatomy of a Murder* (1959), with its great compositions by Duke Ellington and Billy Strayhorn. In the 1970s, Hollywood tried valiantly to make hit movies focusing on jazz with *Lady Sings the Blues* (1972) and *New York, New York* (1977). A decade later, the ambitious biographical jazz films *'Round Midnight* (1986) and *Bird* (1988) drew even smaller audiences.

At the end of the century, the most revealing treatment of jazz could be found in such documentaries as *Thelonious Monk: Straight No Chaser* (1988), *Let's Get Lost* (the 1988 film about the life of Chet Baker), and *A Great Day in Harlem* (1995). But filmgoers could hear bits and pieces of jazz in many Hollywood films, especially in scenes establishing emotional intimacy. Although by century's end jazz had become an art music, in the movies it was still very much the music of romance.

—Krin Gabbard

Singer Anita O'Day and sax player Gerry Mulligan in Jazz on a Summer's Day.

Dave Brubeck

Chet Baker

Not all the white musicians who ventured west sought studio work. Gerry Mulligan wrote the influential *Young Blood* for the Stan Kenton band when he relocated to Los Angeles in 1952, but the move also led him to form a quartet for appearances at a nightclub called the Haig. The group featured an inspired blend of Mulligan's deep yet mobile baritone saxophone and the fragile, unimpeachably lyrical trumpet of Chet Baker, a self-taught newcomer who had impressed no less a figure than Parker himself. Mulligan and Baker would frequently improvise simultaneously, a practice that harked back to early New Orleans music yet took on a modern veneer that was enhanced by the absence of a piano in the quartet's rhythm section. The lean, witty Mulligan sound proved as definitive of West Coast cool as that of any band's, and it turned both Mulligan and Baker into international stars.

Some of the new "West Coast" sounds emerging from California actually *were* created by musicians with roots west of the Mississippi. Saxophonist and clarinetist Jimmy Giuffre, a Texan, had gained early fame as the composer of *Four Brothers* (1947) for Woody Herman's Second Herd (a bebop-oriented follow-up to the swing-heavy band Woody Herman's Herd). After studying advanced compositional techniques, Giuffre began to explore more compact, folkish themes in his intimate Jimmy Giuffre 3, a band that eliminated drums and even, in one unusual clarinet-trombone-guitar configuration, bass. The Giuffre 3 featured the gentle abstractions of guitarist Jim Hall, who had made his debut in the quintet of former Mulligan drummer Chico Hamilton. With its emphasis on flute, cello, and atmospheric percussion, the Hamilton quintet established two Los Angeles natives, Hamilton and woodwind master Buddy Collette, among the leading figures in the cool style.

By far the most popular musician to emerge from California was pianist Dave Brubeck, a product of studies with composer Darius Milhaud and experiments in counterpoint and atonality in late-forties San Francisco. Brubeck's first band was an octet that proved too esoteric for popular tastes, but subsequent trio recordings planted the seeds of a mass following that blossomed after the addition of alto saxophonist Paul Desmond made the Brubeck group a quartet. The contrast between Desmond's limpid elegance and Brubeck's weightier complexities, and the conversational improvisations that the pair generated on such recordings as *Over the Rainbow* (1952) and *You Go to My Head* (1952) carried particular appeal for the growing audience that approached jazz as a challenging intellectual experience. With an uncanny sense of where both technology and the public were headed, Brubeck began recording nightclub performances on 33 1/3-rpm long-playing (LP) records, then obtained bookings on college campuses and recorded those concerts as well—an album of them, *Jazz Goes to College,* achieved commercial success in 1954.

Jazz Poetry

For more than three quarters of the twentieth century, poets responded both to jazz and to jazz musicians. While the term "jazz poetry" tends to conjure stereotypical images from the 1950s (coffee houses, black berets, and the like), the complex history of jazz-related poetry offers a far more diverse collection of poetic styles and sensibilities.

The earliest published jazz poems were written by white writers, such as Carl Sandburg, whose *Jazz Fantasia* (1920) was one of the first to appear in print. Many of his contemporaries, including e.e. cummings and Vachel Lindsay, associated racial and sexual anxieties with jazz; much of the poetry from the 1920s displayed an ignorance of the jazz aesthetic. In 1926, however, Langston Hughes published *The Weary Blues,* a collection of poems that, for the first time, embraced jazz as an art form integral to American and African American culture. Hughes published prolifically, including two exceptional jazz-related poetry collections, *Montage of a Dream Deferred* (1951) and *Ask Your Mama: 12 Moods for Jazz* (1961). Although several writers from the 1930s and forties made substantial contributions to jazz poetry—chiefly Sterling Brown and Melvin Tolson—Hughes' achievements outweigh the efforts of any other writer from the first half of the century.

The popularity of bebop generated a stunning number of jazz poems, particularly among Beat poets. In 1957, Lawrence Ferlinghetti and Kenneth Rexroth performed their work with a jazz band in San Francisco, spurring a series of live poetry-read-to-jazz performances and recordings by such writers as Kenneth Patchen and Jack Kerouac. Ultimately, most of the writers and musicians had great reservations about these performances, and the fad virtually died out by the end of that decade. Since then a number of poets—most notably Amiri Baraka (LeRoi Jones) and Jayne Cortez—have more successfully integrated their work with jazz musicians. The 1970s group the Last Poets fused poetry with black pop—and laid the groundwork for 1990s rap music and hip-hop.

Although poets have celebrated hundreds of jazz musicians, two saxophonists dominate the list: Charlie Parker and John Coltrane. Poets in the late 1950s—mainly white writers from the West Coast—repeatedly found inspiration in Parker's artistic innovations as well as his self-destructive lifestyle. Many of these homages conferred a godlike status on Parker and, in doing so, lost the humanity of the man; against the barrage of bad verse, Bob Kaufman worked diligently to make words sound like jazz and best captured some of Parker's magnetism. In the late sixties, African American poets began to identify Coltrane's music with the black civil-rights movement. Major voices from that time—including Don L. Lee (Haki Madhubuti), Baraka, Sonia Sanchez, and Larry Neal—invoked Coltrane's sound as a direct political commentary on race.

Compared to the work from the 1950s and sixties, jazz poems after 1970 were rather quiet in tone and strongly narrative, but the number of jazz poems rose exponentially. Some of the major voices included Al Young, Hayden Carruth, Sherley Anne Williams, Akua Lezli Hope, Yusef Komunyakaa, and William Matthews. The growing volume of activity—combined with increasing critical interest in jazz-related literature after 1990—suggests that poets will continue to explore the unlimited associations between poetry and jazz as long as the music survives.
—Sascha Feinstein

Lawrence Ferlinghetti reading poetry with jazz accompaniment at The Cellar, San Francisco, 1957.

Beyond the Cool

The Modern Jazz Quartet, which was based in New York, made many of the same inroads with college and concert-hall listeners. The MJQ had originated as the rhythm section in Dizzy Gillespie's 1946 big band, where it comprised pianist John Lewis, vibraharpist Milt Jackson, bassist Ray Brown, and drummer Kenny Clarke. Shortly after it began performing as a unit in 1952, with Percy Heath in place of Brown and (beginning in 1955) Connie Kay in place of Clarke, the MJQ cultivated a veneer of chamber-music propriety in such recordings as *Vendome* (1952), *Django* (1954), and *Milano* (1954). The members often appeared in tuxedos and played compositions that recalled Baroque fugues. Yet the jazz bona fides of Jackson, one of the music's most exceptional blues and ballad players, and the rest of the MJQ could not be denied. They were cool-jazz modernists forthright enough in their playing to also connect with the hard-bop style that emerged around the time of Charlie Parker's death.

This cool/hard dichotomy was increasingly the rule as jazz continued to evolve. In this regard, no musician exemplifies the frustrations of drawing stylistic boundaries more vividly than Miles Davis. First an important member of the Parker quintet, then the harbinger of cool with his nine-piece band, Davis also laid the groundwork for the bluesy, percussion-driven hard-bop style in *Dig, Walkin'*, and other studio recordings he made for Prestige and Blue Note in the early 1950s. These investigations of a more assertive and emotional style would hardly exhaust the trumpeter's curiosity or temper the innovations he went on to introduce in subsequent periods. More than any of his peers, more than even his mentors Parker and Gillespie, Davis demonstrated that, as modern jazz came of age, it remained a miraculous engine for change.

The Modern Jazz Quartet (clockwise from upper left): Connie Kay, John Lewis, Milt Jackson, and Percy Heath.

Key Recordings

The Birth of Bebop. Two discs, Charly (UK). A survey of the swing-to-bop transition. Disc one is particularly valuable for including such transitional figures as Charlie Christian, Jimmie Blanton (with Duke Ellington), and Roy Eldridge along with the Billy Eckstine Band and Coleman Hawkins.

Davis, Miles. *The Complete Birth of the Cool.* Capitol. This 1998 release contains all twelve studio recordings made by the historic Davis Nonet in 1949–50, featuring Lee Konitz, Gerry Mulligan, John Lewis, and the writing of Gil Evans and John Carisi. In addition, an equal number of tracks are airchecks from the band's only public appearance, at the Royal Roost, New York, in 1948.

Gillespie, Dizzy. *The Complete RCA Victor Recordings.* Two discs, RCA/Bluebird. The emphasis is on the Gillespie big band, with such 1947–49 watersheds as *Manteca, Cool Breeze, Two Bass Hit, Cubana Be,* and *Cubana Bop.* But the collection also includes 1946 combo versions of the bebop classics *Night in Tunisia* and *Anthropology,* examples of a young Gillespie as a sideman with Teddy Hill and Lionel Hampton, and a 1949 All-Stars session with Miles Davis and Fats Navarro sharing trumpet duties alongside Charlie Parker and Lennie Tristano.

Modern Jazz Quartet. *Fontessa.* Atlantic. Recorded in 1956, after drummer Connie Kay had replaced original member Kenny Clarke, this program captures all of the MJQ's strengths: the fugue *Versailles* and the classically inspired title suite, the strong ballad (*Angel Eyes, Over the Rainbow*) and blues (*Bluesology*) playing of vibist Milt Jackson, and a nod to the group's bebop roots on Dizzy Gillespie's *Woody 'n' You.*

Monk, Thelonious. *The Complete Blue Note Recordings.* Four discs, Blue Note. Three of these discs document Monk's first six sessions as a leader, taped between 1947 and '52 and featuring nearly two dozen of his classic compositions (*'Round Midnight; Ruby, My Dear; Straight, No Chaser; Well, You Needn't*). There are also 1957–58 recordings of Monk in the company of Sonny Rollins and John Coltrane.

The Gerry Mulligan Quartet with Chet Baker. *The Complete Pacific Jazz Recordings.* Four discs, Pacific Jazz. Two discs of the 1952–53 performances by the original pianoless quartet playing such Mulligan classics as *Walkin' Shoes, Five Brothers,* and *Motel;* a disc of collaborations that includes historic 1953 recordings with Lee Konitz; and an entertaining though less momentous 1957 Mulligan/Baker reunion.

Navarro, Fats, and Tadd Dameron. *The Complete Blue Note and Capitol Recordings.* Two discs, Blue Note. Bud Powell's quintet session with Navarro (see below) is duplicated in this collection, but the first disc focuses on thirteen beautiful Tadd Dameron compositions, with the composer/pianist joined by either Navarro or Miles Davis as featured trumpeter. Disc two also includes a Navarro–Howard McGhee trumpet summit and a track in which Navarro is heard with Benny Goodman.

Parker, Charlie. *Yardbird Suite.* Two discs, Rhino. The only Charlie Parker anthology to contain recordings from the Savoy, Dial, and Clef/Norgran labels. Classics from Parker's 1945–52 prime, including *Now's the Time, Ko Ko, Ornithology, Donna Lee, Parker's Mood, Star Eyes, Just Friends*—thirty-eight titles in all.

Powell, Bud. *The Complete Blue Note and Roost Recordings.* Four discs, Blue Note. Half of this collection reaches beyond the scope of this chapter and covers 1957–63, but the first two discs have the pianist in his prime, in sensational trio performances from 1947–53 and sessions recorded by his 1949 quintet with Fats Navarro and Sonny Rollins. *Dance of the Infidels, Bouncing with Bud, Parisian Thoroughfare,* and *Un Poco Loco* are among the classic tracks.

Tristano, Lennie, and Warne Marsh. *Intuition.* Capitol. The historic 1949 session in which pianist Tristano, tenor saxophonist Marsh, and alto saxophonist Lee Konitz provided the definitive examples of the Tristano concept, as well as two totally improvised performances. A 1956 album by Marsh completes the collection and shows how his disciples sustained these ideas after Tristano had shifted his focus to teaching. —*Bob Blumenthal*

Mainstream Jazz

Neil Tesser

The Dave Brubeck Quartet (from left to right):
Paul Desmond (alto saxophone), Joe Dodge (drums),
Dave Brubeck (piano), and Ron Crotty (bass).

The innovations of bebop—at first considered radical—eventually became jazz conventions. And as a growing number of up-and-coming players built on and reacted to those conventions, jazz entered what is perhaps its best-known phase.

It was a time of maturation, a period in which jazz became firmly established and widely embraced as a distinct, deeply developed musical idiom.

And it was a time dominated by jazz "giants"—musicians whose names even a casual observer of jazz history can't fail to recognize. Art Blakey, John Coltrane, Bill Evans, Herbie Hancock, Charles Mingus, the Modern Jazz Quartet, Thelonious Monk, Wes Montgomery, and Horace Silver are just a few of the players who either emerged or reached the peak of their artistry during the 1950s and sixties and whose influence—and many of whose careers—stretched to the century's end and beyond.

It's as difficult to imagine one stylistic description applying to all these musicians as it is to imagine a jazz world without any of them. Nonetheless, much of the music recorded during these years is now identified as "mainstream" jazz. The term emerged in the mid-1950s, and it came to embody the lyrical, cleanly structured music that predominated during that decade and remained central to the jazz experience through the remainder of the century. Within the mainstream, however, surged a number of musical currents—from cool jazz to hard bop and including such offshoots as chamber jazz and modal jazz—that were set in motion by the galvanic impact of bebop.

Miles Ahead

Miles Davis, more than any other single musician, dominated the mainstream era. Although Davis had made his initial reputation working with Charlie Parker, not until the 1950s did he emerge as an innovator of enormous impact. It was during this period that he first evidenced the ability to synthesize emerging jazz sounds into coherent styles that others would embrace as new movements—an ability that would ultimately make Davis the most

Miles Davis, whose influence dominated jazz in the second half of the century.

important jazz figure in the second half of the twentieth century, in the minds of many.

Davis sometimes seemed to be doing it all with mirrors. On such tunes as *All of You* and *My Funny Valentine* (both first recorded in 1956, then burnished in repeated performances through the mid-1960s), Davis played introspective solos in a vulnerable, diffident trumpet voice, which boasted virtually none of bebop's trademark fireworks and clever one-upsmanship. Old-school trumpeters derided his technique, but Davis's style became the template for jazz expression among musicians and audiences for the next twenty years. The bands he assembled were small miracles: many of his musicians would brilliantly execute his concepts, exceeding what anyone expected of them, before going off on their own. Many never made music of the same quality again. Davis himself wrote relatively few songs, but time after time his recording of an old standard or a modern jazz tune became the definitive one, emulated by his contemporaries and successors. (Good examples include the Davis Quintet's 1956 versions of *Bye Bye Blackbird* and *'Round Midnight*.) And no jazz sound could have better mirrored the existentialist philosophy coloring Western society in the 1950s than Davis's lonely, emotionally naked sorties.

Davis often turned his back on his audience or left the bandstand entirely when not soloing (a practice immortalized in singer Eddie Jefferson's lyrics to one of Davis's best-known recordings, the 1959 track *So What*). And he turned his back on jazz entirely as the 1950s began, dropping out of sight and sound for the better part of two years to overcome the heroin habit he'd learned from Parker. But even in absentia, Davis wielded influence: the "cool school" inspired by his nonet recordings became the "new sound of jazz." By the time Davis returned to the scene in 1953, "cool" had begun seeping up from the jazz underground to become the primary concern of American art, from film to fashion to literature to theater. From 1954 on, Davis's bands would brilliantly capture the hard-bop style, but his own trumpet work never abandoned the hooded stance that characterized cool jazz.

The Birth of Hard Bop

In the words of author Joe Goldberg, the cool breezes from the Pacific "went largely unnoticed by musicians in the East, except as an irritant." The cool school had offered its reaction to bebop, but in New York, Chicago, Philadelphia, and Detroit, the jazz of the 1950s derived primarily from bebop to become the style dubbed hard bop.

While such Miles Davis recordings as *Four* (1954) and *Walkin'* (1954) suggest the arrival of hard bop, the real parents were drummer Art Blakey and pianist Horace Silver. In the autumn of 1954, the two formed a cooperative quintet, the Jazz Messengers, and in 1955 they

Two fathers of hard bop: Horace Silver (lower left), the composer of numerous jazz standards, and Art Blakey (below), who nurtured upcoming talent in the long-running band the Jazz Messengers.

Art Blakey's 1958 release Moanin' *contained Bobby Timmons'* memorable title composition.

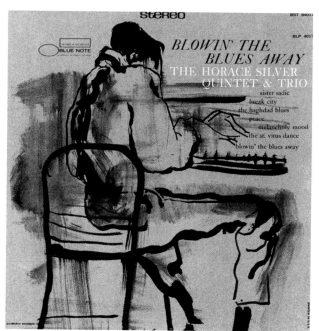

Blues-laced bop permeated Horace Silver's sound; Blowin' the Blues Away (1959) *included the ballad* Peace, *a later standard.*

recorded a jubilee shout in the form of the sixteen-bar blues *The Preacher,* composed by Silver: as Goldberg put it, "The reaction to the reaction had taken place." To be sure, the hard boppers were responding to cool's constraints with their explosive emotionalism. But they were also reacting to the calcifications of bebop.

The hard-bop musicians used much the same vocabulary and grammar as bebop, but they turned the language to somewhat different ends to suit the demands of a new decade. They relaxed the tempos that had often made bebop a breathtaking steeplechase, and they simplified the knotty melodies that had delighted Parker and Dizzy Gillespie. In so doing, the hard-bop players brought back an earthy soulfulness that had receded during the boppers' quest for more "serious" recognition.

This soulfulness had its roots in the ecstasy of church and gospel music, which provided the first listening experience for many black musicians, and which permeates such hard-bop classics as pianist Bobby Timmons' *Moanin',* recorded by the Jazz Messengers in 1958, and keyboardist Joe Zawinul's *Mercy, Mercy, Mercy,* recorded by Cannonball Adderley in 1966. The hard-bop players dug even deeper into the blues than had their bebop predecessors, and minor-key melodies—such as Silver's *Señor Blues* (1956) and cornetist Nat Adderley's *Work Song* (1960)—became increasingly popular. The hard boppers also made use of the new long-playing record format to stretch out on extended solos, and the most important players went further still: they saw in the LP a chance to reconceive the jazz solo as a vehicle for large-scale thematic development.

The most important hard-bop bands all developed under the guidance of bebop veterans: Davis, Blakey, drummer Max Roach, and Silver. In 1956, Silver left the Jazz Messengers to form a quintet concentrating on his own remarkable compositions. Many of these, such as *Doodlin'* (1955), *Nica's Dream* (1956), *Sister Sadie* (1959), and *Song for My Father* (1964), have entrenched themselves in the mainstream repertoire. Meanwhile, Blakey assumed full command of the Jazz Messengers after Silver's departure and proved himself a brilliant leader. The band epitomized hard bop until Blakey's death in 1990; the Messengers became jazz's answer to the Naval Academy, training a steady parade of new recruits to navigate the mainstream as leaders in their own right. The list of prominent Blakey alumni includes (but hardly stops at) trumpeters Lee Morgan, Freddie Hubbard, Woody Shaw, and Wynton Marsalis; saxophonists Hank Mobley, Jackie McLean, Johnny Griffin, Wayne Shorter, and Donald Harrison; and pianists Bobby Timmons, Cedar Walton, Joanne Brackeen, and Mulgrew Miller.

Nonetheless, the most brilliant of the hard-bop bands was the one that bore the closest resemblance to bebop's fire. In 1954, Roach enlisted the startling young trumpeter Clifford Brown, creating one of the most respected

New York Nights

"It was the same every night when we were closing at 4 a.m.," recalled Max Gordon, owner of the venerable Village Vanguard club in New York City. "There were always a few insomniacs and night prowlers left in the place who never wanted to go home."

Chances are, those night owls were still buzzing from the energy of a set by John Coltrane or Miles Davis or Sonny Rollins: the Vanguard, from the 1950s on, was the leading small venue for jazz, launching many an illustrious career and sustaining others that were already aloft. Jazz front-liners from Charles Mingus to Thelonious Monk regularly played there, and some immortalized the stints on LPs (notably Bill Evans' *Sunday at the Village Vanguard*, 1961, and several by Coltrane). Even Monday nights—typically off-nights in the club world—drew crowds, thanks to weekly sets by the Thad Jones–Mel Lewis Orchestra.

The Vanguard was smack in the middle of Greenwich Village, itself a focal point of live jazz following the demise of the 52nd Street nightclub strip in the late 1940s. The emergence of jazz in the Village reflected the growing interest in and identification with the music among college students, artists, and other members of the culturati drawn to that neobohemian neighborhood.

Other downtown clubs that nurtured the latest jazz styles included the Five Spot, which booked such forward-looking players as Cecil Taylor and Ornette Coleman for lengthy residencies that helped their music develop; the Half Note, for nearly twenty years a host to the likes of Charles Mingus, Lennie Tristano, and Coltrane; Slug's saloon on East 3rd Street, where hard bop thrived in the hands of such proponents as Art Blakey, Lee Morgan, and Freddie Hubbard (and where Morgan was shot dead by his mistress on the night of February 19, 1972); and the Village Gate on Bleecker Street, another home of hard bop—and, like the Vanguard, a favored location for live recording sessions. Further uptown, at 1678 Broadway, the post-boppers could get a hearing at Birdland—a club named after their patron saint, Charlie "Bird" Parker.

But more traditional sounds also had their New York show spots, in both the Village and other parts of town. In the mid-1960s, such established stars as Sarah Vaughan, Louis Armstrong, Count Basie, and Lionel Hampton would occasionally take their acts to Basin Street East on 48th Street, and swing veterans Red Allen, Coleman Hawkins, and Roy Eldridge could sometimes be heard at the Metropole, on the western end of that same street. Meanwhile, Dixieland jazz enjoyed an extended life at Nick's, located on Seventh Avenue in the heart of the Village.

Jazz may have livened up Boston, Chicago, Los Angeles, San Francisco, and other locales in the 1950s and sixties. But the surging energy of New York made that town—and still makes the town—the jazz capital of the world. —*Tad Lathrop*

Trumpeter Clifford Brown (right) and drummer Max Roach (below) partnered in the Brown-Roach Quintet, one of the most influential hard-bop bands.

©Herman Leonard

partnerships in jazz history. (It was also one of the shortest lived: thirty months later, Brown died in a car crash that also killed the band's pianist, Bud Powell's younger brother Richie.) "Brownie" played with a honeyed tone, a sunny and exquisite lyricism, and a precision that challenged and at times eclipsed even the virtuosity of his idols, Dizzy Gillespie and Fats Navarro. Roach thought enough of Brown to grant him co-star status, and the Clifford Brown–Max Roach Quintet, with West Coast tenorman Harold Land, achieved overnight success with a sound typified by their take-no-prisoners romp on the bop favorite *Cherokee* (1955). The precocious genius Sonny Rollins replaced Land at the end of 1955, and for the next six months—until Brown's death—this band was fueled by the highest-octane front line in jazz.

Before joining the Brown-Roach Quintet, Rollins had participated in several memorable sessions led by Miles Davis, which produced the first recordings of the classic Rollins tunes *Airegin, Oleo,* and *Doxy* (all 1954). When Davis prepared to form his own hard-bop band in 1955, he thought immediately of the tall, contemplative tenorist, whose playing had already begun to turn heads. But Rollins was unavailable, off in Chicago on the first of three celebrated hiatuses, so Davis turned instead to a relatively obscure saxophonist from Philadelphia, John Coltrane.

Their yin-yang collaboration—with Davis's progressively simpler solos set in bas-relief against Trane's increasingly complicated chromaticism—made this the most influential group of its time. With an unimpeachable rhythm section anchored by bassist Paul Chambers and drummer "Philly" Joe Jones, Davis turned out a series of album masterpieces (*Workin'*, 1956; *'Round About Midnight*, 1955–56; and *Milestones*, 1958) that exemplified the hard-bop style—and transcended it. For in the midst of this decidedly hard-bop landscape stood the distinctly cool figure of Davis himself, turning the band into a bridge between the decade's two prevalent jazz idioms.

West-Coast Bop

Although California was a hotbed of cool jazz, it also supported important musicians who had little to do with the style. But many of these musicians didn't fit the East Coast hard-bop mold, either. Some of them—such as pianist Sonny Clark, trumpeter and flugelhornist Art Farmer, Charles Mingus, tenor saxophonist Teddy Edwards, and drummer Shelly Manne—managed to consolidate key virtues of both schools: Clark, for instance, recorded with the cool-oriented Lighthouse All-Stars before moving to New York, where he worked with Sonny Rollins and led some of the era's most representative hard-bop dates (such as *Cool Struttin'*, 1958).

Other West Coasters—most notably pianist Hampton Hawes and the alto saxophonists Art Pepper and Sonny Criss—concocted a potent version of bebop. This music contrasted sharply with that of their cool compatriots,

Mainstream Jazz Standards

In the 1950s and 1960s, the body of jazz standards mushroomed, giving musicians more choices than ever before. Mainstream standards came from the same kinds of sources as those of the bebop era. Many were contrafacts (tunes based on the chord progressions of other songs)—for example, Horace Silver's *Quicksilver* (1956), based on Sigmund Romberg's *Lover Come Back to Me* (1928); George Russell's *Ezz-thetic* (1961), based on Cole Porter's *Love for Sale* (1930); and Sonny Rollins' *Oleo* (1954), based on George Gershwin's *I Got Rhythm* (1930). A number were blues, such as Thelonious Monk's *Straight, No Chaser* (1951) and Milt Jackson's *Bag's Groove* (1954). Others were pop-song standards, such as *Bye Bye Blackbird* (1926), *Mack the Knife* (1928), *April in Paris* (1932), *Stella by Starlight* (1946), and *Autumn Leaves* (1955). And many more were jazz originals, including Clifford Brown's *Joy Spring* (1954), Benny Golson's *Stablemates* (1955), Eddie "Cleanhead" Vinson's *Tune Up* (1956), Sidney Bechet's *Petit Fleur* (1959), Oliver Nelson's *Stolen Moments* (1961), and Thad Jones' beautiful ballad *A Child Is Born* (1969).

As might be expected, the most dramatic innovations in harmony, form, and rhythm occurred in the category of jazz originals. Harmonically, the mainstream era brought in the use of modes—that is, variations on standard major and minor scales. Form in mainstream pieces became increasingly complex, asymmetrical, and in variance from common song structures. Rhythm became a focal point, as composers increasingly employed meters other than the conventional 4/4, as in Paul Desmond's hugely popular *Take Five* (1961) in 5/4, Toots Thielemans' *Bluesette* (1963) in 3/4, and Charles Mingus's sanctified *Better Git Hit in Your Soul* (1959) in 12/8. A captivating calypso rhythm provides the pulse in Sonny Rollins' *St. Thomas* (1956), a simple but trendsetting piece that opened the door for many imitations.

In part due to its use of modes, Miles Davis's album *Kind of Blue* (1959) was a seminal recording, and *All Blues* and *So What* became its most-played compositions. Musicians also took to Davis's *Milestones* and *Nardis* (both 1958).

John Coltrane's gentle *Naima* (1959) became a perennial among musicians, while his *Giant Steps* and *Countdown* (from the album *Giant Steps*, 1959), were built on frequent shifts of keys that presented new challenges to improvisers and would prove influential.

Pianist Herbie Hancock popularized his *Maiden Voyage* (1964) from the album of the same name—a modal composition using four chords and related scales and employing a rhythmic/harmonic ostinato throughout the entire recording.

Horace Silver's *Nica's Dream* (1956), one of the great jazz compositions, also utilizes a repeating rhythmic figure throughout the solos, and it alternates sections in Latin and swing rhythms. Silver's *Song for My Father* (1964) became his most famous composition, played with great frequency by professional and student musicians alike.

Work Song (1960) and *Jive Samba* (1962) by Nat Adderley are among the most famous of the gospel- and funk-influenced compositions of jazz. Two other notable church- and roots-influenced pieces—Bobby Timmons' *Moanin'* (1959) and Herbie Hancock's *Watermelon Man* (1962)—also joined the rank of jazz standards from this era.

Count Basie's revamped band of the 1950s popularized a handful of tunes among musicians—Neal Hefti's *Cute* and *Li'l Darlin'* (both 1958), Frank Foster's *Shiny Stockings* (1956), and Peter Chatman's *Every Day I Have the Blues* (1950).

The Brazilian songwriter Antonio Carlos Jobim contributed several lilting standards to the jazz repertory—*Girl from Ipanema* (1964), *Wave* (1967), and *How Insensitive* (1963). Also in the bossa nova beat were Luiz Bonfá's *Manha de Carnaval* (1959), Clare Fischer's *Pensativa* (1962), and Kenny Dorham's *Blue Bossa* (1963), while Mongo Santamaria's *Afro Blue* (1958) fell into an Afro-Cuban groove.

Johnny Mandel's pop successes *The Shadow of Your Smile* (1965) and *Emily* (1964) were appreciated by jazz musicians. Finally, Bill Evans' *Waltz for Debby* (1964) found a place with pianists, while the ballads *When Sunny Gets Blue* (1956) and *Spring Can Really Hang You Up the Most* (1955) were favorites among singers.
—David Baker

Miles Davis's versions of songs were often embraced as definitive.

Breaks and Fours

Jazz musicians have developed a number of common practices; two of the best known are breaks and fours. Both provide contrast and drama and allow the soloists to show off.

A *break* is a short solo passage by a single instrument or group of instruments—or, less commonly, a short period of complete silence. During a break the rhythm section lays out, but the meter, tempo, and beat remain intact and are ongoing. Breaks usually occur at the ends of sections, especially in the final phrase of a blues or a multi-strain composition.

The break serves a number of purposes: providing the soloist with a springboard into a solo; briefly changing the texture, which is typically otherwise constant; serving as a structural device to herald the next solo; and creating tension and excitement leading to the beginning of a new section. Breaks were found frequently in early jazz, and Jelly Roll Morton used them brilliantly in such recordings as *Black Bottom Stomp* and *Grandpa's Spells* (both 1926). By the 1940s, breaks had become less common, but Charlie Parker took a memorable one to set up his solo on his Dial recording of *Night in Tunisia* (1946).

Other modern instances of breaks include John Coltrane's *Locomotion* (1957) and Stan Getz's *Night and Day* (1964).

Another venerable tradition in jazz performance is that of soloists' trading improvised phrases. Exchanging phrases of four measures is called *playing fours, trading fours,* or simply *fours,* while alternating phrases of eight bars is called *eights,* and so on. The length of these phrases is usually some equal subdivision of the tune's form. In playing a twelve-bar blues, musicians could exchange complete *twelves,* two *sixes,* three *fours,* or four *threes.* In a thirty-two-bar form, the phrases might be two, four, eight, or sixteen measures in length.

These exchanges most often follow a round of extended solos, affording the soloists space to build on what the previous soloists have played, revisit their own improvisational ideas, engage in friendly musical combat, and collect their thoughts between cyclical occurrences. The exchanges occur in a number of different settings, often between a solo instrumentalist and a drummer. They also frequently take place in a "round robin" of two or three instrumentalists in a small group setting, whereby a competition of improvisation ensues: for example, Dexter Gordon and Wardell Gray on *The Chase* (1947), Johnny Griffin and Eddie "Lockjaw" Davis on *Blues Up and Down* (1961), and trombonists J. J. Johnson and Kai Winding on *It's All Right with Me* (1976). Sometimes a number of like instruments trade phrases, as the saxophones do on Woody Herman's *Four Brothers* (1947).

Trading phrases—quite common in jam sessions—gives participants opportunities to express their personalities through concise statements.
—*David Baker*

Big-band drummer Buddy Rich (shown here in 1954) demonstrated dazzling technique when trading fours or taking long solos.

© Herman Leonard

but it also differed from hard bop, which offered a somewhat relaxed adaptation of bop's frenzy; listening to the aptly named Pepper on such tracks as *Surf Ride* (featuring Hawes, from 1952) and the supersonic *Straight Life* (1954), most people have trouble believing the sessions took place anywhere near the Pacific Ocean. On the other hand, Pepper utilized certain "West Coast" devices to great effect, most notably the studied counterpoint that distinguished the quartet of baritone saxophonist Gerry Mulligan. But Pepper played it hot instead of cool: that same recording of *Straight Life* boasts a fast and furious bit of two-part invention for Pepper and tenor saxophonist Jack Montrose.

Pepper blurred the line further with *Art Pepper Meets the Rhythm Section,* the widely respected 1957 album on which he partnered with perhaps the finest trio unit in jazz—the rhythm section from the Miles Davis Quintet (pianist Red Garland, bassist Paul Chambers, and drummer "Philly" Joe Jones). By this time Pepper had arrived at one of the most compelling styles of the decade, a personal and deeply felt compendium of bebop, cool, California, and New York. A similar description would apply to pianist Hawes, who—on the albums *Hampton Hawes Trio* (1955) and *Four* (1958)—proved himself one of the few pianists able to capture not only the virtuosity but also "the scorching intensity of Bud Powell's pianism," as Ted Gioia put it. "He was, in his own words, the man with the 105-degree fever." Both Hawes (who died in 1977) and Pepper (d. 1982) fought substance-abuse problems their entire adult lives.

Other than the members of Brubeck's and Mulligan's bands, the best-known West Coast jazzmen belonged at one time or another to the Lighthouse All-Stars, a loose-knit amalgam of players associated with the club called the Lighthouse. Just south of Los Angeles in Hermosa Beach, the Lighthouse was a restaurant down on its luck in 1949, when bassist Howard Rumsey convinced the owner to institute Sunday jam sessions. These sessions often displayed the bristling energy associated with hard bop on the opposite coast; nonetheless, as the schedule expanded to every night of the week, the Lighthouse emerged as headquarters for such important cool-jazz musicians as Shelly Manne and saxophonist Bud Shank, who led innovative groups that balanced composition with improvisation. Soon the club and its "house band," the Lighthouse All-Stars—which at various times included Shank, Manne, pianist Claude Williamson, tenor saxophonists Bob Cooper and Bill Perkins, and brass men Conte Candoli, Shorty Rogers, Frank Rosolino, and Jack Sheldon—came to embody West Coast jazz to most listeners.

Meanwhile, the cool trumpet voice of Chet Baker, one of the original West Coast stars, began a fadeout into the jazz background. Drugs took their toll on him, as they had on Pepper and Hawes.

Art Pepper's Smack Up *(1960) capped a decade in which he emerged as an important purveyor of West Coast bop.*

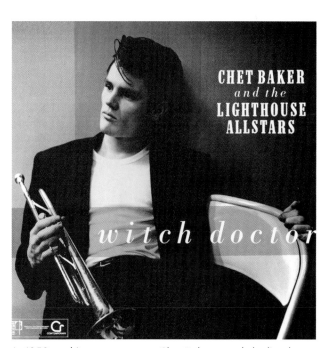

In 1953, cool-jazz trumpet star Chet Baker recorded a live date with the Lighthouse All-Stars, among whom, at the time, were saxophonists Jimmy Giuffre and Bud Shank, bassist Howard Rumsey, and drummer Max Roach.

Three Tenor Torchbearers:
Gordon, Rollins, and Coltrane

The 1950s produced a number of important alto saxophonists—among them Cannonball Adderley, Jackie McLean, and Phil Woods. But the virtuosic genius of Charlie Parker remained an unmatchable benchmark for most alto players, so the spotlight shifted to the tenor sax. The sound of bebop had belonged to trumpet and alto; the sound of hard bop was the tougher, more full-bodied sound of trumpet and tenor. In retrospect, the Sonny Rollins title *Tenor Madness* (1956), which paired Rollins with John Coltrane, could well describe the entire decade.

Both Rollins and Coltrane owed a huge debt to Dexter Gordon, the first important bebop tenorist, whose adaptability made him a vital voice in hard bop as well. Gordon fused the two streams of earlier jazz tenor playing, combining the huge sound and harmonic ingenuity of Coleman Hawkins with the light vibrato and quixotic grace of Lester Young; he also expanded upon Young's narrative abilities, playing solos that almost unfailingly told a story. (Excellent examples include *It's You or No One* from the Blue Note album *Doin' Allright*, 1961, and his solo on Herbie Hancock's famous *Watermelon Man*, 1962.) Gordon's style fed two new streams, represented by Rollins and Coltrane, which then provided the primary inspiration for the next generation or three of jazz saxophonists.

Sonny Rollins (right) playing with his early role model Coleman Hawkins, 1963.

Lee Tanner

Although he was four years younger than Coltrane, it was Rollins who first grabbed the attention of jazz cognoscenti, including Davis: in the section of Harlem in which he'd grown up, his neighbors included such towering figures as Hawkins, Monk, and Bud Powell, all of whom encouraged his interest in jazz. (As a teen, Rollins would wait on Hawkins' doorstep for the chance to see his first idol.) Rollins' first recordings with Powell in 1949—especially *Wail* and *Dance of the Infidels*—showed a youngster still mastering bebop's complexities but already possessing a distinct sound and innovative ideas. Before long, the intense young saxophonist had arrived at a style of unusually cogent thematic development, heard on such tunes as *I'll Remember April* (1956) with the Brown-Roach Quintet. Rollins' best improvisations—heard throughout the albums *Saxophone Colossus* (1956), *Sonny Rollins* (1957), *A Night at the Village Vanguard* (1956), and *The Bridge*

(1962)—gracefully unfolded across multiple choruses. His solos sounded like spontaneous compositions rather than a series of fragments strung between harmonic signposts, and they set a new standard for jazz improvisation.

Coltrane's solos, on the other hand, seemed to burst directly from the horn rather than the head, even though they grew from his deep study of modern harmony; his first professional experience came in rhythm-and-blues bands, and the soulful passion of that music remained with him during his short life (he died in 1967, at the age of forty). Playing with Davis, Coltrane garnered a huge audience for his hell-for-leather style, which featured cyclonic, note-filled solos informed by a relentless appetite for harmonic permutations. Coltrane's albums with Davis, as well as his own *Blue Train* (1957) and *Soultrane* (1958), document the progression of his style, which became increasingly controversial: one reviewer criticized him as "anti-jazz," and Davis supposedly once told him, "Coltrane, you can't play everything at once!" The climax of these investigations came on his 1959 masterpiece, *Giant Steps*, the title track a tricky slalom of careening chords. Afterward, Coltrane set about assembling his own band, which by the end of 1961 had coalesced into his galvanic "classic quartet": McCoy Tyner (one of the period's most influential pianists), bassist Jimmy Garrison, and drummer Elvin Jones. The empathic interplay of the four reached a peak on *A Love Supreme* (1964).

The track *Tenor Madness* (also from *Saxophone Colossus*) is the only on-disc meeting of Rollins and Coltrane, and it remains the perfect starting place to compare and contrast their styles. Both men benefited from Monk's tutelage, and their work under his name—on *Brilliant Corners* (1956) and *Monk with Coltrane* (1957), respectively—further illuminates their different approaches. Coltrane's music altered in the 1960s, and he became an iconic figure of the jazz avant-garde. Rollins also made significant changes, but not until the 1970s, when he unveiled a technique that was bluesier and far less refined than his music of the fifties.

As for Dexter Gordon, his battle with narcotics addiction made him something of a shadow figure in the 1950s: he spent almost six years in jail and recorded only one album between 1951 and 1959. When he re-emerged in the 1960s, he showed that he had big enough ears to appreciate Coltrane and Rollins—and a small enough ego to adapt some of their innovations to his own style, as on *Both Sides of Midnight* (1967). This adaptability allowed Gordon to flourish throughout the 1960s and seventies, and as an "elder statesman" in the eighties, when he made his film debut in *Round Midnight* (and received an Academy Award nomination for best supporting actor).

John Coltrane's complex solos and compositions were the subjects of intense study by later jazz players.

Bop saxophonist Dexter Gordon released Our Man in Paris *in 1963, soon after beginning what would be a fourteen-year stay in Europe.*

Two Takes on the Piano

In the 1950s, most jazz fans would have considered Thelonious Monk and Dave Brubeck polar opposites—in the unlikely event that those two names even showed up in the same conversation. However, Monk and Brubeck played similar roles in their respective musical camps: that of the stubborn iconoclast, the exception that proves the rules. In his book *West Coast Jazz*, Ted Gioia offers a superb analysis of their unexpected similarities, pointing out that instead of the dominant fifties piano style, characterized by horn-like single-note lines and sparse chords, "Brubeck and Monk brought out the intrinsically pianistic and orchestral qualities of the instrument.... Both began adopting more complex harmonic structures than their peers.... Both emphasized (almost to an extreme) the percussive nature of the piano...and focused as much on composing as on playing." And although both men were active in the 1940s, Brubeck and Monk—the second and third jazz musicians to appear on the cover of *Time* magazine, after Louis Armstrong—really wrote their legacies during the fifties.

Brubeck's popularity grew at a steady clip, but he refused to coast on his success, or on the West Coast phenomenon he nominally represented. He continued to develop his classically influenced compositions and to challenge

Thelonious Monk, who had first earned notice as a bop innovator, reached his prime as a composer, bandleader, and one-of-a-kind piano player in the 1950s and sixties.

himself and his listeners with unusual meters. This process culminated in his landmark 1959 album *Time Out*, featuring the famous *Take Five* (written by his saxophonist, Paul Desmond). *Time Out* was the first jazz album to sell a million copies—even though it was almost shelved by its label, Columbia, which thought it too "radical" for the record-buying public.

On the other hand, Monk's success in the 1950s represented a return to grace, as the jazz public began to rediscover his quirky compositions and one-of-a-kind piano style. This resulted from a combination of factors. In 1955 a fledgling jazz label, Riverside, decided to "rehabilitate" Monk's image with two albums designed to show him as less "far out" than generally believed: *Thelonious Monk Plays Duke Ellington* and a standards date, *The Unique Thelonious Monk* (a redundant title if ever there was one). Subsequent albums such as *Monk's Music* (1957) proved his stature, with Monk leading groups that mingled respected veterans with fiery newcomers; meanwhile, a few other musicians (most notably soprano saxophonist Steve Lacy) began to revisit his deceptively simple, elegantly constructed compositions and proselytize for them. In 1957 Monk regained his New York City cabaret card and took up residence at the Five Spot club, leading a quartet that featured the skyrocketing Coltrane and propelling himself into the jazz limelight; in 1959, his compositions were arranged for nonet for a famous concert at Town Hall (released on disc as *The Thelonious Monk Orchestra at Town Hall*). By the early sixties, when Monk established his long-running quartet starring saxophonist Charlie Rouse, he was hailed as one of jazz's true geniuses. Monk tunes were still favorites decades later, having proved adaptable to a wide range of musical settings.

Down Beat and the Jazz Magazines

Jazz magazines come and go with dizzying frequency. More than three hundred jazz periodicals have been published in the United States and abroad, but most long ago ceased publication. At the end of jazz's first century, the best known included *Down Beat, Jazz Times,* and *Jazziz* (all in the United States); *Coda* (Canada); *Jazz Journal International* (United Kingdom); *Jazz magazine* and *Jazz hot* (France); *Orkester journalen* (Sweden); *Musica jazz* (Italy); and *Swing Journal* (Japan).

One of them, *Down Beat,* boasts a special place in jazz history. Of the English-language jazz magazines, it survived the longest: sixty-six years and counting by the turn of the century. And along the way—through jazz's roller-coaster ride through changing sonic landscapes and jumps and dips in popularity—it stayed on track as the magazine that U.S. fans and musicians thought of first when seeking jazz information.

With its record and concert reviews, interviews, readers' polls, and educational features, *Down Beat* not only supported the efforts of working musicians but also inspired new generations to follow in the footsteps of their musical heroes.

The magazine helped launch the careers of some leading jazz writers, among them Dan Morgenstern, Nat Hentoff, and Gary Giddins. It also invited musicians to submit commentary, and many—including Jelly Roll Morton, Duke Ellington, Marian McPartland, Kenny Dorham, and Ornette Coleman—took them up on it, with sometimes controversial results. *Down Beat* ultimately codified musician participation in a feature called the Blind-fold Test, in which musicians would listen to unidentified recordings and offer their critiques.

The magazine rose to popularity during the Swing Era, linking its fortunes with those of the big bands and players it advocated—including Duke Ellington, Benny Goodman, Woody Herman, and Jimmy Dorsey. When those fortunes began to sag, *Down Beat* was left seeking ways to maintain financial viability at a time when jazz—in its new bebop, cool, and experimental incarnations—was becoming a music of the devoted few rather than the general public.

Its answer, in part, was to focus on jazz education: by providing instructional articles, drawing attention to young talent in a "First Chorus" column, co-sponsoring instrumental clinics and music festivals, and conferring scholarships through its Student Music Awards, it would build its future readership. That approach took *Down Beat* into the 1960s and what some observers consider the magazine's heyday, as it was, to an extent, a heyday of mainstream jazz.

The arrival of the rock era and of magazines that chronicled its culture—*Rolling Stone,* for one—brought another turning point. With jazz eclipsed by the popularity of the Beatles, Jimi Hendrix, and other rock stars, the magazine faced the quandary of maintaining its strictly-jazz focus or branching out and covering the many other new popular styles. It chose the latter route, and its decision to do so reflected what many jazz musicians were doing: drawing from increasingly varied musical sources for creative fuel and inspiration. The magazine's broadened focus was but one more indicator of the growing pluralism—and resilience—of jazz itself.
—*Tad Lathrop and John Edward Hasse*

Soul Jazz

As the 1950s drew to a close, one hard-bop strain dominated all others. To be sure, the gospel-tinged but down-and-dirty sounds of "soul jazz"—simple, funky melodies, danceable rhythms, and plenty of the blues—had exerted a strong influence since the idiom took shape. But now, inspired by the successes of Horace Silver's group and the remarkable keyboardist Jimmy Smith, jazz players began turning out one album after another on which they sought to parlay "the funk" into commercial success.

No one had a more important hand in this process than Smith, the Philadelphia pianist who started to play the electric organ in 1951. By 1956 he had mastered his driving, slashing, sophisticated combination of bebop and rhythm and blues. And on his Blue Note Records debut, *A New Sound… A New Star* (volumes 1 and 2) and the follow-up *The Incredible Jimmy Smith*, all recorded in 1956, he established the model for the ultra-streamlined "organ trio" in jazz; it featured only a drummer, either a guitarist or saxophonist, and Smith himself, both hands and feet in constant motion on the organ's keyboards and pedals as he handled the chores of bassist, keyboard accompanist, and dynamic lead soloist. On subsequent albums, Smith was joined by a number of Blue Note hornmen in jam-session performances that fully exploited the new long-playing record format, with tracks that ran fifteen minutes or more.

Jazz and Religion

At first glance, jazz and religion may seem as incompatible as gambling and God. Indeed, early on, jazz and the blues were often denounced as "the devil's music," regarded as disreputable by middle-class blacks and whites alike. Such attitudes took many years to soften. But jazz and religion have been connected in a number of ways—even beyond the obvious link between certain musicians' tastes and their formative experiences hearing church singing.

Early New Orleans jazz musicians performed such religious songs as *Glory, Sing On*, and *Down by the Riverside*. Still, in 1938, Louis Armstrong raised some eyebrows when he made swinging recordings of *Bye and Bye, When the Saints Go Marching In*, and other Negro spirituals.

Some jazz composers went to the spiritual well for inspiration. Duke Ellington composed the ravishing *Come Sunday* for his epic *Black, Brown, and Beige* (1943) and, commissioned by San Francisco's Grace Cathedral, wrote the controversial *Concert of Sacred Music* (1965). Two other sacred concerts followed (1968, 1973).

Bassist-composer Charles Mingus, inspired in part by his mother's visits to Methodist and Holiness churches, wrote *Wednesday Night Prayer Meeting* (1958) and *Better Git Hit in Your Soul* (1959)—raucous, wailing pieces with hand-clapping, shouting, spontaneous bursts of emotion, and simultaneous improvisation. Gospel-influenced pieces such as Horace Silver's *The Preacher* (1955) and Cannonball Adderley's *Sermonette* (1956) echoed call-and-response patterns of down-home African American churches. Pianist Mary Lou Williams composed a cantata, *Black Christ of the Andes* (1963), and three masses, and Django Reinhardt and Lalo Schifrin each wrote a jazz mass.

John Coltrane, after experiencing a religious awakening in 1957, composed and recorded a number of spiritual works that included *Amen* and *Dear Lord* (both 1965) and the mighty *A Love Supreme* (1964). "God," he wrote, "is gracious and merciful. His way is in love.… truly—a love supreme."

Beyond specific religiously inspired pieces, many people found jazz meaningful on a deep, spiritual basis. Perhaps echoing the ancient African integration of music, dance, ritual, religion, and daily life, jazz's "mysterious power to evoke ecstasy" and transcendence, as scholar Neil Leonard observed, made it magical or sacred to countless participants. No wonder many jazz adherents maintain such deep allegiance to the music.
—*John Edward Hasse*

A similar format became a favorite of guitarist Kenny Burrell on such late-fifties "jam" albums as *All Day Long* (1957) and *Blue Lights* (1958). He had already worked on albums by Dizzy Gillespie, John Coltrane, and many of his colleagues from Detroit, which throughout the decade funneled jazz stars from its fertile, vibrant scene into New York's. Burrell's mellow tone and easygoing style made him a leading guitarist of the time; in 1959, and then again decades later, he hooked up with Smith on such exceptional Blue Note dates as *Home Cookin'* (1958–59) and *The Master* (1993).

Smith's organ trio showcased the electric guitar to a degree not often heard in earlier jazz, paving the way for the success enjoyed by two other guitarists, Wes Montgomery and Grant Green. In his hometown of Indianapolis, Montgomery formed a trio with his brothers Buddy and Monk, but before long his virtuosity resulted in an extraordinarily successful solo career, best represented by his Riverside album *The Incredible Jazz Guitar* (1960). Montgomery played with a deep, soulful swing that gave his melodies unusual propulsion, and he was the first guitarist to improvise in octaves, a startling technique that at first made listeners think he'd gone back to overdub his solos. In the mid-sixties, he became one of the most popular jazz performers due to a series of albums with orchestra that emphasized his flowing sound (but not his brilliant solo constructions), as well as a partnership with Jimmy Smith heard on *Jimmy & Wes: The Dynamic Duo* (1966). Green, meanwhile, came out of St. Louis with a ringing, shouting tone—tailor-made for soul jazz—and a powerfully direct style of soloing that placed him in great demand as a member of the Blue Note Records "stable": in 1961 alone, he served as either leader or sideman on nineteen different record sessions, most notably on *Green Street* (1961). These guitarists did much to make the instrument an increasingly strong presence in jazz during the sixties, paralleling the rise of guitar-driven rock.

Around 1960, soul jazz became the preferred description for this branch of hard-bop, after the term was applied to the recordings of alto saxophonist Cannonball Adderley. Adderley, a technically brilliant and emotionally dynamic player, sported a brimming, almost fulsome tone and an impressive bag of expressive tricks. He and his younger brother, cornetist Nat, had moved in 1955 from their native Florida to New York, where jazz aficionados quickly discovered the white-hot talent beneath Cannonball's heavy drawl and country manner. After leaving Miles Davis's band in 1960, Cannonball founded a quintet with his brother; it also starred a noted Jazz Messengers alumnus in pianist and composer Bobby Timmons, and it quickly emerged as the most popular band on the hard-bop scene.

Kenny Burrell's precision, taste, and warm tone embodied mainstream jazz guitar.

Lee Tanner

Wes Montgomery, one of the most significant and influential jazz guitarists, infused bop-blues phrasing with swinging energy.

Coast to Coast *packaged live soul-jazz sets from 1959 and 1962—dates that paired Cannonball Adderley (left) with his brother Nat (right) and such others as Joe Zawinul, Bobby Timmons, and Yusef Lateef.*

Prime examples of Adderley's soul jazz are present on the retrospective album *Phenix* (1975).

Even musicians whose main interests lay elsewhere—the progressive Charles Mingus, the darkly emotional alto saxophonist Jackie McLean, and Lee Morgan (a tough and even menacing presence on trumpet)—recorded famous examples of soul jazz. These include Mingus's *Better Git Hit in Your Soul* (1959), McLean's *Appointment in Ghana* (1960), and Morgan's *The Sidewinder* (1964).

Morgan and Freddie Hubbard (his successor on trumpet in the Jazz Messengers) both came naturally to this idiom, having played a fair amount of "the funk" with Blakey. And both were able to transcend the rapidly accumulating soul-jazz clichés to create rich and lasting albums, including Morgan's *Search for the New Land* (1964), Hubbard's *Ready for Freddie* (1961) and *Breaking Point* (1964), and their 1965 face-off, the aptly titled *Night of the Cookers*.

Many of these albums starred pianist Herbie Hancock, for whom soul jazz held the greatest value. A child prodigy who performed with the Chicago Symphony at the age of twelve, Hancock was a vital member of Miles Davis's progressive 1960s quintet. But on his own, Hancock showed a penchant for soul jazz, beginning with his Blue Note debut, *Takin' Off* (1962), an album that included *Watermelon Man*, which became a funk standard. A prolific and important composer, Hancock hit his stride on the 1965 album *Maiden Voyage*, a jazz exploration of the ocean's mysteries that remains a mainstream milestone.

Soul jazz made dozens of converts, moving mainstream jazz further toward funk (and recapturing some of the audience that had turned to rock and roll). Pioneers and newcomers alike rubbed shoulders in the recording studios of Blue Note, Prestige, and Atlantic Records. Soul jazz even found its way into the relatively few big bands that established themselves during the 1960s as descendants of engines that powered the Swing Era.

In this sector, two important figures rose above the rest. Trumpeter and composer-arranger Thad Jones built upon his experience in the Count Basie Orchestra to add soul jazz to the big-band repertoire; the Thad Jones–Mel Lewis Orchestra, which began as a Monday night "rehearsal band" at New York's Village Vanguard, eventually set the standard for modern big-band power. And saxophonist Oliver Nelson, who had worked for jump-band leader Louis Jordan in the early 1950s, offered imaginatively soulful renditions of his own tunes, notably on the album *The Blues and the Abstract Truth* (1961)—a perennial favorite led by its centerpiece, *Stolen Moments*.

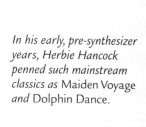

In his early, pre-synthesizer years, Herbie Hancock penned such mainstream classics as Maiden Voyage *and* Dolphin Dance.

Mainstream Jazz Record Labels

For many observers, the names Blue Note, Verve, Prestige, and Riverside have as much historic resonance as some of the jazz sounds they purveyed. These record labels and the people behind them—many of whose names, from Alfred Lion to Rudy Van Gelder to Orrin Keepnews, have acquired familiar rings of their own—were inexorably linked with the pouring forth of mainstream jazz.

These were largely independent specialty labels, created, in most cases, for the express purpose of capturing jazz on vinyl. By contrast, the still-active larger labels—Columbia, RCA Victor—issued jazz discs, too, but primarily as an afterthought to their more commercial strategies. The independents, on the other hand, were often down in the trenches with the players, capturing new sounds, recognizing and shaping movements, and, with their distinctive album covers, aligning jazz with progressive ideas in visual art, photography, and graphic design.

Blue Note, for example, launched by Alfred Lion in 1939, developed into the leading purveyor of soul jazz and hard bop in the 1950s and sixties. It took care in recording—providing paid rehearsal time for its artists—and matched engineer Rudy Van Gelder's "Blue Note sound" with a simple yet striking "Blue Note look." The label became known for its attention to quality and its ability to attract a stable of cutting-edge artists.

Van Gelder also handled recordings for Prestige, a label that began in 1949. Prestige founder Bob Weinstock worked quickly, without rehearsal and with few alternate takes, and emphasized hard-swinging artists and plenty of organ-jazz combos. This gave the label a reputation for being a sort of "poor man's Blue Note" that nonetheless produced a vast quantity of important music.

In 1952, Orrin Keepnews co-founded Riverside Records. It lasted only twelve years but built a strong roster that included Thelonious Monk, Bill Evans, Wes Montgomery, Cannonball Adderley, and Sonny Rollins. In the 1970s, the Riverside and Prestige lines—along with another Keepnews label, Milestone—were acquired by West Coast independent Fantasy Records, creating a catalog of remarkable breadth.

Two other California companies—Contemporary and Pacific Jazz, founded in 1951 and 1952, respectively—became aligned with the cool and West Coast styles, both labels issuing discs by Chet Baker and Art Pepper. Contemporary later branched out, covering more experimental sounds by such artists as Cecil Taylor, before it, too, merged with Fantasy.

Verve, Impulse!, and Blue Note were leading mainstream jazz labels.

Norman Granz, who had built Jazz at the Philharmonic and the label Clef on the momentum of swing and bop, remained a player in the mainstream years. In 1956 he launched Verve, devoting himself to the Ella Fitzgerald "song-book" albums that raised her stature as an American pop icon. Like Blue Note, Verve engaged the services of Van Gelder, and soon assembled an all-star lineup that included Oscar Peterson, Stan Getz, and Billie Holiday.

Verve producer Creed Taylor went on to create his own CTI Records, a company that would achieve commercial success with a glossy sound—again using Van Gelder—and equally glossy, abstract cover art.

Before Verve, Creed Taylor had produced records for Impulse!, a label launched in 1960. After his departure, the new recording supervisor, Bob Thiele, jumped into the mainstream with discs by such stalwarts as Art Blakey and Max Roach. But Impulse! also took a stab at the new and untested. Its records by such musical adventurers as Cecil Taylor, Archie Shepp, and John Coltrane would help carry jazz into an era of full-blown, post-mainstream experiments. —Tad Lathrop and Neil Tesser

Jazz Festivals

The proliferation of jazz festivals—events showcasing multiple artists, sometimes over several days—occurred in tandem with the increasing perception of jazz as music to listen to rather than simply dance, imbibe, or converse to.

Festivals offered audiences and musicians alike an alternative to cramped, noisy, smoky clubs. In often idyllic settings, listeners could enjoy a broad spectrum of artists playing a range of jazz styles—or different approaches to one style if the festival happened to focus on a particular theme.

For musicians, jazz festivals provided an important outlet. With hundreds of such gatherings presented around the globe every year, they added up to an international "circuit" that could keep bands on the road when nightclub gigs were hard to come by.

An International Jazz Congress was held in Chicago in 1926, but the festival idea didn't catch on until the presentation of the Festival Internationale du Jazz, held in Paris in 1949, which offered a wide range of U.S. and European performers. In years that followed, the Newport Jazz Festival (launched in 1954 and captured on film in the 1960 documentary *Jazz on a Summer's Day*) emerged as a leading stateside showcase, as did the Monterey Jazz Festival, founded in 1958 by disc jockey Jimmy Lyons and jazz critic Ralph Gleason. By the end of the century, continuing U.S. festivals included the JVC Jazz Festival in New York, the Concord Jazz Festival in California, the still-active Monterey fest, the Chicago Jazz Festival, and the New Orleans Jazz and Heritage Festival.

Events also cropped up in other parts of the world, including nearly every European country.

Switzerland hosted one of the world's highest-profile yearly jazz events, the Montreux Jazz Festival (over time, mixing jazz with other kinds of pop music); France drew visitors yearly to its Paris Jazz Festival; Germany staged festivals in Berlin, Köln, and Frankfurt; the Netherlands' North Sea Jazz Festival enjoyed a long run and gained a reputation as the world's largest jazz festival; the UK's offerings included an Edinburgh-based event; and Canada staged jazz fests all across the country, from Halifax and Montreal in the east to Victoria and Vancouver in the west.

Theme-based events included the Imatra Big Band Festival in Finland, the Festival of New Orleans Music in Switzerland, and the free-jazz Total Music Meeting in Germany.

By century's end, jazz festivals were held in such far-flung places as St. Petersburg, Istanbul, Melbourne, Tokyo, Beijing, and even the islands of St. Lucia and Jamaica—proving that jazz had truly become a global art form. —*Tad Lathrop*

A mid-sixties Dizzy Gillespie quintet (from left to right): saxophonist and flutist James Moody, pianist Kenny Barron, drummer Rudy Collins, Gillespie (seated), and bassist Chris White.

Lee Tanner

Continuing Traditions

During this period, earlier jazz styles didn't just fold up and die. In fact, every previous idiom not only co-existed but also still thrived—and usually in the work of the musicians who had invented it. In 1955, such legends as Louis Armstrong and Earl Hines were still in early middle age, many of the swing giants maintained rigorous performing schedules, and the bebop rebels had just approached their prime. Jazz had yet to place Duke Ellington and Billie Holiday and Parker and Gillespie on pedestals; fans were too busy checking out their latest records.

In fact, during the 1950s Ellington entered the second great arc of his storied career, during which his fame eclipsed even his previous success. This "comeback" began at the New-port Jazz Festival in 1956, where Paul Gonsalves's intense, twenty-seven-chorus tenor saxophone solo on Ellington's *Diminuendo in Blue*

set the crowd (and then those who bought the *Ellington at Newport* album) on fire. From then until the end of his life (1974), Ellington and Billy Strayhorn spent increasing amounts of time on larger works,

many of which are considered their greatest accomplishments: *Such Sweet Thunder* (1956–57), based on characters and themes from Shakespeare; Ellington's score for the film *Anatomy of a Murder* (1959); their *Far East Suite* (1966); and the *Second Sacred Concert* (1968).

In the work of other artists, the various eras of jazz flowed together, combining aspects of swing, bop, and cool into styles both unique and popular. Pianist Erroll Garner, for example, used an insistent left-hand pulse (à la the 1930s), angular bop syncopations, and richly chorded harmonies in creating perhaps the most popular jazz sound of the 1950s, heard on best-selling records (*Concert by the Sea*, 1955) and network-television variety shows. The song *Misty*, for which Garner wrote the music, is one of the most performed fifties-era compositions. The brilliant tenor saxophonist Stan Getz, previously associated with bebop and cool, reflected both schools in his spectacularly communicative style, at home in both the intimate setting of a quintet, as on *Stan Getz Plays* (1952–54), and the grand stage of orchestral strings, as on his 1961 collaboration with arranger Eddie Sauter, *Focus*.

Cool-jazz man Stan Getz got hotter as the 1950s unfolded.

Jazz on Television

Television may have become a vast wasteland, as critics liked to point out, but jazz fans could occasionally find their music on the "box"—though it wasn't always easy.

In television's early years, traditional jazz styles could be found on *Eddie Condon's Floor Show* (NBC and CBS, 1949–50), with such regulars as Wild Bill Davison and Pee Wee Russell; *Chicago Jazz,* featuring Art Van Damme and the Tailgate 7 (NBC, 1949); and *Adventures in Jazz* (CBS, 1949). The music was upbeat and accessible, and it usually stayed within the bounds of mainstream tastes—and racial preferences.

Pianist Hazel Scott hosted her own variety show in 1950.

But at a time when segregation was still legal in much of the United States, television's increasing use of African American musicians in the 1950s helped chip away at the color line. Black jazz musicians not only performed on television but often did so in integrated groups. Well before the civil-rights movement reached its peak, pianist Hazel Scott had her own network series (Dumont, 1950). What's more, television presented black musicians as artists, not just entertainers. On "The Sound of Miles Davis" (*The Robert Herridge Theater,* CBS, 1958), there was no shucking or jiving, no corny comedy bits; it was filmed with all the dignity and respect given to symphonic broadcasts. In the button-down Eisenhower era, *The Sound of Jazz* (CBS, 1959) enabled Americans to experience the work of such iconoclasts and nonconformists as Thelonious Monk and Lester Young.

Still, there was resistance to jazz on the part of some program sponsors. *The Nat "King" Cole Show* (NBC, 1956–57) featured Ella Fitzgerald, Billy Eckstine, and stars from Jazz at the Philharmonic, including Coleman Hawkins, Roy Eldridge, and Oscar Peterson, but the show was canceled due to sponsors' fears of alienating white southern viewers. Some shows got around such fears by appealing to a more highbrow, presumably more tolerant, audience. *Omnibus* (CBS and ABC, 1953–57), with host Alastair Cooke, is remembered for its sophisticated approach to classical and jazz music; on one broadcast it offered a reunion of the groundbreaking racially integrated Benny Goodman Trio with Teddy Wilson and Gene Krupa.

Musicians Duke Ellington, Steve Allen, and Billy Taylor were instrumental in bringing jazz to a wider TV audience. Ellington was charming, articulate, and telegenic, as evidenced by his appearances on the *Bell Telephone Hour* (NBC, 1959 and 1967); *The U.S. Steel Hour* (CBS, 1957); and *Duke Ellington: Love You Madly* (National Educational Television [NET], 1967). On such shows, he achieved the rare balance of art and entertainment.

Pianist, composer, and comedian Steve Allen also managed to straddle the highbrow-middlebrow divide. *The Steve Allen Show* (NBC, 1956–58) featured jazz artists on a regular basis, including a memorable remote broadcast from Birdland by Count Basie's orchestra.

Pianist Billy Taylor became a mainstay jazz figure on TV, from his musical-directorship of NET's first jazz series, *The Subject Is Jazz,* in 1958, to his ongoing role as arts correspondent for CBS's *Sunday Morning.*

When jazz wasn't the focal point, its sound was used to evocative ends. Crime and detective shows used jazz music to suggest gritty realism or to convey a character's inner thoughts, notably on *Naked City* (ABC, 1958–63), with its theme by Billy May; *M Squad* (NBC, 1957–60), with music by Basie; *Asphalt Jungle* (ABC, 1961), for which Ellington

Woody Herman on Cavalcade of Bands, *which ran from January 1950 to September 1951.*

wrote the opening music; and the highly successful jazz score by Henry Mancini for *Peter Gunn* (NBC and ABC, 1958–61).

In the late 1950s and early 1960s, network television largely ignored jazz, but things were different over at public television. NET—the precursor to the Public Broadcasting System (PBS)—didn't rely on ratings or sponsors, so it occasionally ventured into more modern, even avant-garde territory. Ralph J. Gleason's *Jazz Casual* series, for example, bravely devoted entire programs to performances by the quartets of John Coltrane (1964) and Charles Lloyd (1968). Another NET series, *Music U.S.A.,* presented a program titled "The Experimenters" with groups led by Charles Mingus and Cecil Taylor, including analysis and commentary by critic Martin Williams and novelist Ralph Ellison (1967).

In tandem with America's rightward turn in the Reagan era of the 1980s, PBS programming became more conservative. But jazz continued to find airtime, notably in the series *American Masters* and *Great Performances.*

Meanwhile, jazz found an increasingly hospitable place on commercial cable television, as Bravo, Ovation, and other channels broadcast jazz documentaries by noted filmmakers Don McGlynn, Burrill Crohn, Robert Mugge, and John Jeremy. *BET on Jazz,* backed by Robert Johnson's Black Entertainment Television, became the United

States' most ambitious attempt to create a channel devoted solely to jazz music and its offshoots. However, its twenty-four-hour-a-day mix of documentaries, archival footage, in-studio concerts, interviews, and even a *Jazz Discovery* talent show, was, at the close of the century, still struggling to find an audience and sponsors and was carried only by a limited number of cable systems.

Foreign television—especially in the United Kingdom, France, Germany, Denmark, and Japan—also featured jazz, but not enough to satisfy its fans in those countries. From the 1960s on, European TV—usually government sponsored—routinely broadcast live concert programs from Nice, Montreux, and other festivals. The BBC's impressive *Jazz 625* of the mid-1960s featured leading performers. In the 1990s, European cable and satellite TV offered such programs as *Jazz entre amigos* (Spain), *Muzzik* (France), and the weekly *Talking Jazz,* an American show broadcast exclusively in Europe through NBC's Super Channel.
—*Larry Appelbaum*

The popular Erroll Garner worked television as well as clubs and festivals.

133

Vocalists of the Mainstream Era

The 1950s didn't launch many new vocalists, largely because so many of the "old" ones were still around—and in many cases sounding better than ever. The Swing Era star Ella Fitzgerald reinvented herself not once but twice: in the 1940s she had become a terrific bop singer, and now she recorded a series of "songbook" albums celebrating the great American composers of popular music—including Irving Berlin, Harold Arlen, Rodgers and Hart, and Cole Porter—that made her a national treasure. Sarah Vaughan, meanwhile, had to refashion herself only once: from the bebop rebel who scatted with Bird and Diz to a voluptuously swinging pop star who never lost her jazz roots. Yet when she placed her voice before a symphony orchestra—as on *Sarah Vaughan Sings George Gershwin* (1954–57)—she became the closest thing to an operatic diva jazz has ever known. The work of Mel Tormé, the gifted wunderkind who had achieved fame in the 1940s, gained depth and chiseled his credentials as a great improviser on a par with Fitzgerald (as on *Mel Tormé Swings Shubert Alley*, 1960); the same could be said of Anita O'Day, who had created the mold for cool-jazz singers as a member of Stan Kenton's band in the 1940s and, on such albums as *Pick Yourself Up* (1956), proved herself among the most intelligently swinging vocalists of the 1950s and sixties.

Even Frank Sinatra, en route to establishing himself as the century's symbol of American popular song, reverted to his big-band jazz upbringing, recording a fine album with Count Basie, a fair one with Duke Ellington, and delightful live dates with a quintet led by vibraphonist Red Norvo, heard on *Live in Australia 1959* ("rediscovered" by Blue Note Records in 1997). Sinatra's primary influence, Billie Holiday, continued to record throughout the 1950s. Her voice, ravaged by years of alcohol and heroin, had lost much of its lustre, but hard times had also sharpened her interpretive skills; her many recordings in the 1950s featured noted mainstream instrumentalists, as heard on the album *Billie's Best* (1945–59). Meanwhile, Sinatra passed part of Holiday's torch to the young Tony Bennett, who, like Sinatra, brought his jazz sensibility to a pop context. Although Bennett became primarily associated with such hit pop recordings as *I Left My Heart in San Francisco* (1962) and *If I Ruled the World* (1965), over the years he also took excursions into jazz with such collaborators as Count Basie, Stan Getz, Nat Adderley, and Marian McPartland, and, on two prized albums in 1975 and 1976, the mesmerizing pianist Bill Evans. Deep into the 1990s, as Bennett's time-seasoned sound and interpretive abilities captured a new generation of fans, he issued such acclaimed albums as *Here's to the Ladies* (1995)—with his takes on Billie Holiday's *God Bless the Child* and George Gershwin's classic jazz template *I Got Rhythm*—and *Tony Bennett on Holiday* (1996), his tribute to Lady Day.

Only a handful of vocalists really reflected the hard-bop aesthetic in their music. Three of them sang together as (Dave) Lambert, (Jon) Hendricks, and (Annie) Ross; they perfected the art of vocalese, in which intricate lyrics are fitted to

Billie Holiday, though past her prime, continued to work during the 1950s. Time had diminished her vocal range but seasoned her interpretive abilities.

Frank Sinatra and Ella Fitzgerald, both master song stylists.

Carmen McRae drew inspiration from Billie Holiday but established her own distinctive voice. Noted for the depth of feeling she brought to her performances, McRae remained active—as an actress as well as a singer—through the 1980s.

The much-imitated Anita O'Day.

previously recorded improvised solos; highlights of their work include vocal versions of the Jazz Messengers' *Moanin'* (1959), Horace Silver's *Come On Home* (1961), and John Coltrane's *Mr. P.C.* (1961). Carmen McRae achieved her first success during the 1950s as well, eventually developing a gimlet edge to her singing that echoed the stance of such hornmen as Rollins, Davis, and Jackie McLean: *Carmen McRae Sings Lover Man and Other Billie Holiday Classics* (1961) is an homage to her idol, while her 1972 *Great American Songbook* remains the best snapshot of her piquant personality. Another bop-oriented singer, Betty Carter, first drew attention touring in 1948–51 with bandleader Lionel Hampton, who nicknamed her Betty Bebop. Carter's day wouldn't come till the 1970s and eighties—it took audiences that long to catch up with her edgy, highly improvisatory style. But when recognition came, it happened in a big way: fans hailed her arranging and bandleading skills as well as her voice, and she gained additional respect for starting her own label, Bet-Car Records. The singer's talents are amply displayed on such albums as *I Can't Help It* (recorded in 1958–60), *Look What I Got* (1988), and *Feel the Fire* (1994). Another important hard-bop singer, Mark Murphy, evoked the Beat writers with his cool baritone and ebullient phrasing on such albums as the 1961 *Rah*; his idiosyncratic phrasing continued to evolve through the century's end.

Jazz and Fiction

The impact of jazz on fiction is apparent in two types of writing: works that deal directly with jazz musicians and the jazz life, and works that appear to have been influenced or inspired by the aesthetics or spirit of jazz. In the imaginations of many twentieth-century writers, jazz symbolized liberation from bourgeois social conventions, an intense sense of living in the present moment, and living life dangerously on the edge. In effect, jazz served as a metaphorical frontier in the modern American literary mind.

The two most famous pieces of American fiction dealing with the life of a jazz musician are Dorothy Baker's 1938 novel *Young Man with a Horn* and James Baldwin's 1957 short story "Sonny's Blues." Both works established several conventions about the depiction of the jazz musician hero in fiction: In both books the character is a sensitive victim of dissipation caused by an uncaring, philistine, racist society. He is dedicated solely to his craft, to truth and beauty, to the willingness to endure the pain necessary to bring that

truth and beauty to the world. In short, both writers established the jazz musician as a highly romanticized figure, a martyr. Jazz is presented as an almost spiritual pursuit, a transcendent art, forced to exist in a lowlife or pedestrian setting from which it draws its authenticity and vitality.

Preceding these two defining works were others of both artistic merit and cultural importance. Key books by African American writers include James Weldon Johnson's *The Autobiography of an Ex–Colored Man* (1912), a novel that chronicles the black sporting life and principally the world of ragtime, and Paul Laurence Dunbar's 1902 novel *The Sport of the Gods,* which envisions ragtime as a kind of morally degenerate music. There are vivid depictions of jazz or jazz-like music in many of the black novels of the Harlem Renaissance, including Claude McKay's *Banjo* (1929) and *Home to Harlem* (1928), Nella Larsen's *Quicksand* (1928) and *Passing* (1929), Wallace Thurman's *Infants of the Spring* (1932), and Jean Toomer's *Cane* (1923). Zora Neale

Hurston's famous autobiographical essay, "How It Feels to Be Colored Me" (1928), contains one of the most famous depictions of jazz by a black writer of the era.

Literary writing about jazz became more varied and sophisticated as writers developed a deeper affinity with the creative processes and impulses of the jazz musician. Noted post–World War II works of fiction about jazz musicians include John A. Williams' *Night Song* (1961), William Melvin Kelley's *A Drop of Patience* (1965), Michael Ondaatje's *Coming Through Slaughter* (1976), John Clellon Holmes' *The Horn* (1958), Frank Conroy's *Body and Soul* (1993), Amiri Baraka's much-anthologized story "The Screamers" (1963), Bart Schneider's *Blue Bossa* (1998), and Rafi Zabor's award-winning *The Bear Comes Home* (1997). Another influential book dealing with jazz is Josef Skvorecky's two-novella *Bass Saxophone* (1977). Jazz musicians have also appeared as characters in mystery novels, among them Harper Barnes' *Blue Monday* and Bill Moody's Evan Horne series, about an injured jazz pianist who solves crimes.

The two most significant American novels with a jazz sensibility are Jack Kerouac's *On the Road* (1957)— the novel that defined the Beat movement of the 1950s—and Ralph Ellison's *Invisible Man* (1952). Although neither deals with jazz directly, both exhibit the flow and movement of jazz improvisation. Ellison was also one of the premier essayists on jazz; several pieces appeared in his two collections, *Shadow and Act* (1964) and *Going to the Territory* (1986).

Whether romanticized, demonized, rendered realistically, or invoked as a metaphor, jazz proved a valuable means to various twentieth-century literary ends. —*Gerald Early*

Alternate Currents

While hard bop and cool served as the borders of mainstream jazz, the music contained various other currents.

"Chamber jazz" offered an intimate alternative to big bands and busy combos; the Modern Jazz Quartet exemplified this sound but was hardly alone in making it popular. Taking as their model the hit 1940s recordings of Nat "King" Cole, Oscar Peterson and Ahmad Jamal each led piano-guitar-bass trios that had no drummer. The results couldn't have been more different. In New York, the Canadian-born Peterson floored audiences with his technical prowess, as on *The Lady Is a Tramp* from the remarkable 1957 live album *At the Concertgebouw*. But Jamal, on the recording *Chamber Music of the New Jazz* (1955), created airy, delicate textures in which the spaces between notes had all the impact of the notes themselves; these performances, recorded while he lived in Chicago, exerted a strong influence on Miles Davis.

In California, saxophonist Jimmy Giuffre—a former member of Woody Herman's Second Herd and a Lighthouse regular—spent the 1950s looking both backward and forward for new ideas. On the one hand, he immersed himself in the counterpoint of early New Orleans jazz; yet on Shelly Manne's *The Three*, in 1954, he joined in a trio that featured neither piano nor bass en route to "jazz with a non-pulsating beat," thus anticipating later hybrids of jazz and classical music. California drummer Chico Hamilton, on such albums as *Gongs East!* (1958) and *Man from Two Worlds* (1962–63), explored unusual and intimate textures with a quintet that featured flute and cello and helped shape the music of saxophonists Eric Dolphy and Charles Lloyd. Hamilton's description of the drums as "a very melodic … sensuous feminine instrument" suggests his ability to look beyond conventional strictures in his quest for greater freedom of expression.

In fact, "quest for freedom" would describe the stirrings all around mainstream jazz in the 1950s and sixties. The idea of liberation took many forms, some of them quite subtle. After leaving Miles Davis's group in 1960, Bill Evans conceived a quietly radical trio that would free the piano, bass, and drums from their traditionally assigned roles—a highly democratic unit in which no one element dominated completely, thus allowing each man to steer the music at any given moment. Evans achieved this with drummer Paul Motian and the gifted but short-lived bassist Scott LaFaro, as heard on the 1961 recording *Sunday at the Village Vanguard*. Evans' exquisite lyricism and sonorous harmonies placed his music squarely in the mainstream, where his contemplative but energetic style greatly influenced the next three generations of pianists; these same qualities masked the revolutionary nature of his approach.

©Herman Leonard

Oscar Peterson's keyboard virtuosity earned him legions of disciples.

Bill Evans brought new ideas to the piano-trio configuration.

Jazz and Visual Art

Romare Bearden, Jammin' at the Savoy, *1980. Etching, 15 1/2" x 23 1/2".*

Jazz inspired visual artists to explore primitivism and modernity, to construct racial and national identities, and to invent new styles. It embodied the natural, the exotic.

Realist painters found in jazz bistros a post-Victorian milieu that challenged gender, sexual, and racial boundaries. In Archibald J. Motley, Jr.'s *Blues* (1929) and Reginald Marsh's *Tuesday Night at the Savoy Ballroom* (1930), the female figure and the dancers' intimacy exemplify taboo-breaking sensuality. Jazz was also associated with things African, as in Pablo Picasso's *Three Musicians* (1921), Fernand Léger's set and costume designs for the ballet *La création du monde* (1923), and Arthur Dove's *Primitive Music* (1944).

Jazz was also a machine-age music of the city. While in New York, French painters Francis Picabia and Albert Gleizes worked jazz themes into their work—*Negro Song (Chanson Nègre)* (1913) and *Composition (for "Le jazz")* (1915), respectively—as an expression of modern U.S. culture, as did Otto Dix and George Grosz in Germany. Later, Stuart Davis captured New York's dynamism with jazz-inspired abstract color harmonies and dissonances in *Hot Still Scape for Six Colors—Seventh Avenue Style* (1940). Piet Mondrian merged jazz syncopation with urban energy in *Broadway Boogie-Woogie* (1942–43). In Thomas Hart Benton's *Arts of the City* (1932), the saxophonist personified urban life. An African American perspective on jazz musicians and dancers is reflected in Aaron Douglas's *Song of the Towers* (1934), Romare Bearden's *Alto Composite* (1974), and David Driskell's *Jazz Singer* (1974).

Avant-garde artists equated jazz with creative revolution. Painters produced abstract works inspired by jazz recordings, as Arthur Dove did in *George Gershwin—Rhapsody in Blue, Part 1* (1927). Paris Dada artists in the 1920s considered jazz an unstructured anti-music or an alter ego, if you will, to their anti-art performances. French surrealists saw the music—with its convulsive rhythms and celebration of instinct, seen in Yves Tanguy's *Bar Américain* (1925)—as an example of psychic automatism. Improvisation served as a model for the collage cutouts of Henri Matisse's *Jazz* (1947) and helped inspire Jackson Pollock's drip painting method, exemplified by *Autumn Rhythm (No. 30)* (1950).

Images of jazz and the jazz musician, as in Jean-Michel Basquiat's *Discography II* (1983) and Larry Rivers' *Dick Schwartz, Umber Blues* (1987), have remained popular, guiding artists to create truly modern visual art.
—*Donna M. Cassidy*

A much more blatant attack on convention than that of Bill Evans marks the work of Charles Mingus. Although his fluid and inventive technique raised the bar for jazz bassists, history remembers him mainly as a brilliant (if mercurial) bandleader—and the most important jazz composer after Duke Ellington. A self-professed descendent of Ellington and Monk, Mingus wrote the tenderest of ballads—among them his elegant threnody for Lester Young, *Goodbye Pork Pie Hat*, from the 1959 masterpiece *Mingus Ah Um*—as well as the most roisterous hard-bop anthems (*Haitian Fight Song*, 1955, and *Hora Decubitis*, 1963). Some pieces, such as *The Clown* (from the 1957 album of the same name) combine jazz and poetry; on such tunes as *Wednesday Night Prayer Meeting* (1959) and *Hog Callin' Blues* (1961), Mingus combined soul jazz and satire. Like Ellington, he envisioned jazz on a wider scale than did most of his contemporaries, then used the musical materials of the time—in this case, the sharply angled melodies and vibrant rhythms of hard bop—to realize his vision.

The blind visionary and multi-instrumentalist Roland Kirk created a quite different blend of jazz tradition with the freedom cry. In the mid-1960s, Kirk adopted the name Rahsaan, which he said had come to him in a dream; another dream inspired him to resurrect two archaic reed instruments, the manzello and stritch. These he played simultaneously with his main instrument, the tenor saxophone—three horns at once, with Kirk using countermelodies to accompany himself and circular-breathing techniques to play for minutes at a time without stopping for a breath. His critics saw only a freak show, but Kirk's extraordinary musicianship (as on *The Inflated Tear*, 1968) allowed him to bridge genres and impart a great deal of Mingus-like humor and satire.

But as the fifties closed, it was Miles Davis who once again shifted the mainstream in a new direction. Davis had already combined jazz and classical techniques on a series of Columbia albums, starting with *Miles Ahead* (1957), that reunited him with his *Birth of the Cool* (1949–50) colleague, arranger Gil Evans. These were really jazz concertos, as Evans' limpid, textured writing supported and engaged Davis's trumpet; on the famous *Sketches of Spain* (1959–60), Evans adapted a classical piece, *Concierto de Aranjuez*, penned by Joaquín Rodrigo in 1939.

Among the most idiosyncratic and influential of jazz figures, Charles Mingus combined an expansive musical sensibility with a talent for writing affecting melodies, including his much-performed tribute to Lester Young, Goodbye Pork Pie Hat.

Rahsaan Roland Kirk's innovative experiments of the 1960s would resonate in later decades.

With the 1959 landmark *Kind of Blue,* however, Davis instigated the most significant development in jazz since his creation of *The Cool.* On this album, he fully explored modal improvisation—which had shown up a year earlier on *Milestones* (1958)—instructing his band members to use preselected modes as the basis for their solos. These modes were specific scales named by the ancient Greeks, including but not limited to the standard major and minor; they replaced the chord progressions that had controlled jazz improvisation since bebop, liberating the soloists from bop's "tyranny of chords" and forcing them to look in new directions. (To further spark innovation, Davis presented this new musical puzzle to his players just a few hours before the recording session.)

The aesthetic and commercial success of *Kind of Blue* pointed to new possibilities, specifically for musicians such as Jackie McLean—a fiery alto saxist who had never quite fit in as a hard bopper but who embraced the new freedom with such albums as *One Step Beyond* (1963). McLean's work—and that of his Blue Note Records colleagues vibraphonist Bobby Hutcherson, trombonist Grachan Moncur III, pianist Andrew Hill, and keyboardist Larry Young—widened the jazz mainstream considerably, incorporating the revolutionary spirit that would soon rock every aspect of the 1960s.

Davis himself found it impossible to stand pat. By 1964 he had completely rebuilt his quintet into a band that artfully dodged easy characterization—except for "Miles Davis's greatest band." Its brilliant balance of talents reached an acme on *Miles Smiles* (1966), in performances that remained "mainstream" but reveled in looser song structures descended from Davis's modal music. The music pivoted on the elastic interplay between drummer Tony Williams (who joined Davis in 1963, at the age of seventeen) and pianist Herbie Hancock (only six years older than Williams). Ron Carter's malleable bass glued the rhythm section. And Wayne Shorter's elliptical solos presented a new model for modern tenor saxophonists, while his concise and memorable compositions—among them *Footprints* (1966), *Dolores* (1966), and *Pinocchio* (1967) (along with such earlier tunes as *Witch Hunt,* 1965, and *Infant Eyes,* 1965)—marked him as the most important writer since Monk and Mingus.

With this band, Davis sailed swiftly through the 1960s and seventies, helping to pilot jazz through its most turbulent period in three decades. Others who made their marks in the 1950s and sixties would be there as well, continuing to hone their skills and exploring new ways to apply them. ⌒

Key Recordings

Art Blakey and the Jazz Messengers. *The Big Beat.* Blue Note. No single disc better exhibits the classic Jazz Messengers sound and repertoire, from bluesy stomps to hard-bop potboilers to incipient modal music. This album, recorded in 1960, also sports what many people consider the single greatest Messengers lineup, with Lee Morgan on trumpet, Wayne Shorter on sax, and Bobby Timmons on piano.

The Brown-Roach Quintet. *Clifford Brown and Max Roach.* EmArcy. Although the addition of Sonny Rollins in 1955 gave this band two of the greatest soloists in jazz, its concept was really established two years earlier, with the West Coast tenorman Harold Land providing a slightly cooler approach—as heard in this excellent assortment from the band's early repertoire.

Coltrane, John. *Giant Steps.* Atlantic. Groundbreaking, glorious, at first startling and then mesmerizing, this classic 1959 album—which includes the signature title track and the contemplative ballad *Naima*—has become such a mainstream icon that it's hard to imagine the controversy Coltrane inspired at the time it came out.

Davis, Miles. *Kind of Blue.* Legacy. Decades after its 1959 release, *Kind of Blue* still topped the sales charts and remained one of the most popular jazz albums of all time; it also became a touchstone for the cool culture of the 1950s and, in retrospect, a harbinger of the new jazz freedom that would explode in the 1960s and seventies.

Mingus, Charles. *Mingus Ah Um.* Legacy. Of the nine tracks included on this 1959 recording, four—*Better Git Hit in Your Soul, Boogie Stop Shuffle, Goodbye Pork Pie Hat,* and *Fables of Faubus*—are now considered masterpieces. That's a pretty good ratio, even for Mingus.

Monk, Thelonious. *Brilliant Corners.* OJC. The presence of Sonny Rollins, the freedom of the long-playing record, and the debut of soon-to-be-classics *Bemsha Swing* and *Ba-lue Bolivar Ba-lues Are* all make this one of the very greatest Monk experiences. With this 1956 album, Monk began his "comeback," which included leading a quartet starring John Coltrane.

Pepper, Art. *Art Pepper Meets the Rhythm Section.* OJC. "The" rhythm section—in this case the sidemen of Miles Davis's top-ranked quintet, in Los Angeles to play an engagement with Davis—contracted to back the mercurial and uncategorizable Pepper. The resulting disc, recorded in 1957, captured one of his greatest performances, exemplifying the finest West Coast bop.

Rollins, Sonny. *Saxophone Colossus.* OJC. With its assured and authoritative lyricism and its fearless investigation of mysterious musical nooks and crannies, this 1956 masterpiece established once and for all Rollins' place in jazz history. It contains his most-played composition, the West Indian–flavored *St. Thomas,* and one of his most famous, *Blue 7.*

Silver, Horace. *The Best of Horace Silver, Vol. 1.* Blue Note. The archetypal soul-jazz pianist and composer, Horace Silver issued many worthy albums. Most of his discs feature several great tunes and a couple of maybes, which is why this collection of his best tracks from the 1950s is a good place to start.

Smith, Jimmy. *The Sermon!* Blue Note. Recorded in 1958, this is the best introduction to the classic soul-jazz organ trio, by the man who essentially invented it. Several of Smith's other Blue Note albums from the period feature great horn players in extended jam sessions, but this cuts to the bone with guitar, drums, and Smith supplying both keyboard conniptions and tough bass lines. —*Neil Tesser*

CHAPTER 6

Departures and Explorations

John Litweiler

SIDEBARS

*Sun Ra and his Arkestra performing on NBC-TV's
Saturday Night Live, May 20, 1978.*

Ornette Coleman used the term *harmolodic* for his approach to improvisation, which broke away from the chord-based soloing of bebop and mainstream jazz.

Nineteen fifty-nine brought a turning point in jazz. The spring marked the deaths of three great Swing Era figures—saxophonist Lester Young, singer Billie Holiday, and soprano saxophonist–clarinetist Sidney Bechet. In that same season, the immensely popular Miles Davis Sextet disbanded, leaving two breakthrough albums in its wake: Davis's modal masterwork *Kind of Blue* and the supremely lyrical *Giant Steps* by Davis's departing tenor saxophonist, John Coltrane.

At the time, Ornette Coleman was still an obscure alto sax player, yet the three albums he recorded in California that year were as significant as those other key events. Two of the albums were by his own, carefully trained, pianoless quartet—*The Shape of Jazz to Come* and *Change of the Century*—and they announced a new era in jazz as surely as did Louis Armstrong's Hot Fives and Hot Sevens in 1926–27 or the first Charlie Parker–Dizzy Gillespie groups in 1945. And when the Coleman quartet played its first nightclub gig in New York City, in November 1959, it was the most combustible of all jazz debuts, igniting an explosion of exploratory creative activity by jazz musicians.

Of course, jazz musicians, those notorious nonconformists, have been explorers ever since New Orleans cornetist Buddy Bolden first played ragtime variations. But traditional jazz, swing, and bop improvisations were all based on the harmonic structures—the chord changes—of the songs the players played. Ornette Coleman's greatest innovation, on the other hand, was playing *without* fixed harmonic structures.

What Coleman did wasn't exactly unprecedented. A handful of musicians—among them, woodwind improviser Joe Maneri in Boston in the 1940s and alto saxophonist Joe Harriott in London in the 1950s—reportedly preceded Coleman in abandoning chord changes, though their early adventures weren't documented. Pianist Lennie Tristano's sextet created two notable recordings without preset chord changes in 1949, though the players instinctively imply conventional song form in the more successful piece, *Intuition;* more radical is Tristano's intense, atonal, overdubbed, aptly titled piano solo *Descent into the Maelstrom* (1953). As early as 1933 there were the strange, tumbling key changes of xylophonist-vibraphonist Red Norvo's *Dance of the Octopus,* and during the bebop era there were plenty of works pointing to a world beyond bop. *Dalvatore Sally,* by George Handy for the Boyd Raeburn band (1946); Ellington's atonal theme of *The Clothed Woman* (1948); *A Bird in Igor's Yard,* George Russell's bright fusion of classical composer Igor Stravinsky and bop saxophonist Charlie Parker, played by the Buddy DeFranco band (1949); early experiments by drummer Shelly Manne and reedman Jimmy Giuffre—these are especially noteworthy examples of musicians' stretching the boundaries of jazz. But these works were isolated experiments, even though most of the artists were repeat experimenters throughout their lives.

"The new music," "the new thing," "'outside' jazz," "free jazz"—there was never a universally accepted name, such as swing or bop, for the idiom that grew out of

Coleman's innovations. Early journalists took to the term "free jazz," partly because Coleman recorded an album titled *Free Jazz* (1960) and also because this music's freedom of expression came at a time of great social change.

The changes, in fact, were some of the most far-reaching of the twentieth century: Freedom was in the air. The civil-rights movement—a crystallization of

Jazz: The Sound of Freedom

At the time jazz musicians began freeing themselves from the strictures of traditional harmony, sound, and form, many turned the same impulse toward social issues of the time, especially the burgeoning civil-rights movement. The music and activism that resulted were only the latest manifestations of a desire for individual freedom—and with it, racial equality—that had long been present in jazz. "Jazz was not just a music," Sonny Rollins said. "It was a social force in this country, and it was talking about freedom and people…not having to worry about whether they were supposed to be white, black, and all this stuff."

Not that the racial discrimination coursing through the United States during the twentieth century wasn't also reflected in the world of jazz—and experienced first-hand by its musicians. From the start, the prevailing social order guaranteed inequality of opportunity for black and white players: though black musicians played the first "jass" in New Orleans, it was a white group, the Original Dixieland Jazz Band, that first became famous.

For many years into the evolution of jazz, working conditions remained far from equal for white and black bands. In many parts of the U.S., hotels and restaurants that served black customers were hard to find. And in some areas, particularly the South, black bands faced very real dangers. Cab Calloway recalled a 1931 gig in Virginia Beach, Virginia, in which the mostly white audience grew angry and "somebody shouted, 'Let's take this nigger out and lynch him.' And all this while I was trying to sing."

Integration onstage—pioneered in part by Benny Goodman's employment of a few major black musicians in his small combos—remained a rarity until the bebop era, when the increasing assertiveness of bop musicians began dovetailing with a free-thinking youth counterculture.

But it was in the jazz realm that some of the earliest cracks in the wall of discrimination appeared. From the beginning, the music attracted both black and white

Trombonist Tyree Glenn and tenor saxophonist Chu Berry photographed by bassist Milt Hinton while on the road, ca. 1940.

musicians—and audiences: for many white listeners, racial prejudice began to crumble when they found themselves admiring black jazz players. And exchanges of ideas among musicians of both races were at the core of jazz evolution—in the 1920s, for example, virtually all of the white, Chicago-style musicians were powerfully influenced by Louis Armstrong, while in the 1930s the white Casa Loma Orchestra had a strong impact on black bands of the time.

The jazz world's advocacy of freedom and racial equality ultimately became more overt and direct. In 1950, Duke Ellington vowed that proceeds from his composition *Harlem* would be used to "stamp out segregation, discrimination, bigotry, and a variety of other intolerances." In the 1960s, calls for social liberation—whether in the form of songs such as Eddie Harris's *Freedom Jazz Dance* (1965) or even band names (Charlie Haden's Liberation Music Orchestra)—became plentiful.

To many, the very idea of jazz became synonymous with freedom. "If jazz means anything," Ellington once wrote, "it is freedom of expression."

"Jazz," said Rollins, "has always been the music that had this kind of spirit." —*Tad Lathrop and John Litweiler*

African Americans' growing insistence on equal opportunity and the public's increasing awareness of the value and vitality of African American culture—was at its height, marked by the passing of the Civil Rights and Voting Rights Acts (1964–65). Among jazz musicians, the civil-rights movement had a powerful resonance. Louis Armstrong made headlines with his scalding criticism of President Eisenhower during the Little Rock, Arkansas, school integration crisis (1957); there were civil-rights-inspired albums, including tenor saxophonist Sonny Rollins' *Freedom Suite* (1958), drummer Max Roach's *Freedom Now Suite* (1960), and drummer Art Blakey's *The Freedom Rider* (1961). And the free-jazz musicians, mostly young and mostly black, were unanimous, often vocal, in their support of the struggle for social freedom.

Free-Jazz Ancestors

Of the ancestors of free jazz, two offered especially powerful advances in technique and sensibility: composer-bassist Charles Mingus and composer Bob Graettinger.

Mingus based his music on chord changes and modes, but his passion was certainly a precedent for free jazz. Such Mingus works as *Pithecanthropus Erectus* (1956) and his *Tijuana Moods* album (1957) are volatile, full of complex

As uncompromising in business as he was in music composition, bassist Charles Mingus made numerous career moves to counteract what he saw as restrictive commercialism in jazz. With drummer Max Roach, he ran a record label, Debut, in the early 1950s. In 1960 he and Roach organized Newport Rebels, an alternative to the mainstream Newport Jazz Festival. Such enterprises served as models for later musician-controlled record labels and organizations.

activity and raw-edged playing, foreshadowing the sound of his early 1960s groups with woodwind virtuoso Eric Dolphy; this is music that raises blisters. Along with beautiful melodies, he also composed the socially conscious pieces *Fables of Faubus* (1959), his musical assault on segregationist Arkansas governor Orval Faubus, and *Cry for Freedom (Prayer for Passive Resistance)* (1960). Of Mingus's big-band works, quite the most important is his grand *Epitaph* suite (1962–89), encompassing decades of composition (including reconstruction by composer Gunther Schuller) and not performed until 1989, a decade after his death.

As for Graettinger, the works he composed for Stan Kenton's jazz orchestras bear only passing resemblance to any other jazz or twentieth-century classical music. His large-scale compositions sound like immense dreams. Graettinger's *City of Glass* (1950 version) and *This Modern World* (1951–53) are atonal—without a harmonic foundation—and dense with polyphonic and polyrhythmic movement, lovely instrumental blendings, cold and bleak passages, blazing ensemble climaxes, and fugitive solo moments. These works are almost overwhelming in their complex, ever-changing activity; it's notable that every vivid, beautiful image evaporates.

Free-Jazz Innovations

With all this diverse activity as a precedent, what was it about Coleman that made him such a powerful stimulus? And what is free jazz? To answer the second question first, there were four main areas of innovation in free jazz: sound, harmony, form, and rhythm. New conceptions of all of them grew out of Coleman's early music.

Sonic Freedom

While early jazz and swing were rich with the personal sounds of expressive individuals, bebop's quest for virtuoso lyricism yielded a narrower range of sonorities. You hear this especially in brass instrumentalists. For instance, the smooth sound introduced by J.J. Johnson was pervasive among bop trombonists. In free jazz, on the other hand, the sonic range was unlimited. The emotive trombonist Roswell Rudd, a former Dixieland musician, brought back the rich intonation and slippery slides and blasts of swing, while such successors as George Lewis and Craig Harris went on to further exploit the trombone's power, range, and capacity for expression. Meanwhile, such trumpeters as the vividly dramatic Lester Bowie and the lyrical Leo Smith added new dimensions of humor and sweetness, fire and abstraction, and loud-soft contrasts. It's no accident that Leo Smith was once inspired by Joe Smith's lyric trumpet accompaniments to Bessie Smith, or that Bowie was originally inspired by Louis Armstrong's epic solos; both Bowie and Leo Smith, like other free players, were returning to the quest for personal expression that was at the very root of jazz.

Coleman himself, for a time, played a white plastic alto saxophone, which had a rather dry sound that emphasized the crying quality in his melodies. His sound sometimes changed from phrase to phrase as he soloed

Bob Graettinger composed several large-scale works to supply bandleader Stan Kenton with experimental, "progressive" band scores for concert dates. Kenton played more commercial arrangements in dance halls.

Trumpeter Lester Bowie explored free improvisation and "freak" sounds as a member of both the Association for the Advancement of Creative Musicians and the Art Ensemble of Chicago.

("I realized that you can play sharp or flat in tune," Coleman said). Multiphonics, or split tones (two or more notes at once), and overtones (notes higher than a horn's normal range) became commonplace in the music of Coltrane and Albert Ayler and later among the multitude of saxophonists whom they inspired. Instruments almost wholly new to jazz improvisation appeared from Africa, Asia, and the realm of classical music. The Art Ensemble of Chicago made a deliberate search for new sounds, adding hundreds of gongs, bells, whistles, and toys to the usual instrumentation. Oddly enough, though free jazz coincided with the development of the synthesizer, only bandleader Sun Ra and a handful of others created important work on the instrument. One of those others was trombonist George Lewis, who played duets with a computer he programmed to improvise music.

Years later, when world music and heavy-metal rock were popular, the sounds the free-jazz musicians made didn't seem quite so astonishing as they once had. On the other hand, Lester Bowie, later in his career, proposed forming a *literally* heavy-metal band—with sousaphones, bass saxophones, and steel drums.

Harmonic Freedom

What startled listeners most when they first heard Ornette Coleman was the harmonic structure of his soloing. In swing and bebop solos, chord changes provided emotional shape and tension, and the harmonic tensions were almost inevitably resolved, creating a familiar pleasure for listeners. The singular quality of modal jazz was its reduced structural tension, for modal jazz had slower and subtler harmonic movement, especially in its early years.

Coleman had a third solution. "Before I met Ornette," said his bassist Charlie Haden, "I would sometimes feel to play not on the changes of the song; sometimes I would feel to play on the inspiration and the feeling of the song, and create a new chord structure to it in my solo.... And the first time I played with Ornette, he was *doing* that." Coleman recalled that when he taught his new music to his first quartet partners, Haden, trumpeter Don Cherry, and drummer Billy Higgins, "the most interesting part is: what do you play after you play the melody [theme]? That's where I won them over... finally I got them to where they could see how to express themselves without linking up to a definite maze."

Don Cherry played pocket trumpet in Ornette Coleman's quartet before recording as a leader. In later years Cherry attained renown as a pioneer in world music.

Formal Freedom

Without chord changes, did Coleman's solos turn into chaos, as detractors once claimed? Quite the contrary: his music's formal unity was an important source of its power. He structured his solos by using fragments of melody, which he would alter and incorporate into virtually every phrase. This theme-based method was widely influential, though a good many alternatives followed. There were the free-association forms of Eric Dolphy; the cyclic forms of Coltrane; the grand architecture of pianist Cecil Taylor's solos; the meticulously mounted lines of saxophonist Steve Lacy; the dramatic shapes of Roscoe Mitchell and Lester Bowie; the freely moving lyricism of saxist Fred Anderson—there were even vestiges of the classic building-climax-anticlimax swing and bop form in the sonic adventures of tenor sax player Albert Ayler. Free jazz implied not freedom *from* form but freedom *to choose* form.

An alumnus of Ornette Coleman's Shape of Jazz to Come *quartet (1959), bassist Charlie Haden pursued a range of interests that included work with Gato Barbieri, Carla Bley, Keith Jarrett, and the groups Old and New Dreams and his own Liberation Music Orchestra.*

Bandleader-trumpeter Don Ellis experimented with twelve-tone rows, Indian additive rhythm, microtones, and other departures from standard European harmony and meter. His sixties albums Electric Bath *and* Don Ellis at the Fillmore *were well suited for progressive audiences of the 1960s.*

Rhythmic Freedom

Jazz had typically been played in 2/2 and 4/4 time, or occasionally in 3/4 and 6/4 meters, and the bassist and drummer marked the time. But in *Lonely Woman* (1959) only the drummer of the Ornette Coleman Quartet kept time, while the trumpeter and saxophonist played the haunting melody in freely changing tempos and the bassist strummed spaced, arrhythmic accents. And after the balladlike theme of *Beauty Is a Rare Thing* (1960) the Coleman quartet improvised together in freely moving lines with no fixed tempo or meter at all. Like free harmonic structure, free rhythmic structure was here.

Trumpeter Don Ellis's early combos played free-time pieces, and Jimmy Giuffre's trio created the daring *Free Fall* (1962), an album of free-time, "outside" improvisations. Ellis went on to compose big-band scores using complex Indian rhythmic patterns, while four drummers—Sunny Murray, Andrew Cyrille, Milford Graves, and Rashied Ali—took the more radical step of abandoning fixed rhythm entirely, instead playing pure accent and momentum. What those drummers did was certainly revolutionary. And why not? Coleman's example was leading musicians to question the foundations of the entire jazz tradition.

Giuffre's and the drummers' explorations led to unaccompanied horn solos and free improvisation, which evolved largely in Chicago and England in the late 1960s. In free improvisation, soloists or groups (almost always small groups) of musicians improvised without themes, harmonic or rhythmic structures, or fixed forms.

Free-Jazz Players

The force behind Ornette Coleman's spearheading of free jazz came from the emotion in his music. He played without chord changes because it was in his nature to do so. "I think jazz should express more kinds of feelings than it has up to now," he said, and among his classic early pieces, *Peace* (1959),

Ornette Coleman played violin and trumpet as well as plastic saxophone.

150

Compassion (1959), and *Sadness* (1962) convey the emotions of his song titles with a subtlety new to jazz. There is also the optimistic swagger of *Ramblin'* (1959), the electricity of *Free* (1959) and *Forerunner* (1959), the stark blues of *Lonely Woman* (1959), the sorrow of *Lorraine* (1959), the anger of *Kaleidoscope* (1960) and *Blues Connotation* (1960), all shown in sharp relief. In his early solos he achieved rhythmic tension as acute as Charlie Parker's, though his own broken phrases are rhythmically simpler than Parker's. Like Parker's, Coleman's melodies are rich with blues; his angular note choices and shifting keys added further tension, as did the accompanying interplay of harmonically ambiguous bass and drums. Coleman also pioneered collective improvisation, most notably in the forty-minute *Free Jazz,* with eight musicians bandying lines back and forth over a fixed tempo—a kind of far-out Dixieland.

By the mid-1960s Coleman was also playing violin and trumpet, both with wild, spontaneous phrasing and unorthodox, self-taught technique. Over the years he retired from public performing several times, usually to compose. Few of his orchestral or chamber-music compositions have been performed; the best known is his *Skies of America* (1972) for symphony orchestra and improvisers. Following the mid-1970s he played most often with his band Prime Time—which employed electric guitars and drums—in a hybrid jazz-rock idiom that he invented. These unique fusion-music adventures were rhythmically stimulating, but little of his latter-day music had anything like the power and excitement of his early recordings on the Atlantic and Contemporary labels.

Eric Dolphy's playing exuded warmth, humanity, and intelligence, notably in his innovative work on the bass clarinet.

The commotion over Coleman at the start of the 1960s drew attention to two other highly advanced jazzmen: Eric Dolphy and Cecil Taylor. The almost human sounds—squawks, grunts, cries, blurts, mutters—of Dolphy's bass clarinet and Charles Mingus's bass in improvised mock arguments (*What Love,* 1960) were a fabulous spectacle, as was Dolphy's soaring, biting alto sax soloing (*Original Faubus Fables,* 1960): here at last was a passionate interpreter to match Mingus's own passion. Dolphy played with a full, clear sound on all his horns—and on the flute—and employed wide harmonic leaps and dissonances that often sounded atonal, even though he maintained that "every note I play has some reference to the chords of the piece." He went on to record often with George Russell, Booker Little, Coltrane, Coleman, and others before his untimely death from diabetes at the age of thirty-six.

Even before Coleman, Cecil Taylor was playing piano solos so dissonant and free they sounded atonal. Such classical composers as Béla Bartók and Igor Stravinsky influenced his music, as did Ellington and modern-jazz pianists; a good introduction is his album *The World of Cecil Taylor* (1960). After that, turmoil grew in his highly complex solo forms, which often used fragmentary phrases to generate grand designs; he also composed knotty pieces with many mood changes and stops and starts. By the late 1960s, he was playing violently, as fast as humanly possible (and Taylor may be the most virtuosic of all jazz pianists), with dissonances crashing like thunder through the high ("astral" he called it), middle ("surface of the earth"), and low ("abyss") registers of the keyboard. He usually overpowered the horn soloists who played with him. He also improvised long, intense, unaccompanied pieces, full of detail, almost as demanding for the listener as for the performer; "To feel is the most terrifying thing in this society," he said. A lyrical side of his music subsequently grew in importance, especially in the 1980s. The most remarkable recording project built around a free-jazz artist was *Cecil Taylor in Berlin '88*, a collection of eleven solo, duet, trio, and big-band albums in which he was joined by a succession of excellent, mostly European players.

John Coltrane was by far the most popular "outside" jazz artist, in large part because he had, according to Taylor, "great insight, a feeling for the hysteria of the times, and a conception that goes beyond that of his own horn." After 1960, Coltrane's solos became long, passionate conflicts in which he alternated lyrical playing with longer cycles that became progressively more removed from the central harmony, leading to further cycles of multiphonics and overtone screams. These were terrifically intense solos, and much of Coltrane's tension derived from his harmonic straining against his pieces' modal non-structures. His tone was tender in his occasional ballad solos (as on the album *Ballads*, 1961–62) and iron-hard in his longer virtuoso pieces (*Traneing In*, 1957, and *Good Bait*, 1958). Sometimes he soloed on soprano saxophone for variety, as in his famous interpretation of the Rodgers and Hammerstein song *My Favorite Things* (1960) from their musical *The Sound of Music*. Typical Coltrane quartet pieces featured extensive duets in which the powerful Elvin Jones played dense, multiple rhythms on a resonant drums-and-cymbals kit, creating huge waves of sound around the tenor saxophone.

After the spiritual turmoil of his album *A Love Supreme* (1964), Coltrane progressed to his greatest extremes of violent sound and harmony; *Interstellar Space*, recorded shortly before his death in 1967, consists wholly of duets with drummer Rashied Ali. Coltrane recorded often, and he liked to encourage younger free-jazz players; his quartets and quintets rivaled Miles Davis's quintet as the most popular jazz groups of the mid-1960s.

Jazz Underground

Controversy followed this music, far more and far longer than it did bop in the 1940s. Miles Davis's comment on first hearing Ornette Coleman is famous—"Hell, just listen to what he writes and how he plays. If you're talking psychologically, the man is all screwed up inside." A *Down Beat* reviewer called a Coltrane-Dolphy performance "a horrifying demonstration of what appears to be a growing anti-jazz trend," and jazz magazines were filled with columns about how "outside" jazz would destroy or save Western civilization.

At the same time that controversy was stalling the careers of free musicians, the sixties rock-music industry was having a devastating effect on jazz. Motown Records artists, the Beatles, Bob Dylan, and other pop stars were winning over the young generation that had accounted for a large portion of the jazz audience. On a downswing from the height of modern jazz's popularity at the beginning of the 1960s, jazz clubs closed in cities all over the U.S.

Cecil Taylor's stormy atonality drew on twentieth-century European music as well as jazz.

The Loft Scene

Each jazz era brought its characteristic venues. During the Swing Era, dancers flocked to ballrooms to hear big bands; after World War II, nightclubs, concert auditoriums, and outdoor festivals became the centers of bebop-era jazz. The jazz recession of the early 1960s, coinciding with the emergence of a generation of free-jazz musicians, pointed to a need for different kinds of performance settings—ones where adventurous musicians could ply their trade without the pressures imposed by more commercial nightclubs.

At the south end of Manhattan, where many of the most renowned "outside" musicians lived, the most daring music of the sixties could be heard at coffee houses, little theaters, and especially in the large lofts where musicians maintained rehearsal spaces. Among the leading artists who conducted their early careers in these settings were pianist Cecil Taylor; saxophonists Albert Ayler, Archie Shepp, and Marion Brown; trumpeter Don Cherry; drummer Sunny Murray; and trombonist Roswell Rudd.

Lofts and other alternative venues offered informal surroundings, tended not to serve alcohol, and charged low admission prices. Attendees were typically young and liberal. Writer-poet LeRoi Jones noted in 1963 that "many serious young jazz listeners now seem more willing to go sit on the floor in a loft and hear good music than go to the formal clubs downtown and hear well-known chumps." Due in part to the close connection between artists and listeners fostered by the loft scene, the new music became the center of an underground community.

In the early 1970s, Ornette Coleman led his band in occasional concerts at his rehearsal space, Artists House, below his living quarters at 131 Prince Street. The veteran tenor saxophonist Sam Rivers and his wife, Bea, opened Studio Rivbea, 24 Bond Street, in 1971. Other jazz lofts followed, including several operated by musicians—Ladies' Fort (singer Joe Lee Wilson), Ali's Alley (drummer Rashied Ali), and the Brook (saxophonist Charles Tyler) among them. The lofts provided key support for noncommercial musicians. When Edward Blackwell needed money for a kidney operation in 1973, fellow drummers Billy Higgins and Roger Blank organized benefit concerts, featuring a parade of top jazz artists, at Artists House. Several lofts joined forces to present festivals that competed with the annual Newport Jazz Festival in New York; the festivals showcased important musicians who had been excluded from the Newport bash.

Loft jazz wasn't confined to New York City; other centers included Philadelphia, Detroit, Chicago, Vancouver, and the San Francisco Bay Area. The roots of free improvisation, in fact, are traceable to the activities of drummer John Stevens and his cohorts in the 1960s at the aptly named Little Theatre in London.

What kind of music was played in the lofts? It wasn't always free jazz. Also heard were jazz veterans, now out of fashion at a time when nightclubs were few and their fare was limited. Ex-Basie arranger-tenorist Frank Foster led his Loud Minority big band in lofts, and a number of boppers such as Clifford Jordan, Sheila Jordan, Lee Konitz, and Hank Mobley alternated with a colorful variety of free players. Coleman and Konitz recorded albums at Artists House, saxophonists Tyler and Arthur Blythe recorded albums at the Brook, and five noted recordings

Lee Tanner

Saxophonist Sam Rivers and his wife, Bea, founded the Studio Rivbea loft.

from Studio Rivbea documented the 1977 Wildflowers festival that Rivers produced, which featured leading "liberated" musicians from California, Chicago, Philadelphia, and New York.

Most lofts disappeared after a few years. The longest lasting, Studio Rivbea, survived and even thrived until 1978, when a dispute with the landlord brought the music to an end. New York theaters and nightclubs were regularly presenting "outside" jazz by 1981, when Sam Rivers said, "Now there's not much need for loft spaces anymore except for rehearsals and for students." Since then, lofts have served as occasional concert spaces in New York and other principal cities, even as the audience for free jazz grew and small nightclubs, theaters, universities, and other venues emerged to accommodate musicians and listeners.
—*John Litweiler*

Saxophonist Archie Shepp studied drama and played in R&B bands before emerging as a key free-jazz player via work with John Coltrane, Cecil Taylor, and others. His later work reflected his view of jazz as an expression of black culture and freedom.

Pharoah Sanders' fat, raspy tenor saxophone sound brought him a modest degree of commercial success; his 1969 album Karma, *recorded with yodeling singer Leon Thomas, reached the pop charts.*

The remaining club and festival producers struggled with the new jazz economics by booking bop and swing acts that had already been dependable attractions. All of the leading jazz record companies, each with hundreds of LPs in its catalog—Riverside, Savoy, Contemporary, Pacific Jazz, Blue Note, Prestige, Verve—scaled down operations drastically, went out of business, or were sold, usually to rock record tycoons. Significantly, the new Impulse! label, unlike its competitors, embraced new jazz wholeheartedly; it issued Coltrane albums about every three months and thrived.

All of this meant that Taylor and the younger free players found work only irregularly, and the music became an underground art in the sixties. Coleman; his liberated, lyrical trumpeter Don Cherry; and especially Coltrane became father figures to a lively underground New York scene that included the dramatic tenor saxophonist-poet-playwright Archie Shepp, alto saxman Charles Tyler, tenor player Pharoah Sanders, trumpeter Bill Dixon, and pianist Paul Bley, among others.

The new underground musicians, by and large, shared the social concerns and liberal attitudes of their jazz predecessors, and some—reflecting the era's social and political unrest—carried these attitudes further. "Outside" jazz musicians offered works that reflected uniquely African American experiences, while Coltrane's *Alabama* (1963) and Shepp's *The Funeral* (1963) and *Rufus* (1965) mourned victims of racist murders. Some young free musicians and audiences went on to favor black nationalism, violent revolution, and even Marxism, for which poet, author, and critic LeRoi Jones (later known as Amiri Baraka) was the most militant spokesperson on the jazz scene: "We want poems that kill!" he wrote.

Other Free Instrumentalists

Some players normally oriented toward chord changes, including tenor saxophonist Sonny Rollins, experimented with free playing. Even Miles Davis moved to Coleman-like freedom in his mid-sixties quintet, which had a remarkable rhythm section centered around the impulsive young drummer Tony Williams. Younger modal players, notably vibraphonist Bobby Hutcherson and pianist Andrew Hill, conducted several daring free-jazz adventures. The change from "inside" to "outside" playing was permanent for some, including soprano saxman Steve Lacy. "It happened in gradual stages," he said. "There would be a moment here, a fifteen minutes there, a half hour there, an afternoon, an evening, and then all the time." A highly influential artist, the prolific Lacy ranged from sweet melody to high overtone abstraction on his instrument, in contrast to the narrower soprano sax sounds employed by latter-day jazz traditionalists and newly emerging "fusion" players. Lacy and pianist Mal Waldron were unusual for their alternately free and bop-era repertoires.

Critics mocked free jazz as "outer-space music." But composer, bandleader, and poet Sun Ra might have considered that a compliment. "I've chosen intergalactic music, or it has chosen me," he said. "Intergalactic music concerns the music of the galaxies.... I'm actually painting pictures of infinity with my music.... The real aim of this music is to coordinate the minds of people into an intelligent reach for a better world, and an intelligent approach to the living future." Sun Ra's shows were always spectacles, with his Arkestra, as he called it, in vivid, glittering robes and space helmets, parading and dancing through nightclubs and concert halls chanting "Next stop, Jupiter! Next stop, Jupiter!"

Sun Ra, born Herman Poole Blount, combined an outer-space mythos—he claimed to have been born on the planet Saturn—with over-the-top music and costumed big bands variously known as the Solar Arkestra, the Intergalactic Research Arkestra, the Cosmo Drama Arkestra, or, often, just the Arkestra.

Sun Ra was among the first composers to work extensively with modal structures in the 1950s. His Arkestras employed exotic sounds, at least for jazz: oboe, piccolos, timpani, throbbing percussion, paired baritone saxes. By 1965 and *The Magic City,* a long, completely improvised piece, he was conducting spontaneous compositions by signaling his musicians to play in changing groupings. The climaxes of his shows were often his own extended solos on the synthesizer: dissonant, crashing, virtuosic, they were sustained explosions of sound.

"It's late now for the world. And if I can help raise people to new plateaus of peace and understanding, I'll feel my life has been worth living as a spiritual artist," said Albert Ayler. The most radical free jazzman of the 1960s, he tried to reinvent the entire jazz tradition. The themes he composed—as in *Bells* and *Spirits Rejoice* (both 1965)—were like nineteenth-century pop songs, hymns, and bugle calls that sounded to writer Dan Morgenstern "like a Salvation Army band on LSD." Ayler played with a big tenor saxophone sound ("the biggest human sound I ever heard," critic Larry Kart said) and a wide, quavery vibrato. At fast tempos—and Ayler was another who played in the fastest tempos

humanly possible—he did not play notes at all; rather, he approximated notes with distorted sounds, multiphonics, overtone screams, and wild, long, careening phrases. "It's a matter of following the sound," said his brother and trumpeter Donald Ayler, "…the pitches, the colors, you have to watch them move." Albert drowned, apparently murdered, in 1970; his own style became almost as influential as Coltrane's and Coleman's.

Terrifically fast tempos, dissonances and extreme sounds, and long, furious, exhilarating collective improvisations all characterized late-sixties New York free jazz—"energy music"—inspired by Coltrane, Ayler, Shepp, and Taylor. But energy music was emotionally narrow, even obsessive, compared to the music that was emerging in Chicago, where free jazz could be lyrical, soft as well as intense, simple as well as complex, composed as well as improvised, even swinging or humorous. The Chicagoans—members of the cooperative AACM (Association for the Advancement of Creative Musicians)—played in big bands led by veteran pianist-composer Muhal Richard Abrams as well as in small groups.

One of them, the trio of altoist Roscoe Mitchell, trumpeter

Lester Bowie, and bassist Malachi Favors created musical lines that included "freak" sounds (bells, whistles, and toys) and silences. In time they were joined by Joseph Jarman—who had achieved an unparalleled virtuosity in his alto saxophone's extreme ranges—and drummer Don Moye, and they took the name the Art Ensemble of Chicago.

Like them, altoist Anthony Braxton explored free improvisation and unaccompanied soloing (his 1968 *For Alto Saxophone* album inspired a generation of horn players to play a cappella solos); like them, Braxton went on to master a number of different horns and became a prolific composer. More than the rest, he returned often to the bebop-era repertoire, with bop accompanists. To the early concept of free jazz— freedom from traditional harmonic, rhythmic, and formal restraints— the Chicagoans added a crucial element: freedom of choice.

Free Spaces

Where could the new musicians play? With nightclubs vanishing in Chicago, the AACM was formed to produce concerts by its member musicians. Churches, art galleries, high schools and colleges, neighborhood taverns, a lodge hall, and a historic settlement house became concert sites for the AACM players,

Tenor saxophonist Albert Ayler tempered his honking, screaming sound with the implied serenity of such album titles as Spiritual Unity.

Jazz Cooperatives

The Association for the Advancement of Creative Musicians (AACM)

The notion of musicians cooperating in business was a long-held one in jazz; members of early jazz bands often pooled income and shared responsibilities and decision making. But as jazz developed along less commercial lines, some musicians found it desirable to take more active steps to ensure their creative and economic survival. This inclination gave rise to jazz cooperatives—organizations formed for their members' mutual benefit.

In 1960, bassist Charles Mingus and drummers Max Roach and Jo Jones formed the Jazz Artists Guild, to produce their own musical events. Though the Guild didn't last long, it planted an important seed: the idea that musician-run enterprises could work.

The Jazz Composers Guild, formed by trumpeter Bill Dixon in 1964, included a number of New York free-jazz artists, among them Archie Shepp, Cecil Taylor, Sun Ra, and Paul and Carla Bley. The Guild produced weekly concerts in a New York City loft and sought to negotiate members' contracts with clubs and record companies. Its efforts led to the formation of the Jazz Composers Orchestra Association (JCOA), which lasted through much of the 1970s. The JCOA performed and recorded large-scale, big-band compositions by its directors, composers Mike Mantler and Carla Bley, and other "outside" composers; its New Music Distribution Service distributed albums of free jazz produced by small labels, some of which were musician-owned.

There were other musicians' cooperatives, based outside New York. In 1961, pianist-composer Horace Tapscott formed the Union of God's Musicians and Artists Ascension (UGMAA) to produce concerts by his big band in Los Angeles. The Association for the Advancement of Creative Musicians (AACM), the most successful cooperative, had its base in Chicago. Its longevity rested in part on its school, which produced the organization's later generations of musicians and teachers.

Inspired by the AACM, Oliver Lake, Julius Hemphill, and other St. Louis musicians formed the Black Artists Group (BAG), which was active at the turn of the 1970s; like the AACM, it emphasized the sharing of creative discoveries as a vital by-product of cooperation. In the 1980s, in Chicago, came a music lovers' cooperative, the all-volunteer Southend Musicworks, which produced a variety of jazz and even contemporary classical concerts.

Grants from the National Endowment for the Arts (founded in the mid-sixties), state arts councils, and private philanthropies helped support the teaching and performance programs of the AACM and its successors. In time, as free jazz found its way into a growing number of venues, and as the music gained favor with a younger generation of listeners, the need for cooperative efforts declined. And as individual musicians arrived at different levels of musical and popular success, the cooperative, all-for-one feeling often dissipated. Nevertheless, for a number of important modern-jazz artists, participation in cooperatives marked a crucial stage of their careers. —*John Litweiler*

Benny Carter listens to student Joshua Redman at a Harvard University workshop.

©Ken Franckling

If anyone had told Charlie Parker that colleges would someday offer courses in jazz, he'd likely have shaken his head in bewilderment. In his time, jazz musicians got all the education they needed by hanging out in nightclubs or dance halls and waiting to sit in with the greats. But with the shrinking of the jazz audience and the closing of scores of clubs and ballrooms, opportunities for young players to prove themselves onstage decreased dramatically. As the century ended, more and more musicians were learning their craft—and honing their chops—in academic settings.

By the late 1990s, aspiring jazz musicians could major in the art form at more than 120 music schools and universities nationally, including the Berklee College of Music and the New England Conservatory of Music in Boston, the University of North Texas in Denton, Florida State University in Tallahassee, the University of Miami, the Manhattan School of Music, the New School in New York City, and Indiana University in Bloomington.

The best high school and college programs, rather than attempting to create clones of past masters, gave young musicians the tools and encouragement to find their own voices. Guitarist Hiram Bullock, a successful sideman and solo artist who studied with Pat Metheny at the University of Miami, concluded that "the point of a teacher is not to stylistically mold students into carbon copies of himself but to take what a student has and make it more." Other notable beneficiaries of academic training include such distinctive artists as trumpeter Roy Hargrove, guitarist John Scofield, and tenor saxophonist Joshua Redman (the latter a graduate of the outstanding program at Berkeley High School in Northern California).

Jazz schools also generated networks of alumni that served as sources of work. "[Bassist] Mark Egan, [drummer] Danny Gottlieb, and [keyboardist] Gil Goldstein were all at the University of Miami at the same time," Bullock said, adding that he worked with them on his first union gig. "It was playing *Godspell....* The band was Metheny, Gottlieb on drums, and Egan on bass. Metheny quit the show and got me the gig."

As recently as the early 1970s, some college and university music programs were biased against jazz and threatened to expel students who preferred to improvise. Jazz was thought to violate the European musical values that those institutions sought to instill.

But times changed, and as jazz became established in academic circles, some eminent jazz artists gained appointments as professors of the music, among them vibraphonist Gary Burton, drummer Max Roach, composer David Baker, alto saxophonist Jackie McLean, bassist Richard Davis, saxophonist Marion Brown, and guitarist Kenny Burrell.

The increasing number of jazz instructors created an important new jazz constituency. The International Association of Jazz Educators, founded in 1968, became a strong advocate; by 1999 the Kansas organization had more than eight thousand members in thirty-five countries.

Classrooms will never replace clubs—the ultimate gauge of jazz artistry will always be audience response. But academia has become increasingly important in guiding bright new performers onto the scene. —*Calvin Wilson*

who booked, advertised, and sold tickets for concerts, then swept the floors and turned out the lights once the music was over. The AACM was not the first self-producing effort by musicians, but it lasted arguably the longest, and for over three decades, beginning in the late 1960s, it ran a music school for inner-city youth; some excellent musicians, including saxophonists Douglas Ewart and Edward Wilkerson and trombonist George Lewis, were graduates.

In New York, jazz musicians and music lovers converted lofts in old factory buildings into concert sites; the best known of these were Artists House, owned by Ornette Coleman, and Studio Rivbea, operated by saxophonist Sam Rivers. In this respect, too, free jazz was revolutionary. Just as swing thrived primarily in ballrooms and bop in nightclubs, free jazz became a music of concert venues and performance spaces. And if free jazz began as underground experiments, in time it was played often enough at jazz festivals and major concert halls.

Without a dominating figure such as Armstrong or Ellington or Parker, free jazz took off in many different directions. Unlike leading postwar combos (the Modern Jazz Quartet, Horace Silver, Art Blakey, Miles Davis, Dave Brubeck, Thelonious Monk), the most popular free-jazz groups were only intermittently active—their members had too many other musical interests. So, for example, the members of the Art Ensemble of Chicago and the multisaxophone virtuosos of the World Saxophone Quartet (originally David Murray, Julius Hemphill, Hamiet Bluiett, and the brilliant, Dolphy-inspired Oliver Lake) also maintained individual careers as composers, sidemen, and leaders of small and large groups.

Similarly, the free-jazz scene was geographically dispersed. New England and Upstate New York (notably the Creative Music Studio, a school in Woodstock) were new-music centers, and handfuls of musicians sparked activity in Houston, Toronto, New Orleans, Detroit, and a number of other cities throughout North

America. In San Francisco were the far-ranging ROVA Saxophone Quartet, which played works by its members and commissioned music by others. In Los Angeles two of Ornette Coleman's former associates, Bobby Bradford, a wonderful lyric trumpeter, and John Carter, who brought the clarinet back to jazz, formed a long-time team. Carter also composed a series of five suites—including *Castles of Ghana* (1985) and *Fields* (1988)—interpreting the historic black experience in the United States.

Fred Anderson and Hal Russell, two pioneering free players, were catalysts in reviving the Chicago scene, beginning in the late 1970s: Anderson led bands and played endlessly creative, lyrical, blues-rich tenor sax, and the late multi-instrumentalist, composer, and teacher Russell led the freewheeling, often hilarious N-R-G Ensemble. None of the later AACM generations were much influenced by the innovations of the first generation, except for Anderson's protégés, especially saxophonist Douglas Ewart.

The Art Ensemble of Chicago (from left to right): Don Moye (drums), Roscoe Mitchell (woodwinds), Lester Bowie (trumpet), Joseph Jarman (woodwinds), and Malachi Favors (bass).

Jazz on Radio

Aside from the sound recording, radio has been the most important dissemination medium in jazz. While records, tapes, and compact discs took jazz into homes, and permitted the control over playback ideal for focused, repeated listening, radio granted listeners exposure to a broad repertoire of jazz recordings, for free.

As radio and jazz developed simultaneously, they proved mutually beneficial: Radio took jazz to a mass audience and promoted sales of jazz recordings; in earlier years it provided work for musicians in radio orchestras, and, in later years, it kept older styles of recorded jazz in the public ear when record companies showed little inclination to reissue their early jazz sides. Jazz, in turn, served as important content for radio broadcasts.

But the story of jazz on radio is also one of an often complex and challenging music getting decreasing airtime as, over the decades, talk and populist programming gained favor

among stations eager to attract the largest possible audiences.

During the 1920s, when radio first emerged as a mass medium, broadcasters relied heavily on jazz-flavored dance music. At that time, "sweet" (as opposed to "hot") dance bands dominated the schedules of most local stations. Jazz programming was hampered by the exclusion of African Americans from the broadcasting studios, though a few of the great black jazz pioneers still managed to get on the air thanks to "remotes"—microphones and wires installed to carry live performances from big-city nightclubs to radio studios for broadcast. WHN in New York, for example, aired Fletcher Henderson's band direct from the Roseland Ballroom beginning in 1924.

When, during the later 1920s, radio stations organized into national networks such as the National Broadcasting Corporation (NBC), Duke Ellington quickly moved into that influential arena. In 1928, the Columbia Broadcasting Company (CBS)

shot Ellington into the big time when it began broadcasting his orchestra directly from the Cotton Club. CBS and NBC continued to carry remote broadcasts from the Cotton Club until at least 1938, also bringing Cab Calloway to national fame. These and similar broadcasts were the first encounters that many white listeners had with African American music.

When the Great Depression decimated the record business, radio became "the poor man's phonograph." Radios poured out free music to an estimated 60 million listeners in U.S. homes. Light variety shows ruled the day, but radio also helped usher in the Swing Era by featuring the big bands that were active in the 1930s and forties. NBC aired the Benny Goodman Orchestra—playing mostly swinging versions of pop songs, greatly enlivened by Fletcher Henderson's arrangements—as the last portion of its *Let's Dance* program. Network remotes also produced national audiences for Count Basie, the Dorsey brothers, Artie Shaw, and Glenn Miller.

During the late thirties, radio stations turned increasingly to recorded music as captured on "electrical transcription" discs, which carried a full fifteen-minute show on one side and often featured swing bands.

In ensuing years, radio would become primarily a record-playing medium, in part because television's early variety shows replaced those of radio, siphoning off live bands. Radio's reliance on records, combined with its selling of airtime to powerful advertising agencies, leading to increasingly simple, generic, and primarily vocal musical programming, marked the beginning of the end of jazz radio's heyday.

In the meantime, government-backed radio began playing a role

Pianist Billy Taylor maintained a high profile on jazz radio, especially as host of the long-running Jazz Alive *program on National Public Radio.*

Radio played a key role in popularizing Duke Ellington (left), beginning with remote radio broadcasts of his orchestra performing at the Cotton Club in the late 1920s.

in jazz broadcasting. During World War II, the Armed Forces Radio Network installed outlets in the European and Pacific theaters and spread the sound of jazz-flavored big-band music around the world.

In the 1940s and 1950s, some stations were still airing live remotes—hosted by such personalities as "Symphony Sid" Torin, noted for his programs emanating from Birdland in New York. As the playing of records replaced live broadcasts, jazz disc jockeys developed their own followings in different parts of the country: Don Manning, Mort Fega, and William B. Williams broadcast from New York City; Oscar Treadwell out of Philadelphia; Willis Conover and Felix Grant in Washington, D.C.; Dick Martin out of New Orleans; Al "Jazzbo" Collins from a series of cities; and the hip Daddy-O Daylie out of Chicago.

Starting in 1955, and continuing through the Cold War, the U.S. government radio service Voice of America aired jazz programming hosted by Conover. The programs proved highly popular, further building the international audience for jazz.

The 1960s brought the rise of frequency-modulation (FM) broadcasting, which yielded a clearer, more reliable audio signal than that of the established amplitude-modulation (AM) technology. FM radio proved hospitable to jazz and brought a number of important jazz oases, particularly on National Public Radio, founded in 1971.

In 1977, Steve Rathe and Tim Owens began producing Jazz Alive with Billy Taylor; the program featured jazz in performance and became the show carried by the most NPR affiliates. Marian McPartland's Piano Jazz, produced by Shari Hutchinson, got under way in 1979. As a direct result of these programs, the number of hours of jazz programming on local stations increased considerably; jazz became the third leading public-radio format after classical music and news. A major grant from the Lila Wallace Readers' Digest Fund to strengthen jazz programming on NPR generated the American Jazz Radio Festival and, starting in 1992, JazzSet with Branford Marsalis. Jazz from Lincoln Center, produced by Rathe and Ron Gibson, with Wynton Marsalis as

artistic director, began airing in 1994. A year later, Owens developed Billy Taylor's Jazz at the Kennedy Center and Jazz Profiles, the latter hosted by jazz vocalist Nancy Wilson.

A sister network, Public Radio International, also carried a number of jazz programs. The most popular was Riverwalk, which began in 1989, produced by Margaret Moos Pick and Lynne Cruise.

Syndicated jazz programs included Jazz Revisited with Hazen Schumacher (1970–98) and Jazz with Bob Parlocha (beginning in 1997), heard on more than two hundred stations.

In the 1990s, jazz lost ground on U.S. airwaves as public radio stations found it more lucrative to broadcast news and public affairs programming, and some major stations in Washington, Philadelphia, Los Angeles, and San Francisco dropped their jazz format. But jazz stations were still swinging in such major markets as Newark/New York, Miami, Atlanta, Seattle, Los Angeles, San Francisco, and San Diego. New technologies, however, helped to take up the slack: Long Beach, California's KLON radio added home satellite capability in 1990, cable and satellite TV services added jazz audio options, and a number of jazz radio stations "webcast" their signals on the World Wide Web, making them available far beyond their normal listening areas. JazzWorks—a highly automated, technologically advanced, twenty-four-hour-a-day programming service, gained popularity—an indication that jazz remained viable on noncommercial radio. Meanwhile, the accessible format of "smooth jazz"—which many jazz aficionados regarded as rather empty—gained favor in the commercial arena. —William H. Kenney, John Edward Hasse, and Tad Lathrop

Gunther Schuller, a later president of the New England Conservatory of Music, introduced the notion of "third stream" music, a fusion of classical and jazz ideas.

Anthony Braxton's compositions, titled with diagrams instead of words, reflected his interest in the mathematical aspects of music.

Experimental Composers

One of the most radical departures of the era was undertaken in the traditional-jazz idiom by the Australian jazz and ragtime composer David Dallwitz. The subject of his *Ern Malley Suite* (1975) is a notorious Down Under literary hoax. Imagine a singer like the young Billie Holiday warbling surreal lyrics ("Come, we will dance sedate quadrilles/A pallid polka or a yelping shimmy/ Over these sunken sodden breeding-grounds!…/Culture, forsooth! Albert, get my gun") while a fine Dixieland band plays strange ragtime melodies.

"Outside" experiments came from the realm of classical composition as well. In the 1950s, composer Gunther Schuller had conceived of "third stream" music, a fusion of the classical and jazz traditions. Two of his 1959–60 works are considered modern landmarks: *Abstraction* offers a string quartet playing an atonal piece in pyramid form with, at the apex, an unaccompanied Ornette Coleman alto solo; in the four *Variants on a Theme by Thelonious Monk* (*Criss Cross*), improvisers including Coleman, Dolphy, and bassist Scott LaFaro enjoy interplay with each other and with a string quartet.

Other classical composers, some encouraged by Schuller, contributed new works. They included Milton Babbitt's *All Set* (1958) and Krystof Penderecki's *Actions* (1971); John Cage created inconclusive collaborations with Joseph Jarman and Sun Ra. The score of the 1997 opera *Amistad* by Anthony Davis included free-jazz improvisers with the orchestra's symphonic musicians. Pianist-teacher Ran Blake advanced the third-stream idea to include the fusion of any ethnic and art-music traditions, whether improvised or composed.

Variations of the third-stream concept pop up in most extended pieces by free-jazz artists, including Coleman. Carla Bley composed her "chrono-transduction" *Escalator over the Hill* (1968–71) for a crowd of improvisers, singers, and reciters. For Charlie Haden's Liberation Music Orchestra, Bley's suites, such as *Dream Keeper* (1990), link Spanish and Latin American folk music with original pieces; her best scores for her own big bands, including

Spangled Banner Minor and Other Patriotic Songs (1977), are notable for balancing distinctive elements and for a recurring whimsical humor. Cecil Taylor's large works for big band fuse composition and improvisation in grand polyphonic designs, as in *Alms/Tiergarten (Spree)* (1988). AACM artists, including Abrams, Jarman, Leroy Jenkins, Douglas Ewart, and Henry Threadgill, all composed large works. The largest is Anthony Braxton's *For Four Orchestras* (1978); among the most musically successful are Braxton's jazz-band scores and Leo Smith's *Return to My Native Land II* (1981).

Some other composers worked specifically within jazz traditions. The big band, octet, and saxophone ensemble scores of Julius Hemphill, David Murray, and Edward Wilkerson (especially for his group Eight Bold Souls) gained vigor from Ellington sonorities and swing and bop phrasing. The potent trio Air (Henry Threadgill, woodwinds; Fred Hopkins, bass; Steve McCall, drums) created free interpretations of Scott Joplin rags as well as of Threadgill themes. In the eighties Threadgill went on to compose works—such as *Subject to Change* (1984) and *Theme from Thomas Cole* (1986)—with memorable melodies and countermelodies, rich harmonies, expressive soloing, and constant, ongoing, nervous activity for his sextet. As a composer, Roscoe Mitchell made some of the most far-reaching innovations of jazz form, including *Nonaah* (1976), originally a saxophone solo that he recomposed several times for wind and string ensembles. He created *L-R-G* (1978) for himself (woodwinds) and two brass instrumentalists (Leo Smith and George Lewis), in ever-mobile disparities; *The Maze* (1978), by contrast, contains the interactions of eight percussionists. In these works—Mitchell called them "sound collages"—form and musical line evolve from the unique sounds created by the performers.

Despite the artistic success of these big-band and orchestra compositions, most were seldom performed because of the expense of paying so many musicians. Self-contained orchestras, including Sun Ra's Arkestra, whose members lived together in Philadelphia, or local phenomena like the AACM big band (Chicago) and Either/Orchestra (Boston) were rare. Needed were repertory ensembles dedicated to playing new music, just as the Lincoln Center and Smithsonian orchestras would focus on playing earlier jazz. In fact, for a time in the 1970s, trumpeter Mike Mantler maintained the Jazz Composers Orchestra as a workshop for New York composers. But most orchestral performances of jazz works were ad hoc, often resulting from grants by arts philanthropies. The largest arts foundation, the National Endowment for the Arts, provided significant support for jazz composition in the 1970s and eighties.

Performances by composer Carla Bley's big bands were often as entertaining and humorous as they were challenging.

The Growing Role of Women in Jazz

Trumpeter and bandleader Valaida Snow.

The jazz world, for all its sophistication and liberal-mindedness, proved to be largely male-dominated through most of its first century, leaving women underrepresented and underreported—particularly as instrumentalists.

Prior to the emergence of jazz, the most socially acceptable instrument for women was the piano, and the acceptable places to play it were the parlor and the church. Apart from signs of professional activity by women in ragtime—they composed music, demonstrated ragtime and pop sheet music at department stores, and played accompaniment in silent-movie theaters—there is scant evidence of working female jazz musicians in the early years of the twentieth century.

In the 1920s and 1930s, cutting contests and band battles further established jazz as a male-controlled enterprise. With rare exceptions, such as pianist Lil Hardin Armstrong, female jazz players were relegated to the sidelines. Women found themselves struggling against age-old strictures holding that while singing was suitably feminine, instruments that made them alter their facial expressions or stances were not "ladylike." A particularly challenging hurdle for women was gaining acceptance as drummers and as brass and reed players.

Excellent performances and the ability to survive the rigors of the road weren't enough to override the prevailing sentiment that women were too weak for such men's work. Consequently, musically committed women sometimes had to resort to extreme measures to secure opportunities to play. Trumpeter Valaida Snow, disgusted by her lack of acceptance in the U.S., toured with Jack Carter's band in Shanghai from 1926 to 1928, eventually leading her own outfit in Europe from 1935 to 1940. Some women even cross-dressed, and one—Dorothy Tipton—masqueraded for fifty years as "Billy Tipton," passing as a male piano player and bandleader until her death in 1989.

In the 1940s, as jazz developed larger audiences and greater commercial potential, the contributions of women did increase—if they were vocalists. Audiences for big bands demanded female singers—or "chippies," as *Down Beat* termed them. Both familiar and obscure white "chippies" graced the magazine's covers, but the extraordinary talent and beauty of Billie Holiday, Ella Fitzgerald, and Sarah Vaughan were not deemed worthy of equivalent exposure during the same period. Also, fewer African American than white men were featured on covers or in photographs; ultimately this was noticed more than the absence of women, just as the issue of racial equality has tended to overshadow the subject of gender equality in jazz.

When the United States entered World War II, women took over the jobs vacated by soldiers—except in the music industry. Lacking opportunities to occupy the vacant chairs of musician inductees, women formed all-female groups, including the International Sweethearts of Rhythm and Virgil Whyte's "All-Girl" Band, to tour the United States and perform in USO shows. Despite their excellent musicians, they were often viewed as mere novelty acts; most of them folded when men returned to civilian action.

Accounts of the rise of bebop after World War II have mostly ignored the contributions of women—for example, the impact of Mary Lou

Influential pianist and composer Mary Lou Williams.

The International Sweethearts of Rhythm

Williams as a mentor to bebop pioneers Charlie Parker, Thelonious Monk, Dizzy Gillespie, and Bud Powell. Male journalists gravitated toward the new sound emanating from Minton's Playhouse and New York City's 52nd Street nightclubs to fraternize with their male idols while many women musicians—wary of the encroaching drug lifestyle—stayed home. And so, as jazz became more "modern," women continued to be overlooked and underrecorded (unless under the aegis of Moses Asch, Leonard Feather, and a few other producers).

Significant change began to occur in the 1960s and seventies, when colleges and conservatories began replacing big bands and jam sessions as the learning centers for jazz musicians. On the more level playing fields of academic institutions, women and men developed their skills together; men were exposed to the full range of women's musical abilities and developed an appreciation of and a natural rapport with their female colleagues.

Women became more prominent in jazz of the 1960s and 1970s, with such pianists as Joanne Brackeen, Carla Bley, and Toshiko Akiyoshi leading bands that showcased their own compositions. By late in the century the climate for female jazz musicians had vastly improved: government grants were increasingly being awarded to subsidize their careers as performers and composers; changed attitudes stemming from the women's movement and the declining cachet of drug use among jazz musicians had made the atmosphere more conducive to interaction and collaboration between women and men.

At century's end, women were providing their own formal support systems and networks. In 1996, the Kennedy Center in Washington, D.C., began holding an annual Mary Lou Williams Women in Jazz Festival as a forum for discussing gender-related problems in the business and as an opportunity for women to perform on the same stage. Musicians as dissimilar in style as pianists Geri Allen and Marian McPartland; as diverse as soprano saxophonist Jane Ira Bloom and drummer Cindy Blackman; and as powerful as the Maria Schneider Jazz Orchestra, Maiden Voyage, and Diva—No Man's Band have performed and informally jammed with new talent at the festival. Still, "the discrimination is now all subtle," according to pianist Rachel Z. "It's more like being left out." Perhaps the twenty-first century will see women widely welcomed into jazz. If so, when the second century of jazz is chronicled, a sidebar about women's contributions will be viewed as a twentieth-century anachronism.
—*Ann K. Kuebler*

Composer and bandleader Toshiko Akiyoshi.

The experimental big bands led by composer Muhal Richard Abrams yielded future members of the AACM and the Art Ensemble of Chicago.

European jazz composers fared better than their U.S. counterparts. For over two decades, beginning in 1966, the Globe Unity Orchestra, comprising the best European free players, gathered almost annually to tour and debut new works by leader Alex Schlippenbach and other members. Bassist Barry Guy formed and re-formed the London Jazz Composers Orchestra often, from 1970, to play his massive settings (including *Harmos*, 1989) for band and top British improvisers; the Italian Instabile Orchestra served as a similar showcase for Italian players.

Guy, who maintained dual careers as a jazz and classical musician, was one of a number of Europeans advancing the third-stream concept. Other successes included the fiery Brotherhood of Breath, 1970s South African exiles and English musicians who merged free jazz with black South African folk-pop; Pierre Dørge's New Jungle Orchestra (Denmark), fusing Ellington, free jazz, and West African music; and Willem Breuker's Kollektief (Holland), playing the leader's mad, satiric mélanges of jazz, classical, folk, and dance musics.

Staying Free

In the late 1990s, the best places—and some of the only places—to listen to live free-jazz were music festivals. The leading U.S. free-jazz festival was the one hosted by the famous New York City nightclub the Knitting Factory for two weeks each spring. The name of the event changed frequently—in 1999 it was called the New York Jazz Festival.

While the U.S. government encumbered visiting European artists with red tape, Canada had few such restrictions, so festivals such as those in Vancouver, British Columbia; Edmonton, Alberta; and Victoriaville, Québec, annually presented international free-jazz performers. Several European festivals, including the Total Music Meeting and Moers annual affairs (both in Germany), also showcased artists who played the new music.

U.S. radio coverage of experimental jazz, which had always been limited, became more so in the 1990s. In keeping with that decade's fashion for conservative playlists, a good many public radio stations eliminated innovative jazz entirely, leaving college and university stations to pick up the slack.

Buyers of jazz compact discs needed to be alert, because the five rock-music conglomerates that controlled over 90 percent of the recording industry in the late nineties tended to yank jazz albums off the market a few months after release. On the other hand, independent labels in the U.S. and Europe, such as Leo, FMP, HatART, and Silkheart, a number of them musician owned, released many albums, and their CDs remained available.

All of which served to underscore what had always been the case: the farthest reaches of jazz, whether deep underground or way out in space, are populated thinly, but with a determined group of explorers willing to do what it takes to expand the music's boundaries.

Key Recordings

The Art Ensemble. *The Art Ensemble 1967/68.* Five discs, Nessa. Recorded in 1967–68, here are songs, strange sounds, humor, sweeping solos, clever collective improvisations, high flights, and low blows—the very best performances by the players who became (in 1969) the Art Ensemble of Chicago, plus guests. Alternatives: The Bomba label (Japan) has issued two CDs from this collection. Lester Bowie, *Numbers 1 & 2* (Nessa) and Roscoe Mitchell, *Old/Quartet* (Nessa), both recorded in 1967. Roscoe Mitchell Sextet, *Sound* (Delmark), recorded in 1966, is the astonishing debut of Mitchell, Bowie, and bassist Malachi Favors.

Ayler, Albert. *In Greenwich Village: The Complete Impulse! Sessions.* GRP. Recorded in 1966–67. An indescribable mixture of agony and ecstasy, sentimentality and hysteria, by the most influential saxophonist since Coltrane. **Alternative:** *Spirits Rejoice* (ESP, Germany), recorded in 1965, is the best album by an Ayler group, although only thirty-two minutes long.

Coleman, Ornette. *Beauty Is a Rare Thing: The Complete Atlantic Recordings.* Six discs, Rhino. Includes performances from 1959–61 by the classic quartet of Coleman (alto sax), Don Cherry (trumpet), Charlie Haden (bass), and Billy Higgins or Edward Blackwell (drums), and their first brilliant successors; also, Coleman's tenor sax solos and Gunther Schuller's *Abstraction* and *Variants* and the "double quartet" collective improvisation *Free Jazz.* **Alternatives:** *The Shape of Jazz to Come* (Rhino, 1959) and *Change of the Century* (Atlantic, 1959), the first two albums by a free-jazz group, containing some fine solos and the first versions of several standard songs, including *Lonely Woman.*

Coltrane, John. *Coltrane.* Impulse. An outstanding introduction to Coltrane in the sixties, this 1962 recording showcases his diversity and includes the brilliantly played and highly influential *Out of This World.* Coltrane recorded several other equally fine albums with a group that included drummer Elvin Jones, bassist Jimmy Garrison, and pianist McCoy Tyner. Among them is *A Love Supreme* (Impulse), recorded in December 1964, which includes more difficult works and is essential to an understanding of the artist.

Charlie Haden Liberation Music Orchestra. *Dream Keeper.* Blue Note. A 1990 recording of Latin American folk music, original compositions, Langston Hughes lyrics sung by a children's choir, and a hot version of the South African national anthem, all arranged by Carla Bley (one of her finest projects) and beautifully played.

Sun Ra and His Solar Arkestra. *The Magic City.* Evidence. On this 1965 recording, Sun Ra, "from the planet Saturn," conducts difficult, wholly improvised music that ranges from moody to exciting. The title piece is a key work among Sun Ra's many recordings.

Taylor, Cecil. *Looking (Berlin Version) Solo.* FMP. The pianist conjures a range of moods that seems to encompass heaven, hell, and earth. An important 1989 recording by one of the most visionary and distinctive performers in jazz.

Henry Threadgill Sextet. *Easily Slip into Another World.* Jive/Novus. Sounds that range from bluesy to tough and thorny, recorded in 1987 by a top composer and his interpreters. **Alternative:** Air, *Air Time* (Nessa), recorded in 1977. Bold yet sensitive music by three of the best "outside" improvisers: Threadgill, saxophones, flute, hubcaps; Fred Hopkins, bass; Steve McCall, percussion.

Mal Waldron Quartet with Steve Lacy. *The Super Quartet Live at Sweet Basil.* Evidence. From closely constructed melodies to high, fanciful flights, Lacy is at his best on this 1987 effort—but Lacy has often performed as well in widely diverse settings with U.S. and European cohorts, playing either highly composed or freely improvised music.

World Saxophone Quartet. *Revue.* Black Saint. Virtuosity with a smile, in a 1980 recording by the four exceptional saxophonist-composer-arrangers Hamiet Bluiett, David Murray, Oliver Lake, and Julius Hemphill. —*John Litweiler*

Jazz Worldwide

Kevin Whitehead

Cuban percussionist Machito and his orchestra, with lead trumpeter–musical director Mario Bauzá (seventh from left), created some of the earliest Latin jazz in the 1940s.

Tenor saxophonist Jan Garbarek brought distinctively Nordic elements to his jazz improvising.

It's a rainy Sunday in December. The bassist Lelio Giannetto is at Palermo's airport on the Sicilian coast, where incoming flights are running late. He keeps looking at his watch.

Giannetto is an organizer of a three-day meeting—called "Dreamin' California"—of free improvisers from Sicily and the San Francisco Bay Area, starting in a downtown theater tomorrow evening. Yesterday, he'd recorded with early arrival Tim Perkis, whose basic equipment is a laptop computer from which he coaxes abstract blurps and squeaks. Expected within the hour is Tom Nunn, who plays homemade instruments and has written a three-hundred-page treatise on free improvisation, in which jazz is barely mentioned.

Think we're off the jazz map yet?

Then ask Giannetto why he keeps checking the time. His answer: he has a different kind of gig this afternoon, an hour or so away in the town of Salaparuta, with the Sicilian Jazz Dixielanders. In the nineteenth century, he explains, there was regular ship traffic between Salaparuta and New Orleans, a boat going out loaded with oranges and maybe a few hopeful immigrants and coming back full of cotton.

One couple who took the boat to New Orleans had a son who grew up to be Original Dixieland Jazz Band cornetist Nick LaRocca. All those Italians in old New Orleans were one reason opera was in the air, helping inspire Louis Armstrong's dramatic high-note endings.

Moral: You don't have to be American to see yourself in jazz. By the end of the twentieth century, jazz was nearly everywhere, coming back around the bend just when you thought you'd left it. Colleges all over Europe were teaching it, wealthier European countries were subsidizing it. Even Beijing had launched an annual jazz festival, where musicians converged from the United States, Australia, Japan, Europe, and China itself—including the People's Liberation Army Big Band. But then, Shanghai had begun hosting itinerant jazz musicians as far back as 1926.

Early Jazz Abroad

Jazz went international early—no later than the fall of 1914, when the Original Creole Orchestra from New Orleans, including cornetist Freddie Keppard, toured western Canada for five weeks. They passed through again in 1916. The year after that, two homegrown Canadian jazz bands turned up, one in Vancouver and one in Hamilton, Ontario. Others quickly followed, in cities from Winnipeg to Montreal. (And Americans kept coming: pianist Jelly Roll Morton made Vancouver his base from mid-1919 through 1920.) In many ways, what happened in Canada set the pattern for jazz's reception

The Original Dixieland Jazz Band, billed as "the creators of jazz" and "the sensation of America," played the Palladium and other London halls in 1919. They are shown here at London's Palais de Danse.

in the rest of the world: the music was popular immediately, even if newspaper critics were hostile; musicians quickly attempted to do it themselves; a few African American musicians elected to stay around, because racial attitudes were less oppressive than in the States; many Canadian musicians got a good education listening to and playing with U.S. talent. As a practical matter, this meant working bands were racially integrated in Canada in the 1920s, rather earlier than in the U.S.

Jazz began crossing the oceans even before it turned up on records back home, to judge by *Down Home Rag,* recorded in London in 1916 by the Versatile Four, an American vaudeville band. Their drummer, Charlie Johnson, was already swinging.

In 1918, Australia's first jazz band was a smash hit in Sydney. In 1919, the Original Dixieland Jazz Band visited England and stayed a year. Around 1920, the Blue Band, from Holland, recorded in Berlin and London. Dutch colonials were playing jazz in Java by 1922; by 1926 they'd been joined by native Indonesians and itinerants from the Philippines.

The first great U.S. jazzman in Europe was clarinetist Sidney Bechet, who appeared in London in 1919 with Will Marion Cook's ragtimey Southern Syncopated Orchestra. Swiss conductor Ernest Ansermet heard them often and wrote a now-famous review singling out Bechet as a

harbinger of music that would sweep the world. Ansermet was astute enough to praise the quality of Bechet's blues, at a time when the conductor may have had little knowledge of that style. When Cook's band broke up, its musicians scattered as far afield as Norway.

Back then, when the "jazz" label got pasted on any music that moved, there was some confusion abroad about just what jazz was. Was its essence syncopation or improvisation? Was it futuristic noise music, or a novelty act with drummers doing tricks with sticks? Was it folk music or a more refined expression?

For that reason, American musicians on foreign soil were enormously important locally, even if little remembered back home. Take drummer Louis Mitchell, who in 1918 or 1919 took a jazz band to Paris and stayed over a decade. To quote John Szwed, jazz was "the shock to the system the French had been waiting for": modern, energetic, exotic. By 1922, composer Darius Milhaud was taking notes in Harlem nightspots, an influence you can hear on his *La création du monde* (1923).

On the Continent, black American musicians were suddenly in demand, and more than a few at home—encouraged by stories of racial tolerance told by black GIs returning from World War I—took the boat abroad. One pianist lured to Paris by an offer of $50 weekly was soon in London making $750 a week.

When U.S. musicians left a local band, or a group showed up a few players short, locals began filling in. One such precocious French player was trombonist Leo Vauchant, born in 1904. Hearing Mitchell's band, he quickly grasped that improvisation was the point and soon figured out how to do it himself. In 1924 Vauchant began exchanging music lessons with symphonic composer Maurice Ravel, who wanted to know about jazz. Relying on his practical experience, Vauchant formulated loose guidelines for what worked or didn't, what was hip and what wasn't—an early glimmering of "jazz education" (but not the only one: jazz instruction books were sold in England by 1926, and by 1927 the Frankfurt conservatory was offering a jazz performance class). Surreal postscript: In 1931 Vauchant traveled to the States as a dance-band arranger. On one band's bus tour in Louisiana, he and a guitarist went out in a field during a rest stop to play impromptu blues for African American cotton pickers. By age thirty he'd glimpsed both jazz's intellectual future and its romantic past.

By the mid-1920s, jazz records were being distributed overseas, and before long England and France (like the United States) had jazz critics. Pianist Claude Hopkins, in Paris to accompany singer Josephine Baker in 1925, found local musicians had been studying the latest Armstrong sides: "Some of the European bands were so like Louis's band, you could hardly tell the difference.... The tone and the range weren't as good but the overall picture was pretty similar."

Still, for many outside the U.S., such records posed more questions than they answered. Labels on 78s typically gave no or misleading information about who the players were, and when and where they recorded the disc—information necessary to fit fragmentary pieces of the jazz puzzle together. Thus were born the jazz discographers, tracking down dates and personnel, often by peppering visiting Americans with vexing questions about sessions long past. Over the years, many of jazz's most diligent discographers have come from outside the U.S.: France's Charles Delaunay, whose 1936 *Hot Discography* was a stylistic model for many later examples; England's Brian Rust; Denmark's Jørgen Grunnet Jepsen; Belgium's Walter Bruyninckx; and Canada's Tom Lord.

Charles Delaunay, an influential jazz discographer, played a key role in helping jazz thrive in France. He launched Jazz hot *magazine in 1935, presented concerts, and directed the recording programs of the Swing and Vogue labels.*

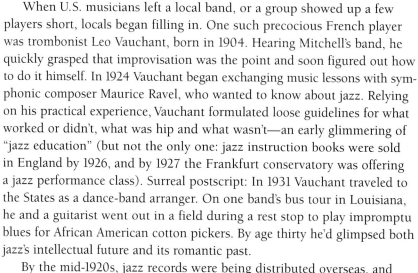

Le Jazz Hot: Jazz in Paris Between the World Wars

Fats Waller (third from right) at the popular Paris nightclub run by Bricktop (far right).

Jazz was born and raised in America, but in Paris between the wars it found its home away from home. Long a cosmopolitan city that encouraged personal and artistic freedom, the City of Light attracted hundreds of U.S. writers, painters, and classical and jazz musicians.

World War I jump-started Parisians' infatuation with syncopated music. In August of 1918, they discovered American Lt. James Reese Europe and his jazzy Hellfighters military band. Americans, thanks to their strong participation in the war, were loved by the French.

African Americans found a far more welcoming environment in Paris than in their native United States and drank in the greater freedom. When Mitchell's Jazz Kings recorded in Paris in December 1921, they made the first non-ragtime jazz disc by blacks in Europe. The St. Louis–born singer and dancer Josephine Baker achieved overwhelming success in *La revue Nègre* (1925) and overnight became the darling of the French, while the African American singer Bricktop (Ada Smith) ran a highly successful nightclub in Paris (1928–39) where many top musicians performed.

In 1920, Parisians had an opportunity to hear their first jazz artist of wide renown, Sidney Bechet, playing with Benny Peyton's Jazz Kings. In 1925, Bechet returned with *La revue Nègre* and in 1928 played the nightclub Chez Florence, but then was expelled from the country for getting into a gunfight.

Bandleaders Paul Whiteman (1925) and Noble Sissle (1928) also played and made their marks in Paris, and at the end of the decade, many young, talented white Chicago musicians went to the city, among them Bud Freeman and drummer Dave Tough. France was also producing homegrown jazz musicians—the most important of the 1920s were trombonist Léon (Leo) Vauchant, trumpeter Philippe Brun, and pianist Stéphane Mougin, while the most outstanding orchestras were those of Ray Ventura and Grégor.

In the 1920s, jazz was terrifically in vogue, but in the early thirties, the mass audience seemed to turn its back. Still, *Jazz tango* magazine emerged in June 1930. And in 1932, a handful of amateurs established the Hot Club of France to offer concerts under the direction of critic Hugues Panassié and jazz activist and discographer Charles Delaunay. American records were widely distributed, and radio followed timidly.

In the first half of the 1930s, most young Parisian jazzmen were still works-in-progress. But their music took a flying leap thanks to their microscopic analyses of the best jazz recordings; live concerts (Duke Ellington in 1933 and 1939, Louis Armstrong in 1934); and jam sessions with leading American jazzmen. Europe's *crème de la crème* burst forth in 1934 with the Quintet of the Hot Club of France, centered around guitarist Django Reinhardt and violinist Stéphane Grappelli. Emerging around the Quintet were, among others, violinist Michel Warlop and saxophonists Alix Combelle and André Ekyan.

Thanks to Delaunay, the second half of the decade saw the debut in 1935 of the bilingual (French and English) magazine *Jazz hot* (continuous, except for a wartime hiatus, until century's end) and in 1937 of the label Swing, which captured marvelous encounters between French jazz artists and visiting U.S. jazzmen.

In 1939, as the German army advanced into France, American musicians fled Paris; jazz would take a lower profile until after World War II.
—*Philippe Baudoin*

Canadian pianist-composer Gil Evans.

French violinist Jean-Luc Ponty.

Austrian keyboardist Joe Zawinul.

Foreign-Born Musicians in the States

Jazz musicians crop up all over the world, and many get the itch to soak up the music and test their skills and ideas in the land where it began, often in the music's business capital, New York. Many of these foreign-born musicians have been part of the fabric of the scene so long—a first-call bass player (Dave Holland), the guiding light behind Weather Report (Joe Zawinul), the composers of the *Mission: Impossible* theme (Lalo Schifrin) and *Lullaby of Birdland* (George Shearing)—that it's easy to forget the strong international component of the jazz we hear every day.

What follows is a partial list of some stateside worthies who began life on other shores. —*Kevin Whitehead*

Toshiko Akiyoshi	pianist, composer	Japan
Mario Bauzá	trumpeter	Cuba
Seamus Blake	tenor saxophonist	Canada
Paul Bley	pianist	Canada
Paquito D'Rivera	saxophonist	Cuba
Urszula Dudziak	singer	Poland
Eliane Elias	pianist	Brazil
Gil Evans	pianist, composer	Canada
Victor Feldman	pianist, vibraphonist	England
Jean Goldkette	pianist, bandleader	France
Dave Holland	bassist	England
Abdullah Ibrahim	pianist	South Africa
Adam Makowicz	pianist	Poland
Hugh Masekela	trumpeter, flugelhornist	South Africa
Marian McPartland	pianist	England
Ralph Moore	tenor saxophonist	England
Airto Moreira	percussionist	Brazil
George Mraz	bassist	Czechoslovakia
Mike Nock	pianist	New Zealand
Jean-Luc Ponty	violinist	France
Chano Pozo	percussionist	Cuba
Flora Purim	singer	Brazil
Renee Rosnes	pianist	Canada
Luis Russell	bandleader, pianist	France
Arturo Sandoval	trumpeter	Cuba
Mongo Santamaria	conga player, bandleader	Cuba
Lalo Schifrin	pianist, composer	Argentina
George Shearing	pianist	England
Joe Temperley	baritone saxophonist	Scotland
Toots Thielemans	harmonica player, guitarist	Belgium
Lorenzo Tio, Sr.	clarinetist	Mexico
Carlos Ward	alto saxophonist, flutist	Panama
Joe Zawinul	keyboardist	Austria

The line dividing discographers and critics from active jazz promoters and producers was thin enough for several Europeans to cross, just as John Hammond did in the U.S. Delaunay and French writer Hugues Panassié both produced numerous recording sessions; together, they directed the A&R program of the French label Swing. Critic André Hodeir both played and produced jazz, in addition to writing several noteworthy books on the subject.

If European musicians at first emulated the Americans stylistically, by 1934 the seeds were planted for an alternative approach. That's when guitarist Django Reinhardt and violinist Stéphane Grappelli put together their Quintet of the Hot Club of France. Grappelli's violin, notably on *After You've Gone* and *Limehouse Blues* (both 1936), was as sweet, urbane, and sophisticated as Parisian café music. Reinhardt, a Belgian gypsy who couldn't read music and who had limited use of his fire-damaged fretting hand, proved a phenomenal jazz-guitar innovator. He had a stinging attack and improvised complex single-note lines broken up by short series of charging chords that goosed the music forward—all rendered with distinctive flair (*Swing Guitars*, 1936, and *Minor Swing*, 1937). Traveling Americans who heard and played with him related to it, even as they recognized that his harmonic and melodic vocabulary reflected his own roots at least as much as it echoed the blues.

Reinhardt was the model of the successful non-American jazz improviser. The Quintet inspired similar groups around the continent, and he belatedly spawned a raft of French or French-speaking pickers, including Raymond Boni, Philip Catherine, Boulou Ferre, Bireli Lagrene, and Belgium's electric-guitar wizard René Thomas. To date, no foreign-born jazz musician who didn't move to the U.S. has commanded nearly as much stateside attention or respect as Reinhardt.

Guitarist Django Reinhardt (below left) and violinist Stéphane Grappelli (below) were partners in the Quintet of the Hot Club of France from 1934 to 1939, each exerting a lasting impact on jazz. Although Reinhardt died in 1953, Grappelli kept performing into the 1990s.

© Herman Leonard

Controversies Abroad

Naturally the music encountered resistance. Italians circulated an anti-jazz petition in 1923. One French composer explained that collective improvising was mathematically impossible. Swedish critics denounced Louis Armstrong when he visited in 1933.

In post-revolutionary Russia, folks had fiercely debated jazz's merits—even before they'd heard any jazz. Abroad as at home, there was always someone ready to argue what the music should or shouldn't be.

In 1926, two contradictory visions of jazz came to Russia. Bandleader Sam Wooding, criss-crossing Eurasia with the theatrical revue *Chocolate Kiddies*, championed Paul Whiteman's symphonic jazz. Drummer Benny Peyton's Jazz Kings, with Bechet on board, backed the hot alternative. Predictably, the music establishment backed the dead-end former approach, while grass-roots musicians supported the latter.

Jazz, like any art form, must be free to develop as it will; it does not take orders from the top. But in the Soviet Union, where the official line on any matter could reverse itself in an instant, jazz was a small boat on a high sea.

Examples? In 1934, a pro-jazz movie swept Russia. In 1936, the newspaper *Pravda* denounced jazz, then reversed itself, but sister paper *Izvestiia* continued the attacks. In 1937, some jazz musicians were hauled off to labor camps, or simply disappeared. In 1938, a sanitized, forty-three-piece State Jazz Orchestra was organized, its musicians paid twice the compensation of their classical counterparts—a grand if grim exception to the rule that jazzers always make less money. Hip audiences booed anyway. In 1939, subsidized regional swing orchestras cropped up. During World War II, army and navy jazz bands entertained the Russian troops.

The reception accorded Sam Wooding (seated, center) and his band in travels through Eurasia and South America in the 1920s wasn't matched in the U.S., where the returning Wooding found that other pre–Swing Era bands had staked claim on the domestic listenership.

Trumpeter Buck Clayton (center) took his 14 Gentlemen of Harlem to the Canidrome club in Shanghai, China, in 1934. The band split up there; Clayton stayed on until he'd earned enough money to return to the States, where he joined Count Basie's band.

In Germany, the situation was similarly tragic and absurd. The Nazis portrayed jazz as Jewish-Negro degeneracy—and declared syncopated music incompatible with marching!—but because of existing trade agreements were obliged to allow in Armstrong records.

The Germans unwittingly helped the cause of European jazz in 1935, when they forbade Coleman Hawkins and the British band he was touring with from entering the country. Stranded in Holland, Hawkins worked and recorded with the capable swing band the Ramblers and with expatriate pianist Freddy Johnson, in Europe since 1928.

Johnson, by the way, was one of a few American musicians locked up by the Germans in the early 1940s, another being Valaida Snow, the most widely traveled jazz woman of the prewar years. She traveled from Sweden to Shanghai and hit a lot of stops between. When her fellow trumpeter Buck Clayton spent two years in Shanghai in the mid-thirties—at the instigation of pianist Teddy Weatherford, who'd been bouncing around Asia for years, and would spend his final years playing in India—he found that Snow had taught some Shanghai chefs how to cook soul food.

Hawkins was naturally much in demand, and he stayed in Europe until 1939, playing with locals in Holland, France, Switzerland, England, and Scandinavia. That the father of the tenor saxophone found European musicians acceptable colleagues gave them a strong psychological boost. He was impressed by Reinhardt; by his own French admirer, tenor saxophonist Alix Combelle; and by at least one chart the Ramblers brought him. Having him around also helped the Europeans see how a musician's life and art intertwine—how the choices made on the bandstand relate to the kind of day a musician's having, for example.

The War Years and After

In Germany even before the Second World War, and in occupied countries during it, musicians were encouraged to play good European music rather than "degenerate" jazz—never mind how bad the proposed alternatives sounded. The occupation government in Holland and at least one German district issued regulations for improvisers—riffing was limited or forbidden, plunger mutes and scat singing were off-limits, and other restrictions applied.

American tunes were outlawed, too, but musicians found ways around that. If the French lament *La tristesse de St. Louis (The Sadness of St. Louis)* sounded oddly like the Czech patriot's anthem *The Song of Resetová Lhota* or the German *Das Lied vom Heiligen Ludwig (The Song of Saint Louis)* it's because all of them were *St. Louis Blues.*

Jazz continued to be played in Berlin itself. Germans put jazz into propaganda broadcasts aimed at the British, and vice versa. There was even a jazz band, known as the Ghetto Swingers, at the Czech Terezín concentration camp, and it's said there was one at Buchenwald. For some in Germany and occupied countries (as in the Soviet Union), jazz became a symbol of freedom and resistance; then and there as now and elsewhere, however, to be a jazz fan was no sure sign of liberal politics. There were jazz fans in SS uniforms too.

In the long run, the war had much to do with the dissemination of jazz around the world. Armed Forces Radio played a conspicuous role in spreading jazz in Europe and Asia, both during and after the war. U.S. soldiers also played an important part. During wartime, they shared their "fake books"—informal sheet music—with Russian allies, who picked up on harmonic refinements they'd been missing. (But as the Cold War dawned, the Soviets flip-flopped again, confiscating saxophones in 1949.)

Postwar U.S. service folk in Germany and Japan gave the defeated powers a taste for the music. (Those aforementioned radio broadcasts helped too.) In 1948, Takatoshi Kyogoku reported from Japan to *Down Beat* magazine that jazz had "swept over this country like wildfire since the end of the war." In Europe, homegrown musicians got work entertaining off-duty U.S. troops. One, German trombonist Albert Mangelsdorff, later developed a method of coaxing harmonies from his horn by playing one note and humming another, a technique now widely used by other trombonists; he may have been the most influential European jazz musician after Django Reinhardt.

There was a major jazz festival in Paris in 1949, with bebop players Charlie Parker, Miles Davis, Tadd Dameron, and Kenny Clarke among featured performers. After Bechet played at the festival, music stores

Although preceded a year earlier by an event in Nice, the Festival Internationale du Jazz, held in Paris in 1949, gave weight to the concept of large multi-artist festivals. Charlie Parker and Miles Davis performed, as did Django Reinhardt and an international array of others.

CH. DELAUNAY

Jazz Under the Nazis

The German jazz band Weintraub's Syncopators (shown here in 1931) appeared in the 1930 film The Blue Angel, *which rising Nazi official Josef Goebbels denounced as "offal."*

To many Germans of the 1930s who subscribed to the notion of a superior Aryan race, jazz—because of its black origins and its loose, danceable rhythm—was widely considered to be counter to German moral and cultural standards. Thus, immediately after the Nazi takeover in March 1933, Germany's new rulers banned jazz from all radio programs on the grounds that it was a form of musical decadence. Josef Goebbels, the Third Reich's Minister for Public Enlightening and Propaganda, referred to jazz as "talentless and unimaginative juggling with notes" (a position that didn't prevent him from employing a jazz band, Charlie and His Orchestra, in propaganda broadcasts to North America and Great Britain).

In many ways jazz was the antithesis of Nazi regimentation and a symbolic threat to the regime's control. The authorities disliked it not only because they associated it with despised racial minorities, including Jews, but also because it emphasized freedom, spontaneity, and individualism.

Under Nazi rule, Jewish dance and jazz musicians were unable to pursue their professions and were forced to leave the country. (One émigré, Francis Wolff, launched a record company in the U.S. that would one day become almost synonymous with jazz: Blue Note.)

The German government discouraged the public from playing, listening, or dancing to jazz, but the ban was difficult to enforce. American jazz recordings were readily available until the U.S. entered the war in 1941. Afterward, until 1944, the German companies Odeon, Brunswick, and Imperial pressed hot-jazz records for sale in neutral and occupied countries, but the discs found their way back into Germany and were unofficially available "under the counter."

Not surprisingly, jazz became a symbol of resistance. In order to fool informers and the secret police, jazz fans and musicians organized clandestine sessions, cut off telltale composers' names and song titles from sheet music, and misled the censors by disguising jazz standards under new names.

Despite the repressive climate, jazz enjoyed unprecedented popularity during the Nazi years, not only in such occupied countries as Norway, France, the Netherlands, and Czechoslovakia but also in Germany. And jazz musicians somehow continued to play and evolve. Some of Germany's finest jazzmen—including Kurt Hohenberger, Heinz Wehner, Freddie Brocksieper, Max Rumpf, Ernst Höllerhagen, Helmut Zacharias, and Benny de Weille—emerged, played, and recorded under Nazi rule. And their ranks were supplemented by such visiting foreign players as Kai Ewans, Fud Candrix, Teddy Stauffer, Thore Ehrling, Jean Omer, Eddie Tower, Cesare Galli, and Tullio Mobiglia.

By the time the war ended with the Nazis' defeat, jazz was in Germany to stay. —*Rainer E. Lotz*

United States Musicians Abroad

Artists from the States, including jazz musicians, have always gravitated to Europe and elsewhere in pursuit of greater racial tolerance, a less hectic pace, or a chance to measure their own culture against others. What follows is a roster of some U.S. jazz musicians who spent significant amounts of time abroad.

In the table, a "d" before a second date means the musician died while abroad. Parentheses around the name of a country signal a relatively short stay. Note that dates in a few cases are approximate, since expatriation or repatriation is sometimes a gradual process.

—*Kevin Whitehead and John Edward Hasse*

Arranger Quincy Jones.

Singer Dee Dee Bridgewater.

Louis Armstrong	trumpeter, singer	1933–35	France and elsewhere
Chet Baker	trumpeter, singer	1960–61	Italy
Sidney Bechet	saxophonist, clarinetist	1919–22	England
		1925–30	France, Germany
		1951–d.59	France
Lester Bowie	trumpeter	1968–71	France
Dee Dee Bridgewater	singer	1984–	France
Don Byas	saxophonist	1946–d.72	France, Netherlands, Denmark
Donald Byrd	trumpeter	1963–67	France
Benny Carter	saxophonist	1935–38	England, Holland, France
Doc Cheatham	trumpeter	1928–30	Europe
Don Cherry	trumpeter	1970–74	Sweden
Kenny Clarke	drummer	1956–d.85	France
Buck Clayton	trumpeter	1934–36	China
Art Farmer	trumpeter	1968–	Austria
Bud Freeman	saxophonist	1974–80	England
Stan Getz	saxophonist	1958–61	Denmark
Dexter Gordon	saxophonist	1962–77	Denmark
Johnny Griffin	saxophonist	1963–	France, (Netherlands)
Coleman Hawkins	saxophonist	1934–39	England, France, Holland, Switzerland, Scandinavia
Quincy Jones	trumpeter, arranger	1957–59	France
Steve Lacy	saxophonist	1967–	(Italy, Germany), France
James Moody	saxophonist, flutist	1948–51	France
Oscar Pettiford	bassist	1958–60	Denmark
Bud Powell	pianist	1959–64	France
George Russell	composer	1963–69	Sweden
Valaida Snow	trumpeter, singer	1926–28	China
		1935–40	England, France
		1940–42	Denmark (prison)
Rex Stewart	cornetist	1947–51	(Europe, Australia)
Dave Tough	drummer	1927–29	France, Germany
Mal Waldron	pianist	1965–	(France, Italy) Germany, Belgium
Ben Webster	saxophonist	1963–d.73	Denmark, Netherlands
Randy Weston	pianist, composer	1968–72	Morocco
Sam Wooding	pianist, bandleader	1925–27	Germany, Scandinavia, Russia, Turkey, Romania, Hungary, Italy, England, (South America)
		1928–31	Germany, Scandinavia, France, Italy, Spain, Belgium
		1968–69	Germany

Sidney Bechet (right), one of the earliest U.S. jazz players in Europe (1919), spent his last years in France.

reported a run on soprano saxophones. Bechet moved to France in 1951; he'd record there often through the 1950s (*Olympia Concert*, 1955, and *La légende de Sidney Bechet*, 1949–58), and would become a national hero. The French—like the Italians, mindful of old New Orleans' cultural makeup—considered jazz part of their own cultural legacy.

Along with tenor saxophonist Don Byas, Bechet was in the first wave of postwar expatriates who gravitated to Paris, Rome, Copenhagen, Amsterdam, and other cities where they could find work, respect, and the good life. By 1965 there were so many American jazz musicians in Paris, the French musicians' union complained the Yanks were getting all the good gigs.

Not that Americans there neglected their French colleagues. Drummer Kenny Clarke often played with bassist Pierre Michelot, sometimes backing temporary Parisian Bud Powell, as on the pianist's albums *Cookin' at Saint Germain* (1957–59) and *The Complete Essen Jazz Festival Concert* (1960). (Powell's experiences in Paris were part of the inspiration for *Round Midnight*, one of several feature films focusing on jazz abroad.) For twelve years, Clarke also co-led a successful pan-European big band with Belgian pianist Francy Boland, heard on the albums *Two Originals* (1967–68) and *Three Latin Adventures* (1968).

When Miles Davis visited in 1957 to tour with Clarke, Michelot, pianist René Urtreger, and tenor saxophonist Barney Wilen, director Louis Malle asked Davis to score his film noir *Ascenseur pour l'échafaud (Lift to the Scaffold)*. Jazz soundtracks were then a French fad;

Drummer Kenny Clarke, 1946.

Worldwide Jazz Films

Jazz and the movies were no less mutual symbols of twentieth-century progress in Europe than they were in the U.S. Abroad, movies dealt best with jazz not head-on, but in passing.

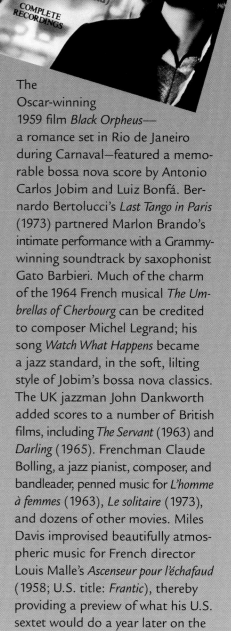

les parapluies de cherbourg
un film de Jacques demy
mis en musique par michel legrand

Weintraub's Syncopators, arguably the first good German jazz band, appear briefly in *The Blue Angel* (1930), with Marlene Dietrich as a living symbol of the perils nightclubs offer.

The Parisian nightclub itself is the real star of Martin Ritt's 1961 *Paris Blues;* its only real competition is the Ellington-Strayhorn music. The film, which was shot in Paris, depicts a jazz setting still found in Europe: a noisy room packed with laughing, drinking, smoking jazz fans.

An examination of the relationship between European fans and American musicians is at the core of Bertrand Tavernier's *Round Midnight* (1986), which captures the proprietary sense many European fans have about jazz and their occasional idolatry of American musicians. After a just-okay performance by Dexter Gordon's character, our Parisian-fan hero goes home to report, "Dale Turner played like a god tonight."

One of the segments in 1964's *Dr. Terror's House of Horrors*—a trashy but entertaining British horror-anthology film—reflects vexing unresolved social issues. In the film, an English trumpeter goes to Haiti and eavesdrops on a secret voodoo religious ceremony. When he's discovered notating the drum rhythms, he is strictly enjoined from repeating them—which of course he does, in a nightclub back in London, with predictably dire, supernatural results. This segment is one of the better commentaries on the potency of rhythmic material for its own sake, on white anxiety and guilt over "stealing" black music, and even on the ethics of world music.

In the Russian film *My iz dzhaza* (1983), a.k.a. *Jazzmen,* directed by Karen Shakhnazarov, a jazz-loving music student struggles to form a Dixieland band. The triumphant ending reproduces the hoariest Hollywood jazz cliché: the People's Music shows it has "arrived" by getting the highbrow symphonic treatment.

Some films have used jazz-flavored scores to add poignancy, color, and romance to small-scale character studies and love stories.

The Oscar-winning 1959 film *Black Orpheus*—a romance set in Rio de Janeiro during Carnaval—featured a memorable bossa nova score by Antonio Carlos Jobim and Luiz Bonfá. Bernardo Bertolucci's *Last Tango in Paris* (1973) partnered Marlon Brando's intimate performance with a Grammy-winning soundtrack by saxophonist Gato Barbieri. Much of the charm of the 1964 French musical *The Umbrellas of Cherbourg* can be credited to composer Michel Legrand; his song *Watch What Happens* became a jazz standard, in the soft, lilting style of Jobim's bossa nova classics. The UK jazzman John Dankworth added scores to a number of British films, including *The Servant* (1963) and *Darling* (1965). Frenchman Claude Bolling, a jazz pianist, composer, and bandleader, penned music for *L'homme à femmes* (1963), *Le solitaire* (1973), and dozens of other movies. Miles Davis improvised beautifully atmospheric music for French director Louis Malle's *Ascenseur pour l'échafaud* (1958; U.S. title: *Frantic*), thereby providing a preview of what his U.S. sextet would do a year later on the influential *Kind of Blue* album.

By the way: the most famous saxophone voice in the movies—the slithery tenor saxophone on most of the *Pink Panther* soundtracks—belongs to England's Tony Coe.
—*Kevin Whitehead and Tad Lathrop*

John Lewis, Art Blakey, and Duke Ellington also did one each—respectively, *Sait-on jamais* (*No Sun in Venice*) (1957), *Des femmes disparaissent* (*The Disappearing Women*) (1958), and *Paris Blues* (1961).

Blakey, by the way, was later quoted as saying about jazz, "It's American music, and no one else can play it." But that didn't stop him from hiring, over the years, such musicians as Russian trumpeter Valery Pomonarev, Australian saxophonist Dale Barlow, or Japanese bassists Isao Suzuki and Yoshio Suzuki—or from recording in the fifties with drummers from Senegal, Nigeria, and Jamaica.

International Influences on American Jazz

While American jazz musicians were emigrating, foreign-born musicians had been seasoning American jazz. By far the most influential came from the Caribbean. Jelly Roll Morton had observed that jazz got its snap from its "Spanish tinge," its hint of Latin rhythms—rhythms ultimately derived from Iberia and Africa. New Orleans music at the time jazz evolved felt the sway of Cuban and (to a lesser extent) Mexican music.

Latin musicians have been a constant in jazz ever since. Ellington trombonist Juan Tizol came from Puerto Rico; Chick Webb's lead trumpeter and, later, musical director in the 1930s was Cuba's Mario Bauzá; in 1929, shortly after arriving in New York from Cuba, Alberto Socarrás recorded what may have been the first flute solo on a jazz record (*Have You Ever Felt That Way*), issued under Clarence Williams' name.

In 1939, Bauzá joined Cab Calloway and met Dizzy Gillespie, one of the best friends Latin or "Afro-Cuban" jazz ever had. On Bauzá's advice, in 1947 Gillespie hired conga player Chano Pozo for his big band, yielding such fiery Latinized pieces as *Ool-Ya-Koo* and *Good Bait* (both 1947). Gillespie's band wasn't alone. In California, bandleader Stan Kenton, attracted to the over-the-top excitement of Latin orchestras, recorded many Cuban-flavored numbers; one, *Machito* (1947), was named for the percussionist and bandleader with whom Charlie Parker would soon record. (In 1952 Bird also did a combo date with a Latin flavor, playing, among other tunes, *La cucaracha*.) After that, Latin influences permeated the work of far too many bands to list completely.

In the 1970s a new wave of Cubans came along, notably the Havana fusion band Irakere. Its breakout star, who later defected to the States, was Paquito D'Rivera, whose sizzling alto saxophone sound, heard on *Why Not* (1984) and *Who's Smoking?* (1991), became almost a Latin stereotype. Onetime Irakere pianist Gonzalo Rubalcaba stayed in Cuba; the U.S. discovered him in the 1990s. Like other Latin pianists Rubalcaba could be flashy for flash's sake, but he could also hold his own on a straight-jazz program—as on *Diz*, a 1993 disc dedicated to Dizzy Gillespie.

Gillespie also dug the lilt of West Indian calypso music. He used the singers Fred Strong and the Calypso Boys on *We Love to Boogie*, a tune he recorded in 1951,

Cuban percussionist Chano Pozo's work with Dizzy Gillespie in 1947–48 helped embed Afro-Cuban sounds in jazz, where they would remain often-used rhythmic and melodic ingredients.

© Herman Leonard

Paquito D'Rivera's role in the Cuban group Irakere brought him to the U.S., where he remained to forge his own Latin-bop sound.

Latin Jazz

Latin musical concepts have flavored the jazz repertoire since its earliest days.

The music of such early piano pioneers as Scott Joplin (*Solace: A Mexican Serenade,* 1909); Jesse Pickett (*The Dream,* unpublished though recorded by others); and Jelly Roll Morton (*New Orleans Joys,* recorded in 1923) attests to the presence of the early Cuban *habanera* form, which many believe was first brought to New Orleans by the Eighth Cavalry Mexican Band around 1884. Morton claimed that it was the "Spanish tinge" that differentiated jazz from the earlier ragtime style of New Orleans music. W.C. Handy toured Cuba and picked up a number of musical ideas and practices, which influenced many of his compositions. Notable was his *St. Louis Blues* (1914), which incorporated the habanera rhythm (♫ ♫) in the middle of its three sections. One of the most significant recordings of this landmark piece was made in 1929 by Louis Armstrong, and it became one of his famous vehicles. The next year, Don Azpiazú released his recording of Cuban songwriter Moisés

Simons' *El manicero (The Peanut Vendor),* which was also recorded by Armstrong and eventually became one of the most-played standards in American music.

By the 1930s, however, another vein was being established in this Latin and jazz encounter. Juan Tizol, the Puerto Rican trombonist enlisted by the Duke Ellington orchestra, co-composed with the maestro a tune that would shake and change the world of jazz: *Caravan* (1936), featuring an alternation of a rumba/habanera based on strict clave—the rhythmic heartbeat of Afro-Cuban dance music (♪♪ ♪♪ ♪♪| ♪ ♪♪ ♪♪). Ellington would continue to experiment with Latin concepts, eventually composing an extended work called *The Latin American Suite* (1968).

Much of the credit for introducing what became known as Latin jazz has been laid at the feet of trumpeter-bandleader Dizzy Gillespie and Cuban percussionist Chano Pozo for their historic interaction during the bebop period of the late 1940s. In large part, however, Gillespie and Pozo followed what had already been established by the orchestra

of Machito (Frank Grillo), under the musical supervision of trumpeter Mario Bauzá—who, like Machito, had emigrated from Cuba to New York City during the 1930s. Machito's *Tanga* (1943) with its mambo-based structure, Ellingtonian palette of orchestral colors, and Basie-like blues-inspired riffs, is considered by many aficionados to be the recording that best defines the emergence of Latin jazz.

During the 1960s, especially in California, another movement emerged, characterized by the music of Cal Tjader, a vibraphonist who contracted such major New York-based percussionists as the Puerto Rican–descended Willie Bobo and the Cuban émigré Mongo Santamaria. Both Santamaria (*Afro-Roots,* 1958–59) and Bobo (*A New Dimension,* 1968) became leaders and innovators of the newer Latin jazz that combined the Cuban forms of the mambo and cha cha cha with bebop, rhythm and blues, and the progressive-jazz currents of the time.

Latin jazz during the last thirty years of the twentieth century thrived in the hands of a range of musicians. They included timbales drummer Tito Puente, who led both a large Latin orchestra and a smaller jazz band (*Oye como va,* 1962); the Puerto-Rican American bandleader and conga drummer Ray Barretto (*Taboo,* 1994); the Mexican American conga drummer Poncho Sanchez (*Para todos,* 1994); the Cuban American trumpeter and percussionist Jerry Gonzalez (*Crossroads,* 1994). Also active were pianist Gonzalo Rubalcaba (*The Blessing,* 1991); trumpeter Arturo Sandoval (*I Remember Clifford,* 1992); and alto saxophonist Paquito D'Rivera (*Paquito D'Rivera Presents: Forty Years of Cuban Jam Session,* 1993).
—Steven Loza

and in 1964 he recorded the calypso-flavored, delightfully silly LP *Jambo Caribe.* Calypso, which, like the mambo and the cha cha cha, was one of the Caribbean crazes that infected American music in the fifties, was perfect fare for the warm, relaxed delivery of singer Nat "King" Cole, too, as on *Calypso Blues* (1949) and *When Rock and Roll Came to Trinidad* (1957). But the classic jazz calypso is undoubtedly Sonny Rollins' 1956 version of the traditional *St. Thomas.* Most every jazz tenor saxophonist who's played a calypso since (Rollins included) pays it an audible debt.

Other tenor players furthered the Latin American cause later. One came from Argentina, where jazz was first heard in the 1920s—peripatetic Sam Wooding again on the case—and which had already produced jaunty swing guitarist Oscar Alemán. At his peak in the late 1960s and through the mid-seventies, Buenos Aires's Gato Barbieri commanded a blatantly passionate, raspy saxophone sound that epitomized macho romanticism, as on *Latino America* (1973) and *Chapter Three: Viva Emiliano Zapata* (1974).

The tenor most associated with South American trends was that of the United States' Stan Getz, who in the early sixties popularized bossa nova, a Brazilian synthesis of cool jazz and the samba. The movement was foreshadowed nearly a decade earlier, when Laurindo Almeida, a Brazilian guitarist living in California, made some records on which altoist Bud Shank blew limpid improvisations over guitar sambas and *baiaos* (reissued as *Brazilliance, Vol. 1,* 1953).

Many of Brazilian guitarist Antonio Carlos Jobim's compositions—including One-Note Samba, Triste, Corcovado, Desafinado, *and* Meditation—*have become cornerstones of the standard jazz repertory.*

Getz was introduced to bossa nova by guitarist Charlie Byrd, who'd heard it on tour in Brazil. Byrd got Getz to record the new music with him, on the album *Jazz Samba* (1962). The saxophonist's breezy, floating improvisations fit the gentle underlying rhythms perfectly. By the end of 1962, bossa nova was an enormous fad in the States—literally dozens of jazz musicians hopped on the bandwagon—and before long Getz was recording with the Brazilian innovators themselves, notably guitarists Antonio Carlos Jobim and João Gilberto. On one session Getz persuaded Gilberto's wife, Astrud, to sing, although she had a small, untrained voice; one of the numbers they cut made the bossa even bigger: *The Girl from Ipanema* (1963), which became a hit single.

Byrd's tour of Brazil was undertaken at the instigation of the U.S. State Department, which in the mid-fifties had perceived jazz as a potent symbol of democracy in action and had been sending musicians around the world. Said Louis Armstrong, "The second happiest moment of my life" was playing for Kwame Nkrumah in 1959, on the eve of Ghana's independence. (The radio service Voice of America began broadcasting jazz to grateful fans around the world in the same period.) Also touring for the State Department were Dizzy Gillespie, who in 1956 went to Europe, the Near East, the Middle East, and South America; Duke Ellington, who recorded his impressionistic *Far East* and *Latin American* suites on his return; Benny Goodman, who toured the Far East in 1956–57 and the Soviet Union in 1962;

Astrud Gilberto (left) sang on the memorable recording of The Girl from Ipanema, *accompanied by her husband, Brazilian singer-guitarist João Gilberto (below).*

Airto Moreira rode into jazz on the 1970s Brazilian-percussion wave.

saxophonist Paul Winter, who began incorporating world-music elements into his jazz in the early sixties and toured Latin America in 1962; and Dave Brubeck, who in 1958 went to Turkey and other Middle Eastern countries, where irregular time signatures like 5/8 or 9/8 are common, and in 1959 recorded his most popular odd-meter piece *Blue Rondo à la Turk.*

The next Brazilian wave began in the late sixties, when percussionist Airto Moreira and his wife, singer Flora Purim, came to the United States. Airto's success—playing numerous and mostly coloristic Brazilian percussion instruments with Miles Davis (*Live-Evil,* 1970); Weather Report (*Weather Report,* 1971); and Return to Forever (*Light as a Feather,* 1972)—set the seventies fashion for employing exotic percussion, played also by fellow Brazilians Paulinho da Costa, Guilherme Franco, Nana Vasconcelos, and others. Wayne Shorter's 1974 album *Native Dancer,* a notable mix of Brazilian music and American jazz, showcased the Brazilian guitarist and vocalist Milton Nascimento.

Willis Conover: Voice of America

For many years during the Cold War, the world's most-heard "voice of jazz" was the mellifluous baritone of Willis Conover, who broadcast his six-night-a-week *Music USA* jazz program, sponsored by the U.S. government radio service Voice of America, throughout Europe, Africa, Asia, and Latin America.

Jazz musicians who lived "behind the Iron Curtain"—in the communist-ruled former Soviet Union, its Eastern European satellites, and Cuba—considered Conover's broadcasts a godsend. In their countries, where government policies restricted access to Western culture—and where jazz in particular was decried as a symbol of Western decadence—information about jazz was hard to come by. Conover's programs—*Music USA, The Voice of America Jazz Hour,* and *House of Sounds*—served as local musicians' sole exposure to a wide variety of jazz styles, performers, and songs. Some players would gather around their radios and try to quickly notate whatever sounds they could pick up through the crackling interference caused by military jamming of radio signals. "The broadcasts of Willis Conover were our best instruction manuals," recalled Lithuanian musician Vladimir Tarasov. In Poland, as James Lester wrote, the "best-known musicians all assert that *Music USA* provided the foundation of their education in jazz." (When Conover visited Poland,

he was hoisted on the shoulders of adoring fans and treated as a hero.) Cuban saxophonist Paquito D'Rivera said the program *Jazz Hour* was one of his main sources for the jazz that helped him grow as a musician.

But Conover's broadcasts are also viewed as having had an even broader impact. To many who lived under repressive regimes, jazz—with its looseness, spontaneity, excitement, and individualism—felt like the antithesis of regimentation; it was the very sound of freedom. And that said something about its country of origin. To the extent that jazz attracted listeners to the Western way of life, Conover, as the personality who most frequently brought jazz abroad, was one of the United States' most effective diplomatic and foreign policy tools during the Cold War.

From his first *Music USA* broadcast in January 1955 to his last more than 40 years later, Conover may have done more for the global spread of jazz than any other single person, earning him the official recognition of the U.S. House of Representatives, an honorary doctorate from Berklee College of Music, and the lifelong gratitude of musicians who studied in the "Conover school of jazz."

Conover died in 1996, and reruns of his show were broadcast for about a year. Afterward, a program called *Jazz America* took its place. —*Tad Lathrop*

World Music and Jazz

The indigenous sounds of cultures worldwide have played an important role as source material for new, regional conceptions of jazz as well as thematic material for jazz played by Americans.

Sidney Bechet's tours in the 1920s had also taken him to Sweden, Spain, France, Italy, Hungary, Czechoslovakia, Greece, and Egypt; his biographer John Chilton said that later in life Bechet surprised listeners by playing various folk themes he'd heard in such places long ago; he was in the vanguard yet again, as interest in world music was beginning to build. In post–World War II Japan, there was a fad for jazzing up traditional themes. In 1951, Stan Getz, in Sweden with a local rhythm section, recorded a Swedish folk tune that became a jazz standard as *Dear Old Stockholm*. Within a few years, Sweden's celebrated baritone saxophonist Lars Gullin began recording original pieces with a folk flavor.

By now, foreign musicians had a good understanding of jazz as a reflection of the United States' cultural mix and of players' own experiences. It was inevitable that some would ask: If U.S. jazz builds on indigenous materials like the blues, shouldn't our jazz reflect our culture and upbringing?

With that question, jazz abroad began to grow up—and out, beyond imitation of American models. Not that outlanders didn't still look to the U.S. for new directions. Australians after World War II, for example, shadowed successive American trends—New Orleans revival, bop, cool, modal, free, and jazz-and-poetry—and produced the brilliant neo-bebopper, lightning-quick alto saxophonist Bernie McGann. But they, too, were mindful of what they brought to the table: around 1960 there was even an Australian TV series called *Jazz Meets Folk*.

A regional conception of jazz was developing in England too, where the growth of jazz had been complicated by a decades-long protectionist blockade of U.S. talent—which didn't stop Americans from making English bandleader Ray Noble's *Cherokee* (1938) and its chord changes into jazz evergreens. The long-running feud between stateside English musicians' unions had made it impossible for jazz musicians from either country to play the other, from 1935 to 1956—a crucial period in the States, encompassing the full flowering of the Swing Era and the birth and assimilation of bebop. The English scene lagged behind American developments, yet the ban also inspired a certain cocky, do-it-yourself attitude, heard in such period notables as trumpeter Nat Gonella. While the French continued to play with visiting Americans, the English made their own music.

That sense of independence bore fruit mostly in the years after the ban was lifted. In England, the folk-jazz connection was abetted by several factors: jazz musicians working in blues and folk-revival groups, several of which played Charles Mingus tunes; an influx of West Indians, including saxophonist Joe Harriott and trumpeters Shake Keane and Harry Beckett, who brought island rhythms along; and the presence of black and white South Africans in exile, notably drummer Louis Moholo, pianist Chris McGregor, bassists Harry Miller and Johnny Dyani, trumpeter Mongezi Feza, and altoist Dudu Pukwana. The latter's "township jazz," a blend of jazz sonorities, catchy tunes, and simple chord schemes (heard on *In the Townships*, 1973), had a significant effect on the English jazz scene.

Curiously, polycultural South Africa remains the most jazz-oriented African country—a sign, perhaps, of the pronounced impact of European culture there. But that didn't stop such U.S. musicians as pianist Randy

Swedish baritone saxophonist Lars Gullin, whose greatest impact was in the 1950s, recorded with such U.S. musicians as Stan Getz, Clifford Brown, and Zoot Sims.

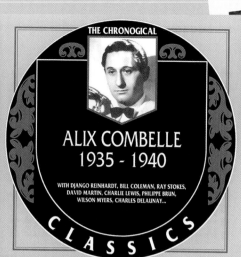

With the spread of jazz around the globe came the rise of numerous jazz-oriented record companies based outside the United States. They typically served two purposes: to showcase local jazz and to locally distribute U.S. jazz.

In France, critics Hugues Panassié and Charles Delaunay provided artist-and-repertoire (A&R) direction for the Swing label, founded in 1937, which recorded guitarist Django Reinhardt in addition to Benny Carter and other U.S. players. The label's successor, Vogue, also directed by Charles Delaunay, carried out a similar program. The Blue Star label, launched in 1945, issued discs by local and U.S. musicians as well as French editions of records from the vaults of Norman Granz's Clef, Norgran, and Verve labels.

England's Tempo and Esquire labels emerged within a year of each other, in 1946 and 1947, respectively. The former offered such British jazzmen as saxophonist Ronnie Scott (later the owner of London's leading jazz club), trumpeter Dizzy Reece, and pianist and vibraphonist Victor Feldman, while Esquire recorded Scott, British saxophonist John Dankworth, and, later, U.S. jazz players.

Scandinavia hosted one of the earliest Euro labels, Sonora, which emerged in 1932 with a swing emphasis and went on to showcase local players and such visiting Yanks as trumpeter Valaida Snow. European musicians, including harmonica player Toots Thielemans, saxophonist Lars Gullin, and violinist Svend Asmussen found a Swedish outlet at Metronome Records (launched in 1949) and later at Sonet (founded in 1956).

While these early ventures tended largely to follow the leads of their U.S. counterparts, later enterprises offered more adventurous repertoires.

London's Black Lion Records (launched in 1968) issued discs by the edgy band of Sun Ra along with more mainstream fare.

Munich's ECM Records, founded by Manfred Eicher in 1969, built its worldwide reputation on crystal-clear recording quality and a roster of performers—from such Euro artists as saxophonist Jan Garbarek and guitarist Terje Rypdal to States-based players Chick Corea and Keith Jarrett—who mixed originality with accessibility. Another German company started in 1969, FMP, emphasized free jazz with discs by local pianist Alex Schlippenbach and tenor saxophonist Peter Brötzmann.

The large roster of the German label MPS (from 1968) included trombonist Albert Mangelsdorff and the Clarke-Boland Big Band. Experimental jazz found more open ears in Europe than in the U.S., and lengthy commitments to such new music could be found in two Italian labels run by Giovanni Bonandrini: Black Saint (established in 1975) and Soul Note (inaugurated in 1979). Between them, they provided homes to such boundary-pushing U.S. artists as Roscoe Mitchell, Anthony Braxton, and the World Saxophone Quartet. Switzerland's Hat Hut (founded in 1974) also recorded Braxton as well as pianist Cecil Taylor and saxophonist Steve Lacy, and the UK label Ogun (started in 1973) promoted British-born free jazz, with saxophonists Evan Parker and Trevor Watts among its artists. Taylor discs also turned up on Germany's ENJA Records, launched in Munich in 1971, which also offered locals Mangelsdorff and the Ganelin Trio and leading Japanese musicians.

In Japan, the local branches of Columbia/CBS and RCA Victor (known there as JVC) recorded both Japanese and American jazz musicians, sometimes releasing albums that were unavailable in the States.

Some of the most consistent efforts to reissue U.S. jazz came from outside the U.S. The British labels Realm and Spotlite, the French branches of RCA and CBS records, and the French labels Classics (launched in 1990) and Masters of Jazz (1991) all issued a considerable amount of music from the first half-century of jazz.

—*Tad Lathrop and John Edward Hasse*

Weston, trumpeter Lester Bowie, multireedist Yusef Lateef, saxophonist Ornette Coleman, and drummers Max Roach and Ronald Shannon Jackson from going to various other African countries to play with local musicians or to investigate their music. And a number of U.S. musicians, including Weston, Lateef, Roach, and clarinetist John Carter, have deployed percussionists from North or West Africa on record as well.

The trend toward homegrown jazz styles really took off in the mid-sixties. Its Pied Piper and Johnny Appleseed was cornetist Don Cherry, one of several American modernists—among them, saxophonist Steve Lacy and pianist Mal Waldron—wandering Europe then, looking for work and partners. Cherry discovered Gato Barbieri, in Paris; sought out and studied with exiled South African pianist Dollar Brand, later called Abdullah Ibrahim, and whose rolling polyrhythms—as on *African Piano* (1969) and *African River* (1989)—can suggest an African percussion choir; went to Milan to play with the remarkable pianist Giorgio Gaslini after reading about him in London; and

spent many years off and on living and recording in Sweden, particularly inspiring musicians there.

Where most previous Americans in Europe sought out, not always successfully, musicians who could play on American terms, Cherry encouraged Europeans to be themselves: he was an avatar of world music, writing compositions flavored by various south-of-the-equator cultures. From 1978 to 1984, he was in a fine co-op trio, Codona, with Brazil's Vasconcelos and American sitarist and tabla player Colin Walcott, of the groundbreaking world-jazz group Oregon, a spinoff of Paul Winter's band.

After 1970, the Scandinavians got another boost, from the German record label ECM, which favored quiet, almost meditative music adorned with atmospheric studio echo. ECM's northern discoveries included pianist Bobo Stenson—whose out-of-tempo intros leading up to playing over a steady pulse reflected his interest in the music of India—and tenor saxophonist Jan Garbarek, who had played with Cherry and with U.S. composer George Russell. Garbarek worked with Norwegian folk materials in all manner of settings—one album featured a Nordic wind harp—and his pinched, restrained sound has been much imitated. In the 1970s he was in pianist Keith Jarrett's "European quartet" with Swedish bassist Palle Danielsson and the graceful Norwegian drummer Jon Christensen.

"What I'm playing today—whatever it is—I'm playing because I once learned the language of jazz," Garbarek said, "...but we also have our own blues equivalents, our own folk music."

This Nordic consciousness was taken even further by Kristian Blak, a pianist from Denmark's remote Faroe Islands, who in 1984 recorded a jazz LP, *Concerto Grosso,* by his group Yggdrasil in a cave formed by the sea, to the accompaniment of crashing waves.

Other strong ethnic influences came from India, a country with no strong jazz tradition, but where improvisation is central to music-making. Indian music was a full-blown fad in the 1960s: the Beatles and other rock bands adopted sitar and tabla; saxophonist John Coltrane recorded *India* (on *Live at the Village Vanguard,* 1961), albeit no more than a vague impression of droning Carnatic music; West Coast sax player Bud Shank recorded with sitar master Ravi Shankar on the album *Fire Night* (1962); British saxophonist Joe Harriott mixed jazz and Indian players in an *Indo-Jazz Fusions* (1966). In the seventies, John Handy draped rhythmically supple alto saxophone improvisations over simplified Indian rhythmic cycles on the album *Karuna Supreme* (1975). Indian strings and percussion had been used for exotic color—as on some electric Miles Davis recordings from 1970—but India's contribution to the jazz vocabulary has been primarily rhythmic, its fiendishly complex additive rhythm patterns stimulating jazz much the way Latin rhythms have.

South African pianist Abdullah Ibrahim (a.k.a. Dollar Brand) followed mid-sixties ventures into free jazz with a return to African musical ideas, yielding music of great harmonic and rhythmic variety and emotional depth.

The most important figure in this connection was English guitarist John McLaughlin, with his strong feel for South Indian music and the blues, two traditions with the shared characteristics of string bending, floating pitches, and elaborations on basic compositional forms. His electric Mahavishnu Orchestras of the 1970s—which at various times included Czech keyboardist Jan Hammer and French violinist Jean-Luc Ponty—hinted at Indian influences on such albums as *The Inner Mounting Flame* (1971) and *Birds of Fire* (1972). The influences were more on the surface in McLaughlin's later acoustic group Shakti, which employed Indian violinist L. Shankar and percussionist Zakir Hussain and played fast and fiery jazz ragas. In the 1980s and nineties, whippet-fast Indian hand-drummer Trilok Gurtu played with many Western musicians and groups, including Oregon and Jan Garbarek.

Asia's most developed scene emerged in Japan, where listeners were as enamored of jazz as they were of other forms of Western music. There, however, image at times won out over content. Fans and even jazz magazines occasionally invented fanciful jazz-player histories unencumbered by the facts. One gets the feeling Japanese jazz's best days are ahead—which is not to slight such accomplished individualists as big-band composer Toshiko Akiyoshi, a resident of the States, whose penchant for flutes suggested her roots; pianist Yosuke Yamashita, who combined Japanese-sounding materials with a hard-edged attack; and Toshinori Kondo, a free-jazzer capable of blasting earthy trumpet lines like an old New Orleans hero.

British guitarist John McLaughlin brought rock power to jazz in his group of the early 1970s, the Mahavishnu Orchestra. Later sojourns led him to a blend of Indian music and jazz in the group Shakti.

190

Free Jazz Worldwide

Even nowadays, American soloists touring Europe sometimes encounter incompatible rhythm sections (although Stan Getz, who lived in Copenhagen from 1958 to 1961, found a compatible bassist in the U.S. expatriate Oscar Pettiford). In 1963 a strange album from Copenhagen rang in new changes from just such incompatibility: the rhythm section (which included bass prodigy Niels-Henning Ørsted Pederson, who'd go on to work with pianist Oscar Peterson) played with a smooth sense of swing, but the visiting American seemed to be fighting the players all the way. That record, *My Name Is Albert Ayler,* announced the European debut of free jazz, which had even more profound consequences there than in the United States. If Americans could break free of their jazz past, so could Europeans. In England, alto saxophonist Joe Harriott had already made Europe's first free-jazz record—*Free Form* (1960)—on which he sometimes sounded strikingly (if coincidentally) like Ornette Coleman.

By the late sixties numerous Western Europeans had declared they no longer played jazz; rather, they were playing "European improvised music," employing scant if any predetermined material. It was a thoroughly transnational movement, with musicians crossing borders looking for like-minded souls. As English saxophonist Evan Parker put it, "It really was reassuring to know you weren't alone, you weren't crazy. Or if you were crazy there were other people who were just as crazy as you."

The major players came mostly from Germany (including saxophonist Peter Brötzmann, who personified his country's roaring high-energy take on the concept); England (where Parker and guitarist Derek Bailey helped define a quieter, more cooperative model); and Holland, where pianist Misha Mengelberg, drummer Han Bennink, and saxophonist Willem Breuker brought a sense of subversive fun to the music. A key contributor, Danish-Congolese saxophonist John Tchicai, had already made a dent in the United States, recording with Archie Shepp and with Coltrane on the latter's roiling album *Ascension* (1965).

That European movement eventually mushroomed into a worldwide circuit of free improvisers, many of whom recognized no kinship with jazz but (like Garbarek) wouldn't be doing what they did without its example.

The Dutch model proved particularly attractive to some observers, because it embraced swing rhythm, while the German and English tended not to. The playing of Bennink—one of the heaviest swingers in or out of Europe, even while performing such visual stunts as bouncing his sticks off the floor—even harked back to vaudeville drummers. (A theatrical side also popped out in the Lithuanian trio that personified the new, liberal Soviet jazz of the eighties: keyboardist Vyacheslav Ganelin, saxophonist Vladimir Chekasin, and drummer Vladimir Tarasov.)

Mengelberg—born in Russia, of temporarily transplanted Dutch and German parents—composed music that reflected his conservatory training, a finely honed sense of the absurd, and an admiration of Thelonious Monk and pianist Herbie Nichols. (Monk loomed large on the European scene when he was overlooked in the U.S.; some pianists who bore his stamp included Germany's Alexander Schlippenbach, Switzerland's Irene Schweizer, England's Stan Tracey, and Russian-born nomad Simon Nabatov.) For this writer at least, Mengelberg's (and Bennink's) Instant Composers Pool Orchestra, usually an octet, offered one of the world's finest mixes of jazz chops and conceptual smarts; the group could twist Ellington, Nichols, and Monk

Danish bassist Niels-Henning Ørsted Pederson emerged as one of Europe's most in-demand jazz players.

Dutch drummer Han Bennink, a colleague of Misha Mengelberg and Willem Breuker in the Dutch Instant Composers Pool, leavened his rhythmic versatility with absurdist humor.

tunes into elegant pretzels, as the album *Bospaadje konijnehol (Forest Path Rabbit Hole)* (1986–91) attests.

Italy produced more than its share of good jazz musicians, ready to play with visiting American soloists—Chet Baker recorded with many of them. And Italy had no shortage of lyrical horn players, the best known of whom was trumpeter Enrico Rava. Still, in terms of developing a national jazz identity, Italy lagged behind Western Europe. Chalk it up to national disorganization rather than lack of ambition. Giorgio Gaslini, in particular, tried about all there was to try: bop just after World War II, cool and free jazz, jazzed-up folk songs, and reconciliations of jazz and twelve-tone music.

International jazz festivals offered audiences and musicians alike an idyllic alternative to cramped, smoky, noisy nightclubs. The hundreds of festivals presented every year—in such cities as Oslo, Paris, Berlin, and Edinburgh—also added up to an important source of work for jazz bands.

OSLO JAZZFESTIVAL 5–10 AUGUST 1997

For a period in the 1990s Gaslini played piano in the Italian Instabile Orchestra, the first successful attempt to bridge the musical gap between the industrial north and rural south. It brought in musician-composers from all over the boot and provided a setting in which a pan-Italian sound could discover itself. The group offered a rich mix, including Rava; multireedist Gianluigi Trovesi, who combined jazz and folk elements in a natural way; the manically comic trumpeter (and IIO founder) Pino Minafra; and elder statesman and squirrelly altoist Mario Schiano. He began free-improvising in 1960 and said later he didn't consider himself a jazz musician anymore. Why, then, did he remain so fond of playing such chestnuts as *Moonlight in Vermont* and *Lover Man?* "Nostalgia," he said.

Of all the European scenes, the Italian may be the richest in as-yet-untapped potential, not least because Italy stands at the crossroads of so many cultures that have their own rhythmic and melodic traditions. It's one to watch in the future.

As is Canada, the site of several pockets of independent jazz activity late in the twentieth century. In Montreal—where Oscar Peterson came up before he arrived on the U.S. scene in 1949—an independent crop of French-speaking improvisers, such as saxophonist-flutist Jean Derome and electric guitarist René Lussier, were bringing Québecois consciousness to improvised music's subversive/political aspect. In Toronto, the heart of the Canadian radio industry, and thus the center of big-band activity, trombonist and arranger Rob McConnell led the best known. In Vancouver, such forward-looking improvisers as the percussive but lyrical pianist Paul Plimley and clarinetist François Houle helped keep things hopping. The influx of Asians into western Canada late in the century held the promise of spawning more cross-cultural players, such as the Canadian-Chinese pianist from Toronto, Lee Pui Ming. Which is not to mention the many Canadian musicians, from high-note trumpeter Maynard Ferguson to neobop pianist Renee Rosnes, who made their mark in the States.

A last word: Even improvisers who claim they don't play jazz often play in groups that mimic jazz instrumentation: trumpet, trombone and/or saxophone, piano, double bass, and trap set. They might even (as at that Sicilian festival we started with) lapse into swinging at times. Jazz is part of what almost every modern improviser knows and draws on, consciously or not. And who'd have it any other way?

One evening in the bar of the Bimhuis in Amsterdam—a jazz club subsidized by the Dutch government since 1974—Evan Parker and the unorthodox German drummer Paul Lovens were having a drink after a gig, when some fifties Sonny Rollins tune came over the speakers. Parker immediately began singing along with the tenor solo, note for note, and Lovens quickly joined in.

"Interesting," an onlooker said. "Inside every free improviser is a jazz musician trying to get out."

Lovens thought it over. "Yes," he said, pausing for effect. "If you're lucky." ⌒

Key Recordings

Barbieri, Gato. *Latino America.* Two discs, Impulse. On these sessions from 1973 and 1974, the tenor saxophonist drapes his own passionate solos over the homegrown accents of bands assembled in Brazil and Argentina. In both cases, he connects with native musicians on an emotional and musical level, even as his own confident solos demonstrate how far he'd traveled from Buenos Aires.

Dyani, Johnny. *Song for Biko.* Steeplechase (Denmark). Jazz inflected by South African kwela music: three musicians who fled apartheid (including alto saxophonist Dudu Pukwana and the bassist leader) team up with the Unites States' goodwill ambassador to world jazz, trumpeter Don Cherry, in 1978.

Ganelin, Vyacheslav, Vladimir Tarasov, and Vladimir Chekasin. *Catalogue: Live in East Germany.* Leo (UK). Rock power-trio antics, exuberant jazz, and Russian heaviness credibly blend, in the hands of the Soviet Union's flagship new-music group during an inspired 1979 performance.

Garbarek, Jan, and Bobo Stenson. *Witchi-Tai-To.* ECM. The much-imitated Norwegian tenor saxophonist and his lyrical pianist are caught in 1973, early in their search for an authentic Nordic jazz sound—although the title tune is a Native American chant by jazzman Jim Pepper.

Gaslini, Giorgio. *L'intégrale no.1 (1948–1963).* Two discs, Soul Note (Italy). A remarkable collection of recordings in which the blossoming Italian composer and pianist takes on bebop, cool, third-stream and other period styles, using each as a vehicle to reveal his own extravagantly Italian musical personality.

Getz, Stan, and João Gilberto. *Getz/Gilberto.* Verve. This 1963 album wasn't the tenor saxophonist's first bossa nova outing, but it's the one that put the movement on the map. Brazilian singer-guitarist Gilberto's wife, Astrud, made her singing debut here on *The Girl from Ipanema.*

Hawkins, Coleman. *Coleman Hawkins in Europe. 1934–1939.* Timeless. A fine survey of the tenor saxophone giant's collaborations with Django Reinhardt, Jack Hylton, the Ramblers, and other Europeans during his years abroad, remastered with excellent sound.

McGann, Bernie. *McGann McGann.* Terra Nova. The quick and canny Australian alto saxophonist is a great bebop musician because he has mastered the trickiest aspect of the beboppers' art: the timing. Here he is in 1994, in an offbeat pianoless quartet with trombone.

Mengelberg, Misha, and the Instant Composers Pool Orchestra. *Bospaadje konijnehol (Forest Path Rabbit Hole) I.* ICP (Netherlands). A major statement from the Dutch pianist and composer, with drummer Han Bennink: an odd but satisfying blend of offbeat Ellington arrangements, lacy chamber music, subversive humor, beautiful melodic writing, and stunning solos from a pocket orchestra of individualists, caught between 1986 and 1991.

Reinhardt, Django. *Django Reinhardt, 1935–1936.* Classics. The amazing Belgian gypsy guitarist is heard with his partner, violinist Stéphane Grappelli, as well as the Hawkins-flavored tenor saxophonist Alix Combelle, expatriate trumpeter Bill Coleman, and other guests.

Shakti, with John McLaughlin. Columbia. In 1975, following his electrified Mahavishnu Orchestra outings, McLaughlin fit his Coltrane-with-a-guitar solo style into a small acoustic ensemble of Indian musicians, with amazing results: they find the common ground between Western and Eastern traditions without obvious strain or compromise—at least when they stick to fast tempos. *—Kevin Whitehead*

CHAPTER 8

Late-Century Tradition and Innovation

Calvin Wilson

Weather Report, led by keyboardist Joe Zawinul (left) and saxophonist Wayne Shorter (right), were at the forefront of electronic jazz in the 1970s.

Wayne Shorter led jazz in electronic and multicultural directions.

Did jazz stop evolving in the late twentieth century? Or, alternatively, did it change so radically that it no longer bore much resemblance to its earlier models? Different listeners have different opinions on the matter.

What is certain is that jazz diversified into myriad offshoots and strains, some of which had little in common except the element of improvisation. And such pluralization, while affirming the continuing vitality of the creative impulse, pointed to the ever-changing nature of what people are talking about when they talk about jazz. Is it strictly bop, swing, and their substyles? Must true jazz be played primarily on acoustic instruments? Can it draw on rock or pop and still be considered jazz? Questions such as these were posed in the years leading up to the new millennium.

"There's a serious transition that's happening right now," said bassist Ray Drummond in 1999. "The jazz tradition has had a kind of singular thread throughout its existence, and that thread right now is being [split] into a number of different strands. That's not to say that it's bad, or any better, but that it's changing."

As the century neared its end, impetus for change came from still-active veterans—saxophonist Sonny Rollins and pianist Herbie Hancock among them—as well as promising newcomers such as pianist Brad Mehldau. And while innovation continued apace, jazz remained steeped in its own traditions.

Jazz Electronic

Miles Davis's influence remained very much a part of the jazz scene in the last decades of the century. The work produced by the esteemed trumpeter during his long career—encompassing bebop, cool jazz, and a range of other approaches—had become a rich resource to be mined by artists of radically different jazz persuasions.

Ironically, Davis became a touchstone both for younger, experimental jazz players working in such new-music showplaces as New York's Knitting Factory and for a neobop movement led by trumpeter Wynton Marsalis. Davis also played a role in the popularization of the 1970s rock and jazz blend that became known as "fusion." As in previous decades, Davis remained a master at culling new sounds from the musical environment and presenting them, in his own reinterpretation, as a "new thing." Davis's imprimatur on an album went a long way toward marking its content as significant.

By the 1960s, Davis had gone as far as he could with standard small-group jazz. On such recordings as *E.S.P.* (1965) and *Nefertiti* (1967) and with his second classic quintet—featuring pianist Herbie Hancock, saxophonist Wayne Shorter, bassist Ron Carter, and drummer Tony

Williams—he sought to shake up the bop-based conventions of jazz, making greater use of sonic space, abandoning the traditional theme-solo-theme approach, and drawing upon the modal lessons of his own *Kind of Blue* album (1959) while also nodding toward the abstractions of free-jazz saxophonist Ornette Coleman.

But it wasn't long before Davis, having taken note of such popular young musicians as guitarist Jimi Hendrix and flamboyant pop-soul bandleader Sly Stone, began to experiment with electric instrumentation. By the time he recorded *In a Silent Way* and *Bitches Brew* (both 1969), he had abandoned the acoustic quintet format in favor of sprawling electronic ensembles. With such albums as *A Tribute to Jack Johnson* and *Live-Evil* (both 1970), Davis had established an entirely new persona that appealed to rock fans, many of whom may have been only marginally aware of his status as a bop icon. And with those albums, the fusion movement gained momentum.

Its first stirrings had been heard from other sources, however. Hendrix—who claimed to be a fan of jazz saxophonist Rahsaan Roland Kirk—had long been shattering the bounds of rock with experimental sounds and techniques. The band the Free Spirits, whose members included guitarist Larry Coryell, recorded an album of jazz improvisation with rock instruments—*Out of Sight and Sound*—in 1966. Coryell went on to explore pop-influenced jazz further with saxophonist Steve Marcus, at which time he professed admiration for rock guitarists' use of "new media…like fuzz-tone and the wah-wah pedal… [and] the sheer loudness of the amplifier." He also joined up with vibraphonist Gary Burton, whose album *Duster* (1967) drew on rock and country music. Another group, Jeremy and the Satyrs, led by flutist Jeremy Steig, purveyed a jazz-rock blend in 1967.

Larry Coryell (left) pioneered a mixture of jazz and rock, starting with the Free Spirits and then the Count's Rock Band, in 1966–67. The Gary Burton (right) album Duster *featured Coryell's brittle guitar work.*

Technically accomplished and musically inventive, Pat Metheny sounded equally at home in vastly different jazz settings.

After Davis issued his roiling, instrumentally dense *Bitches Brew,* musicians who had come through his bands became principal players in the fusion movement. Shorter and keyboardist Joe Zawinul formed Weather Report; pianist Chick Corea helmed two versions of Return to Forever; Williams drove the Lifetime band; guitarist John McLaughlin, a charter Lifetime member, formed his own group, the Mahavishnu Orchestra.

Perhaps the most successful early fusion player was Herbie Hancock, whose experiments with a keyboard-driven experimental band (known after the fact as the Mwandishi group) paved the way for his more commercial Head Hunters group, which had a radio hit with *Chameleon* in 1973.

Jazz-rock fusion had its detractors. Yet some of its performers left a trail of memorable artifacts, including the Mahavishnu Orchestra's *The Inner Mounting Flame* (1971), Weather Report's eponymous first album (1971), and a number of recordings by rock- and country-influenced jazz guitarist Pat Metheny.

Metheny, more than many others, symbolized the flexibility of late-century jazz. In a typical performance, his group drew from bop, Brazilian samba, even the most out-and-out avant-garde jazz, employing virtually any stylistic or sonic element as long as it supported the musical statement being made.

His recording projects also ran the gamut. They included the raucous, uncompromising *Song X* album (1985) with saxophonist Ornette Coleman; the atypically mainstream-jazz Metheny Group album *Quartet* (1996); and sideman dates with the likes of saxophonists Michael Brecker and Joshua Redman and guitarist Jim Hall (*Jim Hall and Pat Metheny,* 1998). In all cases, Metheny proved an improviser of boundless imagination and energy. He also proved one of the most commercially successful jazz musicians of the 1980s, just as the fusion movement reached larger audiences than had the mainstream jazz of preceding years.

"Miles wants you." When musicians got that call, they answered. It was like being anointed.

Post-Mainstream Jazz Standards

While jazz-inclined musicians of the late twentieth century still played earlier swing and bebop tunes, they also acknowledged the enormous body of pop music from the sixties and beyond. Younger bands embraced elements of rock and soul music while adopting the freer stylistic elements made popular by such musicians as Ornette Coleman and John Coltrane.

This new input resulted, most obviously, in a greatly altered role for the rhythm section and the use of more open-ended compositional and improvisational forms. In performances by many post-1960s bands, bass ostinatos and vamps that em-phasize a "pocket" or a groove (as pioneered by the band of sixties soul singer James Brown, Sly and the Family Stone, and others) replaced the traditional swing-derived walk-ing-bass pattern. Familiar chord sequences and changes, such as those used in bop contrafacts, were replaced by a more static harmony. The chord changes were fewer, but often much more exotic.

Post-mainstream standards can roughly be placed within two broad categories: those composed by jazz musicians and songs borrowed from the realms of pop and rock.

Among the more popular jazz compositions were keyboardist Herbie Hancock's *Chameleon* (1973) and his earlier *Dolphin Dance* (1964). Joe Zawinul's 1977 hit *Birdland* evidenced staying power. Musicians also embraced a number of Chick Corea compositions, including the samba-flavored *Spain* and *500 Miles High* (both 1972), and *Windows* (1968). Joe Henderson's *Inner Urge* (1964) proved a favored framework for exploring the exotic-sounding Lydian mode. Ron Carter penned *Eighty-One* (1964) and *Little Waltz* (1966); Freddie Hubbard authored *Little Sunflower* (1966) and *Red Clay* (1970); while Wayne Shorter wrote *Footprints* (1966), *Nefertiti* (1967), and *E.S.P.* (1965). Benny Golson composed the catchy piece *Killer Joe* (1959), and David Frischberg's wry *Peel Me a Grape* (1962) became popular among singers.

Jazz performances employed pop music from such composers as Brian Wilson (of the Beach Boys), the Beatles, Burt Bacharach, Stevie Wonder, and Jimmy Webb. Other music came from widely differing non-jazz sources. Herbie Hancock performed the grunge band Nirvana's *All Apologies* on his album *The New Standard* (1995). A version of the Stylistics' R&B tune *People Make the World Go Around* is included on trumpeter Nicholas Payton's *Payton's Place* (1998). Jimi Hendrix's *Little Wing* and *Up from the Skies* (both 1968) found their way into the repertoire of the Gil Evans big band (initially on *Gil Evans Plays the Music of Jimi Hendrix*, 1975).

Such interpretations—along with jazz musicians' continuing production of their own compositions—promised the growth of a vital and lasting new repertoire. —*David Baise*

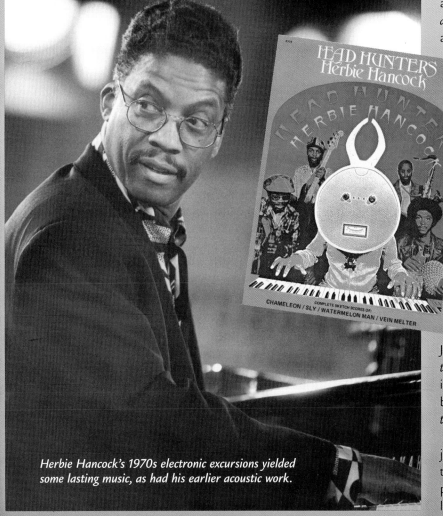

Herbie Hancock's 1970s electronic excursions yielded some lasting music, as had his earlier acoustic work.

Although later fusion at times seemed more pop than jazz, early fusion music had its roots in bedrock jazz values—improvisation, performer interplay, and, most of all, originality of expression. That's because most of the original fusion artists had honed their chops within an acoustic context. They came up in bop and bop-derived bands, and therefore had an understanding of traditional jazz theory and practice.

Aside from Miles Davis, perhaps the best example of a prominent early fusion player with a solid bop background is Wayne Shorter. The saxophonist not only apprenticed with Davis but also played in Art Blakey's Jazz Messengers alongside such mainstream jazzmen as trumpeters Lee Morgan and Freddie Hubbard. On albums for Blue Note Records under his own name, Shorter indulged in the sort of harmonic experimentation upon which his reputation would ultimately be based. This is heard to good advantage on the albums *Juju* (1964) and *Etcetera* (1965). On the former, Shorter is joined by two-thirds of the classic Coltrane rhythm section—pianist McCoy Tyner and drummer Elvin Jones—along with bassist Reggie Workman. The latter album places him in the company of Hancock, bassist Cecil McBee, and drummer Joe Chambers.

Weather Report's Heavy Weather *(1977), the fusion band's most successful album.*

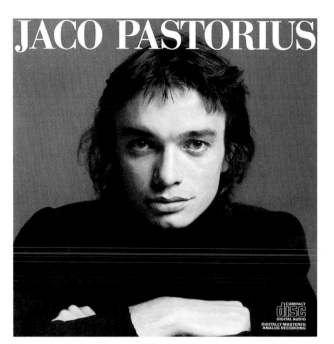

Bassist Jaco Pastorius supplied much of the punch in Weather Report's later music.

Similarly, Joe Zawinul—Shorter's collaborator throughout Weather Report's successful run and a one-time sideman to Cannonball Adderley—also had a thorough understanding of jazz history. Hence, the initial goal of Weather Report was not merely to explore the jazz idiom in a more commercial context, but to use what they and their like-minded colleagues had learned in the acoustic-jazz realm as a basis for more sonically expansive explorations.

That much is evident when one listens to *Weather Report*, the group's eponymous 1971 debut disc. On this album, Shorter and Zawinul seem interested less in melody or harmony than in sound itself: its textures, its colors, its ambience. However, with each successive album, the band became more and more concerned with conventional melodies. Weather Report arguably reached a beatific equilibrium with *Mysterious Traveller* (1973–74). On the other hand, the band had its greatest commercial success with *Heavy Weather* (1977), largely because of the catchy radio hit *Birdland*.

The success of that album also stemmed from the contributions of Jaco Pastorius, the band's bassist at the time. A phenomenal technician with a boundless musical imagination, Pastorius was as capable of firing off rapid, precisely articulated bop phrases as he was of coaxing plaintive, voicelike melodies from his distinctive instrument of choice, a fretless electric bass. He spawned an army of imitators and drew raves as the instrument's most influential practitioner after Jimmie Blanton, Oscar Pettiford, and Charles Mingus. But Pastorius died early—at age 35—from injuries sustained in a beating.

Tradition in Transition

In the 1980s, the United States was in a state of reassessment and retrenchment, and this was reflected in the arts. In jazz, it took the form of renewed interest in earlier—specifically, bop-based—styles.

Throughout the 1980s, bop veterans continued to tour and record. Clark Terry remained active, wielding his trumpet with authority on such albums as *Memories of Duke* (1980) and *Yes, the Blues* (1981). Saxophonist Phil Woods led a quintet that featured Tom Harrell on trumpet and recorded a string of gems including *Heaven* (1984), *Gratitude* (1986), and *Bouquet* (1987). Also active were such standard-bearers for bop as the Heath Brothers (saxophonist Jimmy, bassist Percy, and drummer Albert "Tootie"); saxophonist Johnny Griffin; drummer Elvin Jones; and bassist Ray Brown.

Still, it was largely the excitement surrounding trumpeter Wynton Marsalis—in both the music world and the mass media—that established neobop jazz in mainstream culture.

Marsalis could hardly have been more passionate. When he began to attact attention in the early 1980s, after having worked for both Blakey and Hancock, acoustic bop had slipped out of fashion. Marsalis re-examined and embraced it, bringing to the music his fine musicianship—he was also an accomplished player of European classical music—and fresh enthusiasm. Certainly Marsalis wasn't entirely responsible for the bop revival. Dexter Gordon, for one, had helped to reignite interest in the music through his legendary stint at the Village Vanguard in 1976, after years away from the stateside jazz spotlight,

Veteran bassist Ray Brown.

Dexter Gordon enjoyed renewed acclaim late in his career.

Marcus Roberts, a 1980s "young lion" with an interest in traditional repertory.

Bop-leaning trumpeter Nicholas Payton emerged in the 1990s.

Jazz classicist Wynton Marsalis.

as documented on the album *Homecoming: Live at the Village Vanguard.* But the response to Marsalis undeniably confirmed that bop was back.

On his eponymous 1982 debut album for Columbia, the trumpeter played with exuberance and edge. His subsequent small-group recordings seemed to remap those wide-open musical spaces that the Davis and Coltrane groups of the 1960s had so poetically explored. Later, Marsalis would find inspiration in the works of Duke Ellington and Charles Mingus—influences heard on the albums *Citi Movement* (1992) and *In This House, on This Morning* (1992–93), as well as on the oratorio *Blood on the Fields* (1995), which won the Pulitzer Prize.

Marsalis became a hero to the bop faithful, a standard-bearer for tradition, and a mentor to emerging players.

Record companies began to search for "young lions" to update the bop sound à la the success of Marsalis. One of the more notable discoveries was trumpeter Roy Hargrove, whose debut album, *Diamond in the Rough* (1989), not only displayed his gifts as an exemplary stylist in the spirit of Clifford Brown but also featured fine playing by alto saxophonist Antonio Hart and tenorist Ralph Moore. Hargrove would go on to record such substantial albums as *With the Tenors of Our Times* (1993–94) and, with his band Crisol, *Habana* (1997).

Pianist Marcus Roberts, for a time a sideman in Wynton Marsalis's group, built a solo career marked by deep study of the classic repertoire, reflected on *Gershwin for Lovers* (1994) and *Plays Ellington* (1995). Another newcomer, trumpeter Nicholas Payton, drew the attention of such veterans as drummer Elvin Jones and saxophonist Joe Henderson before recording such bop-inflected albums as *Payton's Place* (1997–98).

Other young players gaining notice during the bop revival included trumpeters Terence Blanchard, Wallace Roney, and Marlon Jordan; saxophonists Kenny Garrett and Donald Harrison; pianists Kenny Kirkland and Benny Green; bassists Christian McBride and Robert Hurst; and drummers Jeff "Tain" Watts and Ralph Peterson.

Institutional Jazz Programs

It's perhaps ironic that jazz—noted for its outside-the-mainstream, antiestablishment ethos—gained a great deal of support from public and private institutions in the last part of the twentieth century.

Some wondered whether institutional involvement would change the music for the worse. But the arguments for such support were compelling: to preserve the growing history of jazz, to give jazz a stronger economic footing, to present it as a music equal in value to any other, and to help it reach new audiences.

Among the first institutions to embrace jazz were Tulane University in New Orleans and Hunter College in New York, each of which set up a jazz archive in the 1950s (Hunter's Institute of Jazz Studies moved in 1966 to Rutgers University in Newark, New Jersey). In 1970, the Smithsonian Institution in Washington, D.C., established a presence in jazz that grew to encompass the world's most comprehensive set of jazz programs, including collections of memorabilia, artifacts, and oral histories and the production of exhibitions, recordings, books, educational material, symposia, concerts, and radio and multimedia programs. The Smithsonian Jazz Masterworks Orchestra, under the baton of David Baker, played the riches of the jazz repertory in the nation's capital and on national and international tours.

In the 1980s and 1990s a number of other institutions got into the act. The Washington-based Thelonious Monk Institute for Jazz focused on nurturing young jazz performers, while the Kennedy Center, under advisor Billy Taylor, began presenting an ambitious series of concerts and school programs. The Library of Congress undertook a program of commissions to jazz composers.

New York's Jazz at Lincoln Center, under the artistic direction of the charismatic Wynton Marsalis, developed its widely touring Lincoln Center Jazz Orchestra as well as the Essentially Ellington high school band contest, a radio series, and lecture and film programs. Carnegie Hall mounted its Carnegie Hall Jazz Band under trumpeter Jon Faddis, while the Brooklyn Academy of Music launched a cutting-edge jazz performance series under clarinetist Don Byron.

Efforts began elsewhere in the United States to create jazz repertory orchestras and homes for jazz performance series and jazz archives. Among the latter were the Chicago Jazz Archive at the University of Chicago and the California Institute for the Preservation of Jazz at California State University, Long Beach.

The National Endowment for the Arts, founded in 1965, provided a modest stream of grants for jazz over the years. In the 1990s, three foundations stepped in to raise the ante: the Doris Duke Foundation, the Louis Armstrong Educational Foundation, and the largest jazz philanthropic donor of the twentieth century, the Lila Wallace–Reader's Digest Fund, whose grants included $7.5 million to the Smithsonian for a ten-year initiative of jazz programs and $6.9 million to National Public Radio.

European institutions included the National Jazz Archive in Amsterdam; the Norsk Jazzarkiv in Oslo; the Jazz-Institut at Darmstadt, Germany; the Institute for Jazz Research in Graz, Austria; and the Danish Jazz Federation in Copenhagen.

—John Edward Hasse

David Baker, artistic director of the Smithsonian Jazz Masterworks Orchestra.

Sonny Rollins' creative well remained full a half century after his first performances.

But by the 1990s record companies had begun to realize that they were overlooking significant veteran performers. Such players as pianists Tommy Flanagan, Hank Jones, and Kenny Barron; saxophonists Gary Bartz, Frank Morgan, and Sonny Fortune; vibraphonist Bobby Hutcherson; trumpeter Eddie Henderson; and trombonist J.J. Johnson recorded new albums and saw their profiles rise.

The case for tradition was also eloquently made in the 1990s by saxophonists Sonny Rollins and Joe Henderson, two of the most esteemed jazz veterans. Although Rollins peppered his work with dashes of pop and R&B, his bop heritage remained audible whenever he lifted his saxophone to his lips, as on the splendid 1996 album +3. Henderson, long a favorite among musicians, finally broke through commercially with his 1991 recording *Lush Life,* a tribute to Duke Ellington's collaborator Billy Strayhorn.

Classic jazz gained champions in several "repertory" bands that emerged in the 1990s. Early in the decade, the U.S. Congress established the Smithsonian Jazz Masterworks Orchestra, which specialized in authentic performances of works by acknowledged masters. The Lincoln Center Jazz Orchestra and the Carnegie Hall Jazz Band were also active.

In that same decade, some of the essential jazz artists died: Miles Davis, Stan Getz, Dizzy Gillespie, Gerry Mulligan, Mel Tormé, Betty Carter, Art Blakey, Cab Calloway, Ella Fitzgerald, Sun Ra, and Sarah Vaughan. Understandably, some longtime fans feared for the future of the music. But as usual, jazz and its audience were changing with the times.

The long career of tenor saxophonist Joe Henderson hit many creative peaks, including the album Inner Urge (1964). *His commercial high point came in 1992 with* Lush Life.

Further Exploration

The edgy territory Weather Report had explored in the 1970s had not been abandoned. Listeners had only to tune their ears to the music emerging on the fringes—much of which had yet to be fully commercialized because it had yet to be fully understood. In the 1980s, New York City served as a base of operation for a handful of artists struggling with new musical ideas. Among them were saxophonists David Murray and John Zorn, keyboardist Wayne Horvitz, and guitarists Bill Frisell and James Blood Ulmer.

Unlike the boppers who had congregated at Minton's Playhouse in Harlem in the 1940s, the work of these artists didn't coalesce into one easily identifiable style. Instead, it reflected an eclecticism that fascinated some listeners while perplexing others.

Murray's octet recording *Ming* (1980) reveals an artist with his ears wide open. The album's aesthetic is one of chaos under control, of manic invention caught in the refining net of form.

Horvitz, on albums with his avant-jazz group the President, such as *Bring Yr Camera* (1988) and *Miracle Mile* (1991), drew on such musical genres as punk rock and Delta blues. He also experimented with compositional form on his album *This New Generation* (1985) and participated in cutting-edge sessions with cornetist Lawrence "Butch" Morris.

Alto saxophonist Zorn became regarded as something of a new-jazz god. In the 1980s, his signature style—heard, for example, on *Naked City* (1989)—was to approach music as a puzzle whose pieces didn't necessarily have to fit. *Spy vs. Spy* (1989) was his nod to his spiritual father, Ornette Coleman. But in Zorn's hands, the album's Coleman tunes became exercises in sonic angst, many of them clocking in at under three minutes but coming on so loud and strong that their impact on the eardrums was palpable.

Ulmer, a onetime sideman to Coleman, for a time had the backing of the mainstream record label Columbia, which flexed substantial muscle in promoting his releases *Freelancing* (1981), *Black Rock* (1982), and *Odyssey* (1983). But the guitarist's raw, angular musings, suggesting guitarist Jimi Hendrix playing the Coleman songbook, straddled the jazz and rock worlds without residing comfortably in either. Even so, he secured a cult following and found support at smaller labels.

Exploratory saxophonist and big-band leader David Murray.

Abstract blues-jazz guitarist James Blood Ulmer.

All-Inclusive Blends

Horvitz and Zorn didn't take these nontraditional paths because of a lack of "straight-ahead"—that is, bop-influenced—chops. Far from it. Their album *Voodoo* (1985–86), on which Horvitz performed solely on acoustic piano, was an involving tribute to the genius of underrated bop pianist Sonny Clark.

With Ray Drummond on bass and Bobby Previte on drums, *Voodoo* was acoustic, bop-informed jazz performed with immediacy and vibrancy.

Indeed, among musicians in the 1980s, looking to bop legends for inspiration seemed a widely traveled route to reaching full musical potential. Accordingly, many musicians were looking both forward and back, acknowledging the jazz tradition while also flirting with new ideas.

One of the more accomplished jazz units of the time was the George Adams–Don Pullen Quartet. Saxophonist Adams and pianist Pullen had both worked for Charles Mingus, and they led their quartet in the envelope-pushing spirit of their former boss. With Dannie Richmond (another Mingus alumnus) on drums and Cameron Brown on bass, the Adams-Pullen unit could thrash one second, only to ruminate the next. The band is in splendid form on its two-volume *Live at the Village Vanguard* recordings (1983).

In the early eighties, bassist Dave Holland formed a group that played "freebop," a jazz approach combining bop-like structures with the anarchic risks of free jazz. On such albums as *Jumpin' In* (1983), *Seeds of Time* (1984), and *The Razor's Edge* (1987), Holland presided over performances of ragged exuberance. His groups featured such players as trumpeter Kenny Wheeler, trombonist Julian Priester, and, early in his career, alto saxophonist Steve Coleman.

The 1980s also saw the artistic ascension of the World Saxophone Quartet, a unit formed in 1976. With reed players David Murray, Julius Hemphill, Oliver Lake, and Hamiet Bluiett performing without a rhythm section, the WSQ focused on creating interesting, overlapping horn textures. Its audacious early albums—such as *W.S.Q.* and *Revue* (both 1980)—eventually gave way to the more measured statements of *Plays Duke Ellington* (1986) and *Rhythm and Blues* (1988).

A similar metamorphosis characterized the adventurous guitarist Bill Frisell's passage from the 1980s into the nineties. Upon hearing his later work, one might have no inkling that he'd ever been associated with an avant-garde. Which is not to imply that his music had been compromised. Rather, the guitarist seemed to have legitimately evolved from maverick to mainstream player.

Indeed, the difference between Frisell's later recordings and the earlier album *Strange Meeting* (1987)—on which he, bassist Melvin Gibbs, and drummer Ronald Shannon Jackson perform under the band name Power Tools—reveals a subtle change in musical attitude. In the 1987 recording of the title composition, the trio performance is wiry and metallic, lean and intriguing. But on *This Land* (1992), the same piece has shed some of its contrariness. In this sextet reading, *Strange Meeting* is more lyrical, less foreboding.

Bill Frisell's musical personality reflected the myriad sounds he'd absorbed.

It's as if Frisell had abandoned the notion of bombast for bombast's sake, choosing instead to embrace a mature grace. The guitarist's 1996 album, *Quartet,* on which he trades phrases with a trombonist, a trumpeter, and a violinist, placed an even greater emphasis on form over effect.

In a sense, the musical adventurousness of a Bill Frisell or a David Murray was prompted by a disintegration of musical categories. Murray, who recorded an album of songs by legendary West Coast rockers the Grateful Dead, and Frisell, who included compositions by folk-rock composer-poet Bob Dylan, bluesman Muddy Waters, and pop singer Madonna on his 1992 album *Have a Little Faith,* were artists unafraid of

A musician of broad interests, clarinetist Don Byron ventured into klezmer, classical, salsa, rock, and jazz.

© Ken Francking

The Big-Band Revival

Nothing delivers the thrill of jazz quite like a big band. And by the late 1990s, fans had a generous choice of listening options.

Some preferred the "ghost bands" that performed the music of such legendary figures as Duke Ellington and Count Basie. Others were enamored of the postbop sounds of such living bandleaders as Carla Bley and Toshiko Akiyoshi.

The classic big-band sound, with its accent on swing and its adherence to smooth ensemble lines, continued to be popular. On any given night, incarnations of the orchestras of Basie, Ellington, Glenn Miller, and other swing bandleaders could be heard performing in towns and cities across the U.S., some with demanding touring schedules.

Even though enthusiastic audiences couldn't get enough of time-tested swing values, big bands in the second half of the century began to absorb elements from classical, rock, and other types of music to create a new kind of swing that was more conducive to listening than to dancing. Such bandleaders as pianists Bley, Akiyoshi, and McCoy Tyner; bassists Charlie Haden and William Parker; saxophonist David Murray; and composer Maria Schneider were among the better-known exponents of this newer approach.

Influences on these innovators ranged from Basie and Ellington to Gil Evans and Charles Mingus. Indeed, the Mingus Big Band, a unit dedicated to the work of its namesake, attracted a devoted following for its surprising and energetic sounds.

Other notable big bands included the Vanguard Jazz Orchestra, which began life as a band co-led by trumpeter Thad Jones and drummer Mel Lewis, and the Sun Ra Arkestra, which carried on in the name of the visionary pianist-bandleader. —*Calvin Wilson*

defying notions of what's acceptable in jazz—just as Louis Armstrong, Charlie Parker, and other jazz innovators had been in earlier decades.

To an increasing number of musicians, the question of mutually exclusive musical categories—say, pop versus jazz, or acoustic versus electric—became irrelevant; they were more concerned with expanding their musical palettes and less worried about fitting into a niche; they were using every sound within earshot.

"Most musicians are listening to music outside of their own categories," said saxophonist David Sanborn in 1998. "They don't think in terms of boundaries."

Clarinetist Don Byron was just such an artist. On his LP *Tuskegee Experiments* (1990–91), he enlisted guitarist Frisell to add the crucial ingredient of unapologetic rock-flavored furor. But on *Bug Music* (1996), the clarinetist paid his respects to the swinging sounds of Duke Ellington, pianist Raymond Scott, and bassist John Kirby. It might be said that Byron, who covered Jimi Hendrix's *If Six Was Nine* on his album *Nu Blaxploitation* (1997–98), was as idiosyncratic in his own way as the better-known guitarist Metheny and pianist Keith Jarrett. It could also be said that, in turn, what Byron, Metheny, and Jarrett had in common was the sort of iconoclastic individualism that had been the signature of leading jazz artists from Jelly Roll Morton to Thelonious Monk.

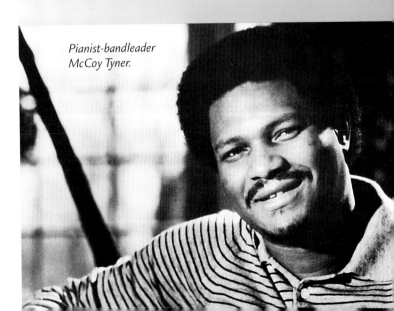

Pianist-bandleader McCoy Tyner.

Jarrett's introspective solo concerts earned him a huge following in the classical world, which probably helped explain the unusually large audience (by jazz standards) garnered by his long-running trio with bassist Gary Peacock and drummer Jack DeJohnette. The pianist was responsible for some of the most impassioned jazz of the late twentieth century, scrupulously eschewing clichés while indulging in the romance of the moment. His more experimental efforts were undertaken in the 1970s—with two groups that came to be called the American and European quartets. The American combo featured Haden on bass, Paul Motian on drums, and Dewey Redman on saxophone; Jan Garbarek handled the saxophone chores in the European unit, which had Palle Danielsson on bass and Jon Christensen on drums.

In his later group with Peacock and DeJohnette, Jarrett's apparent goal was to explore classic songs (along with the occasional original) in an expansive, freewheeling manner not unlike that of the Bill Evans trios of the 1960s.

Jarrett, like other alumni of the Miles Davis groups, had become something of an elder statesman of jazz. Indeed, such musicians as Herbie Hancock, Dave Holland, and Chick Corea were still on the scene actively seeking new ways to express their long-accumulated and time-refined musical thoughts. Their efforts included adapting the results of their avant-garde and fusion explorations to an acoustic context—in essence returning, like prodigal sons, to their points of origin.

Keith Jarrett became noted for long solo piano improvisations—marked by his ecstatic utterances and expressive physicality—and for adventuresome but accessible small-band music.

Hancock impressed critics with his largely acoustic albums *The New Standard* (1995) and *Gershwin's World* (1998), as well as *1+1* (1996), his duo disc with saxophonist Wayne Shorter. Holland veered even closer to the mainstream with his albums *Extensions* (1989) and *Points of View* (1997).

But the veteran artist whose experience was perhaps the most expansive was pianist Chick Corea, whose career encompassed free jazz, fusion, and straight-ahead bop. An alumnus of stints with trumpeter Blue Mitchell, percussionist Mongo Santamaria, and saxophonist Stan Getz, Corea had first emerged as a bandleader in 1968 with the acoustic trio album *Now He Sings, Now He Sobs*, on which he exhibited technical virtuosity and advanced harmonic ideas with a touch of Latin-flavored romanticism. Later, with his Return to Forever bands, he had veered from Brazilian jazz (as on *Light as a Feather,* 1972) to improvisational heavy metal (*Where Have I Known You Before,* 1974).

In the 1980s, Corea simultaneously maintained the Elektric Band—which purveyed fusion on such albums as *Light Years* (1987) and *Eye of the Beholder* (1988)—and the Akoustic Band, a post-bop trio that released an eponymous studio disc in 1989 and a live one in 1991. But in the final years of the nineties, Corea returned to acoustic playing full-time, releasing fine albums that included *Remembering Bud Powell* (1996), a tribute to the bebop pianist, and *Origin: Live at the Blue Note* (1998), the debut disc from Corea's straight-ahead sextet.

The iconoclastic veterans Ornette Coleman and Cecil Taylor also continued to be vital jazz contributors. Coleman's later albums included *In All Languages* (1987), which featured both his electric Prime Time group—a Coleman-esque nod to fusion—and a reunion with his early collaborators Don Cherry, Charlie Haden, and Billy Higgins; *Tone Dialing* (1995), a Prime Time outing; and two simultaneously released quartet albums, *Sound Museum: Three Women* and *Sound Museum: Hidden Man* (both 1996).

Taylor continued to make uncompromising music, as evidenced by the 1984 album *Winged Serpent (Sliding Quadrants)*, which featured a large ensemble; *For Olim* (1986), a solo piano disc; and *Olu Iwa* (also 1986), on which Taylor offers some of his boldest music ever.

Other artists of the 1960s and seventies who remained active at century's end included saxophonists Anthony Braxton, Henry Threadgill, and Dewey Redman; pianists McCoy Tyner, Joanne Brackeen, and Andrew Hill; trumpeter Lester Bowie; bassists Ron Carter and Charlie Haden; and drummers Elvin Jones and Paul Motian.

Chick Corea, leading keyboardist, bandleader, and composer.

Ron Carter, the top-tier post-mainstream bassist.

Rap act Digable Planets' sound included electronic samples of Art Blakey and Sonny Rollins tracks.

The Roots fashioned one of the more successful integrations of hip-hop and jazz.

The Groove Movement

The effect of all this jazz activity—whether that activity was traditionalist or experimental—was an expanded cultural awareness of the music and a resurgence of interest in its commercial potential. Jazz was also taking on new shapes and, as ever, finding new audiences.

In the 1980s, an "acid jazz" movement emerged, with nightclub DJs "sampling"—digitally reproducing—hard-bop grooves in the service of dance beats. Originating in London, the movement quickly crossed the Atlantic. Prime purveyors of this musical strain included the Brand New Heavies, the United Future Organization, and the Groove Collective.

By the 1990s, jazz was becoming prominent in hip-hop, a rhythm-heavy brand of pop music that superimposed spoken rhyming—raps—over collage-like sonic backdrops. The jazz-rap group US3—which took its name from a Blue Note album featuring pianist Horace Parlan, bassist George Tucker, and drummer Al Harewood—charted a hit with the album *Hand on the Torch* (1993) and its successful single *Cantaloop (Flip Fantasia)*, which sampled a Herbie Hancock recording. In fact, *Hand on the Torch,* itself released on Blue Note, enabled the venerable label to take its jazz message to a younger audience than it had previously reached. Other groups that mixed jazz and rap included Gang Starr (whose lead vocalist, Guru, released several solo recordings); A Tribe Called Quest; the Roots; and Digable Planets—the latter scoring a top-twenty hit in 1993 with *Rebirth of Slick (Cool Like Dat)*, featured on the album *Reachin' (A New Refutation of Time and Space)*.

Coming from the jazz side, saxophonists Greg Osby and Branford Marsalis released albums that incorporated rap elements. Both Osby's album *3-D Lifestyles* (1993) and Marsalis's disc *Buckshot LeFonque* (1994) combined a contemporary street sensibility with post-bop aesthetics. Miles Davis's final studio album, *Doo-Bop* (1991), was also a jazz-rap project—not very surprising, given the trumpeter's ever-restless search for interesting new musical material.

M-Base

In the 1980s the neobop movement may have garnered most of the media attention, but not all jazz artists were involved in that trend. Some were exploring the jazz possibilities of more contemporary currents in music, in what came to be known as the M-Base movement. Based in Brooklyn, M-Base was spearheaded by alto saxophonist Steve Coleman, a Chicago native whose eclectic musical tastes were readily apparent in his compositions and performances.

M-Base stands for Macro-Basic Array of Structured Extemporization. In Coleman's music that meant funk that swung, hip-hop that drew on bop, and street rhythms that made room for improvisation. The company he kept in the late eighties was, in retrospect, exemplary: M-Base adherents included such end-of-the-century stars as singer Cassandra Wilson, pianist Geri Allen, and alto saxophonist Greg Osby.

Although M-Base had no formal organization, its flagship was Coleman's group, Five Elements. On albums such as *Black Science* (1991), *Drop Kick* (1992), and *Def Trance Beat (Modalities of Rhythm)* (1995), Coleman updated the sound of Miles Davis's 1970s ensembles and Ornette Coleman's Prime Time band, making a persuasive case that the dance ethic that won jazz its following in the Swing Era yet survived. All that was necessary was that the dance element reflect contemporary styles.

Coleman had developed a strong straight-ahead bop technique before setting out on his own path, having performed in the Thad Jones–Mel Lewis big band and recorded with bassist Dave Holland. In turn,

the M-Base movement exerted an influence on a generation of jazz performers who, while mindful of the music's traditions, were also open to a multitude of ways to express themselves. At the new millennium, that spirit of exploration remained intact as Osby and Allen continued to push the limits of bop, Wilson helped to bring a broader audience to jazz singing, and Coleman remained open to a world of musical possibilities.
—*Calvin Wilson*

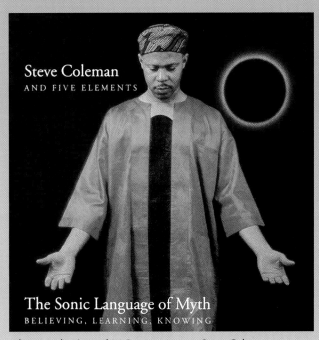

Alto saxophonist and M-Base proponent Steve Coleman.

Access to Jazz

Acid jazz and the sometimes indistinguishable jazz-rap were credited with opening some young people to the notion of listening to more traditional jazz sounds as well. And in the 1990s there was much to choose from, both in record bins and on stages.

Record labels large and small offered an endless outpouring of new albums and reissues. Jazz performances at clubs, concert halls, and festivals were also resurgent.

The Internet provided a new means of connecting jazz with worldwide audiences via networks of online stores, archives, magazines, and educational sites.

To be sure, jazz wasn't so popular that it could compete with rock or country music for radio play or sales. Its share of the music market, like that of classical music,

was small, averaging 4 or 5 percent of album sales in the U.S. Still, jazz had its own strengths in the marketplace. The maturing baby-boom generation held promise as a growing jazz audience. And jazz tended not to go "out of date" as rapidly as ever-changing pop styles of music. Unlike many pop albums, jazz discs tend to have long "shelf lives"—a single record may sell for many years after its initial release, meaning a single jazz album may sell more over its life span than a pop LP. For example, as the century ended, Miles Davis's *Kind of Blue* (1959) was still selling more than 250,000 copies per year in the U.S. alone—and had never been out of print.

As for access to live jazz, opportunities remained plentiful, if somewhat less so than in earlier decades.

Jazz Museums

The movement to preserve the history of jazz was in full force by the end of the twentieth century. As a result, today's seekers of museum exhibits and historic sites have many from which to choose.

In the East, Louis Armstrong's house (3456 107th Street in the Queens borough of New York City) is open to visitors, and a selection of his memorabilia is on display at Queens College. Beginning in 1988, the Smithsonian Institution's National Museum of American History always displayed some of its national jazz treasures, which include the vast, 200,000-page Ellington archive as well as Dizzy Gillespie's angled-bell trumpet, Benny Goodman's clarinet, Buddy Rich's drum set, the band "library" of Jimmie Lunceford, photographs by Herman Leonard and William Claxton, seven hundred films, and papers of Ella Fitzgerald and the Apollo Theatre. In nearby Baltimore, the Eubie Blake National Jazz Institute offers exhibits on Baltimore's own Eubie Blake, Chick Webb, Cab Calloway, and Billie Holiday.

The South offers jazz lovers a growing number of sites. The Louisiana State Museum, in New Orleans, maintains a continuing exhibition on New Orleans jazz, while the city-owned Louis Armstrong Park features statues of hometown heroes Louis Armstrong and Sidney Bechet. In Florence, Alabama, the W.C. Handy Birthplace (602 West College Street) is open to visitors, while the Alabama Jazz Hall of Fame, in Birmingham, honors two hundred native sons and daughters, including Erskine

Hall-of-famer Lionel Hampton.

BEYOND CATEGORY
THE MUSICAL GENIUS OF DUKE ELLINGTON

In 1993, the Smithsonian produced a traveling exhibition of its Duke Ellington holdings.

Hawkins, Lionel Hampton, and Dinah Washington. The Down Beat Jazz Hall of Fame and Museum—launched in 1998 at Universal Studios' CityWalk in Orlando, Florida—features memorabilia borrowed from the families of its inductees, who include Duke Ellington, Count Basie, Miles Davis, John Coltrane, Thelonious Monk, Dizzy Gillespie, and Max Roach.

In the Midwest, Indiana University in Bloomington offers a Hoagy Carmichael Room, displaying his jazz- and song-related memorabilia. The Graystone Jazz Museum in Detroit hosts a modest display and runs outreach programs for students. In St. Louis, you can tour the restored Scott Joplin House State Historic Site (2658 Delmar). In Kansas City, Missouri, the handsome American Jazz Museum, in the historic 18th and Vine District, offers memorabilia of Kansas City jazz, audiovisual programs, and a room for nighttime performances.

Out West, there is a Glenn Miller exhibit, chock-a-block with his memorabilia, at his alma mater, the University of Colorado in Boulder. —*John Edward Hasse*

For the most part, New York City was still the center of jazz. To be a headliner in one of its more prestigious clubs—particularly the Village Vanguard or the Blue Note—was still a significant achievement, an indication that an artist was held in high esteem. The city was also the home of both the traditionalist Jazz at Lincoln Center concert series and the edgy Knitting Factory nightclub; styles in between those extremes could be heard at such long-open venues as Birdland, Iridium, Sweet Basil, and Zinno.

In the 1990s, one of the best places for a new player to get noticed was Smalls, a club in the West Village that could hold only about fifty people but was conveniently located near the Vanguard. Among the notable artists who performed there were pianist Brad Mehldau, bassist Avishai Cohen, and drummer Brian Blade.

But Chicago, which also had a wide-ranging jazz history, was increasingly significant as a place where artists might establish themselves. Saxophonist Ken Vandermark— recipient of a MacArthur Foundation "genius" grant in 1999—hailed from the Windy City, continued to live there, and distinguished himself with such bracing albums as *Target or Flag* and *Simpatico* (both 1998). On some nights Vandermark could be heard at the Empty Bottle, a rock club that also accommodated avant-garde jazz.

Other Chicago jazz venues included the Green Mill and Joe Segal's Jazz Showcase, and other prominent artists on the scene included saxophonist Von Freeman, singers Kurt Elling and Patricia Barber, and the rock-influenced band Isotope 217.

Los Angeles and New Orleans both continued to nurture jazz artists. In L.A., fans could hear the music at such clubs as the Catalina Bar and Grill and Fifth Street Dick's, and new bands, including the B Sharp Jazz Quartet and Black/Note, were constantly emerging. The New Orleans Jazz and Heritage Festival, one of the most popular jazz events in North America, annually attracted hundreds of thousands of music enthusiasts.

In the 1990s, some of the fresher sounds in jazz were heard in San Francisco and Seattle, with performers attracting younger crowds through music tinged with rock, R&B, and funk. Indeed, tenor saxophonist Joshua Redman and guitarist Charlie Hunter—two of the brighter lights of the 1990s—both started their careers in San Francisco. Topping the roster of Bay Area venues were Yoshi's and Kimball's East; both showcased international jazz headliners. Local musicians were more apt to appear at the Up & Down Club, the Elbo Room, Bruno's, and the Café du Nord. Jazz could also be found at the Great American Music Hall and Bimbo's 365 Club. Several of these clubs also hosted "swing nights," in which new bands revived the swing and jump-blues sounds of the 1940s for audiences enamored of vintage fashion and retro dance styles.

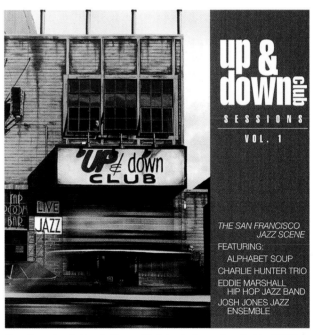

San Francisco's Up & Down Club hosted new jazz in the 1990s.

The Swing Revival

It never completely went away, but swing jazz made an especially powerful comeback in the mid-1990s. Such new bands as the Squirrel Nut Zippers, Big Bad Voodoo Daddy, and the Brian Setzer Orchestra drew audiences and racked up record sales to an extent not seen in swing since the 1930s and 1940s.

Swing's revival was as much a part of a fashion trend as it was a signal of the music's appeal. As the youth-embraced disheveled look of the early-nineties grunge era disappeared into the cultural memory bank, young people seemed suddenly taken with the notion of getting dressed up, 1940s-style, and going out on the town for a glitzy night of martinis and dancing. The ideal musical accompaniment came in the form of large bands—like the audience, dressed to the nines—that blended jump-swing dance music with the high-tech sound processing mandatory for late-century pop.

One of the more popular acts, Brian Setzer (who'd enjoyed prior success in the 1980s with the retro-rockabilly band Stray Cats), issued a representative disc with a remake of Louis Prima's old *Jump, Jive, an' Wail* (1998). Covers of early swing and jump-blues classics peppered albums by others as well. A reworking of Cab Calloway's *Minnie the Moocher* turned up on Big Bad Voodoo Daddy's eponymous 1998 album. Indigo Swing covered Louis Jordan's *Choo Choo Ch'Boogie* on their eponymous disc (1998). The Royal Crown Revue revived the classic *Stormy Weather* on their *King of Gangster Bop* album (1992).

The new mileage gained by those songs—and by swing as a genre—all but ensured even more life further down the road, when 1990s young people reach the age of yearning for the music of their own youth. By which time, most likely, many of them will have long since made the leap to other kinds of jazz.
—*Tad Lathrop*

The swing-revival band Squirrel Nut Zippers.

Although Seattle attracted considerable attention for the 1990s grunge scene that produced the hit band Nirvana, its long jazz tradition still survived. Performers included not only such local bands as the all-female Billy Tipton Memorial Saxophone Quartet (named for the female trumpeter who for fifty years posed as a man) but also former New Yorkers Frisell and Horvitz.

In Kansas City, the storied home of Charlie Parker and Count Basie, local jazz artists continued to perform regularly in clubs and restaurants, occasionally achieving national recognition—as did singers Karrin Allyson and Kevin Mahogany and, before them, saxophonist Bobby Watson.

And of course, jazz continued to be an international phenomenon. Some of the most important jazz festivals were located outside the U.S., key artists hailed from many nations, and foreign labels were increasingly important in providing new musicians—and some older ones—with opportunities to record.

The New Mainstream

In the 1990s, a handful of artists—among them Frisell, Don Byron, saxophonist Joe Lovano, pianist Geri Allen, and drummer Leon Parker—were pushing the envelope, but with a mainstream imprimatur that would have been all but impossible to attain in earlier years.

An all-purpose jazz artist, Lovano seemed equally comfortable playing a jazz standard or heading out for more expansive territory. Perhaps his most representative recording is the double album *Quartets: Live at the Village Vanguard* (1994–95). On one disc, Lovano shares the front line with trumpeter Tom Harrell for a program of avant-leaning excursions; on the other, he's in full bop mode alongside pianist Mulgrew Miller, bassist Christian McBride, and drummer Lewis Nash.

Joe Lovano developed into a masterful, multifaceted saxophonist.

Solo artist and sideman John Scofield, an alumnus of mid-eighties Miles Davis bands.

Lovano also played with guitarist John Scofield (*Time on My Hands*, 1989), perhaps the most popular jazz picker, aside from Pat Metheny, of the 1990s. Fully versed in bop, pop, and blues— all of which had informed his work with such veterans as Miles Davis, Charles Mingus, and saxophonist Dave Liebman—Scofield seemed the heir-apparent to Wes Montgomery, George Benson, and other mainstream guitar masters.

One of those masters, Jim Hall, saw his reputation reach new heights in the final decades of the century. The veteran of 1960s cool jazz made a series of albums as a leader that drew new attention to his understated and elegant guitar style.

Geri Allen's career trajectory was particularly intriguing to observe. On her early disc *The Printmakers* (1984), with Anthony Cox on bass and Andrew Cyrille on percussion,

215

© Ken Franckling

Bobby McFerrin's wide vocal range and ability to quickly shift between high and low registers enabled him to sing both melody and accompaniment.

she achieved a kind of inside-outside synergy that made her music at once accessible and challenging.

Over the years, Allen occasionally flirted with mainstream bop, as on the album *Twenty-One* (1994), with the mainstay rhythm section of bassist Ron Carter and drummer Tony Williams. But even at her most conservative, Allen threw more than enough quirks into the works to keep listeners surprised.

Drummer Leon Parker established himself as a singular voice after releasing only three albums under his own name: *Above & Below* (1994), *Belief* (1996), and *Awakening* (1998). His sensibility embraced what has been termed "world music"; ironically, when his group performed such standards as *In a Sentimental Mood* or *It's Only a Paper Moon,* the listener's attention was drawn to the tune itself more than if it had been played in a traditional manner. As a rhythmist, Parker proved extraordinarily resourceful: he sometimes said more by merely tapping on a pair of high-hat cymbals than another drummer could muster with a full kit.

As always, jazz boiled down to individuality. In that regard, even the more traditional players began to assert themselves as the millennium approached.

Branford Marsalis turned most of his attention to investigating the possibilities of saxophone in a trio setting on such albums as *The Beautyful Ones Are Not Yet Born* (1991), *Bloomington* (1991), and *The Dark Keys* (1996). Alto saxophonist Kenny Garrett took much the same approach with his album *Triology* (1995), then followed up with *Pursuance* (1996), an energetic tribute to Coltrane that showcased guitarist Metheny's wilder side. Joshua Redman and reedman James Carter were two others who attracted mainstream attention, perhaps as much for their unique personalities as their rapidly developing talents. Redman showed off his compositional skills on *Mood-Swing* (1994) and his hard-blowing horn mastery on *Spirit of the Moment: Live at the*

Open-eared and open-styled pianist Geri Allen performed as a leader and with such veterans as saxophonist Ornette Coleman and singer Betty Carter.

Tenor saxophonist Joshua Redman earned acclaim for his mature phrasing and full-bodied tone; media coverage also focused on his decision to pursue jazz rather than study law at Yale.

Village Vanguard (1995). Carter's ability to reconcile bop basics with avant-garde anarchy was heard to fine effect on *J.C. on the Set* (1993) and *Conversin' with the Elders* (1995–96).

In a field of dynamic young pianists that included Eric Reed, Renee Rosnes, and Geoff Keezer, the immensely inventive Brad Mehldau stood out. Mehldau, who played piano on Redman's *MoodSwing*, updated Bill Evans' interactive trio approach with such involving albums as *Introducing Brad Mehldau* (1995) and *The Art of the Trio, Vol. 1* (1996).

Other instrumentalists of the 1980s and nineties who continued to create challenging music included saxophonists Tim Berne, Mark Turner, and David Sanchez; pianists Matthew Shipp and Myra Melford; trumpeters Dave Douglas and Russell Gunn; bassist William Parker; and drummer Brian Blade.

On the vocal scene, Kevin Mahogany, Kurt Elling, and Andy Bey led a sudden and welcome proliferation of male performers. Mahogany, with his rich baritone, was at times evocative of the late Joe Williams at his best. The leading female singers included veterans Abbey Lincoln and Shirley Horn as well as such relative newcomers as Diana Krall, Dee Dee Bridgewater, Diane Schuur, Jeanie Bryson, Karrin Allyson, Rachelle Ferrell, and Patricia Barber. The vocal group Manhattan Transfer continued to charm fans, and singer Bobby McFerrin, who had attained pop success in 1988 with the hit single *Don't Worry, Be Happy*, effectively transcended musical categories.

Cassandra Wilson's eclectic tastes—embracing blues, folk, funk, and rap—brought depth to her jazz singing.

But the most commercially successful jazz vocalist was Cassandra Wilson, due in no small part to her original take on the jazz tradition, one that acknowledged the commonalities between, say, Billie Holiday and folk-rock innovator Joni Mitchell. On such albums as *Blue Light 'Til Dawn* (1993) and *Traveling Miles* (1997–98)—the latter a tribute to Miles Davis—Wilson was smooth without being shallow, smoky without being overwrought.

Not that she was the only jazz performer to parlay individuality into mass appeal. Far from it. The commercial success of McFerrin, Hancock, Corea, and Byron, as well as that of guitarist Charlie Hunter and the jazz-funk unit Medeski, Martin and Wood, revealed the willingness of some listeners—especially younger ones—to tap into the music, even if they'd never heard a jazz artist before.

At the arrival of the twenty-first century, the future of jazz appeared to rest on meeting a twofold challenge: to preserve its time-honored traditions while recognizing that changes in the world inevitably will mean changes for the art form.

It had always been so: change itself was a jazz tradition, and openness to it had enabled musicians and listeners to experience ragtime and Dixieland, the excitement of 1930s swing and the big bands, the awesome flights of bebop, the understated sophistication of cool jazz, the soulfulness of hard bop, and the boundless expressiveness of free jazz—just as the love of those movements had impelled practitioners to keep them alive even as glimmers of new ones lit the jazz horizon.

It was the same impulse—the readiness to accept change, and beyond it, the desire to *create* change—that had led innovators to initiate other social, cultural, technological, economic, and political shifts of the twentieth century, vast transformations for which jazz had served as a musical analog.

If the past is any indication, the future will hold more of the same kind of eclecticism. Emerging artists will continue to pull inspiration from multiple sources and discover that no matter what they need to express, they can say it—and say it eloquently—in the international language of jazz. ⌒

Key Recordings

Byron, Don. *Tuskegee Experiments.* Nonesuch. A stunning debut album on which clarinetist and composer Byron demonstrates a comprehensive knowledge of the jazz canon while applying his personal stamp. Playing mostly originals, he elicits splendid support from his co-performers, including guitarist Bill Frisell, bassist Reggie Workman, and poet Sadiq.

Davis, Miles. *Tutu.* Warner Bros. Regardless of one's preferences in jazz styles, there's no denying the sleek majesty of *Tutu.* Its electronic sheen sets off the trumpeter's yearning sound to stunning effect. The atmospheric title track lingers in the mind, and taken as a whole the album, from 1986, is one of Davis's most alluring musical statements.

Hancock, Herbie. *Head Hunters.* Columbia. After leading an experimental band that blended free jazz and fusion, keyboardist Hancock crossed over to the commercial mainstream in 1973 with this adventure in improvisational funk. Although the hit single *Chameleon* garnered most of the attention, the album in its entirety amounted to a watershed in the evolution of American popular music.

Henderson, Joe. *So Near, So Far (Musings for Miles).* Verve. On this 1992 follow-up to his popular album *Lush Life,* veteran saxophonist Henderson pays tribute to the musical legacy of Miles Davis. With guitarist John Scofield, bassist Dave Holland, and drummer Al Foster, Henderson delivers bracing performances of such tunes as *Side Car* and *Teo.*

Lovano, Joe. *Quartets: Live at the Village Vanguard.* Two discs, Blue Note. Saxophonist Lovano demonstrates his considerable versatility on this 1994–95 recording—with one disc devoted to straight-ahead playing, the other leaning more toward "outside" sounds. Particularly noteworthy is the playing by pianist Mulgrew Miller on the former and by trumpeter Tom Harrell on the latter.

Marsalis, Wynton. *Marsalis Standard Time, Vol. 1.* Columbia. With pianist Marcus Roberts, bassist Robert Hurst, and drummer Jeff "Tain" Watts, the trumpeter fashions entrancing versions of such timeless compositions as *Caravan* and *April in Paris.* This 1986 effort presents a convincing case for jazz as an art form of inexhaustible possibilities.

Murray, David. *Ming.* Black Saint. On an important recording in the history of the avant-jazz movement, saxophonist Murray led an all-star octet: cornetist Lawrence "Butch" Morris, pianist Anthony Davis, altoist Henry Threadgill, trombonist George Lewis, drummer Steve McCall, trumpeter Olu Dara, and bassist Wilber Morris. Not surprisingly, the sounds—recorded in 1980—are sublime.

Redman, Joshua. *MoodSwing.* Warner Bros. By the 1990s, some jazz artists of the younger generation were beginning to search for their own voices. On this 1994 effort, saxophonist Redman leads an impressive quartet featuring pianist Brad Mehldau, bassist Christian McBride, and drummer Brian Blade.

Weather Report. *Heavy Weather.* Columbia. The radio hit *Birdland* (a tribute to the big-band sound) helped make this 1977 album the seminal fusion group's biggest commercial success. With bassist Jaco Pastorius featured as prominently as the bandleaders—keyboardist Joe Zawinul and saxophonist Wayne Shorter—the album broke new instrumental ground while establishing a creative benchmark for pop-jazz.

Wilson, Cassandra. *Blue Light 'Til Dawn.* Blue Note. The singer broke through to the mainstream with this 1993 disc, which reconciles blues, folk, and rock influences without forsaking improvisation. Asserting her individuality, Wilson brings sass and swagger to tunes by Robert Johnson and Van Morrison and a smoky exuberance to her own title track.
—*Calvin Wilson*

100 Essential Jazz Albums

Drawn from the full spectrum of jazz styles, the following is a sampling of the best of the music recorded in the twentieth century. It isn't to be taken as an absolute; judgments of quality are always subjective. But this selection is informed by opinions gathered in an international survey of more than one hundred jazz historians, critics, authors, educators, musicians, and broadcasters (listed after the annotations). As such, it's intended as a reliable compilation of albums that have stood the test of time.

In the survey, the top vote getter by far was Miles Davis's *Kind of Blue*, named by nearly 80 percent of the respondents. The others in the top five were (2) John Coltrane, *A Love Supreme*; (3) Louis Armstrong, *Portrait of the Artist as a Young Man*; (4) Duke Ellington, *The Blanton-Webster Band*; and (5) John Coltrane, *Giant Steps*.

CANNONBALL ADDERLEY

Phenix
Fantasy, 1975

The essence of soul jazz and a kind of career retrospective for the alto saxophonist and bandleader. With Nat Adderley on cornet, Joe Zawinul on keyboards, and Airto Moreira on percussion, such standards as *Mercy, Mercy, Mercy* and *Work Song* take on new zing and rhythmic drive.

LOUIS ARMSTRONG

Portrait of the Artist as a Young Man
Smithsonian/Legacy, 5 discs, 1923–34

This cornerstone set covers Armstrong's early years as a sideman with King Oliver and the Hot Fives and Sevens—when he helped transform jazz into a soloist's art—and as a big-band leader in the early 1930s. Also here: Armstrong as singer.

Louis Armstrong Plays W.C. Handy
Columbia, 1954

Armstrong's long-established style, now burnished golden in its maturity, shines with conviction and eloquence on *St. Louis Blues*, *Memphis Blues*, and others.

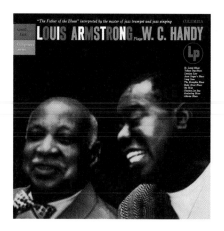

THE ART ENSEMBLE

The Art Ensemble 1967/68
Nessa, 5 discs

Critic Gary Giddins called their music "guerrilla jazz." The players who would become the Art Ensemble of Chicago are caught here in an early incarnation.

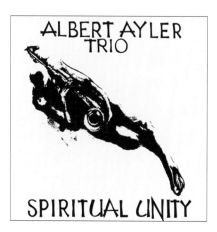

ALBERT AYLER

Spiritual Unity
ESP, 1964

The controversial tenor saxophonist Ayler defied harmonic and rhythmic conventions and broke new ground in the realm of timbre and texture. Here, he, bassist Gary Peacock, and drummer Sunny Murray engage in intense interplay.

COUNT BASIE

The Complete Decca Recordings
Decca, 3 discs, 1937–39

The swinging Basie band at its peak, with its peerless rhythm section, bluesy Kansas City–inspired riffs, and celebrated soloists: saxophonists Lester Young, Herschel Evans, and Chu Berry; trumpeter Buck Clayton; and singer Jimmy Rushing.

SIDNEY BECHET

His Best Recordings, 1923–1941
Best of Jazz

On soprano saxophone, Bechet, perhaps jazz's first great soloist, boasted one of the most identifiable and penetrating sounds in jazz. Includes his soaring solos on *Cake Walking Babies from Home*, *Maple Leaf Rag*, and *Summertime*.

BIX BEIDERBECKE

His Best Recordings, 1924–1930
Best of Jazz

With his clear, chime-like tone, romantic lyricism, and well-conceived solos, Beiderbecke became a musical hero to many. Includes his celebrated *I'm Coming, Virginia; Riverboat Shuffle; Singin' the Blues*; and his piano solo *In a Mist*.

ART BLAKEY

The History of Art Blakey and the Jazz Messengers
Blue Note, 3 discs, 1947–81

Powerhouse drummer and hard-bop patriarch Art Blakey shaped future jazz by shaping future stars in his long-running band the Jazz Messengers. Great lineups—Wynton Marsalis and Wayne Shorter are among the many up-and-comers here—and punchy acoustic jazz make this retrospective a gem.

CARLA BLEY

Escalator over the Hill
ECM, 2 discs, 1968–71

Composer Carla Bley's extended piece for a vast cast of musicians and reciters—with text by Paul Haines—mixes free jazz, rock, scored sections, and musical theater in a triumph of imagination over stylistic restriction.

ANTHONY BRAXTON

Willisau (Quartet)

hatART, 4 discs, 1991

Studio and live discs from reedman-composer Braxton, one of the most intellectual and oft-recorded of jazz musicians.

CLIFFORD BROWN AND MAX ROACH

Alone Together: The Best of the Mercury Years

Verve, 2 discs, 1954–56

In the mid-1950s, drummer Roach and trumpeter Brown co-led the hottest hard-bop band in the land. This anthology of their work includes the often-reinterpreted *Joy Spring* and *Daahoud*.

DAVE BRUBECK

Time Signatures: A Career Retrospective

Sony Legacy, 4 discs, 1946–91

With *Take Five*, the Dave Brubeck Quartet defied the odds, creating an enduring piece in an "odd" meter (5/4). Pianist Brubeck's classically influenced, carefully constructed, and precisely played music proved immensely popular while extending the range of jazz's adaptability.

BENNY CARTER

Further Definitions

Impulse!, 1961, 1966

A showcase for Carter's protean talents as composer, arranger, bandleader, and alto saxophonist. The sax section—with tenor giant Coleman Hawkins and altoist Phil Woods—plays beautifully.

BETTY CARTER

The Audience with Betty Carter

Verve, 2 discs, 1979

Betty Carter honed a unique, instrumentally inspired sound and became an on-the-bandstand teacher to many musicians. Her gift for melodic invention, and song reinvention, is well represented on this album.

CHARLIE CHRISTIAN

Solo Flight

Columbia, 1939–41

No electric guitarist after the 1940s escaped the influence of Charlie Christian. This set, with the Benny Goodman sextet, septet, and orchestra, amply displays his inventiveness, precision, energy, and sense of swing.

ORNETTE COLEMAN

The Shape of Jazz to Come

Atlantic, 1959–60

Pioneering altoist Coleman, here with his classic quartet, shook the foundations of jazz by establishing freedom from chord-based musical structure. Includes the bluesy *Lonely Woman*, his best-known composition.

JOHN COLTRANE

Giant Steps

Atlantic Jazz, 1959

Few improvisers have been able to negotiate the rapidly changing chords of the title piece as successfully as its composer, saxophonist Coltrane. Careening through the obstacle course, he still managed to sound *musical*. The more relaxed and expansive *Naima*—Coltrane's classic ballad—is here as well, along with the bluesy *Mr. P.C.* and other originals.

A Love Supreme

Impulse!, 1964

The "classic" Coltrane quartet—pianist McCoy Tyner, drummer Elvin Jones, and bassist Jimmy Garrison—reached the apex of its surging energy on this alternately ecstatic and contemplative, but consistently passionate, musical statement, considered by many to be among the handful of best jazz albums ever made. It's about spirituality, and Coltrane demonstrates how fully jazz can explore and express it.

Meditations

Impulse!, 1965

Late in Coltrane's career, his harmonic complexity crossed the line into all-out free jazz. This key example of that phase finds him with empathetic colleagues Tyner, Jones, and Garrison, joined by saxophonist Pharoah Sanders and drummer Rashied Ali.

CHICK COREA

Music Forever and Beyond

GRP, 5 discs, 1964–96

An omnipresent figure in late-century jazz, keyboardist-composer Corea employed his prodigious technique and imagination to varied ends. Included here are such enduring compositions as *Spain* and *Windows*, higher-voltage material recorded with his fusion group Return to Forever, and collaborations with Herbie Hancock and other notables.

MILES DAVIS

The Complete Birth of the Cool

Capitol, 1949–50

These epochal recordings by trumpeter Davis and his nonet ushered in a new style that became known as "cool jazz." The orchestrations—by Gerry Mulligan, Gil Evans, and Johnny Carisi—emphasize the darker hues of the lower brass (French horns and tuba).

Miles Ahead

Columbia, 1957

On a series of late-fifties albums, Gil Evans—one of the great jazz orchestrators—painted beautiful settings for Davis's introspective sound. Here, cushioned by a twelve-piece orchestra, the lonely-sounding yet lyrical Davis, on flugelhorn, is the only soloist.

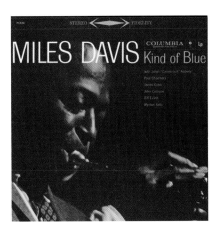

Kind of Blue

Columbia, 1959

The quintessential jazz album: classic, influential, and enduringly popular. In another directional shift, Davis—employing modes rather than the usual rapidly moving chord sequences—provides soloists John Coltrane, Cannonball Adderley, and Bill Evans with new challenges and the listener with a sense of space, freedom, and rightness.

Miles Davis Quintet, 1965–68

Columbia, 6 discs

Davis's second quintet—Herbie Hancock, Wayne Shorter, Ron Carter, and Tony Williams—was one of the great improvising units of jazz. The set comprises the albums *E.S.P., Miles Smiles, Sorcerer, Nefertiti, Miles in the Sky,* and *Filles de Kilimanjaro.* It's modern jazz of the highest order.

Bitches Brew

Columbia, 2 discs, 1969

There had been earlier stabs at rock-infused jazz, but it took Miles Davis—mixing electronic textures, funk riffs, and his own minimalist trumpet work—to provide the impetus for a full-blown "fusion" movement. Sidemen Chick Corea, John McLaughlin, Wayne Shorter, and Joe Zawinul emerged as its torchbearers.

ERIC DOLPHY

Out to Lunch

Blue Note, 1964

Multi-instrumentalist Eric Dolphy (alto saxophone, bass clarinet, flute) straddled the fence between free jazz and "playing the changes" without forfeiting warmth, humor, and humanity. This, his final album, caught him at his peak.

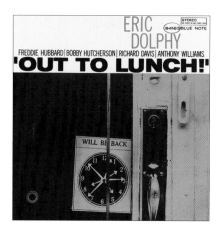

ROY ELDRIDGE

Little Jazz:
The Best of the Verve Years

Verve, 1952–60

Brimming with *joie de vivre,* the passionate swing trumpeter reprises two hits from his stint with the Gene Krupa band—*Rockin' Chair* and *Let Me Off Uptown* (with singer Anita O'Day). Also: the haunting *I Remember Harlem,* the emotive *How Long Has This Been Going On?,* and the boppish romp *Allen's Alley.* Collaborators include Coleman Hawkins and Oscar Peterson.

DUKE ELLINGTON

Beyond Category

RCA/Smithsonian, 2 discs, 1927–67

A retrospective studded with masterpieces, from *Black and Tan Fantasy, Mood Indigo,* and samples of his small-group sides to highlights from his sacred concerts and other 1960s work.

The Blanton-Webster Band

RCA Bluebird, 3 discs, 1940–42

After hiring arranger Billy Strayhorn, tenorman Ben Webster, and bassist Jimmie Blanton, Ellington hit an artistic peak. This set shows Ellington as a tonal colorist, an original harmonic thinker, and a designer of magnificent settings for his soloists.

The Great Paris Concert

Atlantic, 2 discs, 1963

Includes two of Ellington's many suites, *Harlem* and *Suite Thursday,* as well as an excerpt from *Such Sweet Thunder.* Altoist Johnny Hodges shines on *All of Me* and *Things Ain't What They Used to Be.*

The Far East Suite

RCA Bluebird, 1966

Tone paintings of impressions gathered by Ellington and collaborator Billy Strayhorn during travels in the Near, Middle, and Far East, including *Ad Lib on Nippon,* an eleven-minute tour de force for pianist Ellington and clarinetist Jimmy Hamilton.

BILL EVANS

At the Village Vanguard

Riverside, 1961

Evans was one of the most revered jazz pianists ever, and this album indicates why. With introspective lyricism, he spins sensitive musical poetry and leads one of the most interactive of all trios.

ELLA FITZGERALD

Ella Fitzgerald, First Lady of Song

Verve, 3 discs, 1949–66

Fitzgerald's charm, wide range, and excellent pitch control—equally evident on smoky ballads, uptempo swingers, and scat singing—are heard on such tracks as *Mack the Knife* and *How High the Moon.*

ERROLL GARNER

Concert by the Sea

Columbia, 1955

This best-selling disc made Garner—with his trademark behind-the-beat melodies, rhapsodic introductions, joyful drama, and showmanship—a household name.

STAN GETZ

Focus

Verve, 1961

The melodious, floating sound of tenor saxophonist Getz in a string-orchestra setting anchored by bass and drums. The material is a seven-part suite, alternately spiky and lush, penned by Eddie Sauter.

DIZZY GILLESPIE

The Complete RCA Victor Recordings

RCA Bluebird, 2 discs, 1937–49

One of the great innovators in jazz, Gillespie helped pioneer bebop music, extended the range of the trumpet, and popularized Afro-Cuban rhythms. Along with *A Night in Tunisia,* his 1947–49 big-band recordings of *Good Bait, Manteca,* and *Cubana Be, Cubana Bop* are absolute classics. Indispensable.

BENNY GOODMAN

Live at Carnegie Hall 1938, Complete

Columbia, 2 discs, 1938

The "King of Swing" at a career peak—one of the most important jazz concerts ever. Highlights: Goodman's agile clarinet on *One O'Clock Jump;* Gene Krupa's percussion pyrotechnics on *Sing, Sing, Sing;* the Ellington-Basie-Goodman sidemen jam on *Honeysuckle Rose;* and tracks by the Goodman trio and quartet.

CHARLIE HADEN

Liberation Music Orchestra

Impulse!, 1969

The adventuresome bassist, working with such leading lights of the sixties avant-garde as Carla Bley, Don Cherry, and Mike Mantler, transforms social concerns into passionate music. Also on hand: Gato Barbieri, Dewey Redman, and Paul Motian.

HERBIE HANCOCK

The Best of Herbie Hancock
Blue Note, 1962–68

The 1960s music that established keyboardist Hancock as a leading new voice in mainstream jazz, including such signature compositions as *Watermelon Man*, *Maiden Voyage*, and *Dolphin Dance*.

Head Hunters
Columbia, 1973

In his post–Miles Davis years, Hancock applied his keyboard virtuosity to the synthesizer and his compositional skills to a blend of jazz, electronics, and funk. The resulting *Head Hunters* album proved a model of jazz sophistication applied to populist rhythms and sonorities.

JOHNNY HARTMAN

John Coltrane and Johnny Hartman
Impulse!, 1963

A warmer, more intimate- and urbane-sounding, more elegant mainstream jazz recording probably doesn't exist. With vocalist Johnny Hartman's relaxed, soothing baritone supported by an uncharacteristically gentle Coltrane saxophone.

COLEMAN HAWKINS

A Retrospective, 1929–1963
Bluebird, 2 discs

Hawkins, with his big tone and innate musicality, blazed a glorious, wide, and long musical trail. Included here is *Body and Soul*, one of the most celebrated jazz solos ever recorded.

FLETCHER HENDERSON

A Study in Frustration (1923–38)
Columbia, 3 discs

The pioneering bandleader-arranger popularized an approach to big-band arranging and paved the way for the Swing Era. Classics such as *The Stampede*, *King Porter Stomp*, and *Queer Notions* display the attributes for which he, frustratingly, was not accorded full credit in his heyday.

WOODY HERMAN

The Thundering Herds, 1945–47
Columbia

Herman's First Herd, with driving arrangements by Ralph Burns and Neal Hefti, a noted rhythm section, and sparkling performances by trombonist Bill Harris and saxophonist Flip Phillips on *Apple Honey*, *Bijou*, and others. Also, two numbers from the bop-oriented Second Herd.

EARL HINES

His Best Recordings, 1927–1942
Best of Jazz

Hines freed jazz piano from the strictures of ragtime and Harlem stride and became something of a rival to Art Tatum. Highlights of his band and piano-solo recordings include *Fifty-Seven Varieties*, *Piano Man*, and *Boogie Woogie on St. Louis Blues*.

BILLIE HOLIDAY

This Is Jazz, No. 15
Columbia, 1935–58

The quintessential female jazz singer, Holiday ranged freely over the beat, flattened out melodic contours, and slid between speech and song. Includes notable collaborations with tenor saxophonist Lester Young and the first recording of her *God Bless the Child*.

KEITH JARRETT

Köln Concert
ECM, 1975

After a stint with Miles Davis, pianist Jarrett recorded a series of solo concerts—stream-of-consciousness affairs that found him pulling ideas from rock and country music as well as jazz. They irked a few jazz purists but attracted a large audience and spawned an army of Jarrett imitators.

J.J. JOHNSON

The Eminent Jay Jay Johnson, Volume 1
Blue Note, 1953

Johnson modernized the slide trombone, transforming it into an instrument capable of playing rapid-fire bebop articulations. Here he's with an all-star quintet including Clifford Brown and John Lewis.

JAMES P. JOHNSON

His Best Recordings, 1921–1944
Best of Jazz

The "Father of Stride Piano" pioneered an intoxicatingly rhythmic brand of ragtime-derived playing. Includes *You've Got to Be Modernistic*, the finger-busting *Carolina Shout*, and his accompaniment to Bessie Smith's magnificent *Back Water Blues*.

STAN KENTON

Retrospective
Capitol, 4 discs, 1943–68

The variety, audacity, and experimentation of Kenton's bands shine in this compilation, with singer June Christy; soloists Art Pepper, Zoot Sims, and Lee Konitz; and arrangements by Kenton and others.

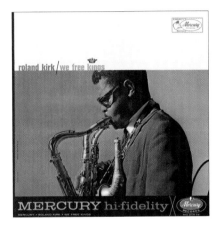

RAHSAAN ROLAND KIRK

We Free Kings
Mercury, 1961

No mere novelty act, the simultaneous-multireed player proved ultimately unclassifiable, except as a player who could draw from the entire jazz tradition in the creation of something new. Here he reaches out to the mainstream audience.

LEE KONITZ

Duets
Milestone, 1967

The altoman forged his own smooth sound—cool, vibrato-free, and long-lined. Here he's teamed in a series of duets that span New Orleans, bop, and free jazz.

JIMMIE LUNCEFORD

Masterpieces, Volume 9
EPM/Jazz Archives, 1934–42

One of the swingingest of swing bands, Lunceford's orchestra embraced polished showmanship and precise musicianship. This French reissue highlights the adroit arrangements of Sy Oliver.

MAHAVISHNU ORCHESTRA

The Inner Mounting Flame

Columbia, 1971

Virtuosity, fiery energy, rock dynamics, and rhythmic complexity—the combination sounded entirely new when guitarist John McLaughlin introduced it. The music's flashiness didn't age well, but the elements that made this record a fusion landmark remain exciting to hear.

WYNTON MARSALIS

In This House, on This Morning

Columbia, 2 discs, 1992–93

Invoking the master tonal colorist Duke Ellington, Marsalis composed this suite to evoke the rich traditions of a down-home black church service. Highlights include "Call to Prayer," "Uptempo Postlude," and "Pot Blessed Dinner."

CHARLES MINGUS

Passions of a Man: The Complete Atlantic Recordings, 1956–1961

Rhino, 6 discs

The fiery bassist, the most important composer in jazz after Ellington, captured during five peak years. Includes *The Clown*, *Pithecanthropus Erectus*, and the raucous, rocking *Better Git Hit in Your Soul*.

MODERN JAZZ QUARTET

MJQ 40

Atlantic, 4 discs, 1952–88

Many of the famed chamber-jazz quartet's most esteemed recordings, including vibist Milt Jackson's *Bag's Groove* and *Cylinder* and pianist John Lewis's *Django*, *Golden Striker*, and his fugal *Vendome* and *Concorde*.

THELONIOUS MONK

The Complete Blue Note Recordings

Blue Note, 4 discs, 1947–52

Monk, the master of dissonance and surprise, is captured in his earliest recordings as a leader, performing such signature compositions as *Ruby, My Dear*; *Well, You Needn't*; *'Round Midnight*; *Misterioso*; *Epistrophy*; *Crepuscule with Nellie*; and *Straight, No Chaser*.

WES MONTGOMERY

The Incredible Jazz Guitar of Wes Montgomery

Riverside, 1960

Propulsive energy, pungent blues-bop phrasing, and distinctive unison-octave melodies made Montgomery the most emulated mid-century jazz guitarist. This album helped establish his reputation.

JELLY ROLL MORTON

The Jelly Roll Morton Centennial: His Complete Victor Recordings

RCA, 5 discs, 1926–39

A seminal pianist and the first great composer in jazz, Morton achieved a striking integration of improvisation, contrast, and variety in his compositions, here performed memorably—after assiduous rehearsal—by his Red Hot Peppers.

GERRY MULLIGAN

Legacy

N2K, 1949–96

The versatile Mulligan developed a fluid, identifiable sound on the baritone saxophone and arranged and composed with great attention to timbres and counterpoint. This set samples recordings with Miles Davis, the early 1950s pianoless quartet, tentette sides with trumpeter Chet Baker, and the Concert Jazz Band of 1960.

DAVID MURRAY

Ming

Black Saint, 1980

The prolific veteran of free jazz and the World Saxophone Quartet leads an octet through adventuresome reconceptualizations of traditional jazz styles.

OLIVER NELSON

The Blues and the Abstract Truth

Impulse!, 1961

The mainstream classic *Stolen Moments* leads off veteran arranger-composer Nelson's most enduring album, boosted by the musicianship of Eric Dolphy, Bill Evans, and Freddie Hubbard.

NEW ORLEANS RHYTHM KINGS

New Orleans Rhythm Kings and Jelly Roll Morton

Milestone, 2 discs, 1922–25

Led by Paul Mares, George Brunis, and Leon Roppolo, this was one of the great ensembles of early jazz. Highlights: an inspired *Eccentric*, a swinging *Tiger Rag*, and, with Jelly Roll Morton, *Milenberg Joys*.

KING OLIVER

King Oliver and His Creole Jazz Band, 1923

Classics

Cornet king Joe Oliver led the greatest New Orleans jazz band of its day. Listen for the inspired interplay between Oliver and cornetist Louis Armstrong, the interweaving clarinet of Johnny Dodds, and the bluesy solos and rhythmic drive on *Snake Rag* and other classics.

ORIGINAL DIXIELAND JAZZ BAND

The Original Dixieland Jazz Band, 1917–1921

Timeless

When it made the first jazz recordings, this quintet set the nation on its ear. They were short on improvising, but long on energy and novelty, as heard here on *Tiger Rag*, *Livery Stable Blues*, and others.

CHARLIE PARKER

Yardbird Suite: The Ultimate Collection

Rhino, 2 discs, 1945–53

Alto saxophonist and bebop innovator Parker revolutionized jazz with his virtuosity, speed, asymmetrical phrasings, and improvisations using "upper partials" of chords. Includes *A Night in Tunisia, Ko Ko, Parker's Mood,* and other classics.

CHARLIE PARKER, DIZZY GILLESPIE, AND OTHERS

Jazz at Massey Hall

Debut OJC, 1953

The legendary concert offered bebop at its best by those who'd created it: Charlie Parker, Dizzy Gillespie, Bud Powell, and Max Roach. Charles Mingus played bass and recorded the date.

BUD POWELL

The Complete Blue Note and Roost Recordings

Blue Note, 4 discs, 1947–63

Powell ushered in modern-jazz piano by playing long lines of melody with his right hand and percussive, stabbing chords with his left. Includes the classic *Ornithology* and such originals as *Un Poco Loco.*

DJANGO REINHARDT/ STÉPHANE GRAPPELLI

Swing from Paris

Affinity, 1935–39

In the 1930s, Frenchman Reinhardt introduced jazz-guitar techniques that are used to this day. These recordings with violinist Grappelli and the Quintet of the Hot Club of France reveal the qualities that made him an object of imitation.

SONNY ROLLINS

Saxophone Colossus

Prestige, 1956

The powerful tenor saxophonist came into his own on this disc, displaying the inventiveness and logic that elevated him to the upper tier of jazz improvisers. Includes his calypso-tinged classic *St. Thomas.*

THE GEORGE RUSSELL SMALLTET

Jazz Workshop

Koch Jazz, 1956

The brilliant, undersung composer and theorist led a sextet performing such unique, surprising compositions as *Ezz-thetic, Knights of the Steamtable,* and *Concerto for Billy the Kid* (with a remarkable Bill Evans piano solo).

ARTIE SHAW

Begin the Beguine

ASV Living Era, 1938–41

The mercurial clarinetist, as cool as Goodman was hot, led one of the top swing bands. Tracks here include *Begin the Beguine, Stardust,* and small-group gems from Shaw's Gramercy Five.

HORACE SILVER

Retrospective

Blue Note, 4 discs, 1952–78

The soulful hard-bop pianist gave jazz some of its most memorable and oft-played pieces, including *Nica's Dream, Song for My Father,* and *Doodlin'.* Those and others are contained in this compilation, boasting such star sidemen as Art Blakey, Hank Mobley, and Joe Henderson.

BESSIE SMITH

The Essential Bessie Smith

Columbia, 2 discs, 1923–33

The Empress of the Blues, with such accompanists as Louis Armstrong and James P. Johnson. Smith's vocal inflections, power, and expressive range remain cornerstones of blues and jazz singing.

JIMMY SMITH

The Sermon!

Blue Note, 1958

Definitive soul-bop Hammond B-3 organ, in trio format and with saxophone and trumpet. Smith's cutting sound and ability to generate excitement made him the man to measure up to for later organists, whether playing jazz, blues, or soul.

MUGGSY SPANIER

1931 and 1939

Jazz Classics in Digital Stereo

Never has revivalist traditional jazz been more compelling than on the 1939 tracks by the Chicago cornetist, leading a band with a driving beat on *Riverboat Shuffle, Livery Stable Blues,* and others.

SUN RA AND HIS SOLAR ARKESTRA

The Magic City

Evidence, 1965

Space was usually the place for self-described Saturnian Ra, and here he staked out a little extra for the lengthy, collectively improvised title track. Over-the-edge jazz from the promulgator of a broad artistic-musical-theatrical vision.

ART TATUM

The Complete Capitol Recordings, Vols. 1 and 2

Capitol, 1949–52

The virtuosic pianist dazzles with his reharmonizations of familiar songs and impressive runs in the right *and* left hands. Includes such gems as *Someone to Watch Over Me, Somebody Loves Me,* and his trademark *Willow Weep for Me.*

CECIL TAYLOR

Unit Structures

Blue Note, 1966

Surging waves of densely clustered tones are building blocks of pianist Taylor's stormy sonic creations, making him a jazz counterpart to such visual Abstract Expressionists as Willem DeKooning and Jackson Pollock. Longtime-colleagues-to-be Jimmy Lyons and Andrew Cyrille are with him here.

JACK TEAGARDEN

His Best Recordings, 1928–1943

Best of Jazz

One of the great trombonists, Teagarden played with deceptive ease and mastered the blues as both instrumentalist and singer. Highlights: *Makin' Friends, Jack Hits the Road, Knockin' a Jug* (with Louis Armstrong), and a bluesy *Sheik of Araby.*

LENNIE TRISTANO AND WARNE MARSH

Intuition

Capitol, 1949, 1956

Low-profile pianist Tristano exerted influence mostly through teaching and such disciples as Warne Marsh and Lee Konitz, emphasizing structure over passion—a "cool" approach to bop-based jazz. Representative tracks are heard here.

SARAH VAUGHAN

Swingin' Easy

EmArcy, 1954–57

Few recordings capture a creative jazz vocalist with a rhythm section better than this one, often acclaimed as Vaughan's best. On *All of Me,* the scat display *Shulie a Bop,* and others, she dazzles with her huge vocal range and virtuosic control of pitch and timbre.

FATS WALLER

The Joint Is Jumpin'

RCA Bluebird, 1929–43

The light-fingered pianist and composer combined two recording careers: as a deft, two-handed soloist (*Carolina Shout, Ain't Misbehavin'*) and as a singer-band-leader who, leading one of the foremost Swing Era small groups, entertained the masses with his infectious, humorous vocals (*The Joint Is Jumpin'*).

WEATHER REPORT

Heavy Weather

Columbia, 1977

State-of-the-art seventies pop jazz from the group led by veteran keyboardist Joe Zawinul and saxophonist Wayne Shorter. This late-career album includes the infectious track *Birdland* and the virtuosic bass work of Jaco Pastorius.

MARY LOU WILLIAMS

Story, 1930–1941

Jazz Archives/EPM

The greatest non-singing woman in jazz, Williams could hold her own with her male counterparts, as revealed by this French survey of her early Kansas City work as pianist (*Night Life, Clean Pickin', Overland*) and as chief arranger for Andy Kirk's blues-and-riff-rich band (*Little Joe from Chicago, Walkin' and Swingin', Moten Swing, Twinklin'*).

WORLD SAXOPHONE QUARTET

Revue

Black Saint, 1980

This avant-garde group—Hamiet Bluiett, Julius Hemphill, Oliver Lake, and David Murray—plays a wide variety of clarinets and saxophones, rich with vocalisms. Here they combine bits of R&B and gospel, group improvisation, and a variety of textures and moods.

LESTER YOUNG

This Is Jazz, Vol. 26

Columbia, 1936–43

Eschewing the big, fat tenor saxophone sound of Coleman Hawkins, Young influentially forged his own cool, airy style showcasing long, flowing lines. Includes such famous solos as *I Must Have That Man* (with Billie Holiday) and *Lester Leaps In* and *Shoe Shine Boy* (with Count Basie).

VARIOUS ARTISTS

Big Band Jazz: From the Beginnings to the 1950s

Smithsonian, 4 discs, 1924–55

Nobody does anthologies as well as the Smithsonian, and this one authoritatively surveys the big-band field from Fletcher Henderson and Paul Whiteman through Dizzy Gillespie and Stan Kenton. Also represents Duke Ellington, Count Basie, Benny Goodman, Earl Hines, and twenty-seven others. Out of print, but worth a trip to the library.

Big Band Renaissance: The Evolution of the Jazz Orchestra; The 1940s and Beyond

Smithsonian, 5 discs, 1941–91

A superb compilation ranging from the bands of Ellington, Basie, Herman, and Kenton through those of Dizzy Gillespie, Thad Jones-Mel Lewis, Muhal Richard Abrams, Quincy Jones, Oliver Nelson, and Sun Ra. Check your library for this one.

A Century of Ragtime

Vanguard, 2 discs

One disc of ragtime pianists—Eubie Blake, Max Morath, Richard Zimmerman, Dick Hyman—and another of orchestras and bands. Rags—some introspective, most infectiously upbeat—composed by Scott Joplin, James Scott, Joseph Lamb, Eubie Blake, William Bolcom, and others.

From Spirituals to Swing

Vanguard, 3 discs, 1938–39

The most celebrated concert in jazz, this Carnegie Hall event and its (1939) sequel showcased jazz and its roots: gospel by Sister Rosetta Tharpe, Sidney Bechet's New Orleans sound, boogie-woogie piano, Sonny Terry's blues, and swing by Count Basie, Benny Goodman, and Lester Young.

The Girl from Ipanema: The Antonio Carlos Jobim Songbook

Verve, 1962–88

The bossa nova influence on jazz is represented in this anthology. Includes Stan Getz's famous reading of the title track, Wes Montgomery's *Insensatez,* Elis Regina, Dizzy Gillespie, Oscar Peterson, Ella Fitzgerald, and Jobim himself.

Jazz Piano

Smithsonian, 4 discs, 1924–78

The piano has a vaunted place in jazz, both in bands and as the supreme solo instrument. This survey ranges from James P. Johnson, Teddy Wilson, and Art Tatum through Thelonious Monk, Mary Lou Williams, Bill Evans, McCoy Tyner, and Herbie Hancock.

The Jazz Singers

Smithsonian, 5 CDs, 1919–94

This wide-ranging survey includes Louis Armstrong, Bessie Smith, Mildred Bailey, Jimmy Rushing, Billie Holiday, Mel Tormé, Frank Sinatra, Anita O'Day, June Christy, Johnny Hartman, Cassandra Wilson, Bobby McFerrin, and others.

Lost Chords, 1915–1945

Challenge, 2 discs, 1920–44

A companion to Richard M. Sudhalter's same-titled book seeking to redress the neglect of early white jazzmen, this set surveys Joe Venuti, Paul Whiteman, Eddie Condon, Red Nichols, *et al.*

More Than Mambo: The Introduction to Afro-Cuban Jazz

Verve, 2 discs, 1949–67

Highlights the Cuban influence on jazz via the work of such leading lights as Noro Morales, Mario Bauzá with Machito, Chico O'Farrill, and the sixties salsa stars Willie Bobo, Cal Tjader, and Eddie Palmieri.

Smithsonian Collection of Classic Jazz

Smithsonian, 5 discs, 1916–81

From the 1970s through the 1990s, this album served as the single best overview of jazz, with canonical recordings of Hines, Armstrong, Ellington, Basie, Parker, Monk, Gillespie, Davis, and many others.

Survey Participants

A.D. Amorosi journalist, *Philadelphia Inquirer, Rolling Stone*
David Baker educator and conductor, Indiana University
Philippe Baudoin pianist and author
Cliff Bellamy jazz reviewer, Durham, N.C., *Herald-Sun*
David Berger composer, conductor, bandleader, educator
Joshua Berrett Mercy College
Robert Boardman *Buffalo Beat*
Michael Bourne *Down Beat,* WBGO-FM
Herb Boyd journalist, author, historian
Jeff Bradley critic, *Denver Post*
Jerry Brock record producer
Stuart Broomer writer, musician
Nate Chinen writer
Thomas Conrad *Down Beat, Stereophile*
James Dapogny pianist; professor, University of Michigan
Chip Deffaa author; jazz critic, *New York Post*
John Diliberto radio producer; journalist, *Echoes*
Richard Domek professor, School of Music, University of Kentucky
Steve Eddy jazz critic-columnist, *Orange County Register*
Ed Enright editor, *Down Beat*
John Ephland music critic
Eric Fidler reporter, Associated Press
Jason Fine senior editor, *Rolling Stone*
Ken Franckling journalist, photographer, UPI, *Down Beat, Jazz Times*
Michael Fremer editor-in-chief, *The Tracking Angle*
Krin Gabbard author; professor, State University of New York, Stony Brook
Phil Gallo music critic, *Daily Variety*
Pete Gershon editor-publisher, *Signal to Noise*
Lew Green musician
Bart Grooms music journalist
Bob Gulla writer
Beto Hale musician; editor, *Músico Pro*
Ed Hazell jazz writer
Nat Hentoff author, journalist
Christopher Hovan writer, *Cleveland Jazz and Blues Report, MusicHound Jazz, MusicHound Swing*
Margaret Howze music producer, National Public Radio

Andy Jaffe jazz artist-in-residence, Williams College
Chris Jisi contributing editor, *Bass Player*
Fred Jung *Korea Times*, 93.5 FM
Elliot E. Kallen jazz writer; contributing editor, *Ultimate Audio*
Bob Karlovits jazz writer, *Pittsburgh Tribune-Review*
Larry Katz music columnist, *Boston Herald*
Bill King co-publisher, *Jazz Report*
Cortland Kirkeby musician, critic
James Lamperetta jazz writer
Terry Lawson staff writer, *Detroit Free Press*, Knight-Ridder
Doug Levine broadcaster, Voice of America
Dave Luhrssen music critic, arts editor, *Shepherd Express Metro*
Rick Mattingly music journalist, *Modern Drummer, Percussive Notes, Jazziz*
Dave McElfresh contributing writer, *Down Beat, Jazz Now, CD Review, Cadence, Goldmine*
Lee Mergner associate publisher, *Jazz Times*
Louis-Victor Mialy senior correspondent, *Jazz hot*
Tom Moon music critic, *Philadelphia Inquirer, Jazziz, Rolling Stone*
Buzz Morison writer, editor
Michael G. Nastos broadcaster, WEMU-FM; journalist, *All Music Guide, Cadence*
Tim Owens senior producer–jazz, National Public Radio
Terry Perkins jazz journalist, *Down Beat, St. Louis Post-Dispatch*
Stephen Phillips *Cleveland Plain Dealer*
Tom Piazza writer
Michael Point *Down Beat*
Sam Prestianni musician, teacher
David Luke Ramsey music feature writer, Syracuse newspapers
Ben Ratliff *New York Times*
Michael J. Renner freelance writer, *Jazziz, St. Louis Post-Dispatch*
Dave Robinson jazz musician; educator, Traditional Jazz Educators Network
Don Rose arts journalist
Tony Scherman writer
Loren Schoenberg conductor and saxophonist; Manhattan School of Music

Gene Seymour jazz critic, *Newsday;* jazz columnist, *Emerge*
Tim Sheridan writer, *Launch, All Music Guide, Stagebill*
Chris Shull classical and jazz music critic, *Wichita Eagle*
Fred Shuster music critic, *Los Angeles Daily News*
Glenn Siegel writer, radio and concert producer; University of Massachusetts, Amherst
Jeff Simon recordings editor, *Buffalo News*
Arnold Jay Smith writer
Bill Smith editor, *Coda*
Bret Sokol music editor, *Miami New Times*
Keith Spore publisher, journalist, *Milwaukee Journal Sentinel*
Richard Spottswood record producer and broadcaster
Tom Staudter freelance writer
Jack Stewart musician, author
Jeff Sultanof composer, arranger, historian, writer
Ronald Sweetman broadcaster, CKCU-FM; writer, *Coda*
Ed Symkus senior arts writer, Community Newspaper Company, Boston
Bruce Talbot record producer
Frank Tirro music historian, Yale University
Jim Trageser *The American Reporter*
Mark Tucker author; professor, College of William and Mary
Michael Ullman jazz journalist; senior lecturer, Tufts University
Joe Vanderford jazz critic, *Independent Weekly*
Michael White musician, bandleader
Ellis Widner deputy features editor, *Arkansas Democrat-Gazette*
Jacques A. Williams publisher, *Strictly Jazz*
Russell Woessner music writer, *Philadelphia Weekly, Down Beat*
Herb Wong jazz media producer, historian, educator
Curt Yeske jazz writer, *The Times of Trenton*
Bob Young *Boston Herald*
Michael Brooks, John Edward Hasse, Tad Lathrop, John Litweiler, Neil Tesser, Kevin Whitehead, and Calvin Wilson

More Recordings

This discography supplements the "Key Recordings" that conclude each chapter and the listings in "100 Essential Jazz Albums." Like the latter, this compilation was informed by an international poll of jazz experts. A number immediately following a title indicates a multi-disc set. OJC stands for the label Original Jazz Classics.

MUHAL RICHARD ABRAMS

The Hearinga Suite	Black Saint, 1989

CANNONBALL ADDERLEY

Somethin' Else	Blue Note, 1958
Mercy, Mercy, Mercy	Capitol, 1996

AIR

Live Air	Black Saint, 1977

TOSHIKO AKIYOSHI

Toshiko Akiyoshi–Lew Tabackin Big Band	Novus, 1974–76
Carnegie Hall Concert	Columbia, 1991

GERI ALLEN

Twenty-One	Blue Note, 1994

RED ALLEN

Swing Out	Topaz, 1929–35

LAURINDO ALMEIDA AND BUD SHANK

Brazilliance Vol. 1	Blue Note, 1953

LOUIS ARMSTRONG

Hot Fives and Hot Sevens (4)	JSP, 1925–29
The Complete RCA Victor Recordings (4)	RCA Bluebird, 1932–56
An American Icon (3)	Hip-O, 1946–68
Complete Town Hall Concert	RCA Tribune, 1947
The Complete Louis Armstrong and Duke Ellington Sessions	Roulette, 1961

ART ENSEMBLE OF CHICAGO

Urban Bushmen (2)	ECM, 1980
Alternate Express	DIW, 1989

ALBERT AYLER

My Name Is Albert Ayler	Black Lion, 1963

DEREK BAILEY

Figuring	Incus, 1987–88

MILDRED BAILEY

The Rockin' Chair Lady	MCA Decca, 1931–50

CHET BAKER

The Best of Chet Baker Plays	Pacific Jazz, 1953–56

GATO BARBIERI

Chapter Three	Impulse!, 1974

CHARLIE BARNET

Cherokee	ASV Living Era, 1939–47

COUNT BASIE

The Essential, Vols. 1–3	Columbia, 1936–41
Count Basie Swings, Joe Williams Sings	Verve, 1955–56
April in Paris	Verve, 1956
The Complete Atomic Basie	Roulette, 1957

SIDNEY BECHET

The Legendary Sidney Bechet	RCA Bluebird, 1932–41
Best of Sidney Bechet	Blue Note, 1939–53

TONY BENNETT

The Tony Bennett Bill Evans Album	OJC, 1975
Here's to the Ladies	Columbia, 1995
Tony Bennett on Holiday	Columbia, 1997

BUNNY BERIGAN

Portrait of Bunny Berigan	ASV Living Era, 1932–37

ART BLAKEY

Art Blakey's Jazz Messengers with Thelonious Monk	Atlantic, 1957

CARLA BLEY

The Carla Bley Big Band Goes to Church	Watt, 1996

PAUL BLEY

Footloose	Savoy, 1962–63
Time Will Tell	ECM, 1994

BOSWELL SISTERS

It's the Girls	ASV Living Era, 1925–31

ANTHONY BRAXTON

Creative Orchestra Music	hatART, 1976

BRECKER BROTHERS

Collection, Vols. 1 & 2	RCA Novus, 1975–81

MICHAEL BRECKER

Michael Brecker	Impulse!, 1987

PETER BRÖTZMANN

Machine Gun	FMP, 1968

CLIFFORD BROWN

Complete Paris Sessions, Vols. 1–3	Vogue, 1953
Jazz Masters	EmArcy, 1954–56

DAVE BRUBECK

Jazz at Oberlin	OJC, 1953
Time Out	Columbia, 1959

KENNY BURRELL

Ellington Is Forever, Vol. 1	Fantasy, 1975

GARY BURTON AND CHICK COREA

Crystal Silence	ECM, 1979

CAB CALLOWAY

Kickin' the Gong Around	ASV Living Era, 1930–31

BENNY CARTER

Elegy in Blue	MusicMasters, 1994

JAMES CARTER

Conversin' with the Elders	Atlantic, 1995–96

CASA LOMA ORCHESTRA

Best Recordings	Best of Jazz, 1930–40

PAPA OSCAR CELESTIN WITH SAM MORGAN

Papa Celestin & Sam Morgan	Azure, 1925–28

DON CHERRY AND JOHN COLTRANE

The Avant-Garde	Rhino/Atlantic, 1960

NAT "KING" COLE

Big Band Cole	Capitol, 1950–58

ORNETTE COLEMAN

At the Golden Circle	Blue Note, 1965
Virgin Beauty	Columbia, 1987–88

STEVE COLEMAN

The Tao of Mad Phat	Novus, 1993

JOHN COLTRANE

Blue Train	Blue Note, 1957
My Favorite Things	Atlantic, 1960
Live at the Village Vanguard	Impulse!, 1961
Ballads	Impulse!, 1961–62
Ascension	Impulse!, 1965
Interstellar Space	Impulse!, 1967

EDDIE CONDON

Dixieland All-Stars	MCA, 1939–46

CHICK COREA

Now He Sings, Now He Sobs	Blue Note, 1968
Remembering Bud Powell	Stretch, 1996

CHICK COREA AND RETURN TO FOREVER

Light as a Feather	Verve, 1972
Return to Forever	ECM, 1972

BOB CROSBY

South Rampart Street Parade	Decca, 1936–42

TADD DAMERON

Fountainebleau	Prestige, 1956

MILES DAVIS

Round About Midnight	Columbia, 1956
Ascenseur pour l'échafaud	Fontana, 1957
Milestones	Columbia, 1958
Porgy and Bess	Columbia, 1958
Sketches of Spain	Columbia, 1960
In a Silent Way	Columbia, 1969
Live-Evil	Columbia, 1970
Aura	Columbia, 1985

JOHNNY DODDS

His Best Recordings	Best of Jazz, 1923–40

ERIC DOLPHY

At the Five Spot, Vol. 1	OJC, 1961

TOMMY DORSEY

Well, Git It	Jass, 1943–46

PAQUITO D'RIVERA

Tico! Tico!	Chesky, 1989

BILLY ECKSTINE

No Cover, No Minimum	Roulette, 1960

ROY ELDRIDGE

After You've Gone	Decca, 1936–46

DUKE ELLINGTON

Early Ellington	MCA/GRP, 1926–31
Duke: The Essential Recordings (3)	Columbia, 1927–61
The Duke's Men: Small Groups, Vols. 1 & 2	Columbia, 1936–38
Black, Brown and Beige (3)	RCA Bluebird, 1944–46
At Newport Complete	Columbia, 1956
Such Sweet Thunder	Columbia, 1956–57
Blues in Orbit	Columbia, 1958–59
Anatomy of a Murder	Columbia, 1959
Back to Back	Verve, 1959
Three Suites	Columbia, 1960
Money Jungle	Blue Note, 1962
Second Sacred Concert	Prestige, 1968

BILL EVANS

Waltz for Debby	OJC, 1961
Conversations with Myself	Verve, 1963
At Town Hall, Vol. 1	Verve, 1966

GIL EVANS

Great Jazz Standards	Pacific Jazz, 1959
Out of the Cool	Impulse!, 1960
The Individualism of Gil Evans	Verve, 1963–64

ART FARMER

Portrait of Art Farmer	OJC, 1958

ELLA FITZGERALD

Best of the Song Books	Verve, 1956–64
Complete Ella Fitzgerald and Louis Armstrong	Verve, 1957
Mack the Knife/ Ella in Berlin	Verve, 1960
Clap Hands, Here Comes Charlie	Verve, 1961

BILL FRISELL

Quartet	Elektra Nonesuch, 1996

JAN GARBAREK

Twelve Moons	ECM, 1992

KENNY GARRETT

Black Hope	Warner Bros., 1992

STAN GETZ

The Complete Roost Recordings (3)	Roost, 1950–54
The Girl from Ipanema: The Bossa Nova Years (4)	Verve, 1962–64

DIZZY GILLESPIE

Gillespiana/Carnegie Hall Concert	Verve, 1960–61
Dizzy Gillespie and the Double Six of Paris	Philips, 1963
Dizzy Gillespie's Big 4	Pablo, 1974

JIMMY GIUFFRE

The Three	Atlantic, 1956
1961 (2)	ECM, 1961

BENNY GOODMAN

The Birth of Swing (3)	RCA Bluebird, 1935–36
Sextet Featuring Charlie Christian	Columbia, 1939–41

DEXTER GORDON

Doin' Allright	Blue Note, 1961
Both Sides of Midnight	Black Lion, 1967

LIONEL HAMPTON

Hamp (2)	Decca, 1942–63

HERBIE HANCOCK

Takin' Off	Blue Note, 1962
Maiden Voyage	Blue Note, 1964
Gershwin's World	Verve, 1998

COLEMAN HAWKINS

Hollywood Stampede	Capitol, 1945–47
Encounters	
Ben Webster	Verve, 1959

JOE HENDERSON

Inner Urge I	Blue Note, 1964

WOODY HERMAN

The V-Disc Years,	
Vols. 1 & 2	Hep, 1945–47
Keeper of the Flame	Capitol, 1948–49

EARL HINES

Grand Reunion (2)	Verve, 1965
Plays Duke Ellington (2)	New World, 1971–75

JOHNNY HODGES

Everybody Knows	
Johnny Hodges	Impulse!, 1964–65

BILLIE HOLIDAY

The Quintessential,	
Vols. 3–4	Columbia, 1936–37
The Complete	
Commodore	Commodore,
Recordings (2)	1939–44
The Complete Decca	MCA/GRP,
Recordings (2)	1944–50

DAVE HOLLAND

Conference of the Birds	ECM, 1972

BILL HOLMAN

Brilliant Corners	JVC, 1997

SHIRLEY HORN

You Won't Forget Me	Verve, 1990

FREDDIE HUBBARD

The Artistry of	
Freddie Hubbard	Impulse!, 1962

ABDULLAH IBRAHIM (DOLLAR BRAND)

African Piano	Japo, 1969

AHMAD JAMAL

Live at the Pershing	Chess, 1958

HARRY JAMES

His Best Recordings	Best of Jazz, 1937–44

KEITH JARRETT

My Song	ECM, 1977

BUNK JOHNSON

1944	American Music, 1944

J.J. JOHNSON

The Trombone Master	Columbia, 1957–60
Live at the	
Village Vanguard	EmArcy, 1988

QUINCY JONES

Pure Delight	Razor & Tie, 1953–64
This Is How I Feel	
About Jazz	Impulse!, 1956–57
The Quintessence	Impulse!, 1961

THAD JONES–MEL LEWIS JAZZ ORCHESTRA

Dedication	LaserLight, 1969–70

LOUIS JORDAN

Best of Louis Jordan	MCA, 1942–45

STAN KENTON

City of Glass	Capitol, 1947–53
New Concepts of	
Artistry in Rhythm	Capitol, 1952
In Hi-Fi	Capitol, 1956–58

ANDY KIRK

Mary's Idea	GRP, 1936–41

RAHSAAN ROLAND KIRK

Rip, Rig and Panic	EmArcy, 1965
The Inflated Tear	Rhino, 1968

LEE KONITZ

Subconscious-Lee	OJC, 1949–50
Live at the	
Half Note (2)	Verve, 1959
Motion	Verve, 1961

GENE KRUPA

Uptown	Columbia, 1941–49

STEVE LACY

Vespers	Soul Note, 1993

LAMBERT, HENDRICKS, AND ROSS

Sing a Song of Basie	Impulse!, 1957
Hottest New	
Group in Jazz (2)	Columbia, 1959–62

YUSEF LATEEF

Anthology (2)	Rhino, 1949–76

GEORGE LEWIS (CLARINET)

Trios and Bands	American Music, 1945

MEADE LUX LEWIS

1927–39	Classics, 1927–39

CHARLES LLOYD

Forest Flower/	Atlantic/Rhino,
Soundtrack	1967–69

LONDON JAZZ COMPOSERS' ORCHESTRA

Ode	Intakt, 1972

JOE LOVANO

Rush Hour	Blue Note, 1995

MACHITO

Mucho Macho Machito	Prestige, 1948–49

ALBERT MANGELSDORFF

Three Originals (2)	MPS, 1975–80

SHELLY MANNE AND HIS MEN

Live at the Blackhawk	Contemporary,
Vols. 1–5	1959

BRANFORD MARSALIS

Bloomington	Columbia, 1993

WYNTON MARSALIS

Live at Blues Alley (2)	Columbia, 1986

DAVE McKENNA

Left-Handed	
Complement	Concord, 1979

JACKIE McLEAN

Let Freedom Ring	Blue Note, 1962

CARMEN McRAE

Sings Lover Man	Columbia, 1961

MISHA MENGELBERG

Who's Bridge	Avant, 1994

PAT METHENY

Song X	Geffen, 1985

GLENN MILLER

The Popular	RCA Bluebird,
Recordings	1938–42

CHARLES MINGUS

Presents Charles Mingus	Candid, 1960
Black Saint and the Sinner Lady	Impulse!, 1963
Let My Children Hear Music	Columbia Legacy, 1971

ROSCOE MITCHELL

| Sound | Delmark, 1966 |

MODERN JAZZ QUARTET

| Dedicated to Connie (2) | Atlantic, 1960 |
| The Complete Last Concert (2) | Atlantic, 1974 |

THELONIOUS MONK

With John Coltrane	OJC, 1957
Thelonious Monk Orchestra at Town Hall	OJC, 1959
Monk Alone (2)	Columbia, 1962–68

WES MONTGOMERY

| Impressions: The Verve Jazz Sides | Verve, 1964–66 |

AIRTO MOREIRA

| The Other Side of This | Rykodisc, 1992 |

LEE MORGAN

| The Sidewinder | Blue Note, 1963 |
| Search for the New Land | Blue Note, 1964 |

JELLY ROLL MORTON

| The Piano Rolls | Nonesuch, 1923–97 |
| Piano Solos | Retrieval, 1923–26 |

BENNIE MOTEN

| His Best Recordings | Best of Jazz, 1923–32 |

GERRY MULLIGAN

| The Concert Jazz Band | RTE Europe, 1960 |

MARK MURPHY

| Rah | OJC, 1961 |

DAVID MURRAY

| Ballads | DIW, 1988 |

OLIVER NELSON

| Jazz Masters Vol. 48 | Verve, 1962–67 |

RED NICHOLS

| His Best Recordings | Best of Jazz, 1927–31 |

JIMMIE NOONE

| Apex of New Orleans Jazz | ASV Living Era, 1923–44 |

RED NORVO

| Dance of the Octopus | Hep, 1933–36 |

ANITA O'DAY

| Pick Yourself Up | Verve, 1956 |
| All the Sad Young Men | Verve, 1961 |

KING OLIVER

| 1923–1930 (2) | Jazz Classics in Stereo, 1923–30 |

KID ORY

| Ory's Creole Trombone | ASV Living Era, 1922–44 |

CHARLIE PARKER

The Immortal Charlie Parker	Savoy, 1944–47
The Charlie Parker Story	Savoy, 1945
The Complete Dial Sessions (4)	Stash, 1945–47
Confirmation: The Best of the Verve Years (2)	Verve, 1946–53

EVAN PARKER

| Imaginary Values | Maya, 1993 |
| 50th Birthday Concert (2) | Leo, 1994 |

LEON PARKER

| Above & Below | Epicure, 1994 |

JACO PASTORIUS

| Jaco Pastorius | Epic, 1975 |

ART PEPPER

| Art Pepper + Eleven: Modern Jazz Classics | OJC, 1959 |

OSCAR PETERSON

| At the Concertgebow | Verve, 1957 |
| The Song Is You | Verve, 1962 |

OSCAR PETERSON WITH CLARK TERRY

| Oscar Peterson Trio + One | EmArcy, 1964 |

PIRON'S NEW ORLEANS ORCHESTRA

| Piron's New Orleans Orchestra | Azure, 1923–26 |

BUD POWELL

| The Complete (5) | Verve, 1949–56 |

TITO PUENTE

| Oye Como Va | Concord Picante, 1982–96 |

DON REDMAN

| Doin' What I Please | ASV Living Era, 1925–38 |

SAM RIVERS

| Waves | Tomato, 1978 |

MAX ROACH

| We Insist! Freedom Now Suite | Candid, 1960 |

SHORTY ROGERS

| The Big Shorty Rogers Express | BMG, 1953–56 |

SONNY ROLLINS

| A Night at the Village Vanguard, Vols. 1 & 2 | Blue Note, 1957 |
| Way Out West | OJC, 1957 |

GONZALO RUBALCABA

| The Blessing | Blue Note, 1991 |

JIMMY RUSHING

| Every Day | Vanguard, 1956–58 |

GEORGE RUSSELL

| Ezz-Thetics | OJC, 1961 |

PHARAOH SANDERS

| Journey to the One | Evidence, 1980 |

MONGO SANTAMARIA

| Afro-Roots | OJC, 1958–59 |

GUNTHER SCHULLER, THE NEW ENGLAND RAGTIME ENSEMBLE

| The Art of the Rag | GM, 1989 |

JOHN SCOFIELD

| Time on My Hands | Blue Note, 1989 |

ARTIE SHAW

| The Last Recordings (2) | MusicMasters, 1954 |

GEORGE SHEARING

| That Shearing Sound | Telarc, 1994 |

ARCHIE SHEPP

Four for Trane	Impulse!, 1964

WAYNE SHORTER

Speak No Evil	Blue Note, 1964
Adam's Apple	Blue Note, 1966
Native Dancer	Columbia, 1974

HORACE SILVER

Song for My Father	Blue Note, 1964

ZOOT SIMS

Zoot Sims and the Gershwin Brothers	OJC, 1975

FRANK SINATRA

The Capitol Years (3)	Capitol, 1953–62

BESSIE SMITH

Complete Recordings, Vols. 1–4 (8)	Columbia, 1923–33

JIMMY SMITH

A New Sound… A New Star (2)	Blue Note, 1956
Walk on the Wild Side (2)	Verve, 1962–73

WILLIE "THE LION" SMITH

1938–1940	Classics, 1938–40

REX STEWART AND DICKIE WELLS

Chatter Jazz	BMG, 1959

BILLY STRAYHORN

Lush Life	Red Baron, 1964–65

SUN RA AND HIS SOLAR ARKESTRA

Jazz in Silhouette	Evidence, 1958
The Heliocentric Worlds, Vols. 1 & 2	Get Back, 1965
Space Is the Place	Evidence, 1972

ART TATUM

The Complete Pablo Solo Masterpieces (7)	Pablo, 1953–55
Tatum Group Masterpieces, Vol. 8	Pablo, 1956

CECIL TAYLOR

Looking Ahead	OJC, 1958
Jumpin' Punkins	Candid, 1961
Silent Tongues	Freedom, 1974
Olu Iwa	Soul Note, 1986

JACK TEAGARDEN

The Indispensable (2)	RCA, 1928–57

FRANK TESCHEMACHER

Muggsy, Tesch and the Chicagoans	Village, 1927–28

CLAUDE THORNHILL

Best of the Big Bands	Columbia, 1941–47

CAL TJADER

Monterey Concerts	Prestige, 1959

MEL TORMÉ

The Mel Tormé Collection (4)	Rhino, 1944–85

LENNIE TRISTANO

Lennie Tristano/ The New Tristano	Rhino/Atlantic, 1956–62

McCOY TYNER

The Real McCoy	Blue Note, 1967
Sahara	OJC, 1972
The Turning Point	Birdology, 1991

SARAH VAUGHAN

With Clifford Brown	EmArcy, 1954
How Long Has This Been Goin' On?	Pablo, 1978

JOE VENUTI

Violin Jazz	Yazoo, 1927–34
Alone at the Palace	Chiaroscuro, 1977

FATS WALLER

Piano Solos/Turn On the Heat (2)	RCA Bluebird, 1927–41
The Middle Years, Part 1 (3)	RCA Bluebird, 1936–38

DINAH WASHINGTON

Story	Mercury, 1943–59

LU WATTERS

The Complete Good Time Jazz Recordings (4)	Good Time Jazz, 1941–47

WEATHER REPORT

I Sing the Body Electric	Columbia, 1972
Mysterious Traveler	Columbia, 1973–74

CHICK WEBB

His Best Recordings	Best of Jazz, 1929–39

BEN WEBSTER

Meets Oscar Peterson	Verve, 1959

RANDY WESTON

The Spirit of Our Ancestors (2)	Verve, 1991

PAUL WHITEMAN

The King of Jazz	ASV Living Era, 1920–36

CLARENCE WILLIAMS

1923–1939	EPM Musique, 1923–39

MARY LOU WILLIAMS

Zodiac Suite	Smithsonian Folkways, 1945
Zoning	Smithsonian Folkways, 1974

TEDDY WILSON

Vol. 4: Fine and Dandy	Hep, 1937

WORLD SAXOPHONE QUARTET

W.S.Q.	Black Saint, 1980
Plays Duke Ellington	Elektra Musician, 1986

LESTER YOUNG

Kansas City Sessions	Commodore, 1938–44
The Complete Aladdin Sessions (2)	Blue Note, 1942–47
The President Plays	Verve, 1952

JOHN ZORN

The Big Gundown	Elektra Nonesuch, 1984

VARIOUS ARTISTS

Anthology of Jazz Drumming, Vols. 1–4	Masters of Jazz, 1904–1938
The Birth of the Third Stream	Columbia, 1956–57
Boogie Woogie Piano (2)	Frémaux, 1924–45
Central Avenue Sounds (4)	Rhino, 1921–56
The Classic Hoagy Carmichael (3)	Indiana Historical Society, 1927–87
Future Jazz	Knitting Factory, 1964–98
Hot Town	Jazz Classics in Stereo, 1926–33
Jazz Fusion, Vols. 1 & 2	Rhino, 1970–81
West Coast Jazz Box (4)	Contemporary, 1950–64

Notes

Foreword

v "[Sincere jazz musicians] aim at excellence": Letter, late 1940s, printed in Eddie Condon and Hank O'Neal, *Eddie Condon's Scrapbook of Jazz*. New York: St. Martin's Press, 1973, unpaginated.

Introduction

ix "If jazz means anything": Quoted in John Edward Hasse, *Beyond Category: The Life and Genius of Duke Ellington*. New York: Simon & Schuster, 1993, p. 399.

Chapter 1

7 "remembering song": Sidney Bechet, *Treat It Gentle: An Autobiography*. New York: Da Capo, 1978, p. 202.

7 "Of all the cities in North America": Berndt Ostendorf, "The Cultural Exceptionalism of New Orleans Music," in Olaf Hanse and Thomas Liesemann, eds., *Demokratie und Kunst in Amerika: Festschrift für Martin Christadler*. Trieste: Edizione Parnaso, 1996, p. 95.

8 "twenty to twenty-five bands": *Metronome*, December 1888, p. 14, as cited in Lawrence Gushee, "The Nineteenth-Century Origins of New Orleans Jazz," *Black Music Research Journal* 14, no. 1 (1994), p. 7.

10 "the raw materials of the blues": Peter Van der Merwe, *Origins of the Popular Style: The Antecedents of Twentieth-Century Popular Music*. Oxford: The Clarendon Press, 1989, p. 145.

10 "framework of melodically sensitive notes": Ibid., p. 118.

11 "laced with more truncated slang": Philip Furia, *The Poets of Tin Pan Alley: A History of America's Great Lyricists*. New York: Oxford University Press, 1990, pp. 35–36.

12 "Syncopations...are characteristic of Negro music": Quoted in Dena J. Epstein, *Sinful Tunes and Spirituals: Black Folk Music to the Civil War*. Urbana: University of Illinois Press, pp. 294–95.

12 "Notice! Don't play this piece fast": Scott Joplin, *Eugenia*. St. Louis: John Stark, 1905.

12 "Don't fake": Artie Matthews, *Pastime Rag No. 1* and *No. 2*. St. Louis: John Stark, 1913. Also Lucian Gibson, arr. Artie Matthews, *Jinx Rag*. St. Louis: John Stark, 1915.

12 "Jazz is the result": Ostendorf, "The Cultural Exceptionalism," p. 98.

17 "There was no end to his ideas": Alan Lomax, *Mister Jelly Roll*. New York: Pantheon, 1993, p. 151.

19 "an extraordinary clarinet virtuoso": Ernst-Alexandre Ansermet, "Sur un orchestra nègre," *Revue romande*, 1919, translated by Walter Schaap for *Jazz hot*, 1938, and reprinted in Robert Gottlieb, ed., *Reading Jazz*. New York: Pantheon, 1996, p. 746.

20 "In the early days...[n]one of the guys took their horns down": As told to Tom Stoddard, *The Autobiography of Pops Foster, New Orleans Jazzman*. Berkeley: University of California Press, 1971, pp. 75–76.

Chapter 2

32 "weren't blown—they were hit": Quoted in John Edward Hasse, booklet accompanying boxed set of recordings, *The Classic Hoagy Carmichael*. Indianapolis: Indiana Historical Society 1988, p. 6.

34 "Most of the night spots were run": Quoted in Nat Shapiro and Nat Hentoff, *Hear Me Talkin' to Ya*. New York: Dover, 1966, p. 288.

40 "Negro melodies or Indian chants": Antonín Dvořák, "Negro Melodies or Indian Chants," *Harper's New Monthly Magazine*, February 1985, p. 428.

40 "the voice of the American soul": George Gershwin, "The Voice of the American Soul," *Theatre*, March 1927.

40 "blues and the snappy number": Quoted in Howard Pollack, *Aaron Copland: The Life and Work of an Uncommon Man*. New York: Henry Holt, 1999, p. 137.

43 "a huge room": Cab Calloway and Bryant Rollins, *Of Minnie the Moocher and Me*. New York: Thomas Y. Crowell, 1976, p. 88.

43 "There were brutes at the door": Quoted in Edward Jablonski, *Harold Arlen: Happy with the Blues*. Garden City, N.Y.: Doubleday, 1961, pp. 53–54.

43 "The soloists, dancers, and singers": Calloway, p. 88.

44 "Tap dancers had a big influence on drummers": Quoted in Burt Korall, *Drummin' Men*. New York: Schirmer Books, 1990, p. 139.

48 "Oh, I stole that from the polka bands": Quoted in Richard Sudhalter, *Lost Chords: White Musicians and Their Contributions to Jazz, 1915–45*. New York: Oxford University Press, 1999, p. 788.

Chapter 3

54 "Swing is not a kind of music": Interview by Manne Berggren, Swedish Radio, Stockholm, April 29, 1939. Issued on the LP *Duke Ellington in Hollywood/On the Air*, Max LMP 1001, undated.

55 "In the middle and late thirties": Barry Ulanov, *Duke Ellington*. New York: Creative Age Press, p. 166.

55 "public dancing in America": Russell B. Nye, "Saturday Night at the Paradise Ballroom: Or, Dance Halls in the Twenties," *Journal of Popular Culture* 7 (Summer 1973), p. 15.

56 "Huge, brilliantly lighted, elaborately decorated": Ibid., p. 17.

57 "The beat is what swing dancing is all about": Quoted in Gerald Jonas, *Dancing: The Pleasure, Power, and Art of Movement*. New York: Abrams, 1992, p. 179.

57 "the rhythm of the dancers comes back to you": Quoted in Nat Hentoff, "Pres," *Down Beat*, March 7, 1956, p. 11.

57 "when they see people moving around": Quoted in unidentified article from the *Cleveland Press*, ca. June 12, 1932, in the Duke Ellington Publicity Scrapbooks, Duke Ellington Collection, Archives Center, National Museum of American History, Smithsonian Institution, Washington, D.C.

57 "that feeling of communion": Ralph Ellison, *Shadow and Act*. New York: Signet, 1966, pp. 237–38.

61 "Three nights a week, we were at the Savoy": Quoted in Jervis Anderson, *This Was Harlem: A Cultural Portrait, 1900–1950*. New York: Farrar, Straus & Giroux, p. 241.

61 "If you didn't swing, you weren't there long": Quoted in ibid., p. 310.

61 thousands "battled mounted cops and patrolmen": "A Great Spectacle," *New York Age*, May 21, 1937, as cited in Anderson, *This Was Harlem*, p. 312.

61 "At one stage, about half the people": Quoted in Anderson, *This Was Harlem*, p. 313.

63 "surely the finest representation of a composer's work": Gary Giddins, booklet notes for the American Jazz Orchestra, *Ellington Masterpieces*. East-West Records, 1989, unpaginated.

63 "the most intricate of all percussionists": John Hammond, Jr., "Ellington on High," *Melody Maker*, December 1932, p. 1055.

66 "We practiced hard between drinks": Quoted in Michael Brooks, booklet accompanying the boxed recording set *Swing Time! The Fabulous Big Band Era, 1925–1955*. Columbia Legacy, 1993, p. 13.

66 "we all admired the Casa Loma band": Quoted in Sudhalter, *Lost Chords*, p. 342.

67 "to avoid having a nervous breakdown": Quoted in George T. Simon, *The Big Bands*. 4th ed. New York: Schirmer Books, 1981, pp. 269–70.

68 "musical vice": Bethany Ewald Bultiman, *New Orleans*. Oakland, Calif.: Compass, 1996, p. 187.

68 "Ellington Refutes Cry": *Down Beat*, December 1937, p. 2.

68 "In Christian homes, where purity and morals are stressed": Leo Oehmler, "Ragtime: A Pernicious Evil and Enemy of True Art," *Musical Observer* 11 (September 1914), p. 15.

68 "Moralists drew a close link": Hasse, *Beyond Category*, p. 66.

68 "You usually weren't allowed to play blues": As told to Mark Tucker, *Jazz from the Beginning*. Ann Arbor: University of Michigan Press, 1990, p. 19.

68 "appealing only to the lover of sensuous and debasing emotions": Quoted in Lawrence W. Levine, "Jazz and American Culture," in Robert G. O'Meally, ed., *The Jazz Cadence of American Culture*. New York: Columbia University Press, 1998, p. 438.

68 a series of suicides: "The 30's," *Down Beat*, September 1989, p. 17.

68 "an atrocity in polite society": Quoted in Levine, "Jazz and American Culture," p. 436.

68 "a return to the humming": Quoted in ibid., p. 437.

68 "if the ban on recording": "The 40's," *Down Beat*, September 1989, p. 28.

68 "Of all the cruelties in the world": Quoted in ibid., p. 27.

68 "bop is ruining music": Quoted in "The 50's," *Down Beat*, September 1989, p. 39.

68 "a horrifying demonstration": John Tynan, "Take 5," *Down Beat*, November 23, 1961, p. 40.

68 jazz represented "a reaction from Puritan repressions": Alain Locke, *The Negro and His Music*. Washington, D.C.: Associates in Negro Folk Education, 1936, p. 88. Cited in Levine, "Jazz and American Culture," p. 439.

68 "the accepted, the proper, and the old": Hoagy Carmichael, *The Stardust Road*. New York: Rinehart, 1946, p. 7.

73 "we do a couple of hundred one-nighters a year": Quoted in Simon, *The Big Bands*, p. 333.

74 "a new arrangement would freshen [*Mood Indigo*] up": Quoted in Gary Keys' documentary film *Memories of the Duke*. Time-Life Films, 1980.

79 "the finest white blues singer": Gunther Schuller, *The Swing Era: The Development of Jazz, 1930–1945*. New York: Oxford University Press, 1989, p. 606.

80 that singer's "imposition of a romantic lyricism upon the blues": Ralph Ellison, *Shadow and Act*. New York: Signet, 1966, p. 238.

80 "the greatest of all jazz vocal groups": Will Friedwald, *Jazz Singing*. New York: Scribner, 1990, p. 156.

81 "She was 17": *John Hammond: From Bessie Smith to Bruce Springsteen*, An American Masters Film, PBS-TV, 1990. Issued on home video by CMV Enterprises.

81 "Scratchy, unmusical voice. Where was the tune?": Ibid.

84 "After the war, families settled down": Bob Blumenthal, unpublished interview with Les Brown, 1997.

Chapter 4

88 "entrenched patterns of segregation": Scott DeVeaux, *The Birth of Bebop*. Berkeley: University of California Press, 1997, p. 27.

89 Hawkins was *the* proto-bebopper: Ibid., esp. Chapter 1.

91 "an integral part of the...entertainment industry": Ibid., p. 29.

92 "the world's greatest junkie": Robert George Reisner, *Bird: The Legend of Charlie Parker*. New York: Citadel Press, 1962, p. 206.

94 "Everybody just flipped": Quoted in Shapiro and Hentoff, *Hear Me Talkin' to Ya*, p. 360.

Chapter 5

115 "went largely unnoticed by musicians in the East": Joe Goldberg, *Jazz Masters of the Fifties*. New York: Macmillan, 1965, p. 45.

116 "The reaction to the reaction had taken place": Ibid., p. 45.

117 "It was the same every night": Max Gordon, *Live at the Village Vanguard*. New York: Da Capo Press, 1980, p. 140.

121 "the scorching intensity of Bud Powell's pianism": Ted Gioia, *West Coast Jazz*. New York: Oxford University Press, 1992, p. 134.

123 one reviewer criticized him as "anti-jazz": Tynan, "Take 5," p. 40.

124 "Brubeck and Monk brought out": Gioia, *West Coast Jazz*, p. 67.

126 "God...is gracious and merciful": John Coltrane, in his liner notes to *A Love Supreme*. Impulse!, 1964.

126 "mysterious power to evoke ecstasy": Neil Leonard, *Jazz: Myth and Religion*. New York: Oxford University Press, 1987, p. 48.

137 "jazz with a non-pulsating beat": Quoted in Gioia, *West Coast Jazz*, p. 234.

137 "a very melodic...feminine instrument": Quoted in ibid., p. 187.

Chapter 6

145 "Jazz was not just a music": Quoted in Ira Gitler, *Swing to Bop: An Oral History of the Transition in Jazz in the 1940s*. New York: Oxford University Press, 1985, p. 303.

145 "somebody shouted: 'Let's take this nigger out'": Quoted in Hasse, *Beyond Category*, p. 176.

145 "stamp out segregation": Quoted in ibid., p. 297.

145 "If jazz means anything": Quoted in ibid., p. 399.

148 "I realized that you can play sharp or flat in tune": Quoted in John Litweiler, *The Freedom Principle: Jazz After 1958*. New York: Morrow, 1984, p. 32.

148 "Before I met Ornette": Quoted in John Litweiler, *Ornette Coleman: A Harmolodic Life*. New York: Morrow, 1992, pp. 59–60.

148 "the most interesting part is: what do you play after you play the melody?": Quoted in Litweiler, *The Freedom Principle*, p. 33.

150 "I think jazz should express more kinds of feelings": Quoted in Martin Williams, liner notes for Ornette Coleman's *The Shape of Jazz to Come*. Atlantic, 1960.

151 "every note I play": Quoted in Litweiler, *The Freedom Principle*, p. 65.

151 "astral," "surface of the earth," "abyss": J.B. Figi, "Cecil Taylor,"

152 *Down Beat*, April 10, 1975, p. 31.

152 "To feel is the most terrifying thing in this society": Quoted in ibid.

152 "great insight, a feeling for the hysteria": Quoted in R. Levin, liner notes for Cecil Taylor's *Hard Driving Jazz*. United Artists, 1959.

152 "Hell, just listen to what he writes and how he plays": Quoted in Litweiler, *Ornette Coleman*, p. 82.

152 "a horrifying demonstration": Tynan, "Take 5," p. 40.

153 "many serious young jazz listeners": LeRoi Jones, *Black Music*. New York: Morrow, 1967, p. 98.

153 "Now there's not much need for loft spaces": Quoted in *Coda*, no. 185 (1982), p. 4.

154 "We want poems that kill!": Litweiler, *The Freedom Principle*, p. 216.

155 "It happened in gradual stages": Quoted in Derek Bailey, *Improvisation*. Ashbourne, Derbyshire, England: Moorland, 1980, p. 73.

155 "I've chosen intergalactic music": Quoted in Victor Schonfield, program notes for Sun Ra concert, London, November 8, 1970.

156 "It's late now for the world": Nat Hentoff, interview of Albert Ayler, *Down Beat*, February 25, 1965, p. 151.

156 "like a Salvation Army band on LSD": Quoted in Litweiler, *The Freedom Principle*, p. 163.

156 "the biggest human sound": Conversation with John Litweiler.

156 "It's a matter of following the sound": Quoted in Litweiler, *The Freedom Principle*, p. 160.

158 "the point of a teacher": Quoted in Tad Lathrop, "Hiram Bullock," *Guitar Player*, September 1988, p. 52.

158 "[Bassist] Mark Egan, [drummer] Danny Gottlieb, and [keyboardist] Gil Goldstein": Quoted in ibid., p. 56.

162 "Come, we will dance sedate quadrilles": From a poem by "Ern Malley" in liner notes for *David Dallwitz/Ern Malley Jazz Suite*. Swaggie LP 1360.

163 "sound collages": Quoted in Litweiler, *The Freedom Principle*, p. 283.

165 "the discrimination is now all subtle": Quoted in Leslie Gourse, *Madame Jazz: Contemporary Women Instrumentalists*. New York: Oxford University Press, 1995, p. 9.

Chapter 7

171 Jazz was "the shock to the system": John F. Szwed, *Space Is the Place: The Life and Times of Sun Ra*. New York: Pantheon, 1997, p. 287.

172 "Some of the European bands were so like Louis's band": Quoted in Chris Goddard, *Jazz Away from Home*. New York and London: Paddington Press, 1979, pp. 290–91.

178 jazz had "swept over this country like wildfire": Takatoshi Kyogotu, "Jazz with a Classical Tint Rules Japan," *Down Beat*, December 1, 1948, p. 15.

179 Goebbels denounced as "offal": Michael H. Kater, *Different Drummers: Jazz in the Culture of Nazi Germany*. New York: Oxford University Press, 1992, p. 23.

179 "talentless and unimaginative juggling with notes": Willi A. Boelcke, ed., *Kriegspropaganda 1939–1941: Geheime Ministerkonferenzen im Reichspropagandaministerium*. Stuttgart: Deutsche Verlagsanstalt, 1966; Horst J.P. Mergmeier and Rainer E. Lotz, *Hitler's Airwaves: The Inside Story of Nazi Radio Broadcasting and Propaganda Swing*. New Haven: Yale University Press, 1997, pp. 136–40.

183 "It's American music, and no one else can play it": Quoted in Gene Lees, *Meet Me at Jim and Andy's*. New York: Oxford University Press, 1988, p. 29.

185 "The second happiest moment of my life": Quoted in Norman C. Weinstein, *A Night in Tunisia: Imaginings of Africa in Jazz*. New York: Limelight, 1993, p. 178.

186 "The broadcasts of Willis Conover were our best instruction manuals": Quoted in James Lester, "Willis of Oz." [http://www.jazzinstituteofchicago.org], August 1999.

186 the "best-known musicians": Ibid.

189 "What I'm playing today": Jürg Solothurnmann, interview of Jan Garbarek in brochure for *Jan Garbarek*. ECM Records, undated.

191 "It really was reassuring to know you weren't alone": Quoted in Kevin Whitehead, *New Dutch Swing*. New York: Billboard Books, 1998, p. 50.

192 "Nostalgia," he said: Unpublished interview by Kevin Whitehead, translated by Elisabetta Jezek, Rome, October 26, 1998.

Chapter 8

196 "There's a serious transition": Interview by Calvin Wilson, 1999.

197 "new media...like fuzz-tone and the wah-wah pedal": Quoted in Tom Phillips, "Larry Coryell," *Jazz and Pop*, September 1968, pp. 18–20.

207 "Most musicians are listening to music outside of their own categories": Interview by Calvin Wilson, 1998.

Essential Jazz Reading

Reference

Feather, Leonard, and Ira Gitler. *The Biographical Encyclopedia of Jazz.* New York: Oxford University Press, 1999.

Kernfeld, Barry, ed. *The New Grove Dictionary of Jazz.* New York: Grove's Dictionaries of Music, 1994.

Lord, Tom. *The Jazz Discography.* 26 vols. Cadence, N.Y.: Cadence Jazz Books, 1992–.

Listening Guides

Carr, Ian, Digby Fairweather, and Brian Priestley. *Jazz: The Rough Guide.* London: Rough Guides, 1995.

Cook, Richard, and Brian Morton. *The Penguin Guide to Jazz on Compact Disc.* 4th ed. New York: Penguin Books, 1999.

Piazza, Tom. *The Guide to Classic Recorded Jazz.* Iowa City: University of Iowa Press, 1995.

Tesser, Neil. *The Playboy Guide to Jazz.* New York: Plume, 1998.

Travel Guide

Bird, Christiane. *The Jazz and Blues Lover's Guide to the U.S.* Updated ed. Reading, Mass.: Addison-Wesley, 1994.

Musical Background of Jazz

Chernoff, John Miller. *African Rhythm and African Sensibility.* Chicago: University of Chicago Press, 1979.

Floyd, Samuel A., Jr. *The Power of Black Music.* New York: Oxford University Press, 1995.

Roberts, John Storm. *Black Music of Two Worlds.* New York: Praeger, 1972.

Blues

Cohn, Lawrence. *Nothing But the Blues: The Music and the Musicians.* New York: Abbeville, 1993.

Davis, Francis. *The History of the Blues.* New York: Hyperion, 1995.

Ragtime

Berlin, Edward A. *Ragtime: A Musical and Cultural History.* Berkeley and Los Angeles: University of California Press, 1980.

Blesh, Rudi, and Harriet Janis. *They All Played Ragtime.* New York: Knopf, 1950. 4th ed., rev. New York: Oak Publications, 1971.

Hasse, John Edward, ed. *Ragtime: Its History, Composers, and Music.* New York: Schirmer Books, 1985.

History and Comment

Balliett, Whitney. *American Musicians: 56 Portraits in Jazz.* New York: Oxford University Press, 1986.

Batchelor, Christian. *This Thing Called Swing: A Study of Swing Music and the Lindy Hop, the Original Swing Dance.* London: The Original Lindy Hop Collection, 1997.

Berliner, Paul F. *Thinking in Jazz: The Infinite Art of Improvisation.* Chicago: University of Chicago Press, 1994.

Collier, James Lincoln. *Jazz: The American Theme Song.* New York: Oxford University Press, 1993.

Dahl, Linda. *Stormy Weather: The Music and Lives of a Century of Jazzwomen.* New York: Pantheon Books, 1984.

Davis, Francis. *In the Moment: Jazz in the 1980s.* New York: Oxford University Press, 1986.

DeVeaux, Scott. *The Birth of Bebop: A Social and Musical History.* Berkeley and Los Angeles: University of California Press, 1997.

Giddins, Gary. *Visions of Jazz: The First Century.* New York: Oxford University Press, 1998.

Gioia, Ted. *The History of Jazz.* New York: Oxford University Press, 1997.

Gioia, Ted. *The Imperfect Art: Reflections on Jazz and Modern Culture.* New York: Oxford University Press, 1988.

Gioia, Ted. *West Coast Jazz: Modern Jazz in California 1945–1960.* New York: Oxford University Press, 1992.

Gitler, Ira. *Jazz Masters of the Forties.* New York: Macmillan, 1966.

Gitler, Ira. *Swing to Bop: An Oral History of the Transition in Jazz in the 1940s.* New York: Oxford University Press, 1985.

Gottlieb, Robert, ed. *Reading Jazz: A Gathering of Autobiography, Reportage, and Criticism from 1919 to Now.* New York: Pantheon Books, 1996.

Gourse, Leslie. *Louis' Children: American Jazz Singers.* New York: Morrow, 1984.

Gridley, Mark. *Jazz Styles.* 6th ed. Englewood Cliffs, N.J.: Prentice-Hall, 1997.

Hadlock, Richard. *Jazz Masters of the Twenties.* New York: Macmillan, 1965.

Hentoff, Nat, and Nat Shapiro. *Hear Me Talkin' to Ya: An Oral History of Jazz.* New York: Dover, 1966.

Hodeir, André. *Jazz: Its Evolution and Essence.* David Noakes, trans. New York: Grove Press, 1956.

Kenney, William Howland. *Chicago Jazz: A Cultural History, 1904–1930.* New York: Oxford University Press, 1993.

King, Johnny. *What Jazz Is: An Insider's Guide to Understanding and Listening to Jazz.* New York: Walker, 1997.

Lees, Gene. *Singers and the Song II.* New York: Oxford University Press, 1998.

Litweiler, John. *The Freedom Principle: Jazz After 1958.* New York: Morrow, 1984.

Mandel, Howard. *Future Jazz.* New York: Oxford University Press, 1999.

Moody, Bill. *The Jazz Exiles: American Musicians Abroad.* Reno: University of Nevada Press, 1993.

Murray, Albert. *Stompin' the Blues.* New York: McGraw-Hill, 1976.

Nicholson, Stuart. *Jazz: The Modern Resurgence.* London: Simon & Schuster, 1990.

Owens, Thomas. *Bebop: The Music and Its Players.* New York: Oxford University Press, 1995.

Pearson, Nathan W., Jr. *Goin' to Kansas City.* Urbana: University of Illinois Press, 1987.

Porter, Lewis, Michael Ullman, with Edward Hazell. *Jazz: From Its Origins to the Present.* Englewood Cliffs, N.J.: Prentice-Hall, 1993.

Ramsey, Frederick, Jr., and Charles Edward Smith. *Jazzmen.* New York: Harcourt Brace Jovanovich, 1939.

Roberts, John Storm. *Latin Jazz: The First Fusion, 1900–Today.* New York: Schirmer Books, 1999.

Rockwell, John. *All American Music: Composition in the Late Twentieth Century.* New York: Knopf, 1983.

Rosenthal, David H. *Hard Bop: Jazz and Black Music 1955–1965.* New York: Oxford University Press, 1992.

Russell, Bill. Barry Martyn and Mike Hazeldine, comps. and eds. *New Orleans Style.* New Orleans: Jazzology Press, 1994.

Russell, Ross. *Jazz in Kansas City and the Southwest.* Berkeley: University of California Press, 1971.

Schuller, Gunther. *Early Jazz.* New York: Oxford University Press, 1968.

Schuller, Gunther. *The Swing Era: The Development of Jazz 1930–1945.* New York: Oxford University Press, 1989.

Simon, George T. *The Big Bands.* New York: Macmillan, 1967.

Spellman, A. B. *Black Music: Four Lives.* New York: Schocken Books, 1970.

Sudhalter, Richard M. *Lost Chords: White Musicians and Their Contributions to Jazz, 1915–1945.* New York: Oxford University Press, 1999.

Turner, Frederick. *Remembering Song: Encounters with the New Orleans Jazz Tradition.* Expanded ed. New York: Da Capo Press, 1994.

Whitehead, Kevin. *New Dutch Swing.* New York: Watson-Guptill, 1998.

Williams, Martin. *The Jazz Tradition.* Rev. ed. New York: Oxford University Press, 1983.

Wilmer, Valerie. *As Serious as Your Life.* London: Quartet, 1977.

Musician Memoirs, Biographies, and Profiles

Basie, Count, and Albert Murray. *Good Morning Blues: The Autobiography of Count Basie.* New York: Random House, 1986.

Bechet, Sidney. *Treat It Gentle: An Autobiography.* London: Cassell, 1960.

Bergreen, Laurence. *Louis Armstrong: An Extravagant Life.* New York: Broadway Books, 1997.

Berlin, Edward A. *King of Ragtime: Scott Joplin and His Era.* New York: Oxford University Press, 1994.

Brothers, Thomas, ed. *Louis Armstrong in His Own Words: Selected Writings.* New York: Oxford University Press, 1999.

Chilton, John. *The Song of the Hawk: The Life and Recordings of Coleman Hawkins.* Ann Arbor: University of Michigan Press, 1990.

Davis, Miles, and Quincy Troupe. *Miles: The Autobiography.* New York: Simon & Schuster, 1989.

Ellington, Duke. *Music Is My Mistress.* Garden City, N.Y.: Doubleday, 1973.

Firestone, Ross. *Swing, Swing, Swing: The Life and Times of Benny Goodman.* New York: Norton, 1993.

Giddins, Gary. *Celebrating Bird: The Triumph of Charlie Parker.* New York: Morrow, 1987.

Giddins, Gary. *Satchmo.* New York: Doubleday, 1988.

Gillespie, Dizzy, and Al Frazer. *To Be or Not…to Bop.* Garden City, N.Y.: Doubleday, 1979.

Hajdu, David. *Lush Life: A Biography of Billy Strayhorn.* New York: Farrar Straus & Giroux, 1996.

Hasse, John Edward. *Beyond Category: The Life and Genius of Duke Ellington.* New York: Da Capo, 1995.

Lees, Gene. *Leader of the Band: The Life of Woody Herman.* New York: Oxford University Press, 1995.

Lomax, Alan. *Mister Jelly Roll.* New York: Duell, Sloan & Pearce, 1950.

Marquis, Donald. *In Search of Buddy Bolden, First Man of Jazz.* Baton Rouge: Louisiana State University Press, 1978.

Mingus, Charles. *Beneath the Underdog.* New York: Knopf, 1971.

Pepper, Art, and Laurie Pepper. *Straight Life: The Story of Art Pepper.* New York: Schirmer, 1979.

Porter, Lewis, ed. *A Lester Young Reader.* Washington, D.C.: Smithsonian Institution Press, 1991.

Russell, Ross. *Bird Lives: The High Life and Hard Times of Charlie (Yardbird) Parker.* New York: Charterhouse, 1973.

Shipton, Alyn. *Groovin' High: The Life of Dizzy Gillespie.* New York: Oxford University Press, 1999.

Sudhalter, Richard, and Philip R. Evans. *Bix: Man and Legend.* New York: Arlington House, 1974.

Tucker, Mark, ed. *The Duke Ellington Reader.* New York: Oxford University Press, 1993.

Picture Books and Illustrated Histories

Claxton, William. *Jazz Seen.* Köln, Germany: Taschen, 1999.

Cooke, Mervyn. *The Chronicle of Jazz.* New York: Abbeville, 1997.

Driggs, Frank, and Harris Lewine. *Black Beauty, White Heat: A Pictorial History of Classic Jazz, 1920–1950.* New York: Morrow, 1982.

Folley-Cooper, Marquette, Deborah Macanic, and Janice McNeil, comps. *Seeing Jazz: Artists and Writers on Jazz.* San Francisco: Chronicle Books, 1997.

Gottlieb, Bill. *The Golden Age of Jazz.* Rohnert Park, Calif.: Pomegranate, 1995.

Leonard, Herman. *Jazz Memories.* Levallois-Perret, France: Editions Filipacchi, 1995.

Jazz for Young Readers

Frankl, Ron. *Duke Ellington.* New York: Chelsea House, 1988.

Gourse, Leslie. *Blowing on the Changes: The Art of the Jazz Horn Players.* New York: Franklin Watts, 1997.

Gourse, Leslie. *Striders to Beboppers and Beyond: The Art of Jazz Piano.* New York: Franklin Watts, 1997.

Gourse, Leslie. *Swingers and Crooners: The Art of Jazz Singing.* New York: Franklin Watts, 1997.

Kliment, Bud. *Ella Fitzgerald.* New York: Chelsea House, 1988.

Seymour, Gene. *Jazz: The Great American Art.* New York: Franklin Watts, 1995.

The Contributors

The Editor

John Edward Hasse is curator of American music at the Smithsonian Institution, founder and former executive director of the Smithsonian Jazz Masterworks Orchestra, and a member of the New Orleans Jazz Commission. He is the author of *Beyond Category: The Life and Genius of Duke Ellington*; the producer of a two-disc set of Ellington recordings, *Beyond Category*; the editor of *Ragtime: Its History, Composers, and Music*; and producer-author of the book and three-disc set *The Classic Hoagy Carmichael.*

Chapter Writers

Bob Blumenthal is a jazz critic for the *Boston Globe* and a contributor to the *Atlantic Monthly*. In addition to writing for *Rolling Stone*, the *Village Voice*, *Down Beat*, and *Jazz Times*, he has authored album liner notes and contributed commentary to radio and television.

Michael Brooks is a four-time Grammy Award–winning record producer and writer with a track record of over two thousand reissue albums, including Time-Life's eighty-seven-disc *Giants of Jazz* series. He worked as an assistant to Columbia's legendary talent scout John Hammond from 1971 to 1976 and is currently an archival consultant to Sony Music.

John Litweiler is the author of *The Freedom Principle: Jazz After 1958* and *Ornette Coleman: A Harmolodic Life*. His writings have appeared in *Jazz Monthly*, the *New York Times Book Review*, the *Chicago Sun-Times*, and *Down Beat*, for which he was also an editor.

Neil Tesser is the jazz critic for *Playboy* magazine. He has written for the *New York Times Book Review*, the *Los Angeles Times*, *Rolling Stone*, the *Chicago Tribune*, *Down Beat*, *Jazziz*, and *Jazz Times* and has served as jazz critic for the *Chicago Daily News*, the *Chicago Sun-Times*, and *USA Today*. He is a visiting professor in the School of Music at Northwestern University and the author of *The Playboy Guide to Jazz*.

Kevin Whitehead wrote the 1998 book *New Dutch Swing*, a detailed study of improvised music in Amsterdam. Since 1987 he's been a jazz critic for National Public Radio's daily program *Fresh Air*. A contributor to such publications as the *Village Voice*, *Down Beat*, *Musician*, *Coda*, *Jazz Times*, *CD Review*, and *Pulse*, he is also an editorial advisor and writer for the upcoming edition of *The New Grove Dictionary of Jazz.*

Calvin Wilson is an arts and entertainment writer at the *Kansas City Star*, where his beats include jazz, film, and books. He was a fellow in the National Arts Journalism Program at Columbia University in 1997–98, and is a contributing writer to *Jazziz* and *Schwann Spectrum.*

Sidebar Writers

Larry Appelbaum is a senior studio engineer in the Division of Motion Pictures, Broadcasting and Recorded Sound at the Library of Congress and a jazz radio host.

David Baise, a guitarist and composer, is the recipient of a Morroe Berger–Benny Carter Jazz Research Grant.

David Baker, Distinguished Professor of Music and Chair, Jazz Department, Indiana University School of Music, is musical and artistic director of the Smithsonian Jazz Masterworks Orchestra and the author of more than seventy books on jazz.

Philippe Baudoin, a jazz pianist, teaches the history and techniques of jazz at the Sorbonne in Paris. He is writing a book on the history of jazz standards.

Donna M. Cassidy is an associate professor at the University of Southern Maine and the author of *Painting the Musical City: Jazz and Cultural Identity in American Art, 1910–1940.*

James Dapogny is a professor of music at the University of Michigan, a pianist and bandleader, and the compiler-editor of *Jelly Roll Morton: The Collected Piano Music* (1982).

Gerald Early is the Merle Kling Professor of Modern Letters at Washington University in St. Louis. He has written extensively on jazz.

Sascha Feinstein is the author of the poetry collection *Misterioso* and two critical books on jazz poetry. He is also the co-editor of two poetry anthologies and the editor of *Brilliant Corners: A Journal of Jazz & Literature.*

Rusty Frank, author of *Tap! The Greatest Tap Dance Stars and Their Stories 1900–1955* and producer of the documentary *Tap! Tempo of America*, is a professional tap dancer, Lindy Hopper, and dance preservationist.

Krin Gabbard is a professor of comparative literature at the State University of New York at Stony Brook and the author of *Jammin' at the Margins: Jazz and the American Cinema.*

Deborah Gillaspie is curator of the Chicago Jazz Archive at the University of Chicago Library. One of her research interests is the history of jazz drumming.

William H. Kenney is the author of *Chicago Jazz: A Cultural History, 1903–1930* and *Recorded Music in American Life: The Phonograph and Popular Memory, 1890–1945*. He is also a professor of history and American studies at Kent State University.

Ann K. Kuebler is an archivist at the Archives Center of the Smithsonian Institution's National Museum of American History. She conducts research into the music manuscripts of Duke Ellington and Mary Lou Williams.

Tad Lathrop, the producer and editorial director of *Jazz: The First Century*, is an editor and co-author of numerous books on music and the performing arts.

Rainer E. Lotz is the author of record album notes, monographs, and scholarly articles and the publisher of the *German National Discography.*

Steven Loza is a professor of ethnomusicology at the University of California, Los Angeles, and the author of *Tito Puente and the Making of Latin Music* and *Barrio Rhythm: Mexican American Music in Los Angeles.*

Jeffrey Magee teaches music history at Indiana University. He contributed the chapter "Ragtime and Early Jazz" to the *Cambridge History of American Music* and is writing a book on Fletcher Henderson.

Jack Stewart, a member of the New Orleans Jazz Commission and a frequent contributor to the *Tulane Jazz Archivist*, is writing a book on the history of New Orleans vernacular music and another on bandleader Jack Laine.

Michael White, a clarinetist and leader of the Original Liberty Jazz Band and a member of the New Orleans Jazz Commission, is heard on more than twenty recordings.

Picture Credits

Courtesy of the American Jazz Museum: 34t, 34b, 35t, 35m, 35b

Archive Center, National Museum of American History, Smithsonian Institution: 42, 63b, 161

Romare Bearden Foundation/VAGA: 138

T. Edward Bowdich, *Mission from Cape Coast Castle to Ashantee*. London: John Murray, 1819. 3rd ed. London: Frank Cass, Ltd., 1966: 3

Michael Brooks: 50

City Lights Books: 109

William Claxton: vi–vii (background), 108b

Down Beat Archive: 33t, 36b, 41 (James J. Kriegsmann), 47m, 47b (Mike Shea), 54 (Bruno of Hollywood), 55 (Philip J. Weinstein), 58, 59, 60b (Bruno of Hollywood), 64t, 70, 72 (Zinn Arthur), 74 (David B. Hecht), 76t (James J. Kriegsmann), 77 (Myron Ehren Berg), 78tl (James J. Kriegsmann), 78tr, 79, 81t, 83 (James J. Kriegsmann), 98br, 100b, 108t (Tom King), 110 (James J. Kriegsmann), 113 (John Brook), 114 (Vern Smith), 115t (Ted Williams), 115b (Veryl Oakland), 118b, 119, 123t (Francis Wolff), 124 (Joe Alper), 127t (Francis Wolff), 128b (Allan S. Flood), 131, 133t (William Kahn), 133b, 135t (Paul J. Hoeffler), 134bl, 134br, 135t (James J. Kriegsmann), 137b (Lawrence N. Shustak), 143 (Alan F. Singer), 145 (Milt Hinton), 148t (Peter Bastian), 149 (Stephen Gunther), 150b (Francis Wolff), 151 (Gösta Peterson), 152 (Tod Papageorge), 154t (Giuseppe Pino), 155b (James F. Quinn), 157 (Ronald Heard), 159 (Enid Farber), 162b (Valerie Wilmer), 163 (W. Patrick Hinely), 165b, 166 (Bill Abernathy), 180t (Benght Malmquist), 181t, 184 (Andy Freeberg), 185t (Gene Lees), 185br, 186 (The Photo Reserve/Jeff Ellis), 189 (Andy Freeberg), 196 (Tom Kopi), 197, 198b (Andy Freeberg), 199l (Hyou Vielz), 201t (Paul J. Hoeffler), 201b (Andy Freeberg), 204b (James Minchin), 209t, 216 (Tom Copi), 217t (Hyou Vielz)

Frank Driggs Collection: 1, 2, 9, 9 (inset), 11b, 16, 17, 18, 19t, 20t, 25, 27b, 28, 29, 31, 32t, 32b, 33b, 36t, 37, 38, 40, 43b, 43t, 44t, 45t, 45b, 46b, 56, 60t, 61t (Baron Timme Rosenkrantz), 61b, 62b, 66, 67, 71, 73t, 78b, 81b, 82, 102, 106t, 106bl, 106br, 107tl, 117t (Popsie Randolph), 117b, 125t, 129b, 146 (Paul J. Hoeffler), 147, 148b, 150t, 164t, 164b, 165t, 169, 171, 172t, 172b, 173t, 173b, 175bl, 175br, 176, 177, 178, 181b, 206 (Bill Smith)

Ken Franckling: 158, 202t, 202m, 202b, 205t, 207t, 215t, 215b, 218

Frank Leslie's Illustrated Weekly, 1867, as reprinted in Leonard V. Huber, *New Orleans: A Pictorial History*. New York: Crown, 1971: 8b

William Gottlieb: vi(l), vi(r), 65, 88, 89, 90, 94, 99b, 104

John Edward Hasse Collection: 8t, 11tl, 11tr, 12t, 12b, 13t, 13b, 14t, 14b, 20b, 22t, 22bl, 22br, 27t, 30t, 30b, 39, 46t, 47t, 48t, 48b, 49, 57 (foreground), 62t, 63t, 68, 69, 73b, 80t, 80b, 84, 91, 93l, 93r, 98t, 98bl (James J. Kriegsmann), 107tr, 107b, 125mt, 125mb, 125b, 130, 132, 135b, 154b, 162t, 174m, 174b, 185bl, 192, 199r, 207b (Phil Bray), 209b, 212l, 213t

Leonard V. Huber, *New Orleans: A Pictorial History*. New York: Crown, 1971: 5b

Institute of Jazz Studies, Rutgers University: 26, 76b (James J. Kriegsmann)

Herman Leonard: 87, 92, 97t, 99t, 100tr, 103, 118t, 120, 137t, 175t, 183

Lopert Films: 182c

National Museum of American History, Smithsonian Institution: 203 (Eric Long)

Bob Parent Archive: 139

Jan Persson: 140, 174t, 180b, 187, 190, 191t, 191b, 198t, 204t, 208, 217b

Don Peterson: 57 (Charles Peterson)

Preservation Hall: 15

Random House, Inc.: 136l, 136r

Redfern/Retna: 170 (Tim Hall)

Retna: 195 (Andy Freeberg)

San Francisco Public Library Picture File: 4, 5t, 6

Duncan Schiedt: 19b, 44l

Smithsonian Institution Traveling Exhibition Service: 212r

SonicNet: 210b (T. Hopkins), 214 (Jay Blakesberg)

Chuck Stewart: 156

Jack Stewart: 7b, 21

Lee Tanner: 122, 127b, 131t, 144, 153

Billy Taylor Collection: 160

Ullstein Bilderdienst: 179

U.S. Library of Congress: 53

William Ransom Hogan Jazz Archive, Tulane University: 7t

Wurlitzer Jukebox Company: 57 (background)

Album Images: Atlantic, 221t; Blue Note, 100tl, 116t, 116b, 123b, 222l, 224t, 225r; BMG/RCA Victor, 211; Capitol, 105b; Classics, 188l; Columbia, 101, 200t, 220b, 221b, 224b; Contemporary, 121t, 121b; Debut, 96b; Decca, 64b; DIW, 205b; ECM, 188r; EmArcy/Mercury, 226l; Epic (CBS), 200b; ESP, 220t; Impulse!, 129m; Jazz Door, 155t; Mercury, 96t, 223r; Milestone, 128t; Pendulum, 210t; Polydor, 209m; PolyGram, 182r; Prawn Song, 213b; Prestige, 225l; RCA Bluebird, 222r, 223l; Roost, 105t; Sony Music Entertainment, 182l; Vanguard, 226r; Verve, 96m, 97b, 129t

Front Jacket Images: Jelly Roll Morton, tl (Frank Driggs Collection); Louis Armstrong, tc (*Down Beat*/Bert Stern); Duke Ellington, tr (*Down Beat*/James J. Kriegsmann); Mamie Smith, ml (Frank Driggs Collection); Bix Beiderbecke, mr (Frank Driggs Collection); John Coltrane, bl (Lee Tanner); Billie Holiday, bc (*Down Beat*/Paul J. Hoeffler); Dizzy Gillespie, br (John Edward Hasse Collection)

Back Jacket Images: Thelonious Monk, tl (*Down Beat*); Lil Hardin, tc (*Down Beat*); Kenny Burrell, tr (*Down Beat*/Francis Wolff); Sonny Rollins, ml (*Down Beat*/Herb Snitzer); Miles Davis Quintet, mc (*Down Beat*/Lars Swanberg); Benny Goodman, mr (Frank Driggs Collection); Betty Carter, bl (*Down Beat*/Darryl Pitt); Benny Carter, br (*Down Beat*)

Jacket Flap Images: Miles Davis Quintet (*Down Beat*/Lars Swanberg)

Index

206, 207, 215, 224
Mingus Ah Um, 139, 141
The Mingus Big Band, 207
Minstrel songs, 7
Minton, M. Henry, 89
Minton's Playhouse (New York), 89, 205
Mitchell, Blue, 209
Mitchell, George, 30
Mitchell, Joni, 218
Mitchell, Louis, 171, 172, 173
Mitchell, Roscoe, 149, 156, *159,* 163, 167, 188
MJQ 40 (Modern Jazz Quartet), 224
Mobiglia, Tullio, 179
Mobley, Hank, 116, 153
Modal playing, 119, 140, 151, 156, 197
Modern jazz, 87–111
The Modern Jazz Quartet, 104, 105, 110, *110,* 111, 114, 137, 159, 224
Moholo, Louis, 187
Mole, Miff, 39, 51
Moncur, Grachan, III, 140
Monk, Thelonious, 10, 32, 89, *89,* 90, 91, 92, 93, 97, 100–101, *100,* 102, 103, 107, 111, 114, 115, 117, 119, 122, 123, *124,* 129, 132, 139, 140, 141, 159, 162, 165, 191–192, 203, 207, 212, 224
Monroe, Clark, 89
Monterey Jazz Festival, 130
Montgomery, Buddy, 127
Montgomery, Monk, 127
Montgomery, Wes, 101, 114, 125, 127, *127,* 129, 215
Montreux Jazz Festival, 130
Montrose, Jack, 121
MoodSwing (Redman), 219
Moody, James, *131,* 180
Moore, Billy, 21
Moore, Ralph, 174, 202
Moreira, Airto, 186, *186*
More Than Mambo, 227
Morgan, Frank, 204
Morgan, Lee, 116, 117, 128, 141, 200
Morgan, Sam, 23
Morris, Lawrence "Butch," 205, 219
Morris, Wilber, 219
Morrison, Van, 219
Morton, Jelly Roll, 4, 7, 8, 13, 15, 16, 17, 18–19, *19,* 21, 22, 23, 26, 29, 30, 31, 37, 49, 50, 51, 68, 77, 82, 84, 120, 125, 170, 183, 184, 207, 212, 224
Moten, Bennie, 29, 34–35, *34,* 51, 66
Motian, Paul, 137, 208, 209
Motown Records, 152
Mougin, Stéphane, 173
Movies, 106–107, 182
Moye, Don, 156, *159*
MPS (record company), 188
Mraz, George, 174
Mulligan, Gerry, 98, 104, 105, *107,* 108, 111, 121, 204, 224
Mundy, Jimmy, 76
Munich, 188
Murphy, Mark, 135
Murray, David, 159, 163, 167, 205,

205, 206–207, 219, 224
Murray, Sunny, 150, 153
Museums, 212
Musica jazz, 125
Music Forever and Beyond (Corea), 221
Music U.S.A., 133, 186
Muzzik, 133
Mwandishi, 198

Nabatov, Simon, 191
Nanton, Joe "Tricky Sam," 42, *42*
Napoleon, Phil, 36, 51
Nascimento, Milton, 186
Nash, Lewis, 215
National Endowment for the Arts, 163, 203
National Jazz Archive (Amsterdam), 203
National Museum of American History, 212
National Public Radio, 160, 161, 203
The Nat "King" Cole Show, 132
Navarro, Theodore "Fats," 98, 99, 100, *100,* 111, 118
Nazis, 177, 179
NBC, 143, 161
The NBC Symphony, 41
Nelson, Oliver, 119, 128, 224
Neobop, 192, 196, 201–202, 204, 211
Nesbitt, John, 48
The New Jungle Orchestra, 166
New Music Distribution Service, 157
New Orleans, 2, 5–9, *6,* 15, 16–22, 45, 49, 80, 82, 108, 137, 144, 183, 212, 213
New Orleans in New Orleans, 23
New Orleans jazz, 13–23, 28, 212
New Orleans Jazz and Heritage Festival, 130, 213
New Orleans Jazz National Historical Park, 15
The New Orleans Orchestra, 23
New Orleans revival, 82, 85
The New Orleans Rhythm Kings, 16, 17, 28, 32, 37, 48, 49, 224
New Orleans Rhythm Kings and Jelly Roll Morton, 224
Newport Jazz Festival, 130, *130*
Newton, Frank, 56, *172*
New York, 1926–1929, Vol. 1, 51
New York City, 22, 36–39, 42, 45, 56, 89, 94–95, 117, 153, 157, 159, 205, 213
The New York Philharmonic, 41
Nicholas, Albert, 45
The Nicholas Brothers, 106
Nichols, Herbie, 191–192
Nichols, Loring "Red," 37, *37,* 39, 51, 79
Nick's (New York), 117, *117*
Nightclubs, 152, 153, 154, 156. *See also* specific clubs
1931 and 1939 (Spanier), 225
Nirvana, 199, 215
Noble, Ray, 77, 187
Nock, Mike, 174
Noone, Jimmie, 30, 31, 82
Norgran (record company), 97, 188
Norsk Jazzarkiv, 203
North Sea Jazz Festival, 130
Norvo, Red, 79, 81, 134, 144

Norway, 189
NPR. *See* National Public Radio
N-R-G Ensemble, 159
Nunn, Tom, 170

Oberstein, Eli, 35
O'Bryant, Jimmy, 37
O'Day, Anita, *107,* 134, *135*
Odd Fellows Hall (New Orleans), 15
Odeon (record company), 179
Ogun (record company), 188
The OKeh Ellington, 51
OKeh Records, 28, 29, 30, 32, 37, 38, 50, 51
Old and New Dreams, 149
Oliver, Joe "King," 10, 15, 17–18, *18,* 28, 28, 30, 31, 32, 37, 42, 49, 51, 82, 106, 224
Oliver, Sy, 70, 73, 77
The Olympia Orchestra, 14, 17
Omer, Jean, 179
Onward brass band, 8
Onyx (New York), 94
Opera, 5, 7, 19
The Orange Blossom Orchestra, 50, 66
Oregon (band), 189, 190
The Original Creole Band, 17, 18, 170
The Original Dixieland Jazz Band, 10, 11, 16, 17, 20, *20,* 21, 23, 28, 29, 49, 106, 145, 170, 171, *171,* 224
The Original Dixieland Jazz Band, 1917–1921, 224
The Original Memphis Five, 36
The Original New Orleans Jazz Band, 16
The Original Superior Brass Band, *x–1*
The Original Tuxedo Jazz Orchestra, 23, 48
The Original Yellow Jackets, 51
Oriole (record company), 37
Orkester journalen, 125
Ørsted Pederson, Niels-Henning, 191, *191*
Ory, Edward "Kid," 13, 14, 18, 82
Osby, Greg, 210, 211
Oslo Jazzfestival, 192
Out to Lunch (Dolphy), 222
Owens, Tim, 161

Pablo (record company), 97
Pacific Jazz (record company), 129, 154
Page, Oran "Hot Lips," 34, *34,* 35, 95
Page, Walter, 34, 35, *35,* 65
Palais de Danse (London), *171*
Palao, Jimmy, 9
Panassié, Hugues, 173, 175, 188
Parades, 8, 9
Paramount Records, 32, 37, 51
Parenti, Tony, 23
Paris, 173, 178, 181, 182
Paris Jazz Festival, 130
Parker, Charlie, 10, 35, 39, 60, 73, 77, *86,* 89, 90, *90,* 91–92, 92, 93, 94, 95, 96, 97, 98, 99, 100, 102, *102,* 103, *103,* 104, 105, 108, 109, 110, 111, 114, 115, 116, 120, 122, 131, 134, 144, 151, 158, 159, 165, 224,

225, 178, 183, 191, 207, 215
Parker, Evan, 188, 191, 193
Parker, Leon, 215, 216
Parker, William, 207, 217
Parlan, Horace, 210
Parlocha, Bob, 161
Pass, Joe, 97
Passions of a Man (Mingus), 224
Pastorius, Jaco, 102, 200, *200,* 219
Pathé-Perfect, 37
Payton, Nicholas, 199, 202, *202*
Peacock, Gary, 208
Peer, Ralph, 29
Penderecki, Krystof, 162
The People's Liberation Army Big Band, 170
Pepper, Art, 105, 118, 121, *121,* 129, 141
Pepper, Jim, 193
Perez, Manuel, 14
Perkins, Bill, 121
Perkis, Tim, 170
Perseverance Hall (New Orleans), 15
Peterson, Oscar, 97, 129, 132, 137, *137,* 191, 192
Peterson, Ralph, 202
Petrillo, James, 83
Pettiford, Oscar, 94, 180, 191, 200
Peyton, Benny, *19,* 173, 176
Phenix (Adderley), 220
Phillips, Flip, 71, 97
Pick, Margaret Moos, 161
Pickett, Jesse, 184
The Pied Pipers, *69,* 70
Pierce, Charles, 37, 51
Piron, Armand J., 14, 23
Plaza Music, 37
Plimley, Paul, 192
Poetry, 109
Pollack, Ben, *33,* 39
Pomonarev, Valery, 183
Ponty, Jean-Luc, 174, *174,* 190
Porter, Cole, 39, 49, 69, 119, 134
Portrait of the Artist as a Young Man (Armstrong), 51, 220
Potter, Tommy, 92
Powell, Earl (Bud), 32, 90, 93, 96, 99, *99,* 100, 101, 102, 111, 118, 122, 123, 165, 180, 181, 225
Powell, Mel, 76
Powell, Richie, 118
Power Tools, 206
Pozo, Chano, 96, 174, 183, *183,* 184
Preservation Hall (New Orleans), 15
The Preservation Hall Jazz Band, 15, *15*
Prestige (record company), 110, 128, 129, 154
Previte, Bobby, 206
Priester, Julian, 206
Prima, Louis, 214
Prime Time, 209
Progressive jazz, 98
Progressive Jazz (company), 98
Puente, Tito, 96, 184
Pukwana, Dudu, 187, 193
Pullen, Don, 206
Purim, Flora, 174, 186
Purvis, Jack, 38

Quartets: Live at the Village Vanguard (Lovano), 215, 219

Race records, 27, 29, 37
Race relations
    color line, ix, 132, 160
    racial discrimination, 16, 73,
        105, 106, 145
    racial equality, 164
    racial integration, ix, 59, 61,
        67, 81, 97, 171
    racial protest, 155
    racial segregation, 88
    racial tolerance, 171, 173
Radio, 27, 96, 160–161, 166,
    178, 179, 186, 192
Radio networks
    Armed Forces Radio
        Network, 160, 178
    CBS, 160
    National Public Radio, 160,
        161, 203
    NBC, 160, 161
    Voice of America, 161, 186
Raeburn, Boyd, 144
Ragas, Henry (H.R.), 20, *20*
Ragtime, 2, 4, 9, 12, 13, 19, 22,
    23, 30, 32, 33, 40, 41, 62, 65,
    84, 162, 163
Ragtime Band (Christian), 14
Ragtime Band (Spanier), 82
Ragtime to Jazz 1 and 2, 23
Rainey, Ma, 10, 23, 37, 46, *46*
The Ramblers, 177, 193
R&B. *See* Rhythm and blues
Rap, 210, 211
Rathe, Steve, 161
Rava, Enrico, 192
Ravel, Maurice, 40, 172
RCA, 29
RCA Victor, 74, 75, 82, 129, 188.
    See also Victor
The Real Kansas City, 1924–1940,
    51
Realm (record company), 188
Recording ban, 91
Recording industry, 27, 32, 42,
    56, 59, 72, 82, 83, 89, 97, 108,
    127, 155, 160, 166, 179, 183,
    205, 211
Recording labels, 29, 37, 129, 188
The Red Hot Peppers, 30, 51
Redman, Dewey, 208, 209
Redman, Don, 36, 48, 50, 54, 65,
    73
Redman, Joshua, 158, *158*, 198,
    213, 216–217, *217*, 219
Red Onion (New Orleans), 15
Reece, Dizzy, 188
Reed, Eric, 217
Regional bands, 48, 50, 54, 59
Reinhardt, Django, 21, 126, 173,
    175, *175*, 177, 178, 188, 193,
    225
The Reliance Brass Band, 16, *17*,
    19
Religion, 126
Religious music, 9, 16, 41, 79,
    131. *See also* Gospel music
Repertory jazz ensembles, 163,
    203, 204
Retrospective (Kenton), 223
Retrospective (Silver), 225
A Retrospective, 1929–63
    (Hawkins), 223
Return to Forever, 186, 198, 209
Revue (World Saxophone Quartet),
    167, 226

Rhythm, 3, 10, 12, 21, 30, 34,
    35, 46, 47, 54–55, 62, 85, 90,
    118, 147, 150, 183, 189, 191
Rhythm and blues, ix, 83, 88,
    123
The Rhythm Boys, 47
Rich, Buddy, 69, *120*, 212
Rich, Fred, 39
Richmond, Dannie, 206
Rinker, Al, 47
Rivers, Bea, 153
Rivers, Sam, 153, *153*, 159
Riverside (record company), 99,
    124, 127, 129, 154
Riverwalk, 161
Roach, Max, 90, 91, 94, 96, 102,
    116, 118, *118*, 121, 122, 129,
    141, 146, 157, 158, 189, 212,
    221
Roberts, Luckeyth, 22
Roberts, Marcus, 202, *202*, 219
Robichaux, John, 14, *14*, 16
Robinson, Bill "Bojangles," 43,
    44, *106*
Robinson, Clarence, 27
Rock music, ix, 88, 197, 199,
    205, 213. *See also* Fusion
Rockwell, Tommy, 29
Rodgers, Richard, 39, 134, 152
Rodney, Red, *90*
Rodrigo, Joaquin, 139
Rodriguez, Tito, 96
Rogers, Milton "Shorty," 98, 104,
    105, 121
Rolling Stone, 125
Rollini, Adrian, 38
Rollins, Sonny, 93, 101, 111, 117,
    118, 119, 122–123, *122*, 129,
    135, 141, 145, 146, 155, 185,
    193, 196, 204, *204*, 210, 225
Romberg, Sigmund, 119
Romeo (record company), 37
Roney, Wallace, 202
Ronstadt, Linda, 101
Roost (record company), 99
The Roots, 210, *210*
Roppolo, Leon, 6, 15, 28
Roseland Ballroom (New York),
    26, 37, 56, 160
Rosnes, Renee, 174, 192, 217
Rosolino, Frank, 121
Ross, Annie, 134–135
Ross, Doc, 48
'Round Midnight, 101, 115
Rouse, Charlie, 124
Rousseau, August, 9
The ROVA Saxophone Quartet,
    159
The Royal Crown Revue, 85, 214
Rubalcaba, Gonzalo, 183, 184
Rudd, Roswell, 147, 153
Rumpf, Max, 179
Rumsey, Howard, 121
Runnin' Wild, 27
Rushing, Jimmy, 23, 34, *34*, 35,
    55, *64*, 65, 80, 85
Russell, George, 41, 105, 119,
    144, 151, 180, 189, 225
Russell, Hal, 159
Russell, Luis, 37, 38, 45, 51, 174
Russell, Pee Wee, 51, 132
Russia, 176, 182
Russo, Bill, 98
Ryan, Jimmy, 95
Rypdal, Terje, 188

Safranski, Eddie, 98, *103*
St. Louis Blues, 10, 11, 46, 178
Sam Morgan's Jazz Band, 23
Sampson, Edgar, 61, 73, 76
Sanborn, David, 207
Sanchez, David, 217
Sanchez, Pancho, 184
Sanders, Pharoah, 154
Sandoval, Arturo, 174
San Francisco, 2, 213
Santamaria, Mongo, 119, 174,
    184, 209
Saratoga Club, 45
Satie, Erik, 40
Satterfield, Tom, 38
Sauter, Eddie, 76, 131
Savoy (record company), 92,
    111, 154
Savoy Ballroom (New York), 42,
    56, 57, 61, *61*
The Savoy Bearcats, 51
Saxophone Colossus (Rollins),
    122, 141, 225
Sbarbaro, Tony, *20*
Scandinavia, 187, 188, 189
Schiano, Mario, 192
Schifrin, Lalo, 126, 174
Schilling, Happy, 14
Schlippenbach, Alexander, 166,
    188, 191
Schneider, Maria, 165, 207
Schubert, Franz, 21
Schuller, Gunther, 41, 79, 85,
    147, 162, *162*, 167
Schumacher, Hazen, 161
Schuur, Diane, 217
Schwartz, Syd, 75
Schweizer, Irene, 191
Scofield, John, 158, 215, *215*, 217
Scott, Hazel, 56, 132, *132*
Scott, Raymond, 207
Scott, Ronnie, 188
Scott, Tony, 94
*Scott Joplin: Piano Works,
    1899–1904*, 23
Seattle, 213, 215
Seeley, Blossom, 47
Segal, Joe, 213
The Sermon! (Smith), 141, 225
Setzer, Brian, 85, 214
Severinson, Doc, 72
Shakti, 190, 193
Shakti, with John McLaughlin, 193
Shank, Bud, 121, 185, 189
Shankar, L., 190
Shankar, Ravi, 189
The Shape of Jazz to Come
    (Coleman), 144, 149, 167, 221
Shaw, Artie, 29, 55, 65, 69, 72,
    74, *74*, 76, 78, 85, 88, 160, 225
Shaw, Woody, 116
Shearing, George, 96, 102, 174
Sheffield, Leslie, 48
Sheldon, Jack, 121
Shepp, Archie, 13, 129, 153, 154,
    154, 156, 157, 191
Shield, Leroy, 29
Shields, Larry, 6, 20, *20*
Shilkret, Nat, 29
Shipp, Matthew, 217
Short, Bobby, 21
Shorter, Wayne, 116, 140, 141,
    186, 196, *196*, 198, 199, 200,
    209, 219
Sicilian Jazz Dixielanders, 170

Silkheart (record company), 166
Silver, Horace, 114, 115–116,
    115, *116*, 119, 126, 135, 141,
    159, 225
Simeon, Omer, 30
Simons, Moisés, 184
Sims, Zoot, 71, 187
Sinatra, Frank, 55, *69*, 70, 83,
    84, 85, 88, 99, 134, *134*
Sissle, Noble, 38, 173
Slug's (New York), 117
Sly and the Family Stone, 199
Slyde, Jimmy, 44
Smalls (New York), 213
Smith, Ada. *See* Bricktop
Smith, Bessie, 10, 11, 23, 29, 31,
    46–47, *46*, 50, 81, 106, *106*,
    147, 225
Smith, Buster, 76
Smith, Clara, 46
Smith, Jabbo, 37, 51
Smith, Jimmy, 126–127, 141, 225
Smith, Joe, 147
Smith, Leo, 147, 163
Smith, Ligon, 48
Smith, Mamie, 27, 29, *29*
Smith, Pine Top, 84, 85
Smith, Stuff, 94
Smith, Willie "The Lion," *29*, 45,
    75
*Smithsonian Collection of Classic
    Jazz*, 85, 227
Smithsonian Institution, 85, 203,
    204, 212, 226
The Smithsonian Jazz Master-
    works Orchestra, 85, 161, 163,
    203, 204
Smithsonian Recordings, 212
Smooth jazz, 161
Snow, Valaida, 164, *164*, 177,
    180, 188
Socarrás, Alberto, 183
The Society Syncopators, 23
Solo Flight (Christian), 221
So Near, So Far (Musings for Miles)
    (Henderson), 219
Sonet (record company), 188
Song for Biko (Dyani), 193
Songs, 65. *See also* Standards
Sonora (record company), 188
Soul jazz, 126–129
Soul Note (record company), 188
The Sound of Jazz, 132
South Africa, 187, 189, 193
Southend Musicworks, 157
The Southern Syncopated
    Orchestra, 171
Soviet Union, 176, 182
Spanier, Muggsy, 23, 29, 30, 31,
    32, 82, 225
"Spanish tinge," 7, 183, 184
The Spirit of Ragtime, 23
Spirits of Rhythm, 94
Spirits Rejoice (Ayler), 156, 167
Spiritual Unity (Ayler), 156, 220
Spotlite (record company), 188
Springsteen, Bruce, 81
The Squirrel Nut Zippers, 85,
    214, *214*
Stafford, Jo, *69*, 70, 84, 102
Stafford, Mary, *31*
Standards. *See also* Songs
    bebop-era, 102
    early, 49
    mainstream, 119